THE ART OF GAY COOKING

A CULINARY MEMOIR

DANIEL ISENGART

FOREWORD BY
JEREMIAH TOWER

ILLUSTRATIONS BY
FILIP NOTERDAEME

Outpost19 | San Francisco
outpost19.com

Isengart, Daniel
        Art of Gay Cooking, The/ Daniel Isengart
        ISBN: 9781944853501 (pbk)

Library of Congress Control Number: 2018935366

Illustrations by Filip Noterdaeme

Cover art by Severin Roesen, *Still Life: Fruit,* 1855. Courtesy The Metropolitan Museum of Art, New York.

OUTPOST19

ORIGINAL
PROVOCATIVE
READING

For Filip

THE ART OF GAY COOKING

A CULINARY MEMOIR

DANIEL ISENGART

CONTENTS

INTRODUCTION

COOKING has always been a natural part of my life, but it had never occurred to me to pursue it as a career before I moved to New York City.

Born in Munich and raised in Munich and Paris I had grown from an avid young observer in my mother's and grandmothers' kitchens to a young adult who found joy and satisfaction in the simple task of preparing home-cooked meals – preferably for friends and family. By the time I reached my early twenties and readied myself to make the leap to New York, with show-business looming much larger in my mind than cooking, I had moonlighted but once in a professional kitchen – a six-month stint as a sous-chef in an Italian restaurant, a job I took on a whim to pay for my ballet classes and voice lessons. Like most of New York's budding performing artists, I found easy part-time employment in the tuxedoed catering industry. A few years later, a summer job in the Hamptons serendipitously put me in charge of producing three meals a day for a group of demanding albeit appreciative gay executive types.

From the very beginning, I did this with the full awareness that preparing food was one of the most intimate things one could do for someone else. This was in the mid-Nineties, several years before America smelled the rosy *rôti* and catapulted its way into a food frenzy that to this day shows no sign of abating. The new obsession with food was propelled by a very American mix of enthusiasm and earnestness, marked by a gender divide that had its female proponents veer towards the precious and its male counterparts adopt a forceful swagger. When the movement hit critical mass in 2007, it became clear to me that something important had gotten lost along the way: the notion that cooking at its best is a deeply personal and generous offering. I watched as this phenomenal American food revolution, started in the Sixties as a counter-cultural impulse to make home-cooking once again a valued part of everyday life, was highjacked by commercial interests inundated by charlatans offering picturesque plates and easy shortcuts. Meanwhile the media overhyped the movement's ideals, pushing people to live out their new culinary dreams – but to do it vicariously, that is, by *imagining* to cook rather than actually doing it. Social media added momentum, starting an avalanche of foodies, do-gooders, self-ascribed restaurant critics and nutty nutritionists. That's how trends and fads began to define American food instead of intimate, shared experiences around the table.

I asked myself, what could I possibly add to this culinary cacophony without falling into the trap of the aggressive self-promotion and competitive posturing I was observing around me? For 20 years, I'd worked as a chef, succeeding, emphatically, off the radar. I knew that I had a perspective; more than a few entertaining, food-related anecdotes; and a good number of recipes I had honed again and again. Perhaps the cultures and languages I had acquired in my childhood could offer some refinement, too. But how could I formulate all of it into a book?

I started to explore the idea that gay men may have a clandestinely particular approach to cooking that sets us apart from the rest. This became a five-part series of essays that took aim at the heteronormative exploitation of cooking as a new form of entertainment and proposed a gay alternative that was insouciantly non-commercial and fun. I called it *The Joy of Gay Cooking*. It was published by *Slate* Magazine in 2015 and is now available as a short book, *Queering the Kitchen*, under this imprint. Only then did I begin to think about writing a culinary memoir.

Tell all the truth but tell it slant, my husband Filip Noterdaeme told me, quoting Emily Dickinson. You are gay, your approach to cooking is gay, why bother trying to write a conventional cookbook?

Back in 2013, Filip had written *The Autobiography of Daniel J. Isengart*, a book about our lives that closely echoed Gertrude Stein's famous memoir, *The Autobiography of Alice B. Toklas*. What you should do, Filip said, is write a sequel to my book, just like Alice B. ended up writing a sequel to Gertrude's. Naturally, he added with a sly smile, you should use that book, *The Alice B. Toklas Cookbook*, as your model.

I tried to picture it.

Alice was, like me, a self-trained home-cook. From the moment she moved in with Gertrude, into the storied apartment on 27, Rue de Fleurus, she devoted her life to making it a safe harbor infused with the spirit of art while upholding the one value that was existentially critical to Gertrude's and her sense of well-being: *domesticity* (or, as Filip likes to call it, *dough-mysticity*). Filip was right: I would not find a better role model. And writing my culinary memoir as a queer adaptation of a classic would not be all that different to what I had done in my last one man show, "The Importance of Being Elvis," in which I had given the King of Rock 'n Roll the Weimar treatment.

So, I decided to write my book as a literary homage to *The Alice B. Toklas Cookbook*, adhering to her structure, mirroring specific passages, and echoing her magnificent voice throughout. I hope fans and scholars will appreciate the parallels. Using her book as a recipe also gave me the delightful opportunity to include, as she did, an entire chapter devoted to recipes from friends. It serves as a wonderful counterpoint to the ongoing popular obsession with the restaurant world, proving that, at least in my social circles, real and unpretentious home-cooking is not a lost art.

What this book does *not* do is analyze what the art of gay cooking is – it merely shows it by example. But if you were to ask me, I would say that the art of gay cooking is the culinary equivalent of the joy of gay sex, or, to broaden the spectrum, the gay joy of sex: something we do for sheer pleasure, driven by passion, backed by knowing what we like (and learning how to go about it), seasoned with a good pinch of curiosity and, most importantly, coupled with an enthusiastic commitment to pay very close attention to the other – in this case, the ingredients we are playing with to bring bliss to the table. It's a joyful, sensual dialogue that, by definition, deserves to be slightly different every time, reflecting the present yet always aiming to hit the spot in delightfully unexpected ways. Incidentally, if I were to ask Filip about his favorite meal, I know what he would answer: Anything prepared by you and that we eat together.

Daniel Isengart
Brittany, August 2017

FOREWORD

BY JEREMIAH TOWER

T HE FIRST TIME my life was imprinted by eating while traveling was in the 1950's when my parents would bring back the menus, stories, and films of their eating their way through the French provinces, always ending with a stop at Fernand Point's La Pyramide, perhaps the most famous restaurant in the world at that time. The second was when in the 1960's I bought my first copy of *The Alice B Toklas Cookbook* (1954). Alice and Gertrude Stein traveling around France in their cars Aunt Pauline and Lady Godiva, the recipes and reminiscences of those meals, the book that she "wrote for America."

For me it was an imprint of how to live and what to cook. Reading through the essays, I traveled to each place in my head, summoning up the perfumes of perfect French butter, boiled crayfish, turbot sauce hollandaise, and *babas au rhum*. I took it to college and traveled again every time I read it while using the hotplate in my freshman dorm room closet. No longer just a luscious description of a perfect omelet somewhere in Lyons, but the actual egg dishes called "Aurore," and "Mirrored," let alone the one called "Picabia" that taught me how to scramble eggs French style and, in this case, to use half a pound of butter to eight eggs. The effect surreal indeed.

Now I am on my fifth copy of Alice's cookbook. The one that goes wherever I do, and the one which I was reading again and talking about while lying on my bed in Merida (Yucatan), drinking cold Pilsner, and relishing the book's cover of Picasso's chicken. That scene was filmed for a documentary about me, and was seen by Daniel Isengart at the film's premiere in New York in 2016. We knew we would end up having a meal, and we did at Buvette in New York City. Over my steak tartare and his Croque Monsieur, Daniel mentioned that he had just finished an adaptation of Alice's cookbook. And would I like to look at it? I did, and I was overwhelmed by its very personal beauty.

As teenager I was smitten with Edith Piaf's song *Non, Je Ne Regrette Rien*. Reading Daniel's manuscript while listening to Piaf I had to disagree with her *"Je me fous du passé,"* because the book and its memories do, in fact, *"allument le feu."* The beacon fire Daniel created burns very bright. A signal one can see for miles. Just as we once honored Alice B. at Chez Panisse in Berkeley.

After graduation from Harvard I traveled in France, England, and across the United States searching for perfect cooking. Then suddenly, I had my first job. The first day of it I was the head chef of Chez Panisse in Berkeley. Much and more has been said about that. The proposed menu that landed me there was:

Oeufs Rémoulade
Consommé Madrilène of Beet and Onion
"Haricot" of Oxtail, Alice B. Toklas

This is not the place to say more, but I will say that I soon realized that to be full all the time we needed not only press, but less of those customers who thought they could make Oeufs Rémoulade at home so why pay for them in the four-course dinner costing $7.50. The idea for the first attention-grabbing event came when my Harvard College roommate, now San Francisco poet Michael Palmer, reminded me that it would very soon be the one hundredth anniversary of the birth of Gertrude Stein. And why not a dinner to celebrate it?

For the February 3, 1974 Stein-Alice B. Toklas dinner, I selected dishes from the *Alice B. Toklas Cookbook,* Michael wrote the menu text, and my only help and sous-chef in the Panisse kitchen, Willy Bishop, designed the menu card with a drawing of an old-fashioned stove that was Gertrude (think the Picasso portrait), with Alice in her oven.

Dining. Dining is west. **Mushroom sandwiches**
Upstairs.

Eating. Eat ing.
Single fish. Single fish single fish single fish.
Sole mousse with Virgin Sauce. I wrote it for
America.
Everyone thought that the syringe was a whimsy.
Mousse and mountain and a quiver, a quaint statue
and a pain in an exterior and silence.
Gigot de la Clinique a cake, a real salve made of mutton and
liquor, a specially retained rinsing and an
established cork and blazing.

Wild rice salad. She said it would suit her.

Cake cast in went to be and needles wine needles
are such. Needles are. **A Tender Tart**. That
doves have each a heart.

Nobody ever followed Ida. What was the use of
following Ida.

Cream Perfect Love.

The poet Robert Duncan read from *The Making of Americans* for after-dinner entertainment, the audience eclectically even more diverse than our usual patrons. High-minded Berkeley street poets, the Birkenstock brigade of both sexes, hunched-over academics from the university, anyone haunted by Gertrude, and the usual troublemakers. Like my sister. When the gay Robert seemed out of his element reading from lesbian Stein, my sister took his place. As she sat down, she unconsciously took the posture of Gertrude in the portrait by Picasso, and a hush fell over the room. Years later my sister described to me those hours: "I have never felt so free, so comfortable and secure, so lovely, and surrounded by acceptance. It was a wonderful evening – a magic dinner." A perfectly gay event.

When I told Daniel that I loved his book, he asked me if I would write a piece for it. Under what circumstances could I refuse? None. We were both untrained chefs, were living our lives like that, and both found a spiritual home and source of inspiration in gay Alice and her book. I would, and did, and was caught up in a hurricane of the double helix of old and new and through Daniel's eyes, I found ever more. Of memories involving all my senses, remembering what it was like to have a marketplace and kitchen providing the perfect chicken pot pie, a Nelly Fritatta, a warm plum tart thirty minutes out of the oven, or a just made Old Etonian. All in this book.

Reading *The Art of Gay Cooking* again I think back to my other (than Alice) previous hero, Lucius Beebe. My hero since college days, who had dropped dead in his Turkish bath a few miles south of San Francisco only a few years before I arrived there and ended up cooking at Chez Panisse. Beebe's column in *Gourmet* magazine called "Along the Boulevards" described a life I wanted to re-create, and the terms on which I wanted to re-create it. "If anything is worth doing, it is worth doing in style and on your own terms – and nobody goddamned else's."

When Alice did, even she had to hear the usual comments one gets when announcing a book project. "How very amusing." And, "But Alice, have you ever tried to write." Alice's final comment in this little bible for cooks, is "As if a cook-book has anything to do with writing."

Well, this book by Daniel Isengart does. And cooking. And, since a human is made of his or her food, also living. Which is cooking.

A NOTE
TO THE COOK

T HE RECIPES INCLUDED in this book have been an integrated part of my life, some of them for as many as forty years. I have purposely written them out as loosely as possible to reflect my personal approach to cooking that always leaves room for what I call *informed spontaneity*. Think of them as *guidelines*: after all, a recipe, no matter how detailed, can never, should never give you all the answers – those are for you to discover on your own, which is all part of the fun.

Elizabeth David, the grand British dame of food writing, once good-naturedly admonished Richard Olney, the hermetic American expat artist and celebrated authority on genuine French cuisine, about his recipe for *Soufflés à la Suissesses* from his cookbook, *The French Menu*, claiming that it had "not worked out at all." To which Richard had replied: "Well, my dear, you must have done something wrong."* It's a gentle reminder that we may learn much from the masters but even more from our own mistakes.

D.I.

---

* This delightful anecdote was related to me by Richard Olney's sister-in-law, cookbook author Judith Olney.

I

THE AMERICAN WAY

THE MODERN AMERICAN approach to cooking is characteristic: Americans bring to the culinary arts the same earnestness, ambitiousness, determination and exuberance that they apply to business, to sports, to entertainment and to politics. By American I mean those who were born here as well as those who immigrated here, for immigrants play a very active part in everything that pertains to American food. I have heard New Yorkers debate the way their mothers prepare *Mofongo*, a dish of fried and mashed green plantains typical for the Dominican Republic, or the way raw tuna must be cut for Japanese sashimi. A restaurant in Brooklyn can be booked solid for months in advance because of the way its chef uses locally foraged ingredients, a very effective way to get attention. Conversations even with strangers in a store or on a subway platform can turn to the subject of restaurant reviews, gourmet shops or popular cooking shows.

The American culinary revolution stems from highly diverse impulses and ambitions and has developed at an accelerating pace over the past fifty years. It has had a tremendously varied impact on the country's culture for these reasons and on account of its exploitation in the media and social networking websites.

As a European expat living in New York City I have observed this development with a mix of awe and amusement but cannot help deploring the American compulsion to turn everything into a competitive sport or business. For example, one cannot open a food magazine without coming across a top ten list. To present a recipe of a particular dish without claiming it is the best of its kind is inconceivable. Still, this compulsive drive to always come out on top has resulted in some remarkable changes that have established America as the new global epicenter of the culinary arts.

New York City's food stores are virtually without limits in regards to the abundant variety they offer year around, and the seasonal local produce sold at farmers' markets is generally of good quality with the exception of potatoes, tomatoes, and most tree fruit. Meat and seafood however are of high grade, locally produced cheeses (formerly subpar) have come a long way in the past ten years and one can even find excellent sourdough bread.

Television and the internet have changed the way of life, habits, markets, and so eventually cooking. For decades, Americans had been intimidated by refined foods and contented themselves with processed foodstuffs they bought at supermarkets and fast food outlets. With the advent of televised cooking shows, a new interest in food preparation as a form of entertainment emerged. The population had been accustomed to convenience and instant gratification for too long, they had never developed a true appreciation of the culinary arts and had forgotten or were ignoring their own culinary traditions. So that even now, preparing a meal from scratch at home is still considered an indulgence.

Affordable transatlantic travel inevitably introduced Americans to the varied cuisines of Europe. Rigid continental traditions aroused the self-determination and ingenuity of young chefs who were either born in America or emigrated here to escape the restrictions of the old world. They sought new inspirations and directives and created a fresh and intriguing new kind of cuisine that is as distinctly American as it is modern.

I feel ambivalent about the commodification of cooking as a form of mass entertainment, about the aggressively entrepreneurial spirit that has infiltrated every corner of America's expanding food world. Nor do I like most of the food that issues from media-hyped restaurants. I insist that it is either too rich or too precious. One may say of the new celebrity chefs what can be said of their customers: they never know when to stop. Since I started cooking professionally in New York I have chosen to limit myself to cooking for private dinner parties and as this is closer to home cooking than to restaurant cooking I would like to share my knowledge.

My cooking style for the use of a home-cook is not hedged around with as many complications as are associated with fine restaurant dining. If trained restaurant chefs permit themselves to indulge in prejudices towards self-taught cooks they should admit the same privilege for us. For example restaurant chefs strain to make their food look decorative, sometimes impressively so, and with a great amount of effort, not only because it has become fashionable but because it "sells" as they say, that is it gets them attention and guarantees press coverage. Which brings us at once to a fundamental difference between my cooking and restaurant cooking. Working alone and preparing every meal from scratch on the day it is served prevents me from spending much time on making it look spectacular on the plate, whilst restaurant food often looks extravagant yet lacks flavor because components of it have been prepped way ahead of time. Restaurants also push their customers to spend as much money as possible. I am getting paid a daily fee and as a rule have an unlimited budget for buying the best ingredients and freshest produce available to execute my menus. Four out of five restaurants are certainly relying on being consistent. Almost every restaurant chef is required to execute each dish countless times without any noticeable changes to satisfy the unreasonable and misguided expectations of diners that this ought to be so. I like to improvise and be playful in the kitchen to keep things interesting for myself as well as for my clients and their guests. Some of my dishes reference national traditions but that does not make them conservative. I never follow culinary trends, nor do I visit food fairs, nor do I routinely eat out at any of the city's innumerable new restaurants, nor do I try to be inventive or innovative. An intuition for the diverse preferences and needs of each of my clients is typical for my flexible approach to cooking, but I always remain true to myself in my style. My subtle ways of both appeasing and educating my clients through food is one of the reasons for my success. This relaxed method, the *innere Ruhe* as we say in German, the inner stillness, is what makes me not only a good cook but a pleasant presence in any kitchen.

Modern American cooking is founded upon the culinary revolution that was started in the Sixties by a handful of individuals, when food and cooking suddenly became a way to articulate one's political progressiveness or epicurean leanings. It was the beginning of great changes and the American approach to cooking has since then been completely redefined and propagated around the world. Dealing with much resistance as any innovative movement must do, new American cookery weathered the influences of industrialized farming in the Twentieth Century and brought forth a surge in sustainable, diversified farming in the Twenty-First Century. But there is in America also a disturbing economic divide between those who can afford organic fresh foods and those who depend on far inferior, industrially produced foods, the consequences of which will no doubt declare themselves in this new century.

To cook as I do one must develop a sense for the sophistication of simplicity. Fussiness is not admissible. Spontaneity and a sense of ease are crucial. Such an approach is not encouraged in the restaurant world but should be considered by the home cook. Over time, any cook can arrive at the blissful state that in the dance world is being referred to as *controlled abandon*.

What is taught in culinary schools and shown in cooking competition shows may be useful for budding restaurant chefs, but it is not necessarily useful for the home cook, the epicurean, the bohemian or the artist.

"This relaxed method, the innere Ruhe, as we say in German, the inner stillness, is what makes me not only a good cook but a pleasant presence in any kitchen."

RED LENTIL STEW
(As cooked regularly by me in our Brooklyn home)

Heat a Dutch oven* on a medium flame; when it is hot add a couple tablespoons of olive oil and 1 finely chopped onion. Stir fry until translucent, then add 1 small knob of peeled

---

*A Dutch oven is a heavy, deep and round pot with a tight-fitting lid than can be used on the stove top as well as in the oven.

and minced ginger, 1 finely diced carrot, 2 finely diced celery stalks and 3-4 finely diced fennel stalks and fronds. Once the mixture is steaming and fragrant, add about 1 tablespoon each of coriander seeds and cumin seeds, lightly crushed between the palms of your hands. Push the vegetables to the sides of the pan, pour a tiny a bit of olive oil into the center of the pan and add about 2 tablespoons of tomato paste. Let it caramelize for about a minute without stirring, then add about 2 cups of red lentils. Stir well and cook for another minute before adding 2 ½ cups of water. Bring to a simmer, turn the heat down to the lowest setting, cover and cook gently until the lentils have absorbed most of the water and are tender but still holding their shape, for 10-15 minutes. Stir occasionally and add more water, no more than ½ cup at a time, if the mixture gets dry before the lentils are done. Season with salt to taste. Serve in individual pasta plates, spooned over steamed Basmati rice and drizzled with fresh lemon juice. Add a dollop of *Labneh** or thick Greek yogurt, sprinkle sliced scallions and chopped herbs like cilantro, parsley, fennel fronds or celery leaves and a tiny bit of olive oil on top. A fresh hot chili pepper, lightly charred on the gas burner, is a pleasant additional condiment for those who like it hot.

STEAMED BASMATI RICE
(A Foolproof Technique)

Pour rice, about ½ cup per person, into a large bowl. Fill the bowl with lukewarm water and gently swirl the rice around with your hand. Wait for the rice to sink to the bottom of the bowl and slowly pour out the water. Repeat this as many times as necessary until the water runs clear, three to five times. Now add enough cold water to cover the rice by an inch and set it aside for at least 10 minutes and up to 3 hours.

Fill a heavy-bottomed pan with water, add a dash of salt and bring it to a boil. Drain the pre-soaked rice and add it to the boiling water. When the water has come to a boil again, stir once to prevent the kernels from sticking together. Parboil the rice for 3-5 minutes, until it is al dente, halfway cooked. Pour out most of the water, holding back the rice with a fine mesh skimmer, leaving just enough water in the pot to barely cover its bottom. Immediately return the pot to the stove, set

* Lebanese, yogurt-based cream cheese. 6

over a medium flame. Push your choice of aromatics (a few cloves, a dried lime, a couple of kaffir lime leaves or bruised fresh lemon grass stalks) into the rice, as well as a tablespoon or more of butter, depending on how many servings you are making. Place a double layer of paper towels over the pot and cover it with a tight-fitting lid (fold in the corners of the paper towels to prevent them from catching fire from the gas flame). Cook over a medium flame for 1 minute before turning the flame to its lowest setting and steaming the rice for another 5 minutes without lifting the cover. Leave it covered for another 5 minutes before gently fluffing it with a fork.

Lessons learned from cooking for others

About the importance of texture, color and brightness in food: Do not overcook vegetables or leafy greens. Only eggplants, potatoes, pumpkins and some starchy squashes are best when cooked until completely tender. Onions are excellent supporters in any state – from raw to caramelized. Fresh herbs, chopped or lightly torn apart with your fingers and sprinkled over any dish right before it is served add an ethereal flavor. Learning to work in a restrained fashion with distinct spices and fiery aromatics like fresh ginger or hot chilies, or getting into the habit of adding to your savory dishes a touch of acidity via a choice vinegar, fresh citrus juice or grated citrus rind or even some acidic fruit like plum or Granny Smith apple will bring a new level of brightness and refinement to your food. Try it.

Oil and butter should be used conservatively, just enough to be absorbed by the food – there should not be any residue on the plate. Neither should ever be heated to the point of smoking.

A few drops of extra virgin olive oil added at the last moment, drizzled and not mixed into it, makes the dish shine and subtly enhances its flavors.

II
FOOD IN
NEW YORK HOMES

FOOD DIFFERS MORE from day to day for a private chef than it does for a restaurant chef, not only in the variety of each day's menu but in the choice of the menu according to the persons to whom it is to be served. A birthday dinner among family members calls for a very different approach than a supper with business partners, and preparing meals in a large loft-style kitchen is a very different undertaking from cooking in a small apartment kitchen that is rarely used for more than making coffee. For example, this is the menu I served at a recent dinner party in an elegant townhouse in Greenwich Village to which the host invited both the CEO of a rapidly growing, Mexican-style fast dining chain and the President of the Italian Academy in Rome.

BAKED WONTON CRISPS
WITH POACHED QUAIL EGG, LEMON CONFIT
AND CHARRED ASPARAGUS TIPS

BRIOCHE POINTS WITH CHICKEN LIVER MOUSSE
AND PICKLED FIGS

SOUP OF RUTABAGA, FENNEL AND APPLE
WITH SORREL CREAM

LEG OF LAMB WITH DEMI-GLACE
AND HORSERADISH SHAVINGS

MASHED RED BEETS AND PEARS

ROASTED SUNCHOKES AND PINK RADISHES

ASSORTED CHEESES AND DRIED FRUIT

BELGIAN CHOCOLATE CAKE
WITH BROWNED BUTTER ICE CREAM

This dinner was accompanied by copious amounts of expensive Champagne, Chablis, a red Bordeaux and Sauternes. The fine linen, classic crystal, French porcelain and antique silver were of the same understated quality as the menu.

CHICKEN LIVER MOUSSE

Clean 2 pounds of chicken livers, removing all membranes, traces of fat, veins and dark spots. Put the livers into a blender

9

and add 3 eggs and the scraped bone marrow of two split veal shinbones. Working swiftly to prevent the mixture from warming up, purée everything and pass it through a fine mesh sieve. Stir in 1 cup of chilled heavy cream and a splash of Cognac. Season the mixture with salt, white pepper and a touch of mace and pour it into a rectangular porcelain terrine (or a loaf pan, greased and lined with parchment paper). Cover with its lid (or aluminum foil) and place it into a baking dish filled halfway with hot water. Bake in a 350° F oven for about 35 minutes, or until a cake tester comes out clean. Refrigerate for at least 5 hours. Serve with toasted Brioche points and

PICKLED FIGS

In a sauce pan place a dozen dried figs, 1 cup each of white wine vinegar and water, a few cloves, a bay leaf, 1 tablespoon whole black peppercorns, 1 tablespoon mustard seeds, 4 tablespoons honey. Simmer over low heat for about 20 minutes, covered. Remove the figs and reduce the liquid to a thick syrup. Store the figs in the syrup.

It does not take as long as it sounds to prepare this dish. The pickled figs offer a pleasant contrast to the liver mousse.

BELGIAN CHOCOLATE CAKE

Melt 2 tablets (or 7 ounces) of good quality dark chocolate and 6 tablespoons butter in a bowl set over simmering water or in a microwave. Using a rolling pin, crush a handful of Belgian Spekuloos cookies (or Swedish ginger cookies) into coarse crumbs and toss them with 1 tablespoon of flour. Beat 4 eggs with ½ cup of brown or raw sugar and a pinch of salt to a firm peak. Swiftly fold in first the slightly cooled chocolate mixture and then the cookie crumbs. Pour the dough into a buttered and floured, fluted 10-inch tart form with a removable bottom, sprinkle a bit of flaky sea salt over it and bake it for no more than 15 minutes at 350° F. Do not over-bake it – the undercooked center will solidify enough once the cake has cooled down. Dust the cake with confectioner's sugar and serve with a few raspberries and a side of whipped cream or

BROWNED BUTTER ICE CREAM

Beat 6 egg yolks with ¾ cups of sugar to a soft ribbon. In a saucepan, melt and cook 2 sticks of butter until the milk solids have turned into brown bits, careful not to burn them. Gradually add the liquid, still warm butter while continuing to whisk the mixture, the way you would add oil to yolks when making mayonnaise. Scrape all the brown bits stuck to the bottom of the pan into the mix as well. Pour 2 cups of milk, 1 cup of heavy cream and three tablespoons of sugar into the same saucepan and bring it to a simmer over a medium flame. Mix 3 tablespoons of cornstarch with a bit of water and add them to the hot milk, stirring constantly. Cook over a low flame for a couple of minutes until slightly thickened, then whisk it into to the yolk and butter mixture. Chill it well, stirring now and then. Churn the mix in a sorbetière or ice cream maker. Add a few pinches of flaky sea salt in the last seconds of churning.

There were twelve guests that night, and from the deceptively simple dessert it is not difficult to imagine the ease and comfort the guests felt at table, even if none of its quality would ever have an influence on the way the aforementioned CEO ran his mediocre fast dining business.

Nor is it difficult to imagine how laborious it was to prepare an entirely different menu the next day at the Park Avenue home of the young heiress to a sugar fortune. The heiress asked for something exotic. She favored light dishes and vegetables and her investment banker husband was fond of rich roasted meats with heavy sauces.

VIETNAMESE RICE CRÈPES
WITH CHICKEN AND SHRIMP

STEAMED RED SNAPPER
WITH TURMERIC BEURRE BLANC

SAUTÉED SPINACH
WITH WATER CHESTNUTS

STEAMED BOK CHOY
WITH GINGER AND BLACK SESAME SEEDS

CARAMELIZED PORK TENDERLOIN

BRAISED EGGPLANT WITH SCALLIONS
CURRIED ASIAN YAM

JASMINE RICE WITH LEMONGRASS
AND FRIED SHALLOTS

PANDAN CRÈME CARAMEL
COCONUT AND LIME COOKIES

The table was elaborately decorated with orchids, the linen, crystal, porcelain and silver were luxurious, quite a bit more precious than the décor at the modernist townhouse in the Village from the previous day, and the service was not done by male models as was customary downtown but by the couple's elderly Paraguayan housekeeper and a young French waitress. The housekeeper was a hardworking woman and always grumpy. On that particular day, she was looking particularly morose, and I asked her what was the matter. I just won the lottery, she said. I thought she was mocking me, but the nanny assured me that it was true. I congratulated her and asked her what she was going to do. She said angrily, what am I going to do with 80 million dollars. Hearing this, the French waitress took her hand, smiled at her and said, my full name is Aurélie Bichon.

There is for any experienced cook no way of understanding the trend of having such attractively designed kitchens that however make it not only impractical but cumbersome to prepare elaborate meals in them. To us a kitchen is a room in which a great deal of preparation for cooking as well as the cooking itself takes place. I have seen many spotless, beautifully designed kitchens that have never been used for more than making protein shakes, placing phone calls and reheating takeout food in a microwave oven. Their pantries reveal a wide array of vitamins pills, several open boxes of breakfast cereals, large containers of protein shake powder, an old bottle each of already oxidized olive oil and cloudy vinegar, and a handful of stale spices in plastic shakers. The cabinets under the counter are largely empty but for a few never-used cheap pots and pans, silent witnesses to less affluent times when home-cooking might have become a necessary option. The kitchen drawers are usually filled with clutter, ranging from pens and store receipts to disposable chopsticks, single-serve packages of ketchup and soy sauce and stacks of stained takeout menus. One drawer will, without exception, reveal a whisk, two large serving spoons, a soup ladle and two oversized spatulas, all from a set made entirely of cheap black plastic. And all this without any logic but exhibiting on the surface the taste that prevails in modern design magazines. Taste here undoubtedly is the deceptively clean modern-design-catalogue taste. It never ceases to puzzle me.

Years ago, a successful business man, having moved into his new home, a townhouse that took 2 years to fully renovate, hired me as his part-time chef so he could finally eat some of his meals at home. For years he had been eating out, night after night. He now eats not only real homemade food in his elegant dining room but even requests the service of a butler. Dinner begins with a variety of hors d'oeuvres followed by an appetizer, a main course, the occasional cheese or salad course, dessert and, of course, cookies. He also asked me to appoint the very large kitchen on the townhouse's lower level with anything I deemed necessary to serve twelve people – he entertains that number as many times a year. In his kitchen, which he rarely wanders into, I have prepared countless meals, including

SEARED STRIPED BASS FILETS

Cut a cleaned and scaled whole striped bass into portion sizes. Brush the pieces with melted butter and season them with salt and pepper and some finely chopped fresh thyme. Sear them, skin-side up, in a frying pan until golden brown and place them, skin-side down, on a parchment-paper-lined sheet pan. Finish cooking the filets in a 400° F oven – 5 minutes should suffice, depending on their thickness. The fish is done once it offers no resistance when pierced with a toothpick. Lift the filets off the paper, leaving the skin behind. Serve with lemon wedges or perhaps a light *beurre blanc* or even a *beurre rouge*.

I often make a light purée to serve alongside this preparation of fish.

PURÉE OF FENNEL AND POTATOES

Wash and peel several Yukon Gold potatoes and steam them along with a quartered fennel bulb over water into which you have added a quartered lemon and several juniper berries. Steam until the tines of a fork enter easily into the potatoes and the fennel is very tender. Purée the fennel with the softened pulp of the lemons, careful to not add any lemon seeds. Push the potatoes through a ricer, add the fennel purée and whip it while adding a bit of olive oil. Season with salt and white pepper.

The purée makes an equally lovely hors d'oeuvre. Whip even more olive oil into it, add some crushed fresh garlic and spoon or pipe it into small, hollowed-out cherry tomatoes. Garnish with chopped parsley.

In New York it is not unusual for men of privilege to not only hire a chef to cook for them in their home but to occasionally ask him or her to replicate a certain dish they have had at some restaurant. Perhaps it is meant as a way to spur on the chef to make a greater effort, or perhaps it is a sign for the employer's lack of imagination or trust in his chef's abilities. A private chef is supposed to fulfill all his employer's culinary wishes. It is rare to find a private chef who has not developed a subtle instinct for his employer's needs. Among the men I have cooked for I have seen several cases who were keen to micromanage every single detail of their lives and who were relieved when I took charge and did not let them interfere with anything pertaining to the kitchen or the food I was preparing for them, reminding them that it was my authority that had convinced them to hire me in the first place.

The first person who ever hired me as a chef was an avid gourmet and very interested in the preparation of food. He was constantly reading up on culinary fads and the city's newest restaurants for information concerning what and when one ought to eat at what places, to be ahead of everybody else. This did not have any influence on the cooking I executed for him. He used to frequently tell me of meals he'd had at some of the city's most renowned restaurants, concluding that he would arrange one day for me to go and eat there on his behalf so I could sample their menus and, as he liked to say, deconstruct the dishes he had in mind so that I could later recreate them for him and his guests. He never followed up on this offer, not once in the several years that I worked for him. Another habit of his was to point out recipes in one of the many food publications he subscribed to and urge me to follow them, a proposition I usually brusquely brushed aside, making it clear that I thought that I could do better. Once at a large lunch party he loudly declared for everyone to hear that the carrot *velouté* I had prepared following his request was better than the one he had once been served at Daniel Boulud's famous flagship restaurant, *Daniel*. The question if he meant to compliment me or rather flatter himself for having hired me still amuses me. Perhaps he needed to convey that his culinary taste was refined enough to distinguish between two Daniels and that it was at his house that carrot *velouté* had reached its absolute zenith.

CURRIED CARROT VELOUTÉ

Peel and cut 3 large carrots and 1 parsnip into irregular diamond shapes. Toss the pieces with a little extra virgin olive oil and a sprinkling of turbinado sugar, spread them out on a parchment-paper-lined sheet pan and roast them at 425° F until they begin to caramelize, about 15 minutes. Peel and thinly slice 3 shallots and 1 small knob of fresh ginger. Gently sauté the two in 1 tablespoon butter, adding a dash of curry powder, cinnamon, ground clove and mace once they are translucent. Add the roasted carrots and enough mild, homemade chicken broth or coconut water to cover. Bring everything to a light simmer and add a small apple, peeled, cored and quartered. When the carrots are fork tender, blend the soup in batches, adding only as much of the broth as necessary to blend it smoothly. Strain it through a fine-mesh sieve. Add more broth if needed to give it a velvety consistency. Season the soup with salt and finely ground white pepper while it is still warm. Adding heavy cream or coconut cream into soups is quite common in restaurants but I usually advise against it, preferring to keep the flavor clean and bright. Serve thoroughly chilled or briefly, gently reheated. It must never come to a boil. If served cold, garnish with diced green apple, marinated in fresh lime juice and a few saffron strands. If served warm, add a dash of lemon juice to the soup just before serving. A dollop of lightly whipped heavy cream, seasoned with salt and nutmeg and spooned over each individual serving is acceptable.

The fish course I served next was simple and straightforward.

BAKED SALMON FILET

Take a whole side of filetted salmon and, using pliers or tweezers, carefully pull out any remaining bones. Generously season with kosher salt and a dense shower of whole fennel seeds. Lay the filet skin-side up on a parchment-paper-lined sheet pan and roast at 400° F for about 10 minutes. Take it out of the oven and remove the skin in one piece, pulling it away from the tail end. Return it to the oven for another 7 minutes. Take it out once more and carefully scrape away the layer of fatty dark meat with a fish knife and discard it. The salmon should still be rare in its center; if it seems too rare at this point return it to the oven for a just few more minutes. Season its exposed flesh with salt and carefully, using the parchment paper to lift it, flip the filet onto a platter in one piece. Serve warm or at room temperature with

HORSERADISH CREAM

Pour a pint of very cold heavy cream into a stainless steel bowl and beat it to a soft peak with a hand whisk. This is done with fair ease when the bowl and whisk have been chilled in the freezer for 30 minutes beforehand or by placing the bowl over a bowl of ice. Fold in 4 tablespoons of very finely, freshly grated horseradish as well as the finely grated zest of 1 lemon. Season with salt and white pepper. Fill into a serving bowl and garnish with sliced chives.

This sauce is also suitable for smoked fish and cold-cut, roasted meats.

At the home of one of my clients' college friends, a Wall Street lawyer and avid collector of contemporary art, I sometimes prepare intimate dinners for a table of eight. She is one of those exceptional Korean-American women who make an excessive effort when they have guests. The table would be set with exquisite linen napkins and modern bone china plates, the glasses are hand-blown Austrian crystal, and she would always ask for a course of assorted cheeses to be passed before dessert and have the finest French chocolates to be served after dessert. Once, to honor her heritage, I proposed to make a French dessert with a Korean touch.

STUFFED KOREAN PEAR WITH
JASMINE TEA-FLAVORED CRÈME ANGLAISE

Score an "X" into the flat side of fresh chestnuts, about 4 per serving. Rinse them with water and place them, still wet, on an aluminum foil lined baking sheet. Roast them at 400° F for about 20 minutes, until the nuts are tender. Peel them while still warm, careful to remove all of the skin along with the shells, and, using your fingertips, crumble them into uneven bits. Mix them with lightly toasted bread crumbs, sugar, cinnamon, powdered ginger and ground clove and some melted butter. Cut a cap off the top of Asian pears (one per serving) and hollow them out with a melon baller or spoon, removing the seeds and core. Stuff them with the chestnut mix, replace the caps onto them and position each pear on a thick orange slice inside a Dutch oven or baking dish. Scatter a few pieces of star anise and a cinnamon stick, broken into pieces, around the pears. Bring a equal amount of sweet rice wine and water to a boil, enough to cover the bottom of the pan by about half an inch, and pour it over the pears. Cover with a lid or a double layer of aluminum foil and bake the pears in a 400° F oven until soft, about 1 hour. Carefully remove the pears and oranges from the pan, pour the pan juices into a sauce pot and simmer them until reduced to a thick syrup. Strain it and set it aside.

Separate 6 eggs. Reserve the egg whites for another use and mix the yolks with ¼ cup of sugar. In a sauce pan, heat 1 ¼ cup of milk, lower 3 tea bags of jasmine-flavored green tea and allow them to steep for 5 minutes. Remove the tea bags, squeezing all liquid from them into the milk, add ¼ cup of heavy cream to it and bring it to a simmer. Temper the yolks with a bit of the hot liquid before adding them to the sauce pan. Heat gently, stirring constantly, until it coats the back of a wooden spoon. Strain the cream through fine-mesh sieve into a bowl set over a larger bowl filled with ice. Stir gently until cooled.

Serve the pears on their orange slices, glazed with the syrup and with a bit of the jasmine tea *crème anglaise* spooned over them.

A German friend (whom I had not met) of a client once booked me to prepare a festive supper for her annual, well-known Christmas Eve party, well-known because she insisted on using real candles on her Christmas tree as per German tradition. It is indeed unusual and possibly illegal to light real candles on Christmas trees in New York – the hostess' way of preempting any possible trouble was to invite the commissioner of the New York City Fire Department as her guest of honor. The address was a grand residence on Manhattan's Upper West Side. The menu and cooking was suitable to the elegant décor and view of Central Park. The ladies in attendance were wearing French Haute Couture, the waiters donned their American tuxedos, the Commissioner arrived dressed in his official uniform, the art on the walls was Japanese calligraphy, the antique porcelain service on which the food was served was real *Meissener* – she had brought it with her from Hamburg – and the Champagne was from France. But the fish course was German.

SALMON TERRINE

Slice away and discard any dark meat from 1 pound of skinned fresh salmon filet. Cut the filet into large cubes and place them in the freezer for 10 minutes. Season the salmon pieces with salt and pulse them in a food processor until they are coarsely chopped. Add ½ cup of very cold heavy cream and 1 tablespoon of tomato paste and rapidly process the mixture to a fine puree without overworking it. Transfer it to a mixing bowl and mix into it 3 lightly beaten egg whites, another ½ cup of cream and 1 tablespoon port wine. Adjust the seasoning with salt, white pepper, mace and powdered ginger to taste and pour it into a buttered terrine dish or 7-inch loaf pan. Cover with aluminum foil, place it into a baking dish, fill the dish halfway with boiling hot water and bake the terrine in a 375° F oven for 35 minutes. Remove the foil, test the terrine's doneness with a skewer and bake for another 5 minutes if necessary. Chill the terrine for 5 hours or overnight, unmold and serve with whipped sour cream seasoned with a few drops of vodka, salt, chopped dill, grated lemon zest, coarsely cracked black peppercorns and a side of salmon caviar.

This is a very elegant dish.

It was a Christmas supper to be remembered.

Another time I was booked by a friend (whom I had never met) of a frequent guest of one of my clients. This time it was on the Upper East Side. If the company was less numerous than the one at the Christmas supper just prescribed, it was more homogenous. I was told that the dinner would have to be kosher. The meat course I decided upon preparing was

BRAISED LAMB SHANKS

Rub lamb shanks, one per person, all over with olive oil and season them assertively with salt and black pepper. Working in batches, brown them on all sides in a very hot Dutch oven. Deglaze the pan between batches with a bit of water and reserve the glaze in a cup. When the shanks have all been browned, wipe out the pan, heat a little bit of olive oil in it and add aromatic vegetables – shallots, peeled carrots and celery stalks, all cut into large chunks; a few lightly cracked garlic cloves with their skins, and a wide strip of orange rind. Thoroughly brown the vegetables in the pan, transfer them to a bowl, add the reserved meat glaze to the pot and place the shanks into the pot, interlaced with a few branches of fresh thyme, a couple of bay leaves and 1 or 2 cinnamon sticks. Scatter the vegetables over the shanks and add just enough fresh-squeezed or bottled non-sweetened pomegranate juice to all but cover the meat.

'The hostess' way of preempting any possible trouble
with the New York City Fire Department
was to invite its commissioner as her guest of honor.'

Bring the liquid to a simmer, place a round piece of parchment paper with a hole cut in its center (to let steam escape) over the meat, cover the pot with its lid and place it in a 300° F oven. Braise the meat for up to 3 hours, until it all but falls off the bone. Carefully remove the shanks and place them on a parchment paper-lined sheet pan. Raise the oven temperature to 400° F. Pour the pan-juices and vegetables through a fine mesh sieve into a sauce pan. Recover just the shallots and carrots and puree them with a bit of liquid in a blender. Brush the shanks with the puree, season them with salt and return them to the oven for 10 minutes. Reduce the reserved sauce to a thick syrup, skimming off any fat or foam, and season it with pepper and salt. Serve the shanks with the sauce, garnished with chopped cilantro and fresh pomegranate seeds.

The hostess had begged me to serve a *béarnaise* sauce with the lamb but I had refused. It had been necessary to make her understand that her own kosher rules forbade me the use of a dairy product for the meat course and that a béarnaise sauce had to be made with butter, real butter and nothing but real butter. But how come then, she asked, he has been served meat with a béarnaise in kosher restaurants. They are probably, I said disdainfully, using a combination of margarine and cornstarch.

Over the years I have had to deal with all kinds of challenges. One client had recently gotten engaged to an interior designer who grew up as part of the jet set of South Beach. She moved into his penthouse on Central Park South and refurnished it with her own, insouciant, sunny sense of style. It was always a pleasure to see them. Alas the kitchen was not pleasurable to cook in. It was very small and disorganized, and the sink was frequently full of dirty dishes when I arrived, usually, around noon to start cooking. The oversized dinner plates were highly impractical, in the shape of large cabbage leaves, and the antique set of silverware stained and incomplete. The fiancé's cat, terrified of the fiancée's terrier, had made it her habit to lounge on the kitchen counter and always fought me vehemently when I tried to get her off the counterspace that I needed so dearly to get any work done. The friendliness and generosity of the hosts redeemed the resulting scratches on my hands and overall difficult working conditions. A few years later, the couple had three children and their oldest son became fascinated by everything pertaining to the kitchen and eager to get involved. He was a quick study and an excellent sorcerer's apprentice. Together, we once made

STUFFED AND FRIED SARDINES

To butterfly fresh sardines, rinse them under running cold water and carefully rub away the scales with your fingers, working from the tail towards the head without damaging the skin. Do this over a colander to catch the scales lest they clog the drain of your sink. To butterfly sardines takes some practice. Make a small incision just behind the sardine's head to expose the spine. Now grab a hold of the exposed spine with both your left and right index and thumb, right hand just below the head. Gently pull with your right hand, literally running the spine through your left thumb and index, which will split the body open through the soft belly as you pull. The head and spine should come away with the guts attached. Pinch off the spine, leaving the fish's tail attached to the now butterflied body. Now remove the little fin in the center of each sardine's back and rinse the sardines in cold water. Fill each sardine with a bit of fresh Ricotta, a few fresh marjoram leaves and a well-rinsed oil-cured anchovy filet, folding the belly over the stuffing to keep it enclosed. Roll the sardines first in flour, then beaten eggs and finally in bread crumbs. Deep-fry them in olive oil heated to 350° F until golden brown and crisp. Transfer to a paper-towel-lined sheet pan to drain off excess oil and serve immediately, sprinkled with chopped fresh parsley and lemon wedges for drizzling.

The seven-year-old boy explained to me that sardines were considered sustainable and that their consumption was thus politically correct. In any case they made for a succulent appetizer. The marjoram and lemon gave it a vibrant aroma.

The joy of working with an intelligent and open-minded child compensated for the burden of other days when I had to cook for less distinguished grown-ups.

The most unexpected combination of menu and setting I ever played a part in took place once (and many times again thereafter) in the home of a very elegant Cuban lady who requested a Bavarian feast. It was the first time anyone had ever asked me to cook Bavarian food. Even though I was technically born in Bavaria I have never considered myself a Bavarian nor do I speak the Bavarian dialect but perhaps one must have lived there to know how to prepare their food well. German dishes in general are looked down upon by the French, and even Germans from the northern part of the country misunderstand and deride the Bavarian cuisine of the south. As for American interpretations of it, the results are barely recognizable to someone in the know. Recently there has been in New York a resurgence in interest in Germanic food, but it is still difficult to find the necessary German ingredients or condiments to prepare any of it at home. This is the menu I proposed.

RED-BEET-PICKLED QUAIL EGGS

MINI CROISSANTS FILLED WITH HAM AND CHEESE

OBATZDA WITH SOFT PRETZELS AND RADISHES

A VARIETY OF BAVARIAN SAUSAGES
WITH ASSORTED GERMAN MUSTARDS

SMOKED CHICKEN BREASTS

BRAISED SAUERKRAUT WITH SMOKED PORK BELLY
AND JUNIPER BERRIES

DUCK-FAT-ROASTED APPLES

MASHED POTATOES WITH FRIED SHALLOTS

PRINZREGENTENTORTE

OBATZDA*

Remove the white rind of a whole, mild camembert or a wedge of brie. Whip it until smooth before gradually adding 1 cup of *Quark,*** a tablespoon at a time, whisking the mixture between each addition until creamy. Season with salt, white pepper and a pinch of crushed celery seeds. Refrigerate until cold enough to hold its shape, form it into quenelles and roll them alternately in sweet paprika powder and in thinly sliced chives. Arrange the quenelles on individual plates garnished with Bibb lettuce leaves, sliced cucumber pickles and quartered pink radishes. Serve with soft pretzels, preferably warmed. To do this, brush them with cold water and place them for 5 minutes in a 350° F oven. The water makes the crust crunchy and the crumb soft and steamy.

---

* Bavarian dialect, literally *pasted on.*
** German-style creamy cottage cheese. If unavailable, use *fromage blanc*, Ricotta or very thick Greek yogurt.

BRAISED SAUERKRAUT

Using your bare hands, squeeze the juice from 2 quarts of barrel sauerkraut into a bowl. In a Dutch oven, sauté 1 thinly sliced, large white onion with 1 tablespoon of butter until light golden. Add the squeezed sauerkraut, sauté some more until it all begins to brown. Deglaze with the sauerkraut juices as well as 1 cup of dry white wine (or leftover Champagne). Fold in 1 heaped tablespoon of dried juniper berries and about 1 teaspoon of caraway seeds.

Add 1 tart apple, cored and cut into sections, and a slab of smoked bacon, its rind spiked with cloves. Submerge the slab halfway in the sauerkraut, rind-side up. Bring the sauerkraut to a light simmer, adding more wine if it seems too dry for a braise, place a round piece of parchment paper with a 1-inch hole cut out of its center directly onto the sauerkraut, add the lid and braise the sauerkraut and bacon in a 300 ° F oven for 3 hours. Before serving, peel off the bacon rind with the cloves and discard it. Slice the bacon crosswise into thick slices.

Serve with pan-fried German-style *bratwursts*, assorted mustards, and mashed potatoes.

This particular preparation of sauerkraut is a pleasant novelty for those used to watery sauerkraut and limp hot dogs that are commonly sold at sidewalk stands all across New York City.

This is a delicious *Torte* that was created in the late Nineteenth Century in honor of Bavaria's then regent, Prince Regent Luitpolt.

PRINZREGENTENTORTE

Beat 2 sticks of softened butter with 1 cup of sugar, 3 drops of almond extract and the scraped seeds of 1 vanilla bean until very light and fluffy. Add 4 eggs, one at a time, beating vigorously until fully incorporated before adding the next. Fold in 1½ cups of cake flour, ⅓ cup of potato starch and 1 teaspoon of baking powder, all sifted together. Evenly spread a scant soup ladle of dough onto a parchment-paper-lined base of a spring form and place it in a 350° F oven for about 8 minutes. Repeat this step until all the dough is used up, lining the base with fresh parchment paper each time. There should be 8 individually baked cake layers.

Melt 5 ounces of dark chocolate in a bowl set over boiling water. In a sauce pan, dissolve 1 cup of sugar in ½ cup of water, add 3 strips of lemon rind and bring to a simmer. Cook until the syrup reaches the thread stage, at 235° F. Remove the lemon rind. In a mixing bowl, beat 3 yolks with ¼ cup of warm espresso or very strong coffee and gradually add the warm syrup, beating constantly. Add the warm chocolate and gradually beat in 1 ½ sticks of butter, 1 tablespoon at a time. Do not refrigerate the cream. Assemble the torte on a rack or turntable by spreading 2 tablespoons of chocolate cream between the cake layers, covering the last layer and the sides with a thin layer of the leftover cream. Chill until fully set.

In a saucepan, whisk 1 teaspoon unsweetened cocoa powder into ½ cup of cold water. Add 10 ounces of chopped dark chocolate and ½ cup of sugar and cook until it simmers. Let it cool down until barely warm and pour it over the cake, making sure the sides are fully covered with glaze. Chill the torte until the glaze is set but serve it at room temperature, with barely sweetened whipped cream on the side. Serving ice cream with a torte would be what Germans call *Stilbruch*, a breech of style.

These traditional Bavarian dishes added variety to the usual elegant French fare commonly served in the Cuban lady's palatial apartment on Park Avenue. Often the mistresses of such households grew up eating rather simple fare and barely touch the rich food prepared by their French caterers. And then there are the dishes that they ask their immigrant housekeepers to prepare for them when there is no one else around. Asking for these secretive favors compensates them for the annoyance of all those social engagements where one must pretend to eat but doesn't for fear of gaining weight.

At the country house in the Hamptons where I got my first break as a private chef, the Columbian housekeeper occasionally prepared Columbian dishes for herself and let me taste them. Once, when I made an upside down pineapple cake, she asked me to save the core and peels for her. She then showed me how use them to make a delectable Columbian drink called

CHICHA DE ARROZ CON PIÑA

Cut the peels and core of 1 pineapple into chunks and soak

them overnight in cold water. The next day, place the peels and core into a non-reactive large pot, add ¾ cups of long grain rice, 1 cinnamon stick, 1 clove, ¼ cup of sugar and 2 quarts of cold water. Bring to a simmer and cook until the rice is tender. Remove the cinnamon stick and blend everything else in batches with the cooking liquid. Pass it through a fine-mesh sieve and discard the solids. Add more sugar to taste and more water if the mixture is too thick to drink. Serve thoroughly chilled. Short of covering the drink with a piece of cloth and leaving it outside to ferment for a couple of days as is tradition in Columbia, a pleasantly sour note can be added to the drink by stirring a couple of tablespoons of apple cider vinegar into it.

The Columbian housekeeper's love of pineapple and cilantro inspired me to make

PINEAPPLE AND CILANTRO SORBET

Chill a very ripe pineapple overnight in the refrigerator, peel and core it, cut it into chunks and place it into a blender with a generous handful of fresh cilantro stems and leaves. Blend until smooth, pass it through a fine-mesh sieve and churn it into a soft-serve sorbet in an ice cream maker. Serve immediately as it looses it unctuous quality once it is deep-frozen.

This is the most refreshing and simplest sorbet in my entire repertoire.

Several years ago, my partner Filip Noterdaeme and I had an unusual dinner in an unusual setting. We had been invited to a party in a penthouse on Park Avenue South near Union Square. We arrived at the address in the early evening and took the elevator to the top floor, where the party was held. The apartment was a luxurious duplex and had just been entirely renovated. The host was the heir of a well-to-do publishing dynasty and known for his decadent all-male parties. A naked servant in a leather choker would handle the buffet-style dinner service. In the living room countless votive candles had been lit. The burly, bearded cook, wearing a blond wig and red evening dress, was helping the server set the table with linen, silver and glasses and putting the last finishing touches on platters of glazed ham, roast turkey, and baked macaroni and cheese. Filip Noterdaeme and I were invited to go downstairs to see the dungeon, a tiled room with a black leather sling and some chains and hooks, paraphernalia for wild doings.

THE ART OF GAY COOKING

Suddenly, there was a warm noisy welcome for a group of arriving guests. Their coats were taken to the bedroom and the wine and Champagne they had brought upraised for dinner. The bottles were handed to the naked servant to be put on ice or decanted into carafes, with some supervision from one or two zealous guests. The atmosphere quickly became as suitably hot as an oven ready for a spit roast. It would not take too long before things got out of hand. The boyfriend announced that dinner was served, and there was a round of late comers arriving when we were all but finished eating. The naked servant was praised for his impeccable service – the host was very proud of having trained him personally – and allowed to eat his dinner next to his master, kneeling on the floor, his hands held behind his back while trying to eat from an immensely precious silver dog bowl.

SAUCE FOR GLAZED HAM
AND OTHER COLD MEATS

In a sauté pan, cook 6 chopped large shallots in 2 tablespoons of butter until translucent. Add a sprig of fresh thyme, powdered allspice and chili flakes to taste, ½ cored, chopped fresh pineapple, 1 cup of raisins, and a tablespoon of brown sugar and cook everything until lightly caramelized. Add ½ cup of ketchup, ¼ cup of Bourbon, ¼ cup of rice vinegar and 1 cup of water, stir and simmer for 15 minutes. Remove the thyme, puree everything in a blender and strain. Season with salt and pepper to taste.

The pureeing and straining can be omitted if a chunky sauce is preferred.

The turkey, repeatedly basted with the juices from the dripping pan and melted butter, had been roasted for exactly as long as the consulted recipe had advised. It was roasted a lot longer than I would have chosen to. Americans dislike to see any pink when turkey is carved, they prefer their steaks and burgers medium rare. The ham and macaroni were cooked to perfection. It was, with the salad and red velvet cake preceding and following the main course, an exceedingly rich meal. After dinner, the guests disappeared one by one into the dungeon, but Filip Noterdaeme and I preferred to leave the party and head to Bar d'O, a very trendy and cosmopolitan cabaret in the West Village to see Joey Arias, Raven O and Sherry Vine perform. Providently I had prepared a French song to perform, *La Bohème* by Charles Aznavour, which was a blessing for the show and a novelty to the Americans in the audience.

There have been over the years countless home-cooked dinners in New York homes of which the far greater number was cooked by me, be it at our own place for our friends or at clients' homes for them and their family and friends. Being invited for dinner served in someone's home has, for us, remained a rarity. But this it not a reproach. With the exception of those who routinely hire caterers or private chefs like me, most New Yorkers have become too shy about their limitations either as cooks or as hosts and prefer to hold their dinner parties in restaurants – and that is their ideal. They enjoy being served and keeping their dwellings private. Unfortunately, they rarely feel compelled to exhibit the fine art of picking up the tab for their guests.

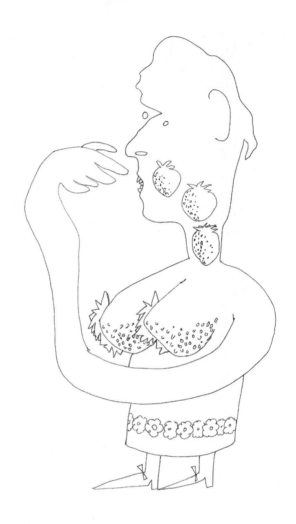

III
DISHES FOR
SOCIALITES

BEFORE MOVING TO NEW YORK, I was a pretty good cook but it was here that I became a chef. When I went to live with Filip Noterdaeme in Brooklyn Heights he said that we would have home-cooked food on most nights, he did not care much for dining out. In my beginnings as a private chef I was recreating dishes I either remembered from my childhood in France and Germany or had tasted in my years of working as a cater waiter – risotto, lamb roasts, filet mignon, chocolate mousse and apple tarts. Then when I got bored with this limited palette I began to explore the city's diverse food markets to develop my own personal interpretations of dishes from all around the world. Filip Noterdaeme not being able to decide whether he preferred my French, German, Korean, Vietnamese, Mexican or Italian experiments, all were kept in rotation. This approach was successful and made my career as a private chef; it gradually became my signature style as I grew more confident and adventurous.

A Dessert for the Allergic Socialite

One day when the private chef of an elderly socialite on Park Avenue asked me for help I taught her some desserts that might please her client. The options were limited as the socialite, who appeared to be anorexic and who kept in her kitchen cabinets a large array of digestive aids and laxatives, claimed that she was allergic to berries, gluten, nuts, and chocolate and possibly many other things. She had made up her mind that any kind of digestive discomfort signified a serious allergy and that all ingredients that had been part of the meal that preceded the discomfort should henceforth be banned from her diet. She demanded that the list be continuously updated. So I made a mild kaffir lime-flavored panna cotta with a grapefruit coulis. I poured 3 cups of heavy cream and 1 cup of milk into a sauce pan and added ½ cup of sugar and 6 fresh kaffir lime leaves, lightly bruised to release their flavor. This was gently simmered for a couple of minutes and then covered and put aside to infuse the cream with the kaffir lime leaf flavor. Then a pack of powdered gelatin was sprinkled over a few tablespoons of cold water. A few minutes later, the cream, gently reheated, was strained into a bowl and the bloomed gelatin added. Once the gelatin had fully dissolved in the mixture, the cream was ladled into eight dessert ramekins and chilled in the refrigerator until fully set, for 4 hours. Four cups of freshly pressed grapefruit juice were strained into a sauce pan and brought to a simmer with several pieces of star anise. The juice was simmered until it was reduced to a syrupy consistency and strained again. The panna cotta would be served unmolded, surrounded by a bit of the grapefruit syrup and garnished with piece of star anise. Then I made an alternative version of the classic Pavlova, a cardamom-flavored meringue filled with blood orange confit and whipped cream, as well as a ginger-spiced mango sorbet that would be served with sugar-encrusted Thai basil leaves. The socialite appeared in the kitchen. She did not acknowledge my presence in any way. She simply said to her chef, I am now also allergic to cream, citrus fruit and mangos.

Many clients asked for diet food; in fact I managed somehow to continue deciding about what to serve at my own discretion and, characteristically, rarely accommodated requests without making substantial changes to them. Most of my clients at the time being gay men everybody was fixated on getting enough protein in those days and that presented a difficulty at first because I did not have much experience in preparing meat dishes, except the inevitable roasted whole chicken. Beef was in constant demand, though the occasional roasted leg of lamb was also received favorably. Or there would be a pork tenderloin, served with ample amounts of sautéed leafy greens, pork being hailed at the time as the "other" white meat and leafy greens being hailed as generally healthy, long before everybody became inordinately obsessed with ordinary kale. But what about occasionally serving a vegetarian meal. I gave it a try. Basmati rice would be rinsed, soaked, boiled and finally steamed with butter and yogurt in a covered Dutch oven, and when sufficiently cooked turned into a hollow dish to reveal a golden crust and served with at least three different chutneys and a wide array of stewed vegetables, chickpeas and lentils. It was my hope that the colorful spread would make the men forget the absence of meat, chicken or seafood. Where's the beef, they said when they stepped up to the buffet.

The only person who ever explicitly asked me to prepare what he called "spa food" was a shareholder in a beach house I cooked at on weekends who always stood first in line at the lunch buffet, always came back for seconds and always asked for ice cream with his dessert. I advised him to diet during the week, arguing that I had not been hired to prepare

EVIAN-STEAMED BROCCOLI

Wash a bunch of broccoli, cut off the thick stem, peel and slice it into thick coins. Cut up the head into mid-size florets, slicing through the thicker stems. Steam the pieces over simmering

Evian water for no longer than 3 minutes and either serve them immediately or submerge them in an ice bath, naturally made of Evian water and Evian ice cubes, to preserve their vibrant green color. This is of course rather plain but dressed with a little fragrant olive oil (walnut, hazelnut, or avocado oil are permitted as a substitute) and seasoned with flaky sea salt and coarsely ground black pepper or chili flakes, the dish acquires a pure and clean flavor that perhaps even strict carnivores will appreciate.

When the first plane hit the North Tower of the World Trade Center on 9/11 I was at home and had no precise idea of what was happening. Our roommate Nick had been awoken by a phone call telling him there was a fire in his office on the 98th floor of the North Tower. Could one grasp the weight of such news. We didn't and turned on the television. We then heard a thunderous noise from across the river. One second later we saw on our little television screen an explosion in the second tower. Then we knew. Not much later everything came tumbling down. This convinced me to act in the way any caring friend should. I would make cookies, little hand-rolled, crescent-shaped Viennese cookies, and get Nick involved in making them to distract him from his distress. I had learned how to make them from my grandmother who had taken her mother's recipe with her to Germany when she was a refugee, in 1945, traveling on foot from Prague to the German border. With these cookies, she once told me, one might not only feel reminded of civilized life but be able to be hospitable. On that terrible day in 2001, we made about 500 of them. We then made our way to the Brooklyn promenade and along with many others looked at the plume of smoke and clouds of dust over lower Manhattan. What were we to do with all those cookies. The next day, we decided to bring them to one of the rescue stations. They seemed madly extravagant for sustenance but I packed them neatly into Chinese take-out containers and handed them to a group of very tired firemen. Later I learned that much of the food that restaurateurs and well-meaning citizens were bringing to the aid centers was either eaten by the countless volunteers or had to be thrown away. More important things than food were needed in those unsettling days in a shaken city.

Throughout this dark period, our friend Joey Arias was still performing several nights a week at Bar d'O in the West Village, the nightclub where I had first met Filip Noterdaeme, a couple of years earlier. That night, back in 1999, Joey had invited me to come to the club and perform a song as his guest. It was a Tuesday night and the club was full of regulars.

Opening the show was Raven O, later very famous as the host of *The Box* nightclub, and there was Sherry Vine with her popular song parodies, and the atmosphere was crisp with excitement. Bar d'O did not have a stage, one simply stood in the middle of the room, leaning against a narrow counter covered in little grey tiles. Raven O's observant eye passed quickly and lightly over the audience. I heard him tell the manager to dim the lights a little bit more before he introduced Joey. But Joey did not sing yet, he merely passed on the microphone to me. I was evidently caught off guard. I was relieved when I caught a knowing look from the manager, who had already cued the music for the song I had decided to sing, *The Best Is Yet to Come*. Later, when Filip Noterdaeme, to show how much he had enjoyed my performance, told me he would like to hear me sing French or German songs, too, I could not help protesting that New York audiences principally preferred to be sung to in English.

I had first seen Joey Arias perform a few years earlier and we had become friends, sometimes performing together; him in drag, me – not. Filip Noterdaeme said that I should convert to performing in drag as well and that it would guarantee me a larger audience. Joey told Filip Noterdaeme that drag was not for everyone and that it would be a drag if everyone were to do it. He told me that I should remain the performer I had always been and continue donning what he liked to call *boy drag*, the look of a woman looking like a boy. Filip Noterdaeme could not resist having the last word and years later asked me to assume the role of Madame Butterfly for his art project, the Homeless Museum of Art, which I refused – until I gave in, one day before the opening.

If Joey Arias was known as an exquisite performer it was not only for his unique style and way to channel Billie Holiday while remaining completely himself or for his gentle character but also for the shows he had done with the late Klaus Nomi. Joey told me that when he and Klaus met, Klaus was engaged as a pastry chef who prepared and delivered delicious cakes to *Windows on the World*, the restaurant on the 106th floor of the North Tower of the World Trade Center. He said that Klaus made the best chocolate cakes. As Klaus was a lover of opera, Joey told me, the two had agreed that Klaus should one day be cast as the Witch in Humperdinck's opera *Hänsel und Gretel*, and I told Joey Arias that if he ever had, everyone would have forgotten everything they had always thought they knew about the part and henceforth wouldn't have wanted anyone but Klaus to sing it.

My enchanting friend was as original in his storytelling as in everything else. Not too long ago, Lukas Volger, the editor of *Jarry*, a new gay food magazine read by those obsessed with food and men, asked me to contribute an article with a recipe for its first issue. When I asked Joey if he would be willing to do a cooking session with me about which I would then write for the magazine he proposed his recipe for

CRUDDY CHICKEN

Marinate 4 organic chicken thighs and 4 chicken legs in enough Tabasco sauce to keep the pieces well submerged for several hours – the longer the better. Pour 2 cups of seasoned flour[5]* into a large brown paper bag and add the drained chicken pieces. Close the bag and toss the chicken pieces around until generously coated with flour. Fry them in batches in corn oil, heated to 350° F, until browned and completely cooked through, for as long as 20 minutes. Drain them on paper towels before arranging them on a parchment-paper lined baking sheet. Pour generous amounts of bottled BBQ sauce and honey over each piece and place the sheet pan in 400° F oven. Bake for about 20 minutes, until the sauce is thickened and bubbly. Ten minutes into baking time, baste the pieces with the sauce, careful to cover them completely. Serve hot, with buttery mashed potatoes and a simple salad of lettuce and tomatoes, dressed with a light vinaigrette.

Everyone thought the amount of Tabasco used in the recipe was an exaggeration, that Joey was pulling their legs. Not at all. A few months earlier Joey had been our official witness when Filip Noterdaeme and I got married at the Guggenheim Museum, and during the intimate seven-course wedding dinner we had with him and our officiant, Penny Arcade, at *Jean Georges*, our favorite New York restaurant for very special occasions, he had kept on taking bites out of a whole fresh jalapeño he was hiding in his handbag. Joey's obsession with hot chilies is documented, it has entered the realm of urban legend.

---

* Seasoned flour is a mix of flour, salt, paprika, pepper, cumin, garlic powder and so on, in which chicken pieces or fish filets destined for frying are coated just before being lowered into the hot oil for crispness and boosted flavor.

IV
MUSIC IN
THE KITCHEN

SINGERS HAVE ALWAYS INTRIGUED and seduced me. Even long before I started out as a dilettante in the cabaret world they were my inspiration, especially the eccentric ones, from opera to pop music, the way renaissance painters and conceptual artists were for Filip Noterdaeme.

Whenever we would see Joey Arias perform, Filip Noterdaeme remarked that it was his particular way of always being in the moment and never taking himself too seriously that made him one of the very best. Goodness knows how much work was required to make it all seem effortless. And so it is in the kitchen. Stress and hesitation are as unpleasant to witness there as they would be anywhere else. One can't, one shan't let it become apparent. Food and performance are much too enjoyable to combine with angst. All the same, efforts, even tremendous efforts, must be made, and we shall see how, before any story of competent cooking begins, a musical sense is indispensable. The same is not necessarily true in reverse. That is why cooking can be such a rewarding pastime for musical people. There is so much melody and rhythm that can infuse a meal. This doesn't of course apply to food that emerges pre-measured, pre-washed and precut in home-delivered boxes from one of those new delivery services that cater to hobby cooks with big ambitions and little time. But the cooking I wish to speak of is an exalted form of home-cooking, and it was through curiosity and fearlessness, which ignore the convenience of shortcuts, that I in due course became an accomplished chef.

In earlier days, memories of which are scattered throughout this book, if indulgent friends or family members on this or that occasion said that the cooking I produced was proof of my talent, it neither charmed nor flattered me into imagining to ever do it professionally. As with performing, the only way to learn how to cook is to cook, and for me, unlike for many professional chefs whose training did not begin until they entered cooking school, it has been an enjoyable and relaxing part of life since I was very young, when my mother kept me in the kitchen for company when she was preparing family meals. It was in this setting of watching my mother that I not only became interested in cooking but eager to get involved, just as, at about the same time, seeing Ingmar Bergmans' film version of Mozart's opera *The Magic Flute* or a French theater troupe perform a French version of the American musical *Godspell* made me want me to become a performer. It was at this time, then, that music in the kitchen began.

My first muse was a very dear and chubby girl who lived next door and whom I invited over to my room for a sing-along performance of *The Magic Flute*. We were both seven years old; she was the first kid I met after we moved from Paris to Munich; she did not know how to sing or act, nor had she ever heard of *The Magic Flute*. I was not in the least deterred by either. I quickly explained everything to her before curtain call. I had by then listened and sung along to my Karl Böhm recording of the opera so many times that I knew the entire opera by heart. Obviously I was going to play the Queen of the Night and she would fill in the other roles. If she could not sing, could she not perhaps at least pretend to and move her lips to the recording? After an appraising glance at my apprehensive new friend it was evident she was perfectly suited to play Pamina. My mother's morning robe came to my mind as the elegant, the perfect costume choice for her, so running, on tiptoes and holding my breath, for my mother might not have been too taken by this idea, I quickly, stealthily got the robe out of my parents' bedroom and draped it all over her. I put on the record and instructed her to move her lips according to Pamina's Aria, *Ach, ich fühl's*. I stood aside and stage-whispered instructions. *Freude schöner Götterfunken*. She killed it, slayed it, bows, curtain calls, flower bouquets. Excited, I wrapped a blue towel around my hair, flipped the record, turned it on, and placed the needle on the part where the Queen of the Night makes her entrance to sing *Der Hölle Rache*. After that aria we both got rather hungry and went into the kitchen to find something edible. There were no cookies to be found but after rummaging through the cabinets I found a chocolate pudding mix. No one in Germany would think of making chocolate pudding from scratch as this handy mix of pre-measured cocoa and starch (and nothing else) is readily available in virtually every supermarket, but if you live in America and care to make an enhanced version of it at home this is my way of preparing

CHOCOLATE PUDDING

In a saucepan, bring 2 cups of milk and ¼ cup of sugar to a simmer. Mix together 2 tablespoons of cocoa powder, 3 tablespoons cornstarch, a pinch of salt, and, if you happen to keep some around, 1 tablespoon of malted milk powder. Add ½ cup of cold milk, whisk everything into a smooth paste and add it to the hot milk while stirring vigorously. When it has thickened and begins to boil, take it off the fire and add ¼ cup of chocolate chips or a few pieces of dark chocolate, stirring until the chocolate has completely melted. Immediately transfer it into portion-sized ramekins or dessert bowls. Serve warm or chilled. Some find the dark skin that forms on top to be the best part.

Many knowledgeable cooks consider the French equivalent to German chocolate pudding just as easy to prepare but even more delectable:

MOUSSE AU CHOCOLAT

In a metal bowl set over simmering water, melt 5 ounces of semisweet chocolate with 1 tablespoon butter. Separate 4 eggs. Add a pinch of salt to the egg whites and beat them to a firm peak. Add the yolks to the melted chocolate and fold in the egg whites in two steps. Fill into ramekins and chill for at least three hours.

It was in a hotel in Times Square some thirty years later that I had to walk through the kitchen in the basement to get to the lounge on the first floor where I starred in *Foreign Affairs*, a weekly cabaret variety show I directed for a couple of years. There is no reason to believe that the show should have been influenced in any way by what I was witnessing in the hotel's kitchen. The chef was a tired alumnus from a large, well-known culinary school and did not try to impress anyone. When the audience cheered and applauded at the end of the night's closing number, I made an exit and walked through the kitchen to the dismal locker room behind it, filled with maids' sensible shoes and dirty chef's whites. In the beginning of the engagement, the management had offered me and the other performers one of the hotel rooms as a dressing room but when the various dancers and singers I engaged from the world of drag and burlesque left behind not-so-innocent traces of makeup and glitter on the bed sheets and the bathroom towels, the hotel maids complained to the management and we were demoted to using the locker room in the basement. I sympathized with the maids. They said we were careless, didn't we know how difficult it was to get glitter off a carpet, didn't we know that lipstick smears on towels were impossible to get out, didn't we possibly do even more unspeakable and perverted things in that room. Couldn't we behave like sensible humane people who go about their job, but no we didn't want to grow up, we preferred to make a mess. Later when we ran into them in the locker room they said nothing. Discussing my guests' misdemeanors had been discouraged by the management. But their unblinking eyes were very eloquent. If the burlesque artists' arsenal of glitter and makeup had not impressed them, they were unquestionably enamored with their shoes, more outrageous and with higher heels than those that could be found at Macy's or even on Eighth Street, which had once been known as Manhattan's shoe store mile and had at the time still but a handful of barely surviving shoe stores.

Later the show's producer moved the entire operation to a club downtown where he and I had a dispute about creative control and where I, after a long period of tensions, withdrew from the show. One day, discussing my cabaret life with Filip Noterdaeme, he told me I ought to do something that no one would expect me to ever do. He said, You have sung the songs of European writers and singers – Bertolt Brecht and Kurt Weill and Edith Piaf and Marlene Dietrich and Jaques Brel and Hildegard Neff and Zarah Leander – and now you should sing the songs of an American icon. He said as a matter of fact the icon should be Elvis Presley, and at first when I thought about rhythm and blues and the difficulty for Europeans to sing on the back beat I wished he hadn't. But Filip Noterdaeme being perceptive and persuasive assured me that I would make it work. It is certainly a mistake to allow a reputation for always making it work to be born and give a partner license to throw the most impossible ideas at you. It is so easy to pretend and hard to prove. An entire new repertoire had to be learned, numbers had to be choreographed, costumes made, musicians hired and promotional photos taken and all this had to be accomplished in a matter of a few months because Joe's Pub, one of the city's best nightclubs, offered me to premiere the show on the night of my 40th birthday, which I could not refuse. If only I had the courage to make Elvis's songs my own. Singing some of them in German might help. This was before a critic told me that in America one must present something that is both familiar and new to ensure success. Until then, I had sung unfamiliar songs from Germany and France in my own translations. Now I was going to diligently perform very familiar American songs in a different style and foreign language. The realization had never come to me before that one could make an audience feel both at ease as well as excited at the same time. It was a most pleasant experience, though as I prepared one song after another there was no denying that I was not accustomed to dancing and singing at the same time. So I rehearsed tirelessly and on opening night suggested that the club put on its menu the following sandwich and name it

THE WEIMAR ELVIS

Lay out 4 thin slices of bacon on a parchment-paper-lined sheet pan and bake them in a 350° F oven until browned and crisp. While still hot, transfer them onto a tray lined with paper towels, cover them with another layer of paper towels and press lightly to blot away as much fat as possible. Take 4 slices of best quality white Pullman bread and spread some non-sweetened but salted, crunchy peanut butter on each slice. Add a few thin slices of ripe banana and one layer of crisped bacon on half the slices and top them with the remaining slices, pressing lightly. Spread the top of each sandwich with a bit of butter and panfry them, buttered side down first, on both sides over medium heat until golden. Cut them diagonally in half and serve them drizzled with honey.

"I rehearsed tirelessly and on opening night suggested that the club put on its menu a sandwich I named the Weimar Elvis."

My next show was a commissioned affair. We had been invited to Kansas City, Missouri, for a weekend of festivities to celebrate Grand Arts, a local non-profit arts organization that was folding after ten years. In Kansas City everything is larger and more spacious than in New York City. People are polite and friendly. In the downtown area everybody is an artist. Many of them had moved there from New York City to concentrate on their work rather than making a living and sometimes one of them managed to build something of a career there and inevitably feel compelled to return to New York. The arts organization's artistic director surprised me by remarking, you're the only one I can think of who could perform a musical tribute to our founder. I knew that the founder, certified dog trainer that she was, was awfully fond of dogs, independently wealthy and quite generous in giving artists the means to realize their projects no matter how large or small. There was going to be a cocktail reception at the Midland, a stately old theater with 3,500 seats, not a bad venue for a performance. The theater was going to be empty but for the 150 invited guests who would all be ensconced at the bar located in the back of the theater's family circle. Perhaps innocently, perhaps not, opinion was divided later, I had been asked to do my surprise performance on the grand stage below. I would have to sing across the vast empty theater to reach the guests far away and high up above. The piano tuner, having been confirmed to come in the afternoon to tune the baby grand that had been rented for me, arrived late. The pianist the organizers had booked as my accompanist (and with whom I had not had a chance to rehearse with yet) and I had no choice but to wait backstage, pacing between the green room and the hallways, hung with signed posters of Tony Bennett, Patti Labelle and other legends who had played the Midland. After a good hour, I told the piano tuner that we were running out of time. Having explained that the pianist and I needed what little precious time there was left before the guests' arrival to run the songs for the first time, I supposed he would hasten to finish. Not at all. Presently he took another thirty minutes to finish. Sir, I said, this will have to do now. We are after all not going to perform a Schubert recital. The pianist and I had a very rushed rehearsal and when it was showtime, there was only one thing to do. I downed a shot glass of vodka to boost my confidence and made a very resolute entrance in a long black coat and black velvet leather over-the knee boots and opened the show with a Grace Jones number. It didn't fail to have an impact on the audience. And then I surprised everyone with my notorious adaptation of Jaques Brel's *"Ne Me Quitte Pas,"* retitled "Let Me Stay with You" and in which I played a dog pleading not to be given away.

The story behind the dog song was a true one. A few years earlier, Filip Noterdaeme and I had adopted a miniature dachshund puppy from one of my clients who had been given two puppies for his birthday and felt unable to keep both of them. What a pity, I had said, such a cute puppy, to which he had replied, why don't you take him. I did not know what hit me until the dachshund had moved in with us. We named him Moby and I almost immediately became completely mad about him, something that had never happened to me before with a dog, much less with what is frequently called a wiener dog. Then our landlord declared that we were not allowed to have a pet in his building and threatened us with eviction. Perhaps he thought this was the easiest way to get rid of us and put the apartment back on the market for a higher rent. After several painful weeks of trials and errors and singing the blues about Moby we finally found a new owner we could trust, a friend of a friend who was visiting from Kentucky. When he took Moby, I felt as if I was giving away

"I rewrote the lyrics to Jaques Brel's 'Ne Me Quitte Pas' to tell the story of a breakup between a dog and its owner — from the dog's perspective."

41

THE ART OF GAY COOKING

my own child. I could not wipe out the memory of this misadventure and rewrote the lyrics to Jaques Brel's song to tell the story of a breakup from the dog's perspective. Moby's new owner returned to Kentucky with Moby and though I never saw him again, it comforted me that he was finally in good hands.

MINI WIENERS IN A BLANKET

In a food processor, pulse 2 cups of flour, 1 dessert spoon of kosher salt and 2 sticks of cold butter into coarse meal. Transfer the mixture into a mixing bowl and quickly fold in 1 cup of *Quark* or well-drained Ricotta cheese. Shape everything into a ball, flatten it into a thick disc, wrap it in cellophane and chill it for at least one hour. Working on a floured surface, roll out the dough to a rectangle of about 1 inch thickness, fold it into thirds (like a letter), turn it ninety degrees and roll it out and fold it in the same manner once again. Wrap and chill the dough for another 30 minutes before repeating the rolling and folding process. Chill it once more before further use. This is called a *Blitz* puff pastry. It is less laborious to make than classic puff pastry yet better than the store-bought kind. It can be used for anything calling for puff pastry.

To make wieners in a blanket, roll out the dough to a thickness of about ⅛ inch and cut it into little squares. Place mini wieners or mini franks diagonally on the squares and tightly wrap the dough around the sausages as you would to shape a crescent. Place them on a parchment-paper-lined sheet pans, brush them with a lightly beaten egg, sprinkle them with sesame, caraway or nigella seeds and bake them at 375° F for about 25 minutes, until puffed and golden brown. Serve warm, with Dijon mustard for dipping.

Many times people with little understanding of either cooking or music have felt compelled to tell me that I could get into television by cooking and singing simultaneously. Once, at an intimate dinner party where I handled not only the cooking but also the service, an obstinate guest tried to challenge me into singing a song as I was bringing out the dessert, a perfect Linzer Tart made with fresh cranberries. I wished that no one had told him that I was also a singer and held the thought of rubbing the cake into his face, but as long as the thought was held the act was not committed. The cake was properly served with cold contempt on the side.

LINZER TART

Pour ⅔ cups of sugar into a bowl. Grate the zest of 1 lemon over it and rub the zest into the sugar with your fingertips. Pour the sugar into a food processor and add 2 cups of whole almonds. Pulse until the almonds are ground to a coarse powder. Add 1 cup of flour, 1 tablespoon of unsweetened cocoa powder, ½ teaspoon of cinnamon, a pinch of ground cloves, and 1 ¼ sticks of cold butter. Pulse until the dough resembles coarse meal. Add one whole egg and process until the dough comes together in a ball. Flatten the dough to disc, wrap it in cellophane and chill it for at least one hour.

Rinse one package of cranberries in cold water and discard all damaged or overripe ones. Transfer them into a saucepan, add a strip of orange peel, a cinnamon stick, a couple of tablespoons of sugar and just enough water to cover the bottom of the pan. Cover the pot and cook the berries over medium heat, stirring now and then, until they are barely translucent. Remove the cinnamon stick and orange peel. Add more sugar to taste.

Roll out the dough on a floured surface and use about three quarters of it to line a greased and floured fluted tart shell. Spread the cooled cranberry compote into the shell and cover it with a lattice made of the rest of the dough. Brush the lattice with a lightly beaten egg and bake the tart at 350° F for 45 minutes. Once it has cooled to room temperature, dust the tart with confectioner's sugar. Serve with barely sweetened whipped cream, never with ice cream

This tart is even better the next day.

Then I met a woman who used to work as a production assistant in television and was looking for fresh content for a video podcast start-up she had just registered. I had an idea for a cooking show parody that would make fun of the deeply earnest and chummy tone that dominated cooking shows at the time. Imperious and alluringly intimidating, the *Foodcommander*, as I would call the character I created for the series, would demonstrate how to prepare very simple dishes, explaining what was right or wrong and good or bad in a staccato tone. He would show how to cook a plain chicken breast, make fresh pesto, select the right ingredients for a composed salad or make a vinaigrette. He would look like a high-strung androgynous scientist who had stepped out of a chemical laboratory. The woman was delighted with the idea. Filip Noterdaeme and I began to film and edit a series of short videos that were promptly featured on her company's website which had at the time little else to offer. Gradually it dawned on us that this collaboration was not as happy as it had seemed in the beginning. I was expected to finance, produce and edit the videos by myself without any compensation whereas she was earning a salary. I decided to end our partnership and asked her to remove the *Foodcommander* videos from her site. She told me that she was not in the business of losing content. This was in 2006 and it was becoming apparent that YouTube was becoming the definite online platform for homemade videos. She was perhaps not so much greedy as desperate. But she refused to remove my video clips until a lawyer friend of ours sent her a cease and desist letter. I then uploaded the videos on YouTube. For a while they got a good amount of attention. One of the most frequently viewed episodes featured my grandmother Nona's recipe for *Hausfreundl*, home guests, the Austrian version of what is more commonly known as

BISCOTTI
(Twice-baked Cookies)

Pour 1 cup of sugar into a mixing bowl. Grate the zest of one lemon over it and with your fingertips rub it into the sugar to flavor the sugar. Add 3 eggs and mix well. Add 1 cup of whole almonds or pistachios, 1 ⅓ cups of flour and 1 teaspoon of baking powder. Stir everything until just combined. Spoon the thick dough in one broad diagonal line onto a parchment paper-lined sheet pan and bake at 350° F until golden brown and dry throughout, 25 to 30 minutes. After removing the sheet from the oven, turn down the oven temperature to 325° F.

When the loaf is cool enough to handle, invert it onto a large cutting board. Peel off the parchment paper in one swift move and replace it on the sheet pan. Carefully flip the loaf around and cut it on the bias into thin slices, no thicker and preferably even thinner than ¼ inch. Align the slices on the sheet pan and toast them in the oven until very lightly browned at the edges and completely dry, about 5 minutes. Do not over-bake them or they will turn bitter.

The first episode of the *Foodcommander* series presented the simplest way of cooking

PLAIN CHICKEN BREASTS

Cut a whole chicken breast in half, remove the bones and all cartilage but leave the skin attached. Carefully pull the chicken "tender" off each of the two breasts. Grab a hold of the end of the white tendon that runs through each tender, press it down with the dull side of a kitchen knife with your other hand and carefully pull it out from the tender. Rub the chicken pieces on all sides with olive oil, season the skin side with salt only and the other sides with salt and pepper and any additional seasoning of your choice (such as fresh, chopped herbs or mashed garlic or fennel seeds.) Set the oven to 400° F and heat a stainless steel or cast iron skillet over a high flame until searing hot. Place the chicken breasts, skin-side down, into the pan without any additional oil. Cook without moving them until the skin is browned, flip them, add the two tenders next to them and immediately transfer the frying pan into the hot oven. Depending on the size of the breasts, they and the tenders will be done after 5-8 minutes. Do not overcook them and let them rest on a plate for a couple of minutes before slicing them.

Here is another dish presented by the *Foodcommander*.

SHRIMP COCKTAIL, TWO WAYS

For Cocktail Sauce I, mix 1 cup of ketchup with finely grated fresh horseradish to taste, a few dashes of Worcestershire sauce and the juice of half a lemon. For Cocktail Sauce II, mix 1 cup of ketchup with finely grated fresh ginger to taste, a few dashes of hot sauce and the juice of half a lime.

Drop medium or large shrimp into boiling salted water, a few at a time. Skim them out once they are floating to the top and immediately transfer them to an ice bath. Peel and devein them, leaving the tail attached. Serve well-chilled with the two sauces for dipping and a bowl for the tails.

One evening as I was arriving at the midtown cabaret where I was to do my newest one man show someone with a notebook was walking in ahead of me and took a seat. A critic? I inquired. From *The New York Post*, the manager answered. I felt uneasy. I had been told that there weren't many reservations that night and felt that I needed a full house to impress the critic. Later in the dressing room the manager came to see me. What is it, I asked. He told me that there had been several last-minute cancellations and that there were going to be only three people in the audience, including the critic. We have to cancel the show, I said in a panic. Oh Daniel, he said, the show must go on and you must honor every single person who comes to see you perform no matter who it is. I sent him away and took a deep breath. I did perform the show, dressed up and elegant as usual, but with overshadowed, darkly brooding eyes, singing to empty tables and the sound of someone taking notes in the dark void behind them.

After the show, I was rather distraught and restlessly roamed the empty streets of midtown, ending up in a nondescript diner on Westend Avenue. There, adding insult to injury, a disinterested waiter served me the worst hamburger I ever ate in my entire life. I sat quietly eating the hamburger and contemplating my fate. What was I going to do. Pick myself up, dust myself off and start all over again. When this plate is empty I shall have forgotten the misery of this night and only remember the comedy of it. Then I tipped the disinterested waiter and left, wondering how difficult it could really be to make a decent

HAMBURGER
(My Way)

Do not buy pre-ground meat. Rather, ask your butcher to coarsely grind a mix of brisket, chuck and a bit of bacon just for you. Wet your hands with cold water and loosely shape the ground meat into beef patties, about 1 ¼-inch thick, careful not to press hard. Using a mortar and pestle or a rolling pin, coarsely crush whole black pepper corns and coriander seeds and gently pat a heaped tablespoon of the mix onto one side of each patty. Chill the meat until ready to use.

Set up all the following trimmings so that assembling the burger can be done quickly. Mash a ripe avocado with a fork, adding a bit of chopped cilantro and salt to taste. Stir a tablespoon of *Gochujang** paste into about ½ cup of mayonnaise. Cut a peeled red onion into thin rings and make little bundles of washed watercress, one per person. Chop Kimchee**, a handful per person, into bite-size pieces. Cut brioche buns, one per person, in half, spread them with a bit of butter and set them aside.

* Korean red chili paste
** Korean-style fermented and spiced Napa cabbage. Buy it ready-made or make your own – a recipe for it can be found in Chapter XIII.

Preheat the oven to 400° F. Season the meat patties with salt and panfry them, peppered side down, in a pre-heated cast iron skillet until crisp and browned on that side. Flip them and immediately place the skillet in the hot oven for a couple minutes to finish cooking them to medium rare. Meanwhile, melt a pad of butter in a non-stick skillet and quickly fry up one duck egg per person, sunny side up. Transfer them to a platter and toast the buns in the same skillet, buttered-side down. To assemble the burgers, spread the lower halves of the buns with a bit of the spicy mayonnaise, add a couple of onion rings and the meat patties, topped by a bit of mashed avocado, Kimchee and a fried egg. Add the upper half of the bun and serve with the watercress bundles, halved red radishes and

BAKED YAM FRIES WITH ORIENTAL KETCHUP

Turn three red bell peppers over a gas burner set on high until their skins are charred. Place them immediately into a paper bag and close it; their steam will further loosen their skins. Once they are cool enough to handle, rub off the skins, remove the seeds and roughly chop the peppers.

Simmer 1 chopped large onion and 2 sliced garlic cloves with ½ cup of water, ½ cup of rice vinegar and ¼ cup of palm sugar until translucent. Add the peppers, mix and cook until softened. Season with salt, chili flakes, 1 tablespoon tamarind puree, 1 teaspoon powdered ginger and a pinch of ground cloves. Puree everything in a blender, strain into a sauce pan and reduce over medium heat until thickened to the right consistency.

Peel several large oriental, yellow-fleshed yams and cut them into sticks as you would for French fries. Coat them thinly with grape-seed or peanut oil and spread them out on a parchment-paper-lined sheet pan. Bake them at 400° F until golden brown, turning them once.

Many times in those years, life between the stage and the kitchen was indeed a cabaret. I often seemed to be reaching for the stars with one hand while washing dishes with the other. With time came experience, maturity and, eventually, freedom. My cooking became more musical and my performing less hungry. I eventually entered a zone of ease where I had nothing more to fear.

There have been very few instances in my life where I did agree to cook and sing at the same time, one being my musical homage to the late great German countertenor and pop star Klaus Nomi, performed one night only at the BAM Café at the Brooklyn Academy of Music. Klaus Nomi had also been a pastry chef and this had given me the idea to include a stylized demonstration of how to make a classic *apple strudel* while singing his hit song, *Simple Man*.

"I often seemed to be reaching for the stars with one hand while washing dishes with the other."

APPLE STRUDEL

Heat an earthen-ware bowl in a 250° F oven until warm. Put 2 ½ cups of flour and a good pinch of salt into a food processor. With the motor running, add ¾ cup of water and 2 tablespoon of neutral-tasting oil like sunflower or grape-seed – never canola – and a few drops of white vinegar. Process everything for 10 seconds more once it has come together in a ball. Transfer the dough onto a lightly oiled large plate, cover it with the warm bowl and set it aside for 20 minutes.

Peel, core, quarter and slice 8 tart heirloom apples, toss them with the juice of one lemon, a pinch of ground clove, a handful of rinsed raisins and about ¼ cup of sugar. Toast 1 cup of bread crumbs and a couple tablespoons of butter in a skillet until fragrant and lightly colored and mix them with ½ cup of sugar, a handful of pine nuts and a bit of cinnamon powder. In a skillet, melt one stick of butter.

Spread a clean bed sheet or tablecloth over a table or kitchen island and lightly dust it with flour. Place the warmed dough in its center and roll it out to a circle of ⅛ inch thickness. Reaching under the dough with lightly oiled hands, stretch out the dough in all directions until it is thin enough to read a Gertrude Stein poem through it. Brush the dough with melted butter, spread the apples over one half of its surface and scatter the bread crumb mixture across the apples in one broad line. Cut off the dough's thick edges with scissors and discard them. Lift the cloth on one end and pull it up so as to make the strudel roll itself into a log (fold over the open ends when it is rolled up halfway.) Lifting the strudel with the cloth, transfer it onto a greased sheet pan (or lined with a silicone pad – do not use parchment paper.) Brush the strudel once again with melted butter and bake it at 350° F for about 40 minutes, until golden brown. Dust it with confectioner's sugar before serving – warm or at room temperature. Exquisite with vanilla sauce.

V
DELICIOUS
COOKIE

CLASSICAL MUSICIANS get to Carnegie Hall by practicing. And here is a note on figuring out the best recipe for a famous cookie. It was as a result of tasting many *Vanillekipferl* throughout the years of my childhood in Germany that I came to the conclusion that recipes through time and personal interpretation can change a great deal. After the first unforgettable tasting of *Vanillekipferl* made by Nona, my grandmother from my father's side, and entirely different but equally exquisite ones had been offered by Oma, my grandmother from my mother's side, trying my hand at making them myself had quickly become of greater importance than school and homework, piano lessons and dance classes. Perhaps Nona's book of handwritten recipes, tattered and stained, would produce the recipe that would answer the burning question of how to make her *Vanillekipferl*. Down to Nona's basement and into the pantry where no husband ever stepped into, looking beyond the Mason jars of homemade jams and compotes, above the shelves lined with hibernating apples were those old square tin boxes filled with the tender, horseshoe-shaped cookies, faintly dusted with sugar and emanating sweet smells of ground nuts, vanilla and butter. I ate without counting, exactly twelve, to learn all there was to learn about their taste and texture. Oh, said Nona, I do not have a written recipe. I listened as she described the necessary procedure to make them and went back to school and homework, piano lessons and dance classes.

Sent by an aunt from faraway Dresden behind the Iron Curtain was another batch of *Kipferl* made with hazelnuts, precious and tiny as a baby's pinky, and a gift bag of sweets on St. Nicholas Day contained a package from a pastry shop with *Kipferl* that had a more vulgar appeal, outrageously buttery. There was nothing to do but scheme a way to occupy the kitchen during my mother's absence and use it as an experimental laboratory. Many years later, a distinguished professor of psychology from Israel, well versed in all things cultural and historical, listened to my story of juvenile obsession with this Viennese cookie. Ah, he said, but you are describing *Sumboosic*, an ancient Lebanese cookie. Before he had time to explain a friend from Greece arrived and upon hearing about the *Vanillekipferl* and *Sumboosic* said, you are describing Greek *Kourabiethes*. Perhaps, said I. It was confusing. She said she was going to ask her mother for a recipe. They were to be sure crescent-shaped like all the others but I did not care for her suggestion to use margarine instead of butter. Then, during a visit to Bruxelles, Filip Noterdaeme and I had Lebanese *Sumboosic*, a really great cookie worthy of its Viennese cousin. But that was not the end. There were Greek *Kourabiethes* in a Greek bakery in Brooklyn; Russian Tea cookies which were not Russian at all but a specialty from North Carolina, produced by the pastry chefs of a famous New York City catering company; Mexican Wedding cookies among the cookie selection of a Manhattan gourmet shop; and *Cornulete* from Rumania that my friend Sanda Weigl, the respected chanteuse and niece of Brecht's wife Helene Weigl, told me about. Yes, indeed it was confusing, until one day it occurred to me that it was evident that all of these hand-shaped nut cookies were not a separate creation but linked through history.

Had the Viennese created the recipe to celebrate their victory over the Ottoman Army in 1683 or had the Turks taught the Viennese to fashion pastries in the shape of the half-moon, symbol of the Orient? Had the moors brought it to Spain from where it travelled to Mexico and had the Eastern Europeans brought it to the Southern States? It is a subject to be pursued. Well, here are six nutty cookie recipes.

VIENNESE VANILLEKIPFERL

Finely grind 1 cup of hazelnuts to a fine powder and toast them in a frying pan until fragrant, careful not to burn them. When they are cooled down, mix them with 1¼ cups of flour, ½ cup of confectioner's sugar and 1 tablespoon of sugar mixed with the seeds scraped out of half a split vanilla bean. Add 1 stick plus 1 tablespoon of softened butter and swiftly kneed everything until it comes together. Shape the dough into a ball, flatten it to a disc, wrap it in cellophane and refrigerate it for a good hour. Cut the dough into small cubes the size of a cherry and, rolling each piece into a little log and curling its ends, shape them into tapered crescents no larger than a curled ring finger. Bake them on parchment-paper-lined baking sheets at 350° F until the tips are golden brown, about 10 minutes. Douse them lightly on all sides with confectioner's sugar.

KOURABIETHES

Beat 2 sticks of softened butter with ¼ cup of confectioner's sugar, 1 egg yolk and 1 teaspoon each of ouzo and vanilla extract until fluffy. Add ¼ cup of toasted and finely chopped almonds and 1 ¾ cups of flour mixed with a teaspoon of baking powder and ½ teaspoon of baking soda. Swiftly kneed everything into a smooth dough, shape it into a ball, flatten it, wrap it in cellophane and refrigerate it for a good hour. Cut the dough into portions the size of a walnut and shape them into plump half moons. Stud each cookie with a whole clove and bake them on parchment-paper-lined baking sheets at 350° F until the tips are just beginning to brown, about 15 minutes. When the cookies are cool enough to handle but still very warm, roll them twice in sifted confectioner's sugar. Traditionally, the cloves must be removed just before consumption. Alternately, you may add a pinch of ground cloves to the dough.

RUSSIAN TEA COOKIES

Beat 2 sticks of softened butter with ½ cup of confectioner's sugar and 1 teaspoon vanilla extract. Add 2 ¼ cups of flour, ¼ teaspoon of salt and ¾ cup of finely chopped walnuts. Swiftly kneed everything until you have a smooth dough. Shape it into a ball, flatten it, wrap it in cellophane and refrigerate it for a good hour. Cut the dough into portions the size of a walnut and roll them into balls. Press them lightly onto parchment-paper-lined baking sheets and bake them at 375° F for 8 minutes, until their bottoms are just golden brown. When they are just cool enough to handle, roll each cookie in sifted confectioner's sugar until fully coated. Repeat once cookies are cooled.

MEXICAN WEDDING COOKIES

In a food processor, pulse 1 cup of pecan halves with ¼ cup of sugar and ¼ teaspoon of ground cinnamon to a fine powder. Add 1 cup of flour and a good pinch of salt and pulse until combined. Add 1 stick plus 1 tablespoon of softened butter, pulse until the butter is evenly distributed and finally let the machine run until the dough is processed into a ball. Shape it into a disk, wrap it in cellophane and refrigerate it for at least an hour. Cut the dough into portions the size of a walnut, roll them into balls, press them lightly onto parchment-paper-lined baking sheets and bake them at 325° F until they are just golden around the edges, 20 to 25 minutes. Cool them slightly before rolling them twice in sifted confectioner's sugar.

SUMBOOSIC

Make an elastic dough by kneading together 2 cups of flour, 6 tablespoons of softened butter, 6 tablespoons of almond oil, ¼ tablespoon of ground *Mahlab**, ¼ teaspoon of anise seeds, a pinch salt, ½ teaspoon of baking powder, and just enough warm milk to bring everything together, a couple of tablespoons should do. Knead for several minutes. Grind 1 cup of walnut halves and ½ cup of brown sugar in a food processor to a coarse powder. With the machine running, add a few drops of orange blossom water and then, a few drops at a time, almond oil, until the nut meal turns into a thick paste. Roll out the dough on a lightly floured surface, cut out discs about 3 inches wide, spoon a little mound of filling onto each, fold the discs in half, press the edges together and bend the corners to form half moons. Bake them on parchment-paper-lined baking sheets at 350° F for 20-25 minutes until golden. Dust lightly with confectioner's sugar while still warm.

CORNULETE

In a stand mixer with a paddle attachment, beat ½ cup of margarine, 1 stick of softened butter and 8 ounces of cream cheese until well combined. With the machine running on low, slowly add 2 cups and 2 tablespoons of flour and mix until you have a smooth dough. Shape it into a disc, wrap it in cellophane and refrigerate it for least 2 hours. In a food processor, process 3 cups of walnuts, ½ cup of brown sugar, 1 teaspoon cinnamon, a pinch each of powdered cloves and mace with 2 eggs into a coarse paste. Roll out the dough on a sugared surface, adding sugar as needed to prevent it from sticking to the rolling pin. Cut it into 3-inch triangles. Place a little mound of nut paste onto a side of each triangle and roll them up into crescents with lightly curved ends. Brush the tops with a beaten egg and roll them in sugar before lining them up on parchment-paper-lined baking sheets. Bake them at 350° for 12-15 minutes or until lightly browned.

---

* Cherry stone kernels, cherished in Middle Eastern cuisine for their distinct bitter flavor. If you cannot find Mahlab, pound a couple of skinned bitter apricot kernels into a paste, or simply use a few drops of bitter almond essence. However only *Mahlab* will give this pastry its distinct flavor.

A couple of years ago, my own, personalized recipe for *Vanillekipferl*, the result of trials and errors through the years and two continents, may very well have saved us a lot of trouble. Filip Noterdaeme, having completed *Growl*, his provocatively contemporary adaptation of Ginsberg's legendary poem *Howl*, and having dedicated it to the best-selling author Andrew Solomon to mirror Ginsberg's dedicatee Carl Solomon, had sent a copy of the poem to Andrew along with a note. Andrew Solomon, a great non-fiction writer and a great diplomat and a great dandy and a great writer of letters wrote back, gracefully giving the poem his blessings yet also making it perfectly clear that he considered Filip Noterdaeme's decision to name him the dedicatee of *Growl* and make him the subject of the poem's third part not just an honor but perhaps an insult as well. Since he mentioned me as a baker of cookies in his response, I thought it would be appropriate to have a cookie jar filled with *Vanillekipferl* delivered to him to show our appreciation of his appreciation and sportsmanship. This in turn made us the receiver of another letter by Andrew in which he very elegantly stated that my gift had made him not only three times happier but also three pounds heavier.

DANIEL'S VANILLEKIPFERL

Using a nut mill, grind 1½ cups of walnuts to a fine powder. Alternately, finely grind the nuts in a food processor, adding ¼ cup of sugar to prevent them from breaking up and becoming oily and careful to not over-process them. Transfer the nut-meal to a bowl and add ¼ cup of sugar if you haven't already. In the food processor, pulse 2 cups of flour with 1½ sticks of cold butter into coarse meal (or swiftly cut up the butter into the flour with a pastry cutter or two butter knives. Add this mixture to the nuts, add 2 egg yolks and knead everything by hand into a smooth dough. Shape it into a ball, flatten it, wrap it in cellophane and refrigerate it for a good hour. In the meanwhile, make the vanilla sugar: scrape the seeds of 1 split vanilla bean into 1½ cups of sugar and rub them into the sugar with your fingertips.

Cut the dough into small cubes the size of a large cherry and, rolling each piece into a log and curling its ends, shape them into tapered crescents no larger than a curled ring finger. Bake them on parchment-paper-lined baking sheets at 350° F until the tips are golden brown, about 10 minutes. When they are just cool enough to handle, carefully roll them in the

THE ART OF GAY COOKING

vanilla-scented sugar until fully coated. Store them in layers in a parchment-paper-lined tin box, never in a plastic box. They are best after one week but you would have to hide them really well to last that long. Tell us all about it, dear Drosselmeier.

VI
FOOD TO WHICH PLANES
AND TRAINS LED US

WHEN IN 2000 Filip Noterdaeme and I took our first summer vacation together, he was an experienced if not very methodical traveler. He knew how to improvise and didn't care much for planning ahead. He said we would be like adventurers, always free to move on as we pleased. Finding vacancies in hotels in Milan offered no difficulties, for there was practically no tourist staying for very long in the hot city. After two days we decided to take a train down to Corniglia in Cinque Terre, where we would try to find a place to spend a week. It was late by the time that had been accomplished and there was only one small restaurant still serving dinner. The dining room was nearly empty. We were shown to a marble table with a cast iron base. Filip Noterdaeme, sitting with his back rather close to the wall, pushed the table away from him to have more room. This made a loud rattling noise and I protested. It was inconsiderate. I cannot sit comfortably with the table so close to me, he said. Alarmed by the noise, the proprietor promptly came out of the kitchen and leered at us. The first course, a platter of marinated roasted vegetables, was excellent. Filip Noterdaeme once again pushed the table and once again, it made a loud rattling noise. This time the proprietor came to our table and asked us what was the matter with us. Nothing, we said in unison. You are breaking my table, he said. Oh, said Filip Noterdaeme, that I would never do, as if it were a preposterous exaggeration. Perhaps, the owner continued, you would rather go eat somewhere else. Which we didn't. But Filip Noterdaeme was still not convinced that he would have to learn how to properly move a marble table.

If our first dinner in Corniglia had been a tense one, we were soon doing better. We took long walks along the hiking trails along the coast to Riomaggiore and all the way back to Monterosso, and wherever we went, there were many tourists, so it was never easy to find restaurants that were favored by locals. But in a small Trattoria in Manarola they would serve us for lunch a dainty salad of arugula and tomatoes, followed by grilled octopus and a chestnut honey gelato. The distinctly bitter aroma of the chestnut honey prompted me to remark that it was like having the honey and the bee sting all in one.

GELATO AL MIELE DI CASTAGNO
(Chestnut Honey-flavored Gelato)

Italian or French chestnut honey is preferable, though other bitter honeys such as Tasmanian Leatherwood honey can be substituted as a compromise. Regular honey will not yield the intended, spectacular result.

In a saucepan, heat 2 cups of whole milk and 1 cup of heavy cream. Whisk together 6 egg yolks with ½ cup of chestnut honey, ¼ cup of sugar and a good pinch of salt. Temper the yolks with some of the hot milk and cream mixture before adding them into the saucepan. Heat the mixture gently while stirring until it coats the back of a wooden spoon. Do not bring it to a boil. Strain, chill thoroughly and churn in an ice cream maker until it reaches that desirable texture of ice cream. Fill the gelato into a chilled plastic container with a tight fitting lid and store it in the freezer. Serve scoops of it in chilled Martini glasses, drizzled with more chestnut honey and perhaps some crushed waffle cone bits and a smattering of flaky sea salt. This is a simple yet elegant dessert.

As we came upon a plaza overlooking the Mediterranean we stopped to listen to a string quintet whose playing caught my attention. It sounded suspiciously like a Grace Jones song. Classical musicians usually do not play this sort of music. When I later asked the musicians about it, they said it was in fact a piece written by Astor Piazzolla. All these years I had been thinking of *Libertango* as a Grace Jones original, which not only accounted for the quality of her interpretation but for her way of making any song her own. Years later, I would make it my own as well when I launched my own interpretation of it as part of my cabaret act.

We took a train to Como where we intended to stay for a few days. As a popular summer destination Lake Como was famous for its views, so we had chosen a lakeside hotel, a half hour bus ride away from Como. It is the habit in Como to make daily excursions into the region after lunch and return home just in time for tea. It was therefore not surprising that there were no other guests at the hotel when we stepped off the local bus that had taken us there. The receptionist handed us the keys to our room with a view. I cannot say that we cared much for it, and we decided to cancel the reservation and take the next bus back to Como. There, it took us another hour to find a good restaurant that wasn't closed in August as was still customary in many European cities in those forgotten days of less aggressive tourism. The next day we travelled to Venice. As a former center of the spice trade Venice is famous for a number of dishes, so we were looking forward to the choicest lunches and the choicest dinners. The Rialto market had an excellent selection of produce and seafood, and I deeply regretted not having access to a kitchen in which I could have made meals of either. It is the habit of Venetians to avoid tourists but we were adamant and asked locals for guidance until we found a *ristorante* that served locals and appealed to us. The owner was a short compact man in a starched white apron and sharp eyes that tirelessly scanned the room. To welcome newcomers and decide what they should eat was his privilege that he never relinquished. He was an expert judge of character. He determined that we should have

SEPPIE IN HUMIDO COL NERO DI SEPPIA CON POLENTA
(Cuttlefish Stewed In Its Ink with Polenta)

The very best quality of cuttlefish must be used for this ragù, as singers will use only the best musicians for a concert, which is a very smart thing to do. To prepare the cuttlefish, pull the heads off 6-12 bodies (depending on their size), removing the entrails along the way, cut off and discard the eyes, beak and entrails, reserving the tentacles. Pull the hard transparent piece of cartilage from the inside of the bodies and discard it. Pull off and discard the bodies' purple skin, cut the bodies open lengthwise, carefully remove the attached ink sacs, place them in a cup, cover them with water and set them aside. If using more commonly available pre-cleaned squid, you must also get a small tin of squid ink, sold separately.

Rinse the bodies under cold running water and slice them into large strips. Heat a Dutch oven over medium heat, add a couple tablespoons of olive oil, 1 chopped white onion and two sliced garlic cloves and sauté everything until golden. Add the cuttlefish with two diced celery stalks, mix and cook the lot for about 10 minutes. Add a good tablespoon of concentrated tomato paste and enough white wine to cover the cuttlefish halfway. Simmer for a few minutes. With the back of a spoon, press on the ink sacs to release the ink and add them to the pot. This not only tints the ragù deep black but gives it a distinct flavor. Add a couple of bay leaves and a few twigs of fresh thyme, cover the pot with its lid and place it in a 325° F oven for about 45 minutes, until the cuttlefish is very tender. Remove the cuttlefish pieces with a slotted spoon, set them aside in a covered bowl and reduce the sauce over a medium flame until very thick. Season with salt to taste and return the cuttlefish to the sauce. Before serving, pan-fry the reserved tentacles in olive oil with added slices of garlic, chopped parsley and chili flakes and use them as a garnish.

This ragù is traditionally eaten with triangles of pan-fried polenta. The portions we were served that night were diminutive but very rich so that we agreed that it had redeemed us of the culinary disappointments of the past few days. This we told the owner when he stopped by our table. He looked at our empty plates critically, then proudly. He was an artist.

After a few days in Venice we returned to Milan for a couple of days before taking a train to Tuscany. Walking along the Naviglio Grande we selected a pizzeria, filled with locals, to dine in. We were seated next to a wonderfully voluptuous blond woman who sat with her young secretary, a handsome young man with dark hair and romantic eyes and who advised us to order *pizza von acciughe* and *focaccia con lardo*. This was years before *lardo* became a popular ingredient in the United States. I had never tasted Italian *lardo* before but I knew *Speck* from Tyrol. She herself reminded us of the actress Anita Ekberg in a Fellini film – not in *La Dolce Vita* from 1960 but in *Intervista* from 1987. Her name was Anna, and she said she was a make-up artist for a popular Italian television show. The dessert we were served was a simple, chilled chocolate drink called

BARBAJADA

In a bowl, mix ¼ cup of cocoa powder with ¼ cup of sugar and add 1 cup of cold milk. Prepare 1 cup of very strong coffee and pour it over a few pieces of excellent dark chocolate. Stir until the chocolate has melted and whisk the mixture into the milk. Strain and chill. Pour into dessert glasses and top with a generous amount of unsweetened whipped heavy cream.

Risotto in Milan was common, rich and very filling. It was made with white wine and saffron. Once, in New York, when I was still working as a cater waiter, I had been in charge of serving risotto at a fancy luncheon to a table of socialites and had been so eager to please that in rushing to serve them I all but spilled the risotto over the hostess's pink Chanel costume, of which she was so inordinately proud.

RISOTTO MILANESE

Place 2 pounds of chicken backs, necks or wings into a large stock pot, cover them by about 4 inches with water and bring it to a low simmer. Skim off any rising foam. Do not let the water come to a rolling boil. When the water is no longer cloudy, add half an onion; 1 carrot, split lengthwise; 1 halved celery stick; a bay leaf; and a few sprigs of fresh thyme. Lower a small plate into the pot to keep all solids submerged and simmer the broth for up to 1 hour, skimming off any rising foam. Strain, season with white pepper and only a little salt and keep it warm, set over a low flame. In a cup, crush several saffron strands with the back of a spoon and add ½ cup of chicken broth to dissolve them and release their bright orange color.

In a Dutch oven, sweat 6 finely chopped shallots in 2 tablespoons butter over a medium flame until translucent. Add 1½ cups of *Carnaroli* rice. Stir until all rice kernels are shiny and coated with butter. Add 1 cup of very dry white wine. Keep stirring over medium heat until the wine is almost completely evaporated. Repeat with 1 cup of warm chicken broth and the saffron. Keep adding warm broth in increments until the rice is al dente and the risotto has the consistency of runny porridge. Season with salt and white pepper according to taste. Add 2 tablespoons cold butter and lightly whip the risotto until the butter has melted and emulsified the thickened stock residue. Serve with ground – never shredded or grated – Parmesan on the side[9]*. This is the basic recipe. Sadly, it appears that outside of Italy, people are no longer satisfied with it and expect risotto to showcase all kinds of ingredients and flavor combinations. To me, it remains its purest and most satisfying version.

There had been some difficulty in getting a double room in some Italian hotels we were staying at. Filip Noterdaeme did not like to talk to receptionists – he said they, male or female, were snotty. To reserve a room, I usually called the hotels and allowed them to call me Miss Isengart – I am always mistaken for a woman on the phone. What difference could it make to them. We were just two visitors from abroad traveling through.

* To grind fresh Parmesan (or Pecorino), cut off the rind of a large, freshly cut piece of Parmesan (store the rind in the freezer for later use such as flavoring a broth), cut the cheese into chunks and transfer them to a food processor. Pulse the chunks a few times before running the machine until the cheese is ground into medium fine crumbs. This texture is far superior to the texture of shredded cheese.

Once, when we arrived at a small hotel in Tuscany where I had made a reservation for Isengart and Noterdaeme, the receptionist addressed me as "Signore Noterdaeme" and asked to see my and Miss Isengart's passport. It was time to acknowledge who I was. He looked at me sharply with a furor that alarmed me and said, Signore, there is something immoral in this affair. My explanation did not completely reassure him, but Filip Noterdaeme sitting on the terrace and peacefully reading the papers would. I asked him if he wouldn't come outside with me to meet him. He did. Filip Noterdaeme's polite manners calmed him down, and we were given the keys to the romantic suite. It was a delightful hotel. The owner's wife was training a local apprentice to cook as had been done in the region for generations.

The hotel had its own vegetable and herb gardens and an orchard producing fruit and olives. Poultry, meat and dairy came from nearby farms. A fresh delivery had been made that day so we had

CROSTINI DI FEGATINI

In a frying pan, add a tablespoon of olive oil and sauté half of a finely chopped Vidalia onion until translucent. Add 4 rinsed anchovy filets and ½ pound of cleaned and deveined chicken livers. Cook the livers on all sides until browned. Midway, add a couple of lightly torn fresh sage leaves and a tablespoon of salted capers, previously soaked in water and drained. Deglaze the pan with a splash of *vin santo* or dry Marsala. Transfer everything to a food processor and pulse the mixture into a coarse paste. Season with salt and pepper. Serve warm with roasted slices of Tuscan bread and sliced dried figs.

In one of the little side streets of Lucca we discovered a small, remarkably good restaurant that seemed to be a local favorite. After an excellent lunch we decided to ask Filip Noterdaeme's visiting brother to dine there with us. Consulting with the chef, this was the menu we decided upon

PAPPA AL POMODORO

BISTECA FIORENTINA

GELATO DI MANDORLE

CANTUCCI

The chef generously gave me the recipe for the Salsa Verde which accompanied the grilled steak.

SALSA VERDE

Fill a saucepan halfway with water, add a tablespoon of vinegar and bring it to a simmer. Move the pot to create a swirling movement in the water and break 2 eggs into the water. Take the pot off the fire and leave the eggs to poach for 2 minutes. Lift them out of the water with a slotted spoon, transfer them to a blender with 2 slices of stale white sour dough bread, previously soaked in milk, 1 tablespoon drained capers, 4 anchovy filets, 1 peeled garlic clove, 1 bunch of parsley, stems removed, several leaves of fresh sorrel or mint and ½ cup of warm milk. Blend until smooth and transfer to a mixing bowl. Whisking the mixture by hand, slowly add 1 cup of olive oil, beating until the oil is well amalgamated. Doing this by hand is important as emulsifying olive oil in a blender would oxidize it, magnifying its subtle bitter notes. This sauce is a delicious dip for crudités. It is lighter and creamier than traditional salsa verde and quite unique.

We had visited Florence and all the highlights of the region. Having paid our respects to Boticelli, Giotto and Donatello, we bid Italy farewell and returned to New York. A week later, 9/11 happened and the United States began what would be called its war on terror. Traveling would never be the same. That winter, we took a trip to Barcelona for a Christmas holiday. At the John F. Kennedy airport, as we were standing in line for yet another security check – and when did one not in those days – we were told that no liquids of any kind would be allowed in one's hand luggage any longer. It had always been thrilling to come home from trips abroad with artisanal jams, fresh mustard, honey or specialty oils which compared so favorably to the usual fare in America, but as we always travelled with hand luggage only this would now no longer be an option. On the plane, a young American couple sitting next to us overheard that I used to spend much time in Barcelona in the early Nineties. They had dozens of questions to ask, but what they wanted most to know was how far elBulli* was from Barcelona and which Barcelona tapas bars were currently fashionable. Though they were confused by my answers we had a pleasant flight together. It was their first trip abroad.

---

* Ferran Adrià's legendary three-star restaurant in Roses, now closed.

After our arrival, I decided to show Filip Noterdaeme the Boqueria Market where ten years earlier I had eaten my first *Marcona* almonds and anchovy-stuffed green olives. News of the changes in the city were not so encouraging. Since I had last been there the city had become more touristic and gentrified. But the Pinotxo Bar in the Boqueria still existed and Señor Bayen, the owner, was still presiding over the counter. Just as I remembered it, there was no menu and one was well advised to let him decide what one ought to eat. He was a small man, with the diluted eyes and bruised hands characteristic of a chef who for many years has been working face to face with his customers. He inevitably served first-time visitors rather innocuous fare like a Spanish egg *tortilla* with potatoes or fried zucchini blossoms. For us he made

XPIRONS AMB MONGETES
(*White Beans with Squid*)

Choose the smallest, finest dried white beans you can find. Discard any bruised or broken ones and soak 1½ cups of them overnight in cold water in which you have dissolved 1 tablespoon of kosher salt. The next day, drain them, pour them into a large cooking pot, add enough water to cover them by an inch and bring them to a simmer, skimming off the foam and adding hot water as needed to keep them covered. Add a bay leaf and a couple of whole, unpeeled garlic cloves. Do not let the water ever come to a full boil. When the beans are almost tender, add 1 teaspoon of salt, turn off the heat, cover the pot with its lid and set it aside.

In a Dutch oven, sauté 6 chopped shallots and one crushed clove of garlic in 2 tablespoons of olive oil until translucent. Add ½ diced fennel bulb, 2 diced celery stalks and 2 sprigs of fresh thyme. Sauté until they begin to brown, deglaze with a splash of white wine and add the cooked beans with just enough of their cooking liquid to barely cover them. Remove and discard the bay leaf and thyme sprigs. Fish out the the softened garlic cloves, squeeze the pulp from their skins, mash it and add it to the beans. Rinse 1 pound of cleaned squid. Slice the bodies into very thin rings, add them to the beans and simmer everything for just a few minutes, until the squid rings are opaque. Meanwhile, pan-fry the tentacles along with a couple of sliced garlic cloves in olive oil until crispy. Season the beans with grated lemon rind, lemon juice, olive oil, salt and pepper and serve warm, garnished with the crispy tentacles and some chopped parsley.

Señor Bayen said it was a typical Catalan dish but we suspected a similar dish might be had in Venice. He also made for us

BLISTERED PIMIENTOS DE PADRÓN

Rinse a handful or more of *Pimientos de Padrón* in cold water and drain them on paper towels until completely dry. Heat a frying pan over high heat before adding 1 tablespoon olive oil and the peppers. Shake the pan to coat the peppers in oil and fry the peppers for just a couple of minutes – they ought to be slightly browned in spots but still crunchy. Season them with flaky sea salt and serve immediately. If you cannot find *Pimientos de Padrón*, the more widely available, milder Japanese *Shishito* peppers are a good substitute. Some find it hard to distinguish between the two.

La Sagrada Familia was in a sad way. Antoni Gaudi, the architect, had died in an accident in 1926, the cathedral had been in an intermittent state of construction for more than a century, the newly added portal and sculptures were severe and lifeless. The cathedral had become a commercial enterprise so that all proceeds from entrance fees could be used to finance the renewed construction. Filip Noterdaeme left the building when a busload of loud tourists poured into the nave. Outside, three nuns from the Convent of the Sacred Spirit of Jerez de la Frontera had set up a little stand where they were selling their convent's traditional confection known as

TOCINILLO DEL CIELO
(Little Bacon from Heaven)

In a saucepan, bring 1 cup of sugar, ½ cup of water and 1 wide strip each of lemon and orange peel to a boil. Cook the syrup to the soft ball stage or until an inserted sugar thermometer reaches 235° F. Let the syrup cool down slightly and remove the citrus peels before the next step. Pour it slowly into 6 egg yolks while stirring constantly, careful to not beat any air into the mixture. Strain and fill into espresso cups or extra small ramekins, previously greased with oil spray. Place the cups into a baking dish, fill it with enough boiling water so that the cups are halfway submerged, cover with aluminum foil and bake at 300° F oven for 30 minutes. Refrigerate for a few hours or overnight before carefully unmolding and serving.*

Floquet de Neu, the famous white albino gorilla and mascot of Barcelona whom I had never felt inclined to go see in all the years I had visited my parents while they were living there, was still alive and residing at the Barcelona Zoo. Filip Noterdaeme insisted that we pay him a visit. Floquet's habitat had a glass wall instead of metal bars and there was a large crowd of tourists gathered in front of it. Everyone was giddy with excitement and taking flash photographs of poor Floquet, who looked very much like an old man with his pink skin and white hair, lying on the floor and looking at us with a blasé expression of utter contempt. Later that afternoon we had coffee at the Café de l'Opera on the Ramblas, sitting next to a tableful of male cross-dressers. The manager of the café, a little potbellied man with a balding head, kept walking over to their table. They were perhaps too noticeably gay for his taste.

The next day – a bit fatigued of seeing the inevitably ornamental architecture of Gaudi everywhere we went – we spent a long afternoon in Mies van Der Rohe's Barcelona Pavilion. This is more to my liking, I said to Filip Noterdaeme. I have an idea I must tell you about, he replied. He pointed to the two white leather *Barcelona* chairs. Mies designed the *Barcelona* chairs with the King and Queen of Spain in mind. However at the opening of the ceremony the royal couple declined to sit down on them. Well, I said, what of it. There is someone who should be brought here to redeem the chairs, he said. We should find a way to send for him. He was speaking of Floquet. He went on to explain that perhaps one could arrange it as an exchange. Floquet could be brought into the pavilion for a day and one of the two white Barcelona chairs would be set up in the zoo in his stead. We contacted the friend of a friend who at the time was involved with the planning of a large cultural forum that was to take place in Barcelona the following year. Filip Noterdaeme, always polite, erudite and soft-spoken, explained to him his vision of the exchange between

---

* In Jerez, the local production of sherry calls for a clarification process with multitudes of egg whites. If the nuns of the convent found a creative solution to make use of the countless left-over egg yolks, you can find a way to use leftover egg whites from this recipe. I often need extra egg whites to clarify stock for a *demiglace*, the recipe of which can be found in chapter X. The most common solution would be to make *meringues*, perhaps for a *Pavlova*, a dessert created in neither France nor Russia but in Australia, in honor of the legendary Russian Ballerina Anna Pavlova, in which case it ought to be shaped like a ballerina's tutu or at least a swan.

Floquet and the Barcelona Chair. The man reacted as if he had reason to believe that Filip Noterdaeme was completely mad. Well, said I, the idea perhaps but not he himself. A few months later, Floquet died of skin cancer without ever having seen the pavilion. This ended the man's concern that we might reference his name in an official proposal. A few months later however Filip Noterdaeme's idea was mentioned in an article about Floquet's life.

On Christmas eve a friend of my parents organized, with the aid of a pair of twins who were visiting from Costa Rica, a luncheon at their house in nearby Figueres. After lunch we went to the Dali Museum. The Mae West Room was as gay as can be imagined but the museum guards were not. Later that day we returned to Barcelona and the pretty twins from Costa Rica asked if they might join us. We arrived at the apartment where we were staying and gave them sheets and blankets to sleep on the sofa in the living room. We had just turned out the light in our bedroom when suddenly a silhouette appeared at the doorstep, evidently naked. May I join you, he asked. Too surprised to answer, we were silent for a moment. The question was repeated, I say, may I join you. Not tonight, thank you, we answered. Of course this was not addressed the following morning, so we never found out which one of the two it had been.

A couple of years later, there was an invitation from my uncle: I have moved to Madrid, come visit. If we had enjoyed the busy stylishness of Barcelona we ought to experience the spontaneous leisure of Madrid. One late spring evening we boarded a flight with Iberia Airlines to cross the Atlantic. We declined to eat the food served on the plane. Madrid was already warm as summer and in the evenings the streets were filled with young Madrilenos, out for a long night of bar hopping, and a certain number of American and German tourists.

Having walked around the city for three days, exciting but tiring, we decided to take a day trip to Toledo to see El Greco's *The Burial of the Count of Orgaz* in the *Iglesia de Santo Tomé*. My uncle agreed to come along and we drove to Toledo in his car. Once inside the city, a group of tourists was walking in the same direction Filip Noterdaeme was leading us. Near the entrance of the church two of the women became unruly, shoving each other. One of the women's cell phone and sunglasses scattered on the road and into the ditch. There was, of course, no way of recovering them. Filip Noterdaeme found the women's behavior so disturbing as to make a visit of the church next to them not only annoying but possibly dangerous. We got back to the car very hungry, it was siesta time and everything was closed, but my uncle sweetly convinced a bodega owner to serve us marinated mushrooms, an unwise choice with dire consequences.

On the road back to Madrid, Filip Noterdaeme got violently ill. He has since then understandably never again been tempted by

SETAS AL JEREZ
(Mushrooms with Sherry Vinegar)

For each person take a handful of oyster mushrooms, cut off the root ends, wipe off any dirt with a wet cloth and carve away any brown spots. Heat a large frying pan and add 2 tablespoons of olive oil and a sliced clove of garlic. Once the garlic is fragrant, add the mushrooms. Brown the mushrooms on all sides, tossing them infrequently. Season with salt and coarsely ground black pepper, add some chopped parsley, toss once more and transfer to a platter. Deglaze the pan with a splash of *Jerez* vinegar, bring it to a brief simmer to concentrate its flavor and spoon it over the mushrooms.

The next day we had to return to New York, feeling a bit sorry for not having had a chance to tour the city's famed tapas bars. When we arrived at the airport there was a problem at Iberia. The flight attendant at the check-in counter in her beige and blue uniform (the company changes the colors of the attendants' uniform every few years) informed us that the flight was overbooked and that Iberia would compensate us with a night in a hotel and a generous per diem. It was more like a dream than reality. We were now going to be able to explore the city's tapas scene.

That evening, we went to Cava Baja, a street in the center of Madrid lined with tapas bars. The area was gearing up for the night, and we began our tapas tour. For several hours we went from bar to bar, savoring small plates and *pinchos* that the barmen kept replenishing. It was exhilarating. The variety and richness of the tapas however was a bit overwhelming. We were well taken care of wherever we went, first in the small *taperías* and later when these became too crowded on the terraces on the street. More and more people arrived. The last thing to get was hot *churros con chocolate*, the classic sweet late-night treat of Madrid. A group of German tourists ate unlimited quantities of them and even asked for some to go. But the most satisfactory tapa of all was classic

OLD-FASHIONED PAPPAS BRAVAS

Peel 2 large russet potatoes, cut them into irregular, bite-size chunks and blanch them in salted water with a few tablespoons of vinegar added for no more than 4 minutes. Strain and set them aside to cool.

In a frying pan, heat ½ cup of olive oil. Add 1 chopped onion. Fry them until translucent, then add a dash of salt, 1 heaped tablespoon of Spanish sweet smoked paprika, 1 teaspoon of hot smoked paprika, and ½ teaspoon of white pepper. Stir and fry for 1 minute before adding 2 tablespoons of flour. Stir and cook the mix for 2 minutes. Add 1 cup of chicken broth and cook for about 10 minutes, stirring now and then. Transfer to a blender and process everything until smooth and creamy. Add more salt to taste.

Heat 2 cups of olive oil in a Dutch oven set over medium flame and add the potatoes. Fry over medium heat for about 5 minutes, turn the fire to high and fry them for another 2 minutes until crisp and pale golden, not any darker. Remove them from the oil with a slotted spoon and transfer them onto a paper-towel-lined tray. Immediately season them with copious amounts of flaky salt. Serve on a warmed platter, with the sauce on the side and wooden picks for dipping.

This is the way to prepare the authentic dipping sauce for *pappas bravas*. Very few places still make it this way, having replaced it with tomato-based sauces and mayonnaise. I sometimes add a few anchovies to the onions. It gives the sauce a certain mystery.

Overall the quality of the tapas was excellent but almost none were made with vegetables. They consisted mostly of seafood, meat, eggs and cheese. Almost everything was deep-fried, to be sure, or pan-fried in olive oil, which was considered a lighter version.

Later that year I returned once again to Europe to perform at a cabaret festival in Vienna. When my accordionist and I landed, we were told that our luggage had been left behind by mistake and would be delivered directly to our hotel the next day. All this without the slightest hint of an apology. Meanwhile the producer had requested that we perform a song at the opening ceremony of the festival that very evening. There was no choice but to make our appearance in our simple traveling clothes. The Viennese, who are very stylish people, thought that I was making an understated fashion statement.

While in Vienna I made a tour of the city's legendary pastry shops where the pastry chefs chefs were still producing the same cakes Vienna had been famous for since the era before the Great War. Everything was still in the Viennese manner, with great elegance and luxury. They continued to obstinately refuse anything modern. It was the memory of the way my Czech-born grandmother Nona had insisted on living come to life again.

At Café Sacher, there was among the usual assortment of *Torten* and *Kuchen*, to my delight, a

"The Viennese thought that I was making an understated fashion statement when I appeared on stage in my traveling outfit."

FÄCHERTORTE

Rub the grated zest of 1 lemon into ½ cup of sugar with an added pinch of salt. Add 1 ½ cups of flour and cut 1 ½ sticks of cold butter into the mixture. Add 1 egg and kneed the dough into a ball. Flatten it into a thick disc, wrap it in cellophane and refrigerate it for 1 hour.

WALNUT FILLING

In a food processor, pulse 3 cups of walnuts with ½ cup of sugar and 1 teaspoon of cinnamon into a coarse powder. Do not over-process the nuts lest they release their oil. Transfer the nut-meal into a bowl and add 1 tablespoon rum and 1 egg. Stir until combined.

POPPY SEED FILLING

Grind 2 cups of poppy seeds to a fine powder using a poppy seed mill or, working in batches, a clean electric coffee grinder. Gently heat 2 cups of milk with 2 tablespoons of butter until the butter has melted. In a bowl, mix the poppy seeds with the scraped seeds of 1 vanilla bean and ½ cup of sugar and stir the warm milk as well as 2 tablespoons of honey into it.

APPLE FILLING

Peel, core and chop 6 sour apples, sprinkle them with the juice of 1 lemon, 2 tablespoons sugar and ½ cup of raisins.

Roll out about two thirds of the dough and line a buttered and floured spring form with it. Pierce the bottom at intervals with a fork and evenly spread first the poppy seed filling, then the walnut filling and finally the apple filling over it. Scatter a few tablespoons of prune *lekvar** on top of the apples. Roll out the rest of the dough and cover the cake with it, pinching off the overhanging excess. Pierce the dough at intervals with a fork and brush it with an egg yolk beaten with 2 tablespoons of milk. Bake at 325° F for 90 minutes. Do not remove it from the

* Eastern European prune butter. Very dark and thick, not to be mistaken with plum jam, which is not an acceptable substitute. If *lekvar* cannot be obtained, use dried prunes, soaked for a few hours in rum-spiked warm water, drained and passed through a food mill or puréed in a food processor.

spring form until completely cooled. Dust with confectioner's sugar and serve with barely sweetened whipped cream.

The next winter Filip Noterdaeme and I spent Christmas with my parents in Munich and then traveled on to Berlin. We landed at Tegel airport the morning after New Year's Eve and by this time the city was deserted. We got off at the wrong subway stop in the former Eastern sector of the city and had to trudge through a decaying grid of GDR-era housing projects to get to our hotel, dragging our suitcases behind us. The streets looked like a battlefield, lined with broken bottles, paper garlands, crushed party hats and the vestiges of fireworks in the dirty snow. It was getting close to midday when Filip Noterdaeme finally asked, Where did you say we were going to lunch; I am starving. We deposited our luggage at the hotel and made our way to Unter den Linden, the avenue that was once again becoming the grandest boulevard of the city. There we came upon a group of people who had just exited an after-hour club. They said if we followed them they would show us a good place to eat. They led us to a corrugated hut and sure enough there was an old woman serving Berlin-style *Currywurst*, the legendary concoction that was allegedly invented by a sausage vendor in the years immediately following WWII, when the city was a devastated rubble field and the exotic, bright flavor of curry powder, added to the familiar local sausages, must have conjured visions of a brighter future. As we finished our *Currywursts* I remembered that I still had in my shoulder bag a little box of Christmas cookies my mother had given us in Munich. They were of her own baking and delicious, the very kind she always used to make for Christmas when I was a child. We shared them with the party revelers whose desperate followers we had been. Here is the recipe for my mother's

CHOCOLATE HAZELNUT SQUARES

Melt 9 ounces of dark chocolate in a bowl set over simmering water. Set it aside to let it cool down to room temperature. In a food processor, pulse 1 ½ cups of hazelnuts with 1 cup of sugar and the scraped seeds of 1 vanilla bean until finely ground. In a mixing bowl, beat 2 sticks of softened butter until fluffy. Add 6 eggs, one at a time, beating the mixture until fully combined each time before adding the next egg. Fold in the hazelnut mixture; ½ cup of flour; ¼ cup of unsweetened cocoa powder; 1 teaspoon of salt; and 1 teaspoon of baking powder, all mixed and sifted together to prevent lumps; and

THE ART OF GAY COOKING

finally the melted chocolate. Stir until just combined and spread the dough evenly onto a parchment paper-lined, deep-set sheet pan. Bake for 30 minutes at 325° F. Do not over-bake, it should still be moist in the center. Melt 8 ounces of dark chocolate with 1 tablespoon of coconut oil added and spread it evenly over the cooled cake. When the chocolate is firm to the touch but not fully hardened, cut the cake into small squares. Store them in tin boxes between layers of parchment paper. These are not like American brownies.

BERLIN-STYLE CURRYWURST

While the Parisians can argue at length about where one can find the best baguette or croissant and New Yorkers discuss which place serves the best hamburger or the best pizza, Berliners will fight about which stand serves the best *currywurst*. This is the authentic way of making it.

In a frying pan, heat 2 tablespoons of sunflower or other neutral-tasting oil and add two links of good quality, pre-cooked pork or beef sausages, cut into thick slices. When they are blistered and begin to brown, transfer the pieces onto a plate and place it in a warm oven. Pour most of the fat out of the frying pan and add ½ finely chopped white onion into the pan. Stir-fry the onions until lightly browned before sprinkling them with 1 teaspoon of curry powder. Cook the mixture on medium heat until it is fragrant, then add a dash of salt, a splash of Worcestershire sauce and 3-4 tablespoons of canned tomato purée. Simmer the sauce until thickened and pour it over the sausages. Serve hot with a warmed Kaiser roll.

Nowadays, ketchup is more commonly used than tomato purée. Arguments about the question if ketchup could indeed have been a part of the original recipe are quite common in Berlin.

We were lunching the next day with friends of mine from Munich, Anja and Philip v. R., who were presently living in Berlin and had proposed to meet us for lunch in a fashionable restaurant in the district known as *Mitte*, the middle. We were staying in Prenzlauer Berg at the *Schall und Rauch* Pension, named after a quote from Goethe's Faust or perhaps after the name of Max Reinhard's famous erstwhile cabaret venue – a sacrilege either way. Prenzlauer Berg is next to Mitte and both neighborhoods were already beginning to morph into the gentrified neighborhoods they are today. Lunch was served with style and simplicity worthy of the Vietnamese owner of the restaurant. Of its menu I have adapted its somewhat unusual

CHICKEN SOUP

Cut up a chicken into 4 parts, place them into a large stock pot and cover them by several inches with cold water. Bring it to a gentle simmer and skim off any rising foam. Once the water is clear, add aromatic vegetables and spices to taste (a halved onion; scallions; parsley; cilantro with stems and roots; carrots; celery stalks or root; bay leaves; star anise; a cinnamon stick; pepper corns; bruised ginger or lemongrass; whole garlic cloves). Lower a plate into the water to keep all solids submerged and gently simmer the soup for 45 minutes, skimming off any rising foam. Strain the soup into another pot. Discard vegetables and spices, skin and bone the chicken and tear the meat into shreds and chunks, careful to remove and discard all fat sacks and cartilage. Set the meat aside and season the broth with salt and white pepper. You may return the bones to the broth and simmer it for up to another half hour or so to intensify its flavor. Strain once again before the next step.

Into large, preheated soup bowls (to heat them up, simply fill them halfway with boiling hot water from a tea kettle and pour it out after a few seconds) add some cooked rice noodles or other noodles of your preference, some of the shredded chicken and any combination of the following: cubed firm tofu; very thinly sliced or julienned raw vegetables – any combination of peeled carrots, celery stalks, Shiitake mushrooms, scallions (cut on the bias), tiny broccoli florets, snow peas, or roughly chopped bok choy, as well as assorted aromatics such as slivers of garlic, diced fresh ginger, sliced hot chili peppers, or a few sprigs of fresh cilantro. Be sure that the vegetables are at room temperature or they will cool down the broth and not blanch properly. Ladle over this enough boiling hot chicken broth until fully covered. Add a few drops of toasted sesame oil and a tablespoon of fried shallots, readily available in Asian markets, and serve immediately. Do not mire the subtle flavor of this soup with soy sauce.

The restaurant also offered a more elaborate version that

included boiled or fried wontons, filled with finely chopped and seasoned chicken meat.

On our last day in Berlin, I confided to Filip Noterdaeme that I was planning to return one day to perform in the city's famous *Spiegeltent*. It would be an adventure and certainly worth risking. It might change our lives. As we walked along the Spree that serpentined through the strangely alluring city, we discussed a future where we would happily go back and forth between New York and Berlin. My naiveté and excitement was undoubtedly to blame for my lack of perspective. I nevertheless began researching the field. We went to see a show at the *Spiegeltent* and I got an opportunity to talk with the impresario. It was from there that he and I began to conceive an exclusive new one man show I would bring to his venue. But it would take 2 more trips to Berlin until we finally came to an agreement.

We were back in New York, more defiant, vital and invigorated than ever. We went about our busy lives. It was very gay, more than a little mad but never boring. We went to art openings, cabaret shows and the opera. Our home was filled with people coming and going. We spoke of each other as husband and "wifey." We were living hand to mouth and it didn't matter that this wasn't going to very likely ever change. We lived our quasi-bohemian lives, dressed in forgiving black, preferring to entertain friends at home to meeting with them in restaurants as was becoming more and more the norm.

New York was teeming with burlesque performers at the time, every girl moving to the city seemed to want to be a burlesque performer. I worked with a great many of them, performing in clubs and theaters and sometimes at private parties. It was at about that time that I was asked to perform with a group of circus artists at the opening of the Playboy Casino in Cancun, Mexico. It was a strange experience. After my opening number, a group of acrobats began twirling around a rotating pole in the great gaming hall, filled with slot machines. Suddenly, the producer of the show asked me to please follow him to the back, something had happened. The two hired *parcours* dancers had had accidents on the red carpet in front of the casino, having been blinded by the photographers' flashbulbs as they ran up the walls and jumped off the roof, as was their wont. They had not anticipated the flashes and, miscalculating their landing, broke or twisted their ankles. Could I help get them out of the building without the guests noticing, through to the backdoor to a waiting ambulance. When I got back to the casino floor the pretty Mexican playboy bunnies were serving excellent

FISHY TACOS
(Yes, that is what they called them)

Take a small pumpkin or acorn squash, peel it, cut it in half, scrape out its seeds and cut the halves into sections. Peel a red onion, cut it half and slice it into sections. Coat the vegetables with a restrained splash of olive oil and a bit of ground allspice, cinnamon, coarsely crushed black peppercorns and coriander seeds and spread them out on a parchment-paper-lined sheet pan. Roast them at 425° F until tender and caramelized.

Remove the stems of a few sprigs of cilantro. Thinly slice the stems and reserve the leaves. Brush a halibut steak or a piece of halibut filet with olive oil and season it with salt, white pepper and the chopped cilantro stems. Loosely fold the fish into a sheet of parchment paper and bake it at 350° F for about 10-15 minutes, until a toothpick inserted into its thickest part meets no resistance. Remove any skin and bones and break up the fish into pieces. Warm corn tortillas on a griddle and arrange on each a little heap of roasted onion, pumpkin chunks and some halibut. Drizzle some whipped, lightly salted sour cream over it and top it with thinly shredded red cabbage, sliced fresh jalapeños, and the cilantro leaves. Serve with lime wedges.

In the spring of 2005, we once again went to Munich to visit my family. After a couple of days in the city, we drove to the country to visit a spa with hot springs, but the tepid pool was full of obese and sallow retirees who reminded us in a somewhat awful way of the *Weisswurst* floating in water-filled claypots that we had been served in Munich when we had had lunch at the Café in the *Valentin Musäum*. On our way back to the city we stopped at an inn. It was on the Isar river, and its traditional Bavarian food was renowned. It was there that we had

SCHWEINSHAX'N
(Roasted Ham Shanks)

Simmer 1 pork shank per person for 1 hour in a pot of water seasoned with a smattering of caraway seeds, several lightly crushed garlic cloves and enough salt to make the water as salty as the sea. Let the shanks cool down in the broth. When they are cold enough to handle, cut several incisions into the skin. Fill a roasting pan with half an inch of the broth, add a quartered onion, place a rack over it, add the shanks and roast them at 350° F for about 1 hour and a half. (Add more water as needed to prevent the pan juices from fully evaporating). Raise the temperature to 425° F and roast for another twenty minutes, turning the shanks once, until their skin is dark amber and crisp all around. Serve with mustard, soft pretzels, and a very light

RED COLE SLAW

Thinly shred 1 small red cabbage with a mandoline. Add 1 coarsely grated carrot, 2 julienned red-skinned apples like Gala or Fuji and season the salad with lemon juice, white wine vinegar, salt, pepper, chopped parsley and coarsely crushed anise seeds. Toss and chill for a good hour before serving. This very refreshing salad does not need any oil in its dressing.

In Bavaria every meal seemed to include pork: there was ham for breakfast, sausages and *leberkäse* (a baked loaf of forcemeat; the recipe for it can be found in Chapter VIII) for lunch, and pork roast for dinner. We tolerated this for a few days before this made us ill. We insisted on vegetarian fare for the rest of our stay. The locally grown vegetables were of such excellent quality that it made us miserable thinking of the lesser quality of produce available in New York. Even organic fruit and vegetables sold at New York's farmers' markets could never match this quality. Things would get a little better in the following years when the American culinary revolution, budding since the Sixties, invigorated a new generation of progressive farmers. But I maintain that Europe's centuries-old biodiversity, unique climate and soil is still yielding better results even though Americans refuse to believe me – with the exception of those who have travelled to Europe, of course.

After we returned to New York, Filip Noterdaeme convinced me that the time had come to transform our apartment into the headquarters of his conceptual art project, The Homeless Museum of Art. He had already presented it as a sly little booth at the Armory Show, where it had gathered some attention as the only non-commercial art project in this most commercial of art fairs. Its reincarnation as a live-in art installation suggested that it was no longer homeless – camping out in a rent-stabilized apartment. It would continue to mock the art establishment to the end.

Gradually, The Homeless Museum was taking shape in our home. There was no limit to how we used every nook and cranny to exhibit interactive installations, art works and wall texts, all of them full of *double entendres* and witty references to the contemporary art world machinery. Our openings, held regularly for the next couple of years, were very clandestine operations, announced exclusively to trusted acquaintances and talked about in hushed tones. Once inside the apartment, visitors were greeted by me, dressed as Madame Butterfly, and asked to step onto a scale so I could calculate their entrance fee, which was met with much resistance, especially by the women. We charged one cent per pound. Next, I handed each visitor a headset with a specially recorded audio tour that commented on the multiple exhibits installed throughout the apartment until they reached the museum's café, Café Broodthaers as we called it, installed at the kitchen counter, where they were offered a very eccentric dish inspired by the works of the late great Belgian conceptual artist Marcel Broodthaers.

ASSIÈTTE À LA BROODTHAERS
(Serves 12 museum visitors)

In a large pot, bring two quarts of water to a simmer. Add 2 heaped tablespoons of baking soda before carefully lowering twelve eggs into the water. Adding baking soda causes the egg white to shrink away from the shell, making it easier to peel the eggs even after a short cooking time that guarantees soft egg yolks. This I first heard about via Wylie Dufresne, who told Eric Ripert about it in the latter's cooking show. If only I had known about it sooner, when peeling 3 dozen boiled eggs for our openings was an ordeal on Sunday mornings.

Cook the eggs for exactly 8 minutes before transferring them to an ice bath. Once they are cool, peel them carefully under running water and store them in a container filled with cold water.

Rinse and scrub a good dozen Prince Edward Island mussels, careful to remove the beard[11]* of each of them. Pour 1 tablespoon of olive oil into a Dutch oven set over high heat, add 1 sliced clove of garlic and a bit of chopped parsley. When the mixture is fragrant and foamy, add the mussels and a splash of (preferably Belgian) brown beer and instantly cover the pot

---

* The tough piece of membrane by which mussels attach themselves to stable surfaces. Remove it by grasping it between thumb and index and pulling it out.

with a lid. Cook the mussels for a few minutes, shaking the pot occasionally. They are done when their shells have opened. Pour everything into a colander set over a bowl to catch the juices. Pluck the mussels from their shells (discard any mussels that have not opened), place them into a small bowl and cover it with plate or cellophane to prevent them from drying out. Rinse the pot and pour the reserved juices back into it, careful to not add any sandy sediments that have settled on the bottom of the bowl. Reduce the juices to a syrupy consistency before adding them to the mussels.

Cut a sliver off the bottom of each egg to level them and place them upright on small plates. Place 1 shelled mussel next to each egg, pierced with a wooden pick, and spoon a bit of juice over them. Serve with a glass of chilled milk and a small bowl of *fleur de sel* on the side.

Our visitors were aghast when they tasted this most unusual combination of flavors. I explained to them that the dish was a symbolic gesture to fill the void that Broodthaers had expressed in his art work by using an array of empty vessels: mussel shells, egg shells and, once, an empty milk bottle. I assured them that even at MoMA's new restaurant, The Modern, they would not get anything comparable. It was not the only moment our visitors were puzzled during their tour of our museum.

We regularly held openings in this fashion for the next two years and then, The New York Times published an article about it. This is how our landlord evidently found out everything about it and he instantly demanded that we shut down the museum. Nothing Filip Noterdaeme said to him was of any avail, he would not relent. Many people who had been amused by the article wanted to come and see the museum but the landlord was not at all amused. Didn't we know that it was an infraction of the law to run a museum out of a rental apartment, particularly on the top floor of an old brownstone, where too much foot traffic going up and down might damage the staircase. Someone could fall and get injured and whose insurance would then cover the medical bills. We tried to explain that this was a misunderstanding, that The Homeless Museum was a private insider project and not a public institution, that we never held more than one opening per month and rarely had more than one or two dozen visitors. Eventually, we had to give in and the landlord got his way. We announced to our followers that the Homeless Museum was once again homeless. I packed the exhibits and artifacts into several large sailor's trunks. Undaunted, Filip Noterdaeme remembered the beginnings of the museum as a little booth at the Armory Show. He asked me to build a new, portable Homeless Museum booth. He said he would take it into the city and set it up wherever he wanted to. The street was where the Homeless Museum truly belonged. This new adventure would dominate the next couple of years of our lives. It has ended since then but those who experienced it still talk about it.

No matter what the circumstances, it was unthinkable that we would ever lead regular, regulated lives. I was performing in cabarets and cooking part-time for wealthy people and Filip Noterdaeme was teaching art history in several colleges and performing his Homeless Museum Director act on the streets of Manhattan. He set up his booth on the Bowery, on Union Square, and under the Highline. In the beginning, he transported everything back and forth on the subway but eventually he conveniently stored it in a storage space in Chelsea. The booth was outfitted with a microphone and speakers and showcased several artifacts from the museum. People always inquired about the taxidermied coyote he set up next to the booth. That is Florence, my director of public relations, was Filip Noterdaeme's reply. The Homeless Museum Booth became quite notorious without the benefit of any support from the art world. The details are chronicled in Filip Noterdaeme's memoir, *The Autobiography of Daniel J. Isengart.*

We were ready for another summer trip. My parents found a lovely villa for us to rent near Aix en Provence. During our brief sojourn in Paris on our way to Provence we found an excellent restaurant in the 9th *arrondissement* called Café Panique which has unfortunately closed since then. There we ate

SALADE AUX FINES HERBES

Wash, stem and tumble-dry one bunch each of fresh parsley, tarragon and chervil. Toast a couple tablespoons of pine nuts until golden. Peel and thinly slice 3 shallots. Just before serving, toss the herbs together with the shallots and pine nuts and dress them lightly with salt, pepper, white wine vinegar, lemon juice and olive oil. This is a wonderful appetizer or side dish for fish or even a roasted rack of lamb.

Once we were settled in the villa near Aix, we delighted in hitchhiking into town every morning to buy fresh produce at the market and return in time for me to prepare a lunch of

TABOULÉ ALGÉRIEN*

Wash a few handfuls of mint, parsley and cilantro. Remove the tough stems of the mint (using the thin parsley and cilantro stems is fine) and purée all the herbs in a blender with 1 chopped seedless cucumber, ½ white onion, 1 seeded and chopped green pepper, 1 quartered ripe tomato, and ½ teaspoon of salt. Pour the mixture over 2 cups of uncooked couscous. Stir, cover and set aside in a cool place for 1 hour. Fluff the soaked couscous with a fork and dress it with lemon juice, olive oil, salt and pepper. Add raisins, toasted pine nuts, pitted dry-cured black olives and diced tomatoes to taste. Serve thoroughly chilled with a side of

CRÈME D'AUBERGINES
(As taught to me by my mother)

Squeeze the juice of 1 lemon into a bowl and reserve. Place the lemon halves into a large pot and add about 2 inches of water and 2 peeled and lightly crushed garlic cloves. Place a steamer over the water and add 2 large, firm eggplants, peeled and cut into large cubes. Cover the pot and steam the eggplant until very tender, about 10 minutes. Puree the eggplant and the softened garlic gloves in a food processor or with an immersion blender. Season it with the reserved lemon juice, salt, white pepper. Whisk ¼ cup of olive oil into the purée by hand, little by little, and beat until the oil is emulsified. Serve chilled.

This is quite different from and much lighter than the popular eggplant dip known as *Baba Ganoush*. It is also an excellent condiment for grilled or roasted vegetables or fish but should not be served with meat of any kind.

Even though the villa was what Filip Noterdaeme's visiting brother and sister-in-law ironically called a love nest, we didn't just stay put. We went to nearby Vauvenarges where Picasso had spent the end of his life and to the foot of Cézanne's famed Mont Sainte Victoire, where we shot the footage for a short film Filip Noterdaeme wanted to make. It transposed the Brother Grimm's "Hänsel and Gretel" fairy tale to Provence, with

---

* This is what the French refer to as *taboulé*. It is quite different from Lebanese *tabouleh*, which is not made with couscous but with bulghur (cracked wheat), and dressed with little else than lemon juice, parsley, and chopped tomatoes and onions.

Picasso as the greedy father and Cézanne as a good witch. To keep us all in good humor during the two days of shooting, I prepared two picnic lunches.

FIRST PICNIC LUNCH: PAN BAGNAT

An Italian-style roll like Ciabatta is sliced in half and some of the crumb is removed. The inside of each roll is drizzled with a bit of olive oil and just a few drops of red wine vinegar. The sandwich is then filled with the following: tomato slices, seasoned with salt and pepper; blanched, skinned and coarsely mashed fava beans, seasoned with lemon juice, crushed garlic and salt; a couple of thin slices each of red onion, radish and green bell pepper; 1 sliced hard-boiled egg topped with an anchovy filet; a few pitted black *Niçoise* olives; and a couple tablespoons of the best oil-packed tuna you can find. Press the sandwiches lightly to flatten, wrap them tightly in cellophane and refrigerate them for at least 1 hour.

For dessert bring a few very ripe peaches, packed in loosely crumpled newspaper so they don't get bruised.

SECOND PICNIC LUNCH: PISSALADIÈRE

The day before the picnic, pour 2 cups of all-purpose flour with 1 tablespoon kosher salt and 1 tablespoon dry yeast into a mixing bowl and add just enough water to bring it all together into a sticky mass – 1 cup should do. Kneed the dough until it is no longer sticky. Shape it into a ball, cover the bowl with cellophane and let the dough rest overnight in a cool spot.

The next morning, thinly slice 4 large Spanish onions and sauté them in a large skillet with a bit of olive oil and a sprinkling of brown sugar. When the onions are completely softened and begin to caramelize, season them with some chopped fresh thyme and white pepper.

Dust the dough with a bit of flour, punch it down, kneed it briefly on a floured surface before dividing it in half and lining two greased and floured tart shells with it (or one sheet pan, greased and dusted with cornmeal). Spread a thin layer of anchovy paste over the dough and scatter the cooked onions over it. Decorate the tarts with a grid of anchovy filets, aligned in a diamond pattern, pitted cured black olives and halved cherry tomatoes. Bake in a 450° F oven until the edges are lightly browned, about 20 minutes. Excellent warm or cold.

If there is no time to prepare a yeast dough and wait for it to rise (overnight or even for just a few hours), it is acceptable to make *pissaladière* with a *pâte brisée*, the buttery short crust that is commonly used for a quiche *Lorraine* (a recipe thereof can be found in Chapter IX). Purists may complain about such an alteration to tradition but no one in my experience has ever refused a second slice of either version.

We frequently took walks in the countryside around the villa. Whenever we ran into neighbors, they would politely address Filip Noterdaeme as *Monsieur* and me as *Madame*. Evidently, they thought that we were husband and wife, something that happened quite frequently in those years, even though we were not officially married until a few years later. In any case, we never bothered to correct them, we didn't see any need for it. Until the morning when the old neighbor who was in charge of watering the plants in the garden of the villa we stayed at saw me in my bathing suit. He promptly left and refused to return to water the plants. What was I to do. His wife appeared and asked what was the matter. Before we knew it, she was arguing with her husband that it didn't matter if I was a woman or not, that it was quite obvious that we were a couple either way and that he should continue watering the plants every morning as he had promised the villa's owner he would. It was an unexpected display of instinctive tolerance and understanding. To this day, I am occasionally mistaken for a woman, but only in France.

That summer in Aix, my parents came to visit us and we decided to take a day trip to a small town on the *Côte Bleue* where we used to vacation in the Seventies. We were going to have lunch at the home of André and Roseline, an interesting couple. First of all, Roseline looked like the great Edith Piaf, just as small and lively, with watery eyes. André had a great knowledge of the history of French poetry from the Seventeenth Century to the present. From her I learned a great deal about Provencal cuisine. She was one of those great French home cooks. Comparing the cooking of a dish to the writing of a poem, it has always seemed to me that however much the cook or poet did to cover up any weakness would not in the least avail. Such devices would only emphasize the weakness. There was no weak spot in the food prepared by Roseline in her summerhouse kitchen in that small town on the *Côte Bleue*.

For lunch we had

FRIED EGGPLANT WITH TOMATO TOPPING

Cut 2 large eggplants into thick round slices, lay them out flat on a kitchen paper-lined sheet pan and sprinkle them with copious amounts of salt. Set them aside for an hour before sponging off the drawn-out moisture with paper towels, pressing lightly. In a heavy casserole, heat about 2 inches of olive oil, add a couple of peeled garlic cloves, fry them until golden brown and remove them (reserve them for later use). Season the eggplant slices with white pepper, coat them with white flour and fry them in the oil in batches. They should be golden brown. Remove them with a slotted spoon and place them immediately onto a tray lined with several layers of paper towels to drain off any extra oil. Peel, seed and chop several ripe tomatoes and fry them in a sauce pan with a bit of olive oil. Cook them until they are just breaking up. Mash the reserved fried garlic cloves with a fork and add them to the tomatoes. Season them with salt, black pepper and add a handful of fresh bread crumbs and stir well. The mixture should have the texture of a custard. Mount a spoon of it onto each eggplant slice. Serve chilled, garnished with chopped fresh basil or parsley and drizzled with a bit of olive oil.

After two weeks in Aix, I had to return to New York for work. Filip Noterdame stayed awhile longer in southern France with his visiting older brother. Together, they went to the coastal village of Hyères, which has always been favored by the fashion crowd, much more than Cannes. There, at a charming little restaurant, the *patronne* personally prepared and served them a very simple pasta dish. Filip Noterdaeme was so impressed with it that he returned the next day to have it once more so he could figure out how to make it. This is the recipe.

SPAGHETTI À L'AIL

Whole unpeeled garlic cloves, several per person, are lightly pressed with the side of a large chef's knife to just crack them slightly and then slowly stir-fried in a heavy casserole with a generous amount of golden, provencal olive oil, until their skins are crispy and the cloves are caramelized to a medium amber. Add spaghetti, boiled in well-salted water until they are just al dente, as well as a splash of the pasta water, some chopped parsley and a few chili flakes. The pasta is then tossed until fully coated with the oil and kept covered for a few minutes to let the aromas infuse the pasta before serving.

Frying the garlic in their skins lends them a particular sweetness and the skins also add flavor. This is a delicious dish if one doesn't mind picking out the aromatic but inedible garlic skins while eating.

Back at the Villa in Aix, Filip Noterdaeme made a simple dish for dinner according to instructions I had given him before leaving.

CHICKEN SALAD

Strip all meat from a roasted chicken and shred or dice it. In a mortar, crush a garlic clove along with a tablespoon of whole black peppercorns and a teaspoon of coarse sea salt. Add 2 handfuls of fresh basil leaves and crush everything into a coarse paste. Stir a couple tablespoons of olive oil into it and scatter the sauce over the chicken. Toss well and chill for several hours before serving.

The confectioners in Aix are proud of their local specialty, the *Calissons d'Aix*, an elegant and very refined treat. Roseline and André used to always bring a large box of them when they came to visit my family in Munich after we had moved there from Paris, and they were hurt if I didn't have at least several. *Calissons* are made of best quality almonds and candied melon. It is impossible to find them in New York City. For years this confection was a puzzlement to me. It wasn't until I found a place that sold imported Italian almonds and *bitter* – not sweet – apricot kernels that I had enough courage to attempt the making of this famous confection. How I first found a recipe for it, long before one could find a recipe for virtually anything on the internet, I do not recall. This is as near as my experiments got me to

CALISSONS D'AIX

On the day before making the *calissons*, soak 4 bitter apricot kernels in cold water. The skins should come loose after an hour. Peel them, refresh the water and soak them overnight.

This removes much of their cyanide and brings out their subtle bitter almond aroma, so crucial for real *calissons*.

Toss 2 cups of imported Italian almonds into a pot of boiling water. After a minute, drain them – their skins will be loose by then, making it easy to pop them off once they are cool enough to handle. Spread out the skinned almonds on a sheet pan and dry them thoroughly in a 200° F oven for about 15 minutes. Let them come to room temperature and cool them briefly in the refrigerator before transferring them into a food processor, adding 1 ½ cups of confectioner's sugar and the apricot kernels (wipe them dry before adding them). Pulse the mixture until coarsely ground, then run the machine until you have a fine powder. Do not over-process or it will turn into an oily, rubbery paste. Transfer the powder into a bowl and place ¼ cup of candied orange peel, a tablespoon of candied lemon peel and 1 cup of candied cantaloupe, all finely diced, into the processor. Pulse the fruit with 3 tablespoons of orange flower water, added in increments, until you have a smooth, fine paste. Add the sweetened almond flour and process everything into a pliable ball. Working in batches, roll out the paste onto sheets of edible paper, using wax paper or cellophane to prevent it form sticking to the rolling pin. Cut out classic lozenge shapes or slice the sheets into diamond -shaped pieces. Glaze each piece with royal icing, made of 2 cups of confectioner's sugar and 1 egg white. When the icing is set, store the *calissons* in a tin box, layered between sheets of wax paper.

This is of course not a dessert but candy. They have a very sophisticated flavor and are quite worth the effort and time it takes to make them.

Years later when we took our first trip to San Francisco I was eager to eat at Chez Panisse in nearby Berkeley, where it is said the American culinary revolution began under the influence of Provencal cooking. I had been invited to San Francisco along with two dozen cabaret singers and burlesque dancers for a couple of special performances at SF MoMA. I had heard so much of Chez Panisse – how likely was it that Alice Waters, the owner, was going to be there. In the city guide it said that the restaurant was always fully booked months in advance but that one might be able to get a table at the upstairs café on short notice. We took a train from San Francisco to Berkeley just in time for an early dinner. When we arrived we were indeed told that we could be accommodated. Alice Waters was sitting in a little nook by the entrance of the upstairs dining room. Like many trailblazing women, she had alert eyes and a well-rehearsed smile. She was clearly a very determined woman. She nodded in appreciation when I told her how happy I was to be there. The café had the casual air of a family operation, there were no table cloths and the sparkling water was made on the premises and offered on the house. We agreed it was all very modern yet warm and welcoming. So did everybody else in the room. I was impressed with the harmonious flow of the service. Lunch would be just as well-balanced.

CHEZ PANISSE-INSPIRED CITRUS SALAD

Sections of several kinds of citrus – oranges, grapefruit, blood orange, pomelo – and a couple of avocado slices are neatly arranged in a pattern on individual serving plates. A few thinly cut red onion rings are scattered over the fruit as well as 3 or 4 split, peeled pistachios and a couple of very thin Jalapeño and pink radish slices. This is sprinkled with a few drops of excellent extra virgin olive oil, seasoned with flaky sea salt, garnished with a cilantro sprig or a few microgreens and served immediately. This is simplicity at its best. And a thing of beauty.

The pomelo, a citrus fruit I had first tasted on my sixteenth birthday when my mother gifted me a basket with exotic fruit, is less tart than grapefruit. Years later, during a trip to the Dominican Republic where I cooked alongside chef Gabrielle Hamilton for a group of millionaires and their friends, I learned that the white pith of the fruit can be soaked in water for several days and then cooked with copious amounts of sugar into a compote, preferably with a stick of cinnamon and a few cloves.

Our cabaret show at SF MoMA was a long one and went until very late, the New York producer having not considered that San Francisco was a conservative town where people go to bed early. To our endless consternation, several audience members got up to leave before the show was over. Later we heard that the overtime pay for museum staff and security was so high that night that it nearly cost the event's curator his job.

The day after the show, Filip Noterdaeme and I wandered through the city and visited the V. C. Morris Gift Shop, a gallery that had taken over a Frank Lloyd Wright-designed building with a curving indoor ramp that is said to be the prototype for the ramp that later became the defining element of the interior of the Guggenheim Museum. The gallery was selling Asian antiques.

The farmers' market on the Ferry Plaza was impressive. It was not as abundant as the market in Aix en Provence and not as precious as the one I had once seen in Zurich, but it was in any case far superior to any market I had seen on the East Coast. In Zurich, I had nearly cried when I saw the perfect green lettuces and colorful vegetables, so crisp and neat and clean as only Switzerland could produce them. In San Francisco I also nearly cried, not because of the quality of the produce but because of the prices.

From Ferry Plaza we walked downtown to have lunch at a small and unpretentious little restaurant that specialized in raw seafood. They served us the freshest

SCALLOP CRUDO

The best scallops to use for this recipe are large "dry" sea scallops. Briefly rinse them in cold water, pat them dry and cut off the tough little muscle band that adheres to the flesh. Cut each scallop against the grain into 4 thin slices, fan them out on chilled appetizer plates and top them with a thin line of very finely diced raw rhubarb. Add a few drops of excellent extra virgin olive oil and season with flaky salt. Serve with crisp toast points.

One winter Filip Noterdaeme's mother was inspired to invite us and the extended Noterdaeme family for a week of skiing in the Alto Adige region of Italy. Filip Noterdaeme's brother took the initiative in locating a suitable *Pensione*. As we were in a haste to get there we took no time to go out of our way to discover new places. We contended ourselves with a two-star hotel in Milan for a night before continuing our trip to the mountains and found it quite wanting. The night was deadly. A young couple in an adjacent room was fighting loudly for hours and the incompetent night concierge refused to do anything about it. In the morning, the more competent daytime concierge directed us to an excellent café around the corner for a *cornetto* and *latte macchiato*. On the cold bus ride to our final destination up a snowy mountain it became obvious that we had not packed the right shoes. Was I or Filip Noterdaeme to blame? In the discussion that followed we came to no conclusion. We would also have to rent skiing equipment. It was an enchanting alpine landscape, snow-covered and interlaced with skiing lifts and gondolas. Our *Pensione* was understated, clean and friendly. Situated next to the slopes, it was very convenient, and every room had a balcony. The food was simple but skillfully prepared. We stayed for a whole week. The owners became very dear to us. *La padrona* was running the front of the house and her husband cooked, shyly but expertly. The first meal he served us was

CARPACCIO DELL' ALTO ADIGE

Arrange very thin slices of *Bresaola** on a platter. Over this, scatter a few thinly sliced Porcini, typically conserved in olive oil and herbs (thinly sliced raw portobello mushrooms may be substituted). Add a few shavings of Parmiggiano cheese and garnish with a few leaves of baby arugula. If baby arugula cannot be found, thin shavings of raw, green asparagus will do. Season with coarsely crushed black peppercorns, a few drops of lemon juice and a generous drizzle of extra virgin olive oil. This is nice served as an appetizer with grilled slices of country bread.

After a few days of skiing we took a bus to explore Bormio, the little town down in the valley we had passed through on our way. We were seduced at once by its pastry shops and cafés. We tasted everything and went on to spend the rest of the afternoon in the ancient thermal baths on the other side of the valley. Wandering its hallways and exploring its steaming warm water caves and more modern amenities, we came upon a dining area where Filip Noterdaeme, who is always interested in food, found the buffet to be a bit excessive for a thermal bath. The cook smiled when he saw Filip Noterdaeme and I arguing and pointed to a platter filled with a regional pasta dish, but I said I would prefer to have it after a day of skiing than in between steam baths. Later that week, at our *Pensione*, we were indeed served

PIZZOCCHERI

Place 1 cup of buckwheat flour and 1 cup of all-purpose flour into a food processor. With the machine running, add 3 eggs, lightly beaten with 3 tablespoons of warm water. Pulse a few times before letting the machine run and process the mixture into a ball (add more water if the mixture is too dry.) Wrap the dough in cellophane and refrigerate it for at least half an hour. If you have a pasta rolling machine, proceed as you would for making Tagliatelle. If not, roll out the dough by hand as thin as

* Dry-cured beef from the Alpine region

possible and cut it into wide ribbons.

Boil a couple of starchy potatoes in salted water until tender. Peel them, break them into uneven chunks and cover them to keep them warm. In a large frying pan, sauté a finely diced, small white onion and chopped garlic to taste until translucent. Add half a white cabbage head, cored and cut into 1-inch squares. Sauté until the leaves begin to wilt and lightly caramelize. Season with salt and coarse black pepper.

Boil the pasta in salted water until al dente. When it is almost ready, add 1 cup of light cream to the cabbage in the frying pan and bring it to a simmer. Add the drained pasta, the potatoes and a generous amount of shredded *Valtellina* cheese. Toss until the cheese is melted. Garnish with chopped parsley and serve immediately.

For Filip Noterdaeme's birthday, a few days later, I ordered this local specialty cake from a bakery in Bormio.

TORTA DI SARAZENA

Pour ½ cup of sugar into the mixing bowl of a stand mixer. Grate the zest of 1 lemon over it and rub it into the sugar with your fingertips. Add 1 stick of softened butter and beat it until the sugar has completely dissolved. Add 6 egg yolks, one at a time, beating in between each addition until fully combined. Sift together 1 cup of buckwheat of flour, ½ cup of potato starch and 1 teaspoon of baking powder, add ¾ cup of ground hazelnuts and fold everything into the buttercream. Beat 6 egg whites to a firm peak, gradually adding ½ cup of sugar, and fold them into the dough base. Divide the dough into 2 cake pans lined with buttered and floured parchment paper and bake at 350° F for about 25 minutes, until a cake tester comes out dry. Unmold the cakes and let them cool off on a wire rack. Stack them together, filled with strained, seedless raspberry jam. Dust the cake with confectioner's sugar and serve with barely sweetened whipped cream to which you may add a drop of Kirsch liquor.

This is a cake of particular interest for those who are eager to omit gluten from their diet as has become more and more fashionable in recent years. It serves as a good basic recipe. The variations are endless. One may use a mix of rice flour and corn flour and almonds or walnuts can be substituted for the hazelnuts. It is a cake that does not advertise its absence of wheat flour.

In the fall, one of my clients, an investment banker who now and then hired me to cook dinner parties at his Central Park South penthouse, told me that he had bought a 2,000 acre property and golf course on the northern coastline of the Dominican Republic and suggested that I should go see it. He wanted me to create the menu for the dream resort he was planning to build there. He was an admirably successful financier and had a gift for locating interesting places and opportunities. When Christmas came, Filip Noterdaeme and I boarded a plane full of Dominicans traveling home with a great many, large, gift-wrapped presents for their families, and headed south. It was indeed a beautiful property, but the constant playing of salsa and meringue music everywhere was too unnerving for the enjoyment of a proper meal. We once went to Pig and Khao, a popular restaurant on Manhattan's Lower East Side. As we were led to our table, we realized that the loud music would spoil our dinner. We decided to instead eat at home, quietly, happily. As Filip Noterdaeme always says, if I cannot hear it, I cannot taste it. However, there are exceptions. One day, we had dinner with friends at Pearl Oyster Bar, one of our favorite restaurants. When more and more people arrived and it became too loud to continue a civilized conversation, they asked him, do you mind the noise. He explained that he never did when food had been prepared by a lesbian chef.

During our stay in the Dominican Republic, Filip and Noterdaeme often discussed whether I should agree to move there and take charge of the kitchen once the planned resort and a new clubhouse were built. The surrounding landscape was enchanting. Our driver took us to Cabrera, a small village up on a hill, where we had a very common local street food snack,

CHULLITOS DE CASSAVA

Peel and finely grate about 2 pounds of yucca root and one white onion. Fold the gratings into a cloth and squeeze out as much of the liquids as possible. Transfer the mix to a bowl, season it with salt and, working with wet hands, press 2 tablespoons of it into the palm of one hand, place a piece of Mozzarella, Monterey Jack or other melting cheese in its center, fold over the dough and seal it, shaping it into a torpedo with pointed tips. Fry the *chullitos* until golden brown in neutral-tasting oil like grape-seed or peanut – never canola – heated to 375° F.

The cooks at the clubhouse on the golf course not quite understanding yet what was expected of them for the next days continued to concern themselves with the preparation of rice, beans and fried chicken for staff meals and the occasional omelet or burger with French fries for a stray golfer. Neither the investment banker nor I found either offering acceptable. What had seduced me was the idea of cooking with tropical fruit and fresh local seafood. My menus would be based on these. The cooks asked me if I had tried Dominican food before. I was obliged to admit that I had. I would adapt it to my own taste. I had not been flown in to prepare traditional local, nor, for that matter, continental food. The club's kitchen was in a sad state. The produce in the walk-in cooler was subpar. Filip Noterdaeme ominously declared that we would never come to live here. The guests were scheduled to arrive the next day and I started by reorganizing the kitchen. There was a lot to be done.

It was very hot and there wasn't much time, but I was assured by the staff's helpfulness and willingness to take directions. I commenced by inquiring about local food stores and markets. After some investigating I concluded the freshest produce and seafood could only be bought directly from local farms and fishermen. This was a political quagmire, but it did not discourage me. There were farms nearby and many fishermen; surely one could figure out a way to work with them.

The cooks were very surprised that I insisted on creating dishes based on their local ingredients yet dramatically differing from their own cuisine. One of them insisted on taking me to two specialty stores in the town of Sosua that certainly would be of interest. We drove to Sosua the next morning. There, he proudly led me first to a German butcher shop where Bavarian-style hams and sausages were sold and then to a German bakery with a display case full of old-fashioned German cakes and tortes. I felt obliged to dissuade the cook from his fixation that any of these exotic offerings would be of use for me.

In the meantime, I got a local fisherman to deliver several dozen freshly caught local spiny lobsters. Here's the dish I made with them.

LANGOSTINOS IN LIGHT COCONUT SAUCE

Shell and devein spiny lobsters or real prawns, 1 to 3 per person, depending on size. Save the heads for the stock and refrigerate the tail meat.

In a large casserole, stir-fry the heads with some neutral-tasting oil and a few chopped shallots and celery stalks until fragrant. Deglaze with a glass of dry vermouth, add a couple of fish heads without gills as well as a few bruised stalks of lemon grass, kaffir lime leaves or a tied-up bunch of well-rinsed cilantro stems. Add enough water to cover the solids by an inch (keep them submerged in the water with an inverted plate) and simmer the stock on a very low flame for about an hour, skimming off any rising foam. Strain the broth through a cheese cloth, discard the solids and bring it back to a simmer. Add a peeled large carrot, cut into chunks, a quartered, white onion, and small knob of peeled fresh ginger. When they are tender, transfer all the vegetables and ginger into a blender, add enough coconut milk to cover them halfway and blend everything to a smooth, thick puree. Strain and reserve. Add some ice cubes to the broth to cool it down (or wait until it has cooled down on its own), add 4 lightly beaten egg whites and the cracked egg shells into it, set it over a low flame and bring to very low simmer. Once the egg whites and shells have solidified to a raft and the broth is clear, strain the *fumet* through a cheese cloth, return it to a clean, non-reactive sauce pan and simmer it until reduced at least by half. Its flavor ought to be quite concentrated. Crush a few saffron threads in a bowl and add some warm broth to release their color. Pour the coconut vegetable cream into a sauce pan. Add the saffron and just enough of the concentrated broth to have a sauce that is about as thick as buttermilk. Season it with salt and white pepper and keep it warm. Do not bring it to a simmer again. Season the lobster tails with salt, white pepper and, if desired, powdered achiote (sometimes called *annatto*) or turmeric powder, and cook them with just a little butter in a frying pan set over medium heat until barely opaque. Add them (and the butter) to the warm sauce. Serve with plain white rice and quartered baby bok choy bulbs, steamed for 3-5 minutes over ginger-infused water.

For the next couple of days, the guests were kept busy with excursions in all directions, returning to the clubhouse for lunch and dinner.

We stayed on in the Dominican Republic for New Year's Eve; it was the end of the rainy season, the dry season would be even more beautiful. Whenever there was a tropical downpour it not only made the ocean jade green but all the landscape more exotic. One day I went to a chicken farm. There were countless rather large white-feathered chickens held in several pens, and I had to point at the ones I wanted them to slaughter for us. It remains one of my more disturbing memories.

All day and night we heard the sounds of birds and insects and the obligatory rather hectic salsa and meringue music from someone's radio. Filip Noterdaeme and I were obliged to sleep with earplugs. No one else seemed to mind the noise. The investment banker and his friends enjoying the exotic timbre all around could not understand why we didn't find it atmospheric. The food at the hotel even on New Year's Eve was wretched. The only thing the little local community produced and that was noteworthy was an array of fruit compotes and confections made of papayas, the aforementioned pomelos, pineapples and caramelized milk curds, but one could not live on that alone. I once went to visit the woman who made them. She had a large copper caldron set over an open fire and stirred several gallons of sweetened fresh milk in it until it turned into a mild caramel, into which she would then pour some fresh lime juice to make it curdle. Like so many good things we tasted on our travels, this confection would not be allowed in our carry-on luggage.

Over the next years, the resort was built and I returned several times to develop a suitable, modern menu for its new clubhouse. Perhaps I was naïve. It was foolish to believe that the Dominican cooks would properly execute my menu in my absence. One day during my last visit, walking through a plowed field where soon several new bungalows would be erected, I was forced to admit that I was wasting my time and that it was best to distance myself from the project. I took a moment to survey the place I had so hoped would showcase my food and then travelled back to New York.

It had become our habit to remain in New York during fall, winter and spring unless we were being invited somewhere, which did not however prevent us from constantly discussing our next summer vacation. At this time my parents told me that they had made up their mind to once again buy a summer house on the little island in Brittany where they used to own a large property and house when I was a teenager. They had sold the first house when it had become too laborious to maintain. Filip Noterdaeme and I had visited them there just once before the sale but he, having suffered severe allergy attacks, had insisted on cutting our stay short. Of all the places we had visited together this had been the only one we had not been in agreement about. However I was able to convince him to give it another try. We decided that on our way there we would make a stopover in Brussels to visit his family.

In late July, we travelled to Brussels, where we would find not only incomparable food but some unchanged places of Filip Noterdaeme's youth. To prove this he took me to lunch at the *Taverne du Passage*, a well-established art deco restaurant in the *Galeries Royales*. Its menu was a distinctly mid-Twentieth Century version of Nineteenth Century Belgian cuisine and eating there was like a trip into a distant past none of us could have known. We asked for a particularly old-fashioned appetizer that isn't served anywhere else in Brussels any longer and that had reportedly been a favorite of the late Belgian artist Marcel Broodthaers. Filip Noterdaeme enjoyed this notion much more than the dish itself.

LA POUTARGUE SUR TOAST

In a saucepan, melt 2 tablespoons of butter and whisk 1 tablespoon of flour into it to make a smooth paste. Whisking vigorously, gradually add 1 cup of milk and bring it simmer. Cook it for a couple of minutes while stirring continuously to prevent lumps. Transfer it to a mixing bowl. When cooled to room temperature, add a handful of shredded Chimay or other tangy semi-soft cheese and 2-4 tablespoons of finely grated Poutargue*. Season with white pepper and a touch of lemon juice.

Cut off the crusts of 2 slices of white bread, lightly toast the slices and top them with a generous amount of Poutargue cream. Place them under a broiler and brown them until golden and bubbly. Serve with a few small leaves of butter lettuce, tomato quarters and split radishes.

From the *Galeries* we walked to the Jacques Brel Foundation, the Magritte Museum and the Sablon Square, where we had for dinner at the famous restaurant Au Vieux Saint Martin

FILET AMÉRICAIN
(Belgian-style Steak Tartare)

Finely ground beef – sirloin, not filet – is mixed with raw egg yolk, tiny capers, Dijon mustard, finely diced shallots, a dash of Worcestershire sauce and homemade mayonnaise and seasoned with salt and black pepper. Thoroughly chilled, it

---

* Pressed and smoked mullet roe, more commonly sold in the States under its Italian name *Botarga*.

is then quickly blended once again to a fine paste in a food processor. This final step is characteristic for a Belgian *filet americain* and sets it apart from the French *steak tartare* which is traditionally seasoned table-side. There is an interesting variation of this dish called *Aller-Retour*, round-trip, where the seasoned, mixed beef paste is shaped into a patty and seared in a very hot pan for just a few seconds on both sides. The name is an allusion to the quick back-and forth flipping of the patty.

The confusing name of this Belgian favorite, confusing to all Americans who are not known for having a taste for raw meat of any kind, stems from the Belgians' cheerfully innate penchant for linguistic misunderstandings. In this case, I suspect the confusion began when the French created a dish of chopped raw and seasoned meat and named it steak tartare after the Tatar people who were too busy riding horses and waging wars to bother cooking the meat they ate. The region closest to where the Tatars stem from is named Armenia. As a matter of fact, the Armenian people have their own version of raw beef named *Chee Kufta*. It may be a long way from Armenia to Belgium but it is only a short way from *Filet Arménien* to *Filet Americain*. At the venerable Brussels diner known as *Au Suisse*, yet another confusing name for a Belgian establishment, *filet américain* is served spread on a long baguette-style sandwich but elsewhere all over town, the dish is always served with Belgian fried potatoes which Americans insist on calling French fries, a shortened version of their actual English name, *Frenched Fried potatoes*, alluding to the style of cutting things into sticks, which is somewhat elaborate and elegant and therefore, from an American point of view, surely French. This reminds me of an American cake named German Chocolate Cake which is not German at all, it merely originated as a recipe on a box for an American chocolate brand named *German's*. There will always be some confusion when food is crossing borders but there is nothing regrettable about this fact. I suspect much innovation has come from it.

At the historical Dandoy bakery close to the Grande Place, Filip Noterdaeme made me taste another delightful example for the muddling of names called

PAIN À LA GRECQUE

Into a stand mixer equipped with a dough hook, pour ¾ cup of cold milk in which 1 tablespoon of fresh cake yeast has been dissolved; 2 cups of flour; 1 teaspoon of salt; ¼ cup of sugar; and cinnamon to taste. Mix until combined and let the machine run for about 10 minutes, until the dough is no longer sticky. Add ½ stick of softened butter and process until it is completely incorporated into the dough. Divide it into 4 portions. Press each piece, top and bottom, into judicious amounts of pearl sugar, fold it over twice and roll it into a log. Roll the logs once again in pearl sugar, sprinkle them with anise seeds, line them up on a parchment-paper-lined sheet pan, cover them and let them rest and rise in a warm spot for about one hour. Bake them at 375° F for about 20 minutes, until bronze colored.

There is nothing Greek about this pastry. Its original Flemish name had been *brood van de grecht* – bread from the canal, indicating a place by the canal where it was commonly sold. The sweet bread sticks, having become very popular with Napoleon's French soldiers after their invasion of Belgium, were soon referenced by everyone in French as *bread in the Greek manner* – pain à la grecque – so named by the invaders who had not bothered to find out the proper meaning of their Flemish name and simply made a phonetic assumption about it.

After a few days, we bid Brussels farewell and took a train, a bus and a ferry to the little island. For our welcoming meal at my parent's new house my mother served us a *loup de mer en papillote* with brown butter, boiled potatoes, a green salad and an apricot tart. It was all delicious. My parents then drove us to the little summer rental they had found for us via the local tourism office. We were enchanted. Though close to the center of one of the island's larger villages it was set back in a little alley. The next morning we got up early and walked to the bakery a few blocks away to get fresh croissants for our breakfast. The little garden behind the house did not have a terrace but a beautiful Mulberry tree with a wooden table and benches set beneath it for outside dining. In the neighboring garden to our right two charmingly pretty children were playing, and Filip Noterdaeme's hay fever that had plagued him on our last visit did not resurface. It was too good to be true. We biked to one of the island's many beaches for a swim and got back to the house for lunch and a siesta. It was only then that we realized that the children were still playing in the neighboring garden, loudly. We were hopeful that peace and quiet would eventually settle in. The neighbor – she was their grandmother and did not for a moment consider telling them to be mindful of their neighbors – when she heard we were going to stay on for the month brought us a basket of the prettiest, most delicious plums from her garden.

Everything else about the island was so much to our taste that we tried to be indifferent to the children's loud playing each morning and afternoon. It would probably not improve. For the moment at least we would not let it spoil our vacation. At the end of our first week however a group of young people moved into the house to our left and proceeded to host rather raucous late-night dinner parties. We were not amused when they shrugged off our plea for some quiet.

We paid a visit to the local tourism office. The agent was very sympathetic to our complaint but could not help us as there were no vacancies.

One day at the local café where we escaped to more and more often a middle-aged woman sat at the table next to ours, her book turned towards us. After several days she suddenly asked, half turning her head, if we enjoyed spending hours in a café, to which we answered that we had no choice. The next day in the same fashion she asked why we had no choice. Filip Noterdaeme told her that we were here to avoid our neighbor's loud grandchildren. Understandable, said the woman. One day we met her on the market square and we stopped to talk. She told us of a friend's house in a very quiet small village on the other side of the island that might be available for rent. Still hopeful for a quiet vacation, we got in touch with the owner and went to visit her. She was a remarkably expressive painter who had had enough of the urban struggles of being a painter and decided to fully retreat to the island. She showed us the house which was full of her paintings and had two picturesque gardens which pleased us even more. It had been a fisherman's house before she had bought and renovated it. Within a short time she had accepted our offer, figuring that she could live in the studio above her gallery in the harbor during the season. Her bohemian household became a perfect vacation home once I had thoroughly cleaned and re-decorated it according to our sense of aesthetics and taste. From my exacting clients in the Hamptons I had learned very well how one went about changing the décor of a summer rental but as we did not want to offend the painter we tactfully paid very close attention to the way everything was arranged before making any changes, taking photographs of every detail, so as to be able to put everything back into its original state before leaving. Good taste is neither learned nor taught, but respect and attention to detail is.

Towards the end of our sojourn we told the painter that we would be enchanted to return to her pleasant house in the following year. She told us with polite regrets that her daughter was going to come stay with her and that she above all intended to convert the mews behind her house into a guest house so as to be able to rent out her entire property for a price twice as high as what we had been able to pay.

We decided that before returning to New York we must find and reserve another house for the next summer. But that was a large order. Most of the summer rentals were meant for large families and unaffordable for us. In the end, it was another two years before we finally found our perfect fit. The following summer we reserved a house that had been recommended but turned out to be very shabby and poorly furnished. We spent a full day cleaning it but after just one night decided that it was still *insupportable*, insufferable. We moved in with my parents for a few days until we found an alternative, a very expensive house with a view of the ocean that was then promptly sold to new owners who would no longer rent it out. We ended up spending our last days searching and asking around without any luck. We were miserable until one afternoon, the day before our departure, we glimpsed the perfect house behind a little forest in the middle of the island. It was not registered with the local tourism office but an old lady in the next village told us that it belonged to a farmer from the Haute Savoie who only visited the island in the fall and spring, during hunting season. That was enough to inspire us. We would convince this farmer that we were the perfect summer tenants, good at keeping things neat and good at not changing a thing about his habitat. We contacted him and he complained about summer renters having once pitched tents in his garden. We told him not to worry, we were only two, we abhorred camping and were coming all the way from New York City. This did not fail to impress him. He accepted our offer, we sent him a deposit and the following year we became the ecstatic tenants of a house we had not even been able to fully inspect.

One year later, three planes, taken in rapid succession, each one smaller than the former, got us to the island in no time and we arrived with our light hand luggage to find the house better than our dreams of it.

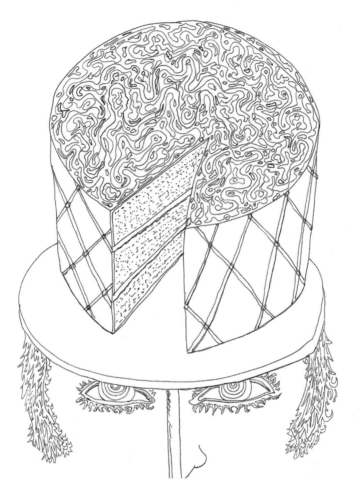

VII

FAVORITES

W HAT IS THE FIRST FOOD you remember, remember eating it and then craving it all the time? Well, the first food I remember craving in my early childhood in Paris in the early Seventies is sweetened condensed milk: sold in tin tubes and preferably sucked directly out of them, little hands squeezing the cool metal tubes until it was all crinkled, stiff and empty. But after that the first food that I clearly remember is pan-fried *Leberkäse**, which of course one could only find in Southern Germany or Austria, never in France. Oma, my maternal grandmother, fortunately made it for my brother and I whenever we travelled from France to visit her in Lower Bavaria. She had become a widow at age forty-six and had since then lived a quiet, reclusive life. Incredibly, she who according to my mother had once been such an energetic and proficient cook of traditional German foods had become accustomed to taking advantage of the modern convenience of processed foods. She was simply tired of kitchen labor. No one in Bavaria would ever think of making *Leberkäse* from scratch since it can be bought in any deli or butcher store but as it is all but impossible to find it in America, here is an easy recipe.

BAVARIAN LEBERKÄSE

Cut 1½ pounds of lean pork shoulder and 1 pounds of pork belly, rind removed, into small cubes. Season the meat with 2 teaspoons of curing salt**, 1 teaspoon of regular salt, 1 teaspoon of ground white pepper, 1 teaspoon of ground dried marjoram and a pinch each of powdered ginger and mace. Add half a small white onion, diced, as well as a smashed garlic clove and chill everything in the freezer for a good hour. Wrap 2 dozen ice cubes into a towel and, using a mallet, pound it until the ice is very finely crushed. Store it in the freezer until ready to use. Grease a pan loaf with lard or butter and place it in the freezer. Working rapidly in two batches, pulse and finally process half the meat mixture in the food processor

---

* Literally meaning "liver cheese," it contains neither liver or cheese but is simply a baked loaf of very fine forcemeat.
** A special salt containing Sodium Nitrate, also known as Prague Powder. This is an obligatory ingredient that conserves the *Leberkäse* and turns the cooked meat appetizingly pink.

with half the amount of crushed ice until you have a fine-textured homogenous sticky paste. Do not overwork the paste to the point that it warms up from the machine's fast motor rotation. Fill it into the chilled loaf pan, pressing down, return the pan to the freezer and repeat the procedure with the rest of the meat and ice. Add the second batch into the loaf pan, press down to remove any air bubbles, smooth the top with wet fingers, draw a grid into it with a wet knife and place the loaf pan in a baking dish halfway filled with hot water. Bake it at 325° F for 75 minutes or until a tester comes out dry. Place the *Leberkäse* under the griddle for a few additional minutes to brown the top thoroughly. Serve warm slices of it on a Kaiser roll smeared with medium or hot mustard, or pan-fry slices of it on both sides until well browned and serve with a pan-fried egg, roasted potatoes and creamed spinach.

Oma's *Rohrnudeln** are still remembered. She usually made them once a week and placed half of each baked batch in the freezer for the second half of the week. Kneading the dough became a chore with age. How she would have loved a kitchen machine with a dough hook. But then, she would also have rebuffed it as an unnecessary luxury as she was a very humble woman who denied herself anything she would have deemed too precious. It therefore wasn't ever easy to find a sensible Christmas present for her. I remember how pleased she was when I once gave her an extra-long shoehorn that finally allowed her to put on her shoes without bending over.

OMA'S ROHRNUDELN

Cut 6 firm-cooking, "Italian" plums in half and remove stems and pits. In a sauce pan, bring ¼ cup of water, 2 tablespoons of sugar and a cinnamon stick to a boil, add the plums, close the lid and cook over medium heat for 5 minutes, shaking the pan occasionally. Transfer the cooked plums to a bowl so they cool down faster.

Gently warm ⅔ cups of milk with ½ stick of butter. When the butter has melted, beat 2 eggs into the liquid and add it to 4 cups of flour mixed with 1 pack of dry yeast. Knead all the ingredients until the dough is no longer sticky. Cover it with a kitchen towel and place in a warm spot for an hour or

* Bavarian specialty, literally "oven noodles" but in fact sweet yeast buns.

until the dough has doubled in volume. Punch it down and knead it once more. Divide the dough into 12 portions, flatten them and roll each portion around half a cooked plum into a ball. Transfer the dough balls into a buttered baking dish, they should touch each other just lightly. Cover and set aside in a warm place for another half hour or until they have doubled in size. Brush them with melted butter and bake them at 350° for about 35 minutes, until golden brown. Serve warm with vanilla sauce or *crème anglaise*, a recipe for which can be found in Chapter IX, or plain at room temperature.

I realize, recalling these two of Oma's specialties, that they may not be in sync with today's culinary fashions. These days, every recipe must be more ambitious and innovative than a previous one to get any attention. If true sophistication is akin to simplicity, the rejection of the latter in today's culinary world is neither encouraging nor inspiring. There is too much of everything going on. But if cooks are increasingly obsessed with the visual, fads, and the media, this book will, I hope, offer an alternative approach that is less about the competitive exploitation of cooking than the relaxed joy that one can find in the kitchen.

My fascination with cooking began with the making of sweets – cookies and puddings, creams, cakes and tarts – double evidence of my epicurean leanings. For when one is young, one seeks to repeat the easy thrill of the sugar rush: savory dishes are for grown-ups. So this is one of the easiest ones.

WHIPPED QUARK*

Soak a good handful of dark raisins in warm water. Meanwhile, separate 3 eggs and beat the yolks with ⅓ cup of sugar, the grated zest of 1 lemon and the scraped seeds of 1 vanilla bean until a soft ribbon forms. Beat the 3 egg whites with a pinch of salt to a firm peak. Whisk 3 cups of *Quark*, *fromage blanc* or thick, full-fat Greek yogurt into the egg yolk mixture, add the drained raisins and fold in the egg whites.

This is also used as a traditional filling for *Palatschinken*, Austrian pancakes. Spread the *Quark* mixture on thin, fluffy

---

* Quark is a German kind of mild and creamy fresh cheese made with rennet. Less suitable as a substitute than French *fromage blanc* or thick Greek-style yogurt, Ricotta is an acceptable alternative but it must first be passed through a fine-mesh sieve and beaten to a creamy consistency with a bit of added milk.

pancakes, roll them up or fold them twice in half, place them into a buttered baking dish and bake them in a 350° F oven for about 20 minutes, until lightly browned and puffed up. Serve warm, dusted with confectioner's sugar.

The recipe for whipped *Quark* was never written down in our family, it was simply taught to me by my mother.

Another old favorite of mine has for the last twenty-three years been known amongst my American friends as

DANIEL'S "LITTLE RASCALS"
(Spitzbuben)

In a food processor, pulse 2 cups of whole almonds with 1 ¼ cups of sugar and the scraped seeds of 1 vanilla bean until finely ground. Transfer to a mixing bowl and add 3 cups of unbleached white flour and 3 sticks of softened butter. Kneed everything into a ball, divide it half, shape the halves into discs, wrap them in cellophane and chill them for one hour. For the filling, heat 2 cups of red currant jam and pass it through a sieve to remove all skins and seeds. Fill the jam into a pastry bag with a round tip, or into a squeeze bottle. Roll out the dough in batches to about ⅛ inch thickness and cut out an equal numbers of rounds and rings, about 1 ½ inches in diameter. Bake them at 350° F on parchment paper-lined sheet pans until light brown, about 8 minutes. Do not over-bake them lest they turn bitter. Flip the rounds, squeeze a bit of jam onto each of them and top them with the ring-shaped cookies. Make a sugar glaze by slowly stirring 2 tablespoons of melted clarified butter or coconut oil and 2 tablespoons rum into 2 cups of confectioner's sugar. Fill the glaze into a pastry bag and squeeze a ring of glaze onto each cookie. When the glaze is dry to the touch, store the cookies between layers of parchment paper in a tin box. They are at their best after a week but keep for several weeks.

As these cookies are very laborious to prepare, they are usually made only around Christmas time. A more ordinary though no less popular treat, this one from France, is

PAIN D'ÉPICES
(Spiced Honey Cake)

Gently heat ¾ cup of dark, flavorful honey with ½ cup of
of milk and 6 tablespoons of butter, just long enough for the
butter to melt. Once the mix has cooled down again to room
temperature, mix with 2 eggs and gradually stir the liquid into a
blend of ½ cup of sugar, ¾ cup of flour, ¾ cup of rye flour, ¼
cup of ground almonds and ½ tablespoon of baking powder
mixed with a pinch of salt, cinnamon, ground clove and grated
nutmeg. Pour the dough into a parchment-paper-lined loaf
pan, careful to not fill it beyond two thirds as the cake will rise
considerably. Pour any extra dough into ramekins. Bake at 375°
F for 45 minutes (less for the ramekins) or until a cake tester
comes out clean. *Pain d'épices* is best at room temperature, sliced
and slathered with nothing but salted butter.

In France, *pain d'épices* is considered a pantry staple, and no one would
consider making it from scratch since a variety of good quality *pains d'épices*
can be found in virtually any French supermarket. Which brings me to an
important distinction between the French and the Americans.

The French have a deeply ingrained respect for the centuries-old
craftsmanship of baking and pastry making. They would consider it
audacious to bake bread at home and *déclassé*, even tacky, to serve one's
guests homemade versions of such refined and complicated classic
pâtisseries as a *Saint Honoré*, a *Paris Brest* or an *Opera* cake, wisely choosing to
leave such tasks to trained professionals. A French home-cook ought to
know how to make any of the classic French sauces, but when it comes to
breads and pastries, he or she will demonstrate his or her discriminatory
sense of taste and class through choosing the best *boulangerie* or *pâtisserie* of
her *quartier* to order them from. This can become a lively subject at table.
The French can therefore not comprehend the Germans' and Americans'
can-do attitude that drives them to create in all earnestness baked goods
at home that ape those prepared and sold by professionals. The decidedly
mixed results of this trend can be studied on social media sites such as
Instagram and a myriad of amateur food blogs.

When favorites are things that one must procure from a specific place
they evoke different feelings than homemade favorites. That is, we tend
to treasure things more when they are not always available. Having moved
three times in my life from one country to another, I know the feeling of
yearning for something that is not available, and it was in this way that my

ambition to replicate favorites at home commenced. Over time, it became an aesthetic experience of the highest order, even more engrossing than consuming the results thereof. What more can one say? If one had the choice of being presented with a perfect *éclair au café*, something I dearly missed during my teens in Germany, or having a lesson from a French pastry chef on how to make them, which would one choose?

Let's not noodle around.

PASTA WITH RAGÙ

Heat a a Dutch oven over a medium flame, add 2 tablespoons of olive oil and lightly brown 1 large chopped onion and 2 thinly sliced cloves of garlic in it. Stir-fry for a minute before adding 1 diced carrot and 2 diced celery stalks. When the vegetables begin to caramelize, push them to the sides of the pot, pour a bit of olive oil into the center and add 2 tablespoons of Italian tomato paste. Do not stir it until it begins to brown. Deglaze with a bit of *vino santo*, dry Marsala or white wine. Stir and cook until the liquid has evaporated, then push the vegetables once more to the side and add 2 pounds coarsely ground meat (any combination of pork, beef or veal, according to preference – at times I even revert to using well-drained, imported oil-packed tuna, with excellent results) into the center. Break up the meat and brown it on all sides with the vegetables before deglazing the pan once again with wine. Repeat this step 2 more times, deglazing and reducing the liquid each time, to deepen the flavors. Season with salt and add aromatics (a cinnamon stick, a few cloves, grated nutmeg or mace, 2 bay leaves, and ground pepper) and 1 large can of whole *San Marzano* tomatoes, coarsely crushed by hand. Bring the sauce to a simmer, stir once, place a round piece of parchment paper with a hole cut out in its center directly onto the sauce, close the Dutch oven with its lid and place it in a 325° F oven for 3 hours. Remove the parchment paper and skim off most of the risen fat. Adjust the seasoning, keeping in mind that it should be quite salty to hold up against the plain pasta. Boil durum wheat pasta – *Ziti Rigati* are an ideal shape, much better suited to hold the heavy meat sauce than spaghetti – in well-salted water until al dente. To serve 4, add 2 cups of ragù, a tablespoon of butter and ½ cup of milk into a large sauté pan and bring to a simmer. (Omit the milk if you used tuna.) Add the drained pasta and toss until the pasta is coated with sauce, using a bit of pasta water if it is too dry. Divide the pasta onto 4 plates, sprinkle with chopped parsley and serve with Parmesan cheese – finely ground, never grated – on the side.

SPAGHETTI WITH ANCHOVIES

In a Dutch oven, heat 3 tablespoons of olive oil. Add 6 peeled and sliced garlic cloves and tip the pan to the side, holding it so the cloves swim in the oil and fry more evenly, until they begin to take on some color. Add 6 drained anchovies and a teaspoon of dried chili flakes and stir until the anchovies begin to dissolve. Deglaze the pan with a cup of homemade chicken broth (or white wine or even water), and simmer for a few minutes. Boil enough spaghetti for two in well-salted water until al dente, reserve a cup of the cooking water, drain the pasta and add it to the anchovy sauce. Stir over a medium flame, adding some of the cooking water if necessary, until the spaghetti have absorbed most of the sauce. Serve immediately, topped with coarse, toasted bread crumbs and chopped parsley. For this pasta dish, ground Pecorino is more suitable than Parmesan; it stands up well to the robust flavors of this particular dressing.

In my collection of cookbooks there is one by Daniel Boulud, *Daniel: My French Cuisine*, passed on to me by a client who received it as a giveaway at a benefit gala. The recipes in it are exceedingly complicated. The center of the book is written by Bill Buford, author of *Heat*, an excellent book about Mario Batali's role in the popularization of Italian cuisines in America. In *Daniel*, Buford describes Boulud's and his concerted efforts to recreate legendary dishes of the grand French culinary tradition. The recipe for a *Canard à la Presse* is entirely devoted to an antiquated, rare contraption by which the carcass of a roasted duck is pressed to release its juices for a, we are made to believe, spectacular sauce. For this reason, the recipe is not given here, but since the days I used to work for Boulud's catering company, *Feast and Fêtes*, I have often drawn inspiration from his dishes, including his way of treating fresh tuna like meat, which one day prompted me to create the following dish.

RARE TUNA FILETS WITH FAVA BEANS

Shell fava beans, about 2 pods per person, and blanch the

beans in salted boiling water for just a few seconds before transferring them to a bowl of ice water and, as soon as they are cold enough to handle, pop off their waxy skins. Cut a chunk of tuna filet lengthwise into 4 strips, rub them with olive oil and season them all over with salt, coarsely ground black pepper and chopped fresh rosemary. Sear them on all sides in a very hot frying pan without any extra oil, careful to not overcook them – they must remain rare in the center. Cut one thin slice of pancetta per serving into wide strips and render them in a frying pan. Pour off the fat and add the fava beans and a few thin strips of lemon rind. Toss to just warm them, and add a few fresh mint leaves, torn into pieces. Slice the tuna filets against the grain, season them with flaky sea salt and arrange 4 slices per person on preheated plates. Scatter a few fava beans and pancetta pieces around the tuna and ladle a spoon of warm *demiglace*, a recipe for which can be found in Chapter X, over the tuna. Garnish with crispy fried shallots and serve.

This is my version of a very popular and classic tuna hors d'oeuvre I first tasted at one of *Feast and Fêtes'* events:

TUNA TARTARE ON WONTON CRISPS

Finely dice sushi-grade tuna filet, carefully stripping away all bits of thin white membrane before chopping it. This is best done by scraping off the meat along each layer of membrane with the dull edge of a chef's knife before stripping the membrane away. Season the tartare with finely chopped light green leaves from celery hearts and seeded, finely diced jalapeño pepper to taste, excellent olive oil and a bit of flaky sea salt. Cover and chill until ready to use.

Spray a mini-muffin tin with oil spray. Using a round cookie cutter a little larger than the tin's indentations, cut out rounds of stacks of store-bought wonton or egg roll wrappers and press them into the tins. Spray the dough rounds with oil spray, sprinkle some salt over them and bake them at 350° F for about 4 minutes, until they are crisp and golden brown. Repeat until all wonton wrappers are used up. Fill tartare into cooled crisps and garnish with thin slices of pink radish, chopped chives, a few Nigella seeds or coarsely crushed black pepper corns.

From the same rich fund of memories related to my years of working as a cater waiter at many a festive event there are other recipes to offer, beginning with

BELUGA CAVIAR ON ARTICHOKE HEARTS
WITH QUAIL EGGS

Cook artichokes in salted water aromatized with the juice and halves of a lemon until tender when pierced with a knife, 20 to 30 minutes. Remove them from the water, place them upside down into a bowl and cover. When they are cool enough to handle, cut off the stems and strip away the leaves one by one, reserving them for another use.* Lift off the hairy "choke" by carefully scraping it away with a spoon. Trim the borders and bottoms of the hearts so they are leveled. Into a small sauce pan of boiling water, add a tablespoon of baking soda and carefully lower quail eggs, 3 per serving, into the water. Simmer for 4-5 minutes. Remove the eggs with a slotted spoon and immediately transfer them into a ice bath. When they are cool, carefully peel them and reserve them in a bowl of cold water until ready to serve.

Place a generous heap of beluga caviar into the cavity of each artichoke. Garnish each artichoke heart with halved quail eggs and a dollop of crème fraîche, sprinkled with thinly sliced chives.

The stuffed artichokes were a most luxurious staff meal after a luncheon at the Russian embassy where a good dozen of the invited guests did not show, leaving the fate of many an unserved first course to our discretion. It was accompanied by buttered and toasted brioche points.

From a different event, catered by *Feast and Fêtes*, I once got to take home one of Daniel Boulud's entire lemon raspberry tarts, which I liked so much I commenced to make my own version of it.

MEYER LEMON TART

In a food processor, grind ¾ cup of whole almonds and ¼ cup of confectioner's sugar to a powder. Add 1 cup of flour and

* Short of eating them the traditional way (dipping them into vinaigrette and biting of the soft end of each leaf), you may scrape off the edible part with a spoon and use the lot for a dip, mixed with cream cheese or Ricotta and seasoned with salt, pepper, lemon peel and chives.

1 stick of cold butter and pulse everything into coarse meal. Add one egg yolk diluted with 2 tablespoons cream and a few drops of almond essence and run the machine until everything comes together in a ball, pulsing at first to evenly mix the dry and wet ingredients. Wrap the dough in cellophane and chill it for 30 minutes. Roll out the dough and line a greased and floured tart shell with it. Lightly dust the dough with flour, brushing off the excess with a pastry brush and place it in the freezer for 10 minutes. Cover the crust with an oversized round piece of parchment paper and pour 2 cups of dried chickpeas, dried beans or pie weights over it. Bake the crust at 350° F for 15 minutes.

Lift off the paper with the beans (you can re-use them for a multitude of "blind bakings") and return the tart shell to the oven for another 5-10 minutes, until it is completely baked through yet short of having taken on any color.

Grate the zest of 2 Meyer lemons and one regular lemon into a bowl, carve the white pith off the fruit and slice the pulp into pieces. Remove all seeds from the sliced fruit and along with the zest, 3 eggs, 3 egg yolks, and ¾ cup of sugar in a blender until smooth. Strain through a fine-mesh sieve into a bowl and stir in 1 cup of heavy cream. Dust a pint of fresh raspberries with a tablespoon of confectioner's sugar mixed with a teaspoon of cornstarch and scatter them over the cooled tart crust. Pour the lemon custard mix over them and bake the tart at 325° F for about 35 minutes, until the custard is set. Let the tart cool down completely before removing the fluted ring and sliding the tart onto a cake platter. Dust it with confectioner's sugar just before serving.

The recipe for this simple cake I learned from the wife of a naval captain during a summer vacation in France. Should it therefore not be called

DROWNED PEAR CAKE

Grease a 9-inch round cake pan and dust it with flour. In a mixing bowl, rub the seeds scraped from one half of a split vanilla bean into ¾ cup of sugar. Add a generous pinch of salt and 3 eggs, beat until homogenous and add first 10 tablespoons of melted butter, then 1 cup of flour mixed with

1 teaspoon baking powder and ¼ cup of ground almonds or pistachios. Stir quickly until the dough is not lumpy anymore and pour it into the cake pan. Drain 1 large can of preserved pear halves (reserve the liquid,) cut the pear segments in half and arrange them on the dough in a floral pattern. They will sink to the bottom on their own. Bake at 350° F for about 35 minutes, until a cake tester comes out clean. Immediately pour the reserved liquid over the cake. Serve at room temperature, dusted with confectioner's sugar.

FLOURLESS HAZELNUT CHERRY CAKE

Roast 1½ cups of hazelnuts in a 350° F oven until browned and fragrant. When cool enough to handle, transfer them onto kitchen towel, fold it over and rub the nuts back and forth through the towel to loosen and remove their skins. Finely grind the cooled, skinned nuts to a fine powder in a nut mill or a food processor.

Beat 4 egg yolks with ½ cup of sugar and the grated zest of 1 lemon until a soft ribbon forms. Fold in the ground hazelnuts and a pinch of cinnamon powder. Beat 4 egg whites and a pinch of salt to a soft peak. Gradually add ½ cup of sugar and beat the mixture until shiny. Fold the egg whites into the nut mixture. Drain one large jar of preserved sour cherries and lightly dust them with a tablespoon of cornstarch. Line a cake pan with parchment paper, grease and flour it and pour the dough into the cake pan. Scatter the cherries over the dough – they will sink to the bottom. Bake for about 50 minutes at 350° F until a cake tester comes out clean.

And one more old-fashioned cake with nuts, this one inspired by a recipe by Alice Medrich but made with buckwheat flour – not to make it intentionally gluten-free but to give it a distinct flavor, so it will be called

PRE-GLUTEN-FREE GLUTEN-FREE WALNUT CAKE

In a food processor, pulse ¾ cup of walnuts with ¾ cup of sugar and ½ teaspoon of ground cardamom to a fine powder. Add a pinch of salt, 8 tablespoons of softened butter, 3 eggs, ⅓ cup of buckwheat flour and ½ teaspoon of baking powder and process until just combined. Line a greased cake pan with parchment paper, pour the dough over it and bake at 350° F for about 40 minutes. Unmold when cool, strip away the parchment paper and dust the cake with confectioner's sugar.

And here is a dish my grandmother Nona frequently made during hunting season. The venison meat usually came directly from her husband's, my step-grandfather's, hunting excursions in the woods of Lower Bavaria.

VENISON TERRINE

Sauté one thinly sliced onion and 2 cloves of garlic in 1 tablespoon of butter until translucent. Cut 1 pound of venison shoulder, 1 pound of pork shoulder and 1 pound of veal liver into cubes, season them with pepper, ground clove, cinnamon, ginger, nutmeg, a few juniper berries, dried marjoram, ½ teaspoon of curing salt and the softened, cooled onion. Cover and refrigerate overnight.

In a food processor, pulse 2 cups of flour with 1 teaspoon of salt, 6 tablespoons of butter and 4 tablespoons of lard or duck fat. With the motor running, add 2 egg yolks mixed with ¼ cup of cold milk. Process the dough into a ball, wrap it in cellophane and chill it overnight.

Spread out the meat chunks on a sheet pan and place them in the freezer for 30 minutes. Line a greased loaf pan with parchment paper. Roll out the dough and line the pan with it, leaving enough overlap to fold over the top. Cut off the crusts of 3 slices of stale white bread and soak them in milk. Whisk together 1 cup of heavy cream and 2 eggs. Blend the meat in 3 batches in a food processor, adding one of the bread slices and a third of the cream mixture to each batch. Season with salt to taste. Fill the farce into the loaf pan and fold the overlapping dough over it. Cut off any excess dough and press the seams together. Poke 3 holes into the dough cover and stick into each of them a rolled-up piece of parchment paper as vents for escaping steam. Brush the top with 1 egg yolk beaten with 1 tablespoon of milk and bake the terrine at 350° F for about 90 minutes, until dark golden brown. Sprinkle 1 bag of flavorless gelatin over 1 cup of cold port or sherry. Wait for the gelatin to bloom and gently heat the port until the gelatin is completely dissolved. When the liquid is all but cooled down again, gently pour it through the paper vents into the terrine to fill any crevices. Chill the terrine overnight. Unmold and slice. Serve with this

CUMBERLAND SAUCE

Gently warm 1 jar of red currant jam and pass it through a fine-mesh sieve to remove any skins and seeds. Grate the zest of 1 orange over it and fold in about 1 cup of fine Dijon mustard.

No cookbook is complete without a recipe for roast chicken, even though most people in big cities seem to prefer buying it ready-to-eat from a rotisserie. This is a very witty way to prepare it at home without a fuss. Because of its appearance resembling two mirrored halves, I call it

AMBIDEXTROUS ROAST CHICKEN

Cut a whole chicken in half. Remove the backbone and the arrow-shaped strip of cartilage that separates the breasts. Rub the inside of the chicken with salt, pepper, crushed garlic and chopped thyme leaves. Pushing a few sage leaves, possibly spread with some softened butter and sprinkled with salt, under the skin is an option that greatly improves the end result. Tuck in the wing tips and brush the skin with melted butter before seasoning it with more salt than seems reasonable. In a roasting pan, make a grid of whole celery stalks and a couple of thick onion slices and place the chicken halves over it, skin-side up. Roast at 425° F for about 40 minutes. Transfer the chicken onto an aluminum foil-lined sheet pan and set it under the broiler, just long enough to crisp the skin. In the meantime, remove the celery stalks and onion slices from the roasting pan, deglaze the pan juices with white wine and pour it into a sauce pan. Add ½ cup of heavy cream and bring to a simmer. Serve the chicken with the vegetables, roughly chopped, and the sauce.

This recipe from Nona taught me that short grain and long grain rice must be cooked entirely differently. Besides, this it is a wonderful meal she often prepared for large family luncheons.

NONA'S PORK MEDALLIONS WITH RICE

In a Dutch oven, melt 2 tablespoons of butter. Add 2 cups of Arborio rice and stir-fry it over a medium low flame until fragrant. Add 3 cups of water, salt, a bay leaf and 1 can of corn, drained, and stir. When the liquid has come to a simmer, cover the pot and place it in a 325° F oven for 35 minutes. The rice is cooked when small holes appear on its surface. Turn off the oven, fluff the rice with a fork, cover and keep it in the warm oven until ready to serve.

Cut a pork tenderloin into ½-inch thick medallions, pound them lightly to flatten them, season them with white pepper, salt and chopped fresh rosemary and panfry them on both sides in a little bit of butter until lightly browned. Work in batches, transferring the cooked medallions onto an aluminum foil-covered platter placed in the warm oven. When all medallions have been cooked, deglaze the pan with 1 cup of heavy cream and any juices that have accumulated on the meat platter and simmer the sauce until thickened. The rice, having been pressed into a large ring mold, is now inverted onto a large round platter and dusted with chopped parsley. The centre of the dish is filled with the medallions and the sauce poured over it.

PINXOS (1)

Pinxos are open-faced sandwiches that originated in Basque tapas bars, and these, inspired by my frequent visits to Barcelona and its multitudes of tapas bars during the early Nineties became my specialty when I hosted parties in my little studio apartment in Munich. Several French baguettes were thinly sliced and toasted before being lightly rubbed with a peeled garlic clove. A bit of olive oil was heated in a small frying pan. Several ¼ inch-thick slices of zucchini, enough to cover the bottom of the pan, were fried on one side until mildly browned, then turned. 2-3 lightly beaten eggs, seasoned with salt and black pepper, were poured over it and fried, the pan shaken occasionally to prevent the egg from sticking to the bottom. Before the egg was completely cooked through, the egg tortilla was slid onto a platter and another one was made. Each slice of baguette was topped with a piece of soft egg tortilla and garnished with julienned basil leaves. Well and good. But here is a variation, also called

PINXOS (2)

Soak ½ cup of blanched whole almonds overnight in water. Place 1 whole Vidalia onion and one head of garlic into an aluminum-foil-lined pie dish, brush them with olive oil and roast them at 400° F for 45 minutes. Once cooled, remove the onion peels and squeeze out the garlic cloves from their browned skins. Puree the onion pulp and garlic with the drained almonds, one jar of oil-packed anchovies, drained, 2 tablespoons of capers, the grated peel of one lemon, black pepper and a few fresh thyme leaves. In a separate bowl, beat 1 stick of butter until creamy and gradually incorporate the almond purée until you have a light paste. Spread the paste on baguette slices, brown them lightly under a broiler and garnish with thin shallot rings, quartered cherry tomatoes or sliced radishes.

So we are back to chicken with some recipes for them, simple or elaborate. This one is simple.

HERBED CHICKEN

In a food processor, make a paste out of half a yellow onion, 3 garlic cloves, one bunch of rinsed and drained cilantro, ground black pepper and coriander seeds to taste. Cut up a whole chicken into wings, legs, thighs and breasts (remove the backbone; wrap and store it in the freezer for later use for chicken stock). Debone the breasts, pull out the "tender" (pull out the tendon as instructed in the recipe for plain chicken breasts in chapter IV) and cut the breasts lengthwise in half. Transfer the chicken pieces into a large bowl, season them with salt and pour the onion paste over them. Add a splash of olive oil and toss everything until well coated. Cover and refrigerate for at least one hour. Preheat the oven to 375° F and brown the chicken pieces on all sides in a non-stick frying pan, working in batches, wiping out the pan each time, and transferring the browned pieces onto a parchment paper-lined sheet pan already set in the oven. Begin with the legs and thighs, then the wings. The breasts and tenders need not be browned, just lightly seared on 2 sides. When all parts are in the oven, spoon the leftover marinade over them and bake them for about another 10 minutes. Remove the boneless parts from the oven, set them aside on a covered platter to keep them warm and bake the rest for another 15 minutes or until done. Serve with a light green salad.

This is my way of preparing a famous chicken dish. Its name belies the fact that it is a modern invention rather than a French classic

CHICKEN CORDON BLEU

Cut a pocket into the thick side of boneless skinless chicken breasts and stuff them with a piece of *Comté* cheese, a crustless *bâton* of country bread soaked in a beaten egg, and a whole sage leaf. Season the breasts on all sides with salt, coarse black pepper and chopped fresh rosemary leaves. Wrap each breast in one large slice of Prosciutto, cut slightly thicker than one would usually ask Prosciutto to be sliced. Rub the wrapped breasts with a bit of olive oil and panfry them in a non-stick pan (without adding any more oil) on both sides until lightly browned. Transfer them to a roasting pan and bake them in a 400° F oven for another 15 minutes. Deglaze the roasting pan with balsamic vinegar and a bit of butter and serve the chicken breasts sliced on the bias, drizzled with the juices.

And this fowl braised with pomegranate juice instead of wine –

PINTADE À LA GRENADE

Guinea Hen should not be roasted whole. Like a chicken, it is likely to have either overcooked breasts or undercooked legs. Rather, cut it in half, remove the backbone and cut each half into 4 parts – leg, thigh, wing and halved breasts. Drizzle them with olive oil to coat, season them with salt and pepper and brown them on all sides in a Dutch oven, working in batches and wiping out the pan in between batches. When the last batch is browned, remove the fowl pieces and add 12 small peeled shallots and 3 carrots, peeled and cut into chunks, browning them in the residue oil. Lift them out of the pan and deglaze the pan with 3 cups of fresh-squeezed pomegranate juice (bottled is acceptable as long as it is non-sweetened). Return the fowl pieces to the pot along with a cinnamon stick, 2 bay leaves, a sprig of fresh thyme and 6 dried figs, nestled between the meat pieces. Scatter the vegetables over the fowl pieces – the meat should be halfway submerged (add more juice if necessary.) Place a round piece of parchment paper out of which you have cut a hole in its center directly on the fowl, close the pot with its lid and place it in a 300° F oven for 1 hour. Remove the four breast parts, set them aside in a covered bowl and braise the stew for another hour, by the time of which the dark meat should be tender enough to practically fall off the bone. Remove the guinea hen pieces and strain the juice into a saucepan. Reserve the shallots, carrots and figs and and discard the spices. Bring the sauce to a simmer and reduce it until syrupy, skimming off any rising fat or foam. Remove the breasts' skin and bones and shred the meat. Pull the dark meat off the bones, careful to discard all cartilage and skin. Reheat the combined shredded meat in the sauce with the softened shallots and figs. Adjust the seasoning, adding salt to taste and serve with couscous, steamed with a few crushed cardamom pods and garnished with chopped fresh mint leaves and toasted sliced almonds, and a side dish of sliced zucchini, briefly sautéed with scallions and fresh ginger.

With the exception of their obligatory annual Thanksgiving Turkey, most Americans seem not very keen on fowl served on the bone. Roast turkey should be a staple and it is a pity that is is most often under-seasoned and overcooked, for it can be quite tasty when done right.

The following dish is a royal one and, though laborious, not difficult. In fact, it is one of the most satisfactory combinations of color, flavor and texture.

JEWELED RICE

The Persians knew that rice should not be merely boiled. More attention and detail is required to make rice into a meal fit for sultans and kings. Rinse 3 cups of Basmati rice several times in warm water until water runs clear. Soak it for at least 30 minutes in cold water.

Prepare the condiments.

Peel and cut two large carrots into juliennes – thin carrot

sticks. Using a vegetable peeler, carve the zest off 2 oranges in vertical strips and slice those lengthwise into thin juliennes. Place them into a small sauce pan, cover them with water and bring it to a boil. Repeat this step twice, refreshing the water each time.

In a medium saucepan, bring ½ cup of sugar and 1 cup of water to a simmer. Add several cracked pods of cardamom, the drained orange zest and the carrots sticks. Simmer for 15 minutes, stirring occasionally, cover and set aside.

Stir-fry 2 thinly sliced Spanish onions in 2 tablespoons of butter. When they are translucent, add 1 teaspoon each of ground cumin and ground coriander, ½ cup of well-rinsed dried barberries (or non-sweetened dried cranberries) and ½ cup of rinsed raisins.

In a 350° F oven, toast 1 cup of sliced almonds and ¼ cup of shelled pistachios until fragrant.

In a small bowl, crush several strands of saffron with a spoon before adding 2 tablespoons of rosewater, 2 tablespoons of warm water and 3 tablespoons of honey.

Fill a Dutch oven halfway with water and bring it to a boil. Add 1 tablespoon of salt and the drained, pre-soaked rice. Stir the rice once the water has come to a boil and cook it for no longer than 5 minutes – it must not be cooked all the way. Drain the rice into a colander, rinse out the pot, place it over medium heat with ½ cup of water and 4 tablespoons of butter. When the mixture is bubbly, scoop one third of the rice over the butter, sprinkle a bit of the saffron mixture over it and top it with half the carrot and orange mixture as well as a third of the onion mixture. Repeat this step twice, ending with the remaining rice and saffron mixture and reserving the last third of the onions for garnish. Using the back of a wooden spoon, poke 3 holes into the rice (for steam to escape), cover the pot with a lid set over two layers of paper towels (or a folded dish towel). Cook over a medium flame for 5 minutes before reducing the heat to its absolute lowest setting and steaming the rice for another 30 minutes. Scoop it onto a large platter, scattering bits of the golden crust that has formed on the bottom over it. Garnish with the rest of the sautéed onions, the toasted almonds and pistachios, fresh pomegranate seeds and cilantro sprigs. Serve with any kind of stewed meat.

And this is another attractive and exotic dish.

BURMESE-STYLE COLD NOODLES

Cook fresh *Lo Mein*-style egg noodles (available in most Asian specialty grocery stores) in salted water until al dente, drain them well, submerge them in ice water for just a minute, drain once more. Transfer the cold noodles into in a large bowl, cover it and store it in the refrigerator. Cook Idaho-style potatoes in well-salted water until soft. Skin them while hot and crumble them into uneven pieces. Season them with salt and pepper.

In a food processor, purée 2 shallots, 3 garlic cloves, 1 peeled knob of ginger, 1 tablespoon of seedless tamarind paste, and 2 tablespoons of palm sugar (or brown sugar). Fry this paste in a couple of tablespoons of peanut oil until fragrant, transfer it to a bowl and season it with fish sauce to taste. Fill it into a jar and use it up within one week.

Thinly slice a couple of shallots and fry them until crispy in ½ cup of flavor-neutral oil. Drain the shallots and reserve the oil. Or buy ready-made fried shallots in an Asian specialty store.

Assemble the dish by first carefully dressing the cold noodles and potatoes with some of the cooked paste, fresh lime juice and shallot oil (if you have it) and then adding rinsed bean sprouts; crushed, unsalted roasted peanuts; thinly sliced, fresh red hot chilies; lightly toasted dried shrimp (available in Asian specialty stores); peeled, seeded and julienned hothouse cucumber; and torn-up cilantro leaves. Pile the pasta onto a platter and garnish with thinly sliced scallions and the fried shallots. Serve with lime wedges and hot chili oil on the side.

NASI GORENG
(Malaysian Fried Rice)

Wrap a nugget of *Balachan*, fermented shrimp paste, the size of of cherry, into aluminum foil and toast it by placing it for a short moment over a gas flame. The smell will be infernal. In a food processor, purée the shrimp paste with 4 garlic cloves, 5-8 shallots, 1 tablespoon of palm sugar and 4-6 fresh red hot "Holland" chilies, seeds and membranes removed). If you cannot find Holland chilies, use half a red bell pepper and a couple of sliced Serrano peppers.

Heat 3 tablespoons of neutral oil in a frying pan, add a

couple tablespoons of the paste and fry it until fragrant. Add cold, cooked Basmati rice and stir until evenly coated with the sauce. Add a handful of shredded cabbage, 3 tablespoons of Kecap manis (sweet soy sauce) and 2 tablespoons of regular soy sauce and stir-fry everything until lightly caramelized. Serve with a fried egg, julienned cucumber, and chopped scallions.

GNOCCHI WITH SAGE BUTTER

Bake 4 large russet potatoes in a 350° F oven for about one hour, until soft. Cut them lengthwise in half, scrape out the flesh and push it through a potato ricer. Loosely spread the potato out on a clean large surface. When it is no longer steaming, dust it with flour and loosely fold it over a couple of times. Dust it once more with flour and knead everything until it comes together. Shape the dough into a log and let it rest once more, covered. Working in batches, roll thick slices of dough into thin logs and cut those into bite-size pieces. Dust them with very little flour to prevent them from sticking and chill or freeze them spread out on a dish cloth-covered sheet pan until ready to use. Drop them into rapidly boiling salted water and cook them until they float to the top.

In a non-stick skillet, melt about a tablespoon of butter per serving plus one for the pan and toss 3 torn sage leaves per person into it once the butter is foaming. Using a slotted spoon, transfer the cooked gnocchi to the skillet, toss until coated and serve with freshly ground – never shredded – Parmesan.

Gnocchi can also be served with a more elaborate

CREAMY SAGE SAUCE

In a mortar, pound a bunch of stemmed fresh sage leaves with ½ teaspoon coarse sea salt and a few whole peppercorns into a pulp. Add just enough olive oil to yield a spreadable paste. Transfer it to a glass jar, seal its surface with a tablespoon of olive oil and store it in the refrigerator. Use up within a week.

In a non-stick skillet, bring one tablespoon of the sage paste and ½ cup of heavy cream per serving to a simmer and add the cooked Gnocchi with a bit of their cooking water. Toss everything, set over a medium flame, until coated and serve it immediately, sprinkled with chopped parsley and bespoke ground Parmesan.

If one likes gnocchi one likes all kinds of it, and that is the reason there are so many recipes for their preparation in this chapter.

Here is another and last one:

ROMAN GNOCCHI

In a large saucepan over medium heat, bring 1 quart of whole milk and ½ teaspoon of salt to a simmer and slowly add 1 cup of coarse semolina, pouring it in a thin stream while constantly whisking to avoid lumps from forming. Reduce the heat to low and cook this gnocchi base for several minutes, stirring often and scraping the bottom of the pan, until thickened. Remove it from the heat and stir in 2 tablespoons of butter until completely melted. Season the mass with white pepper and nutmeg and stir in ⅓ cup of ground Parmesan cheese and, once it is no longer steaming hot, 2 lightly beaten egg yolks. Lightly moisten a rectangular baking dish with cold water, pour the warm dough into it and quickly spread it out evenly with a spatula. Once it has fully cooled and set, invert it onto a large cutting board and cut out 1 ½-inch rounds with a cookie cutter (or cut it into squares). Align the pieces in a buttered baking dish, making them overlap slightly, like roof shingles. Brush them with melted butter and sprinkle them with a bit of ground Parmesan. Bake them in a 350° F oven for about 25 minutes, until lightly browned. Serve them with a simple, meatless tomato sauce flavored with several fresh, hand-torn basil leaves.

The recipes in this collection are not limited to any one cuisine and this is intentional. Though my cooking has been shaped by my European background it has been enriched by a modern American approach. Among my favorites I count recipes from the Middle East, Lebanon, India, Vietnam, China, Malaysia, Brazil, Columbia, the Caribbean, and Mexico. It must be confessed that I have never travelled to most of these places, nor have I necessarily eaten at restaurants that serve their indigenous fare. In fact, preparing dishes from around the world is my way of traveling. In other words, it is an adventure. Not very long ago, when several of our invited guests for an upcoming dinner party sent notifications that they had become vegetarians, I decided to serve them a vegetarian Indian feast. It turned out that Filip Noterdaeme and I were the only ones at table who had never travelled to the subcontinent. Everybody agreed that the dinner made them experience India in a way one could not experience it there.

Here is one of the dishes I served:

YELLOW MUNG BEANS WITH MUSTARD SEEDS

In a Dutch oven, melt 1 tablespoon of butter and add 1 chopped yellow onion, a peeled and diced knob of ginger, 3 knobs of peeled and diced fresh turmeric (or 1 tablespoon turmeric powder) and 2 thinly sliced green hot chilies. When the onions are translucent, add 1 ½ cups of yellow split mung beans. Stir-fry them with the onions until shiny before adding 3 cups of water. Stir, bring to a simmer and cook for about 20 minutes. The beans should be soft but still hold their shape.

In a frying pan, melt 2 tablespoon of butter and add 1 tablespoon each of mustard seeds and cumin seeds as well as a handful of fresh curry leaves. When the mustard seeds begin to pop, pour the mixture over the beans. Stir and season with salt to taste. Garnish with thinly sliced scallions. It is a delicious dish.

The Swiss have their own version of carrot cake. It is an old world classic, Americans do not know it. American carrot cake is very different from the Swiss one my grandmother Nona used to make, especially the cream cheese icing. During my very first visit to New York I once ordered a piece of carrot cake in a diner. I simply could not figure out what the icing was made of. Surely it was neither whipped cream, nor white chocolate, nor fondant. When I asked the waitress what kind of icing it was, she said, classic carrot cake icing. When I suggested that she could perhaps ask the pastry chef what it was made of, she was aghast and said that they never, but never, had had a pastry chef at the diner and that all cakes were simply delivered by a cake company.

This is the carrot cake I grew up eating. It is called

SCHWEIZER RÜBLITORTE
(Swiss Carrot Cake)

Peel and finely grate 2 medium-size carrots into a bowl, add 2 tablespoons of Kirsch liquor and a pinch each of cinnamon and ground clove. In a large mixing bowl, beat 7 egg yolks and 1 cup of sugar to a soft ribbon. Stir the carrots into the mixture and fold in ½ cup of flour, 1 teaspoon baking powder, 1 ½ cups of ground almonds, 1 ½ cups of ground hazelnuts and ⅓ cup of fine bread crumbs. Beat 5 egg whites and a pinch of salt to a soft ribbon, gradually add ⅓ cup of sugar while beating and continue beating them to a firm peak. Fold the egg whites into the carrot mixture in three increments, pour the dough into a parchment paper-lined, greased and floured spring form and bake the cake in a 350° F oven for 45-55 minutes, until a cake tester comes out dry. Once it has cooled, invert it onto a platter, strip away the parchment paper and glaze the top with a white icing made of confectioner's sugar and Kirsch and garnish with a ring of little carrots made out of marzipan, with pistachio slivers as their green tops (personally, I don't like to use artificial food coloring but some insist on dying the marzipan orange for the effect. If time allows and the muses speak to you, the marzipan could be died with a bit of turmeric powder and perhaps a drop of red beet juice). Brush the sides of the cake with melted chocolate and press toasted sliced almonds against it. Serve with unsweetened whipped cream.

As this cake takes some time to prepare, it was usually reserved for special occasions like birthdays.

And here is another unusual cake made with a grated vegetable, this one made with yucca – also known as cassava. I had never had Yucca until I tasted it in a Dominican restaurant on Manhattan's Lower East Side, where it was served boiled and garnished with fried garlic. This cake, however, is a Filipino specialty.

CASSAVA CAKE

Peel, de-vein and finely grate one large yucca. Squeeze it over a colander to get out as much liquid as possible. Mix it well with 3 beaten eggs, 1 can of sweetened condensed milk, ½ can of evaporated milk, 1 can of coconut milk, ½ cup of sugar, ½ stick of melted butter, a pinch of salt and 1 cup of shredded, mild Cheddar cheese. Pour it into a buttered baking dish and bake it in a 350° F oven for 50 minutes. Mix the left-over half of the can of evaporated milk with 1 cup of half and half, 1 cup of shredded, sweetened coconut and 4 egg yolks. Pour it over the cake and bake it for another 15 minutes, or until set. Cut into squares when cold.

And here are some more recipes for desserts.

On opening night of my Elvis Presley tribute, *The Importance of Being Elvis*, I almost had what would have been a terrible wardrobe malfunction. At some point in the show, I was to make a mid-song exit for a very fast costume change backstage. The music kept playing and I was to sing the second verse from behind the curtain while slipping out of my black leather Elvis outfit into a white polyester Elvis jumpsuit. However, to my everlasting shame, I realized too late that I had forgotten to take the microphone with me. My impulse was to jump back onstage to get it but I remembered just in time that I was in fact stark naked, having already tossed off the black leather jacket and tight leather pants. I almost missed my cue but thankfully, Filip Noterdaeme arrived just in time, eager to help me with the costume change, and it was he who jumped onstage to get the microphone for me. The name of the song was *Devil in Disguise*. It would also be a suitable alternate name for this dessert,

NUTELLA TART

In a food processor, pulse 1 cup of flour with ¼ cup of unsweetened cocoa powder, ¼ cup of sugar and a pinch of salt. Add 1 stick of cold butter, pulse everything to a coarse meal and, with the motor running, add 1 egg yolk mixed with 3 tablespoons of heavy cream. Process until everything comes together in a ball. Flatten it to a disc, wrap it in cellophane and refrigerate it for an hour.

Sprinkle 1 pack of unflavored gelatin with 3 tablespoons rum. In a mixing bowl, lightly beat 4 egg yolks with ¼ cup of sugar, a pinch of salt and 1 tablespoon of cornstarch. Bring 2 cups of half & half to a simmer, temper the egg mixture with some of it before adding it to the pot. Cook it on a low flame, continuously stirring, until thickened. When it begins to simmer, immediately pour it through a fine-mesh sieve into a mixing bowl. While still hot, stir in the bloomed gelatin and about 1 cup of Nutella.

Roll out the dough and line a buttered and floured fluted tart pan with it. Dust it with flour, pierce it in several spots with a fork and freeze it for 10 minutes. Place an oversized, round piece of parchment paper over it, and weigh it down with 2 cups of dried chickpeas or pie weight and bake at 350° F for 15 minutes before lifting off the paper and chickpeas and baking the crust for 5 more minutes or as long as it takes for it to be completely opaque. Lightly warm 1 cup of *Dulce de Leche* to soften it and spread it evenly over the cooled crust. Sprinkle a bit of flaky sea salt over it. Lightly beat the still warm chocolate custard and pour it over it. Chill the tart for several hours, until completely set. Set a stainless steel or copper bowl over a pot of simmering water, add 4 egg whites and whisk them vigorously over the steam, gradually adding 1 cup of sugar, for about 5 minutes, until firm peaks form and the *meringue* is glossy. Spread the *meringue* over the tart in a decorative pattern. If desired, the peaks of meringue can be caramelized with a blowtorch.

When I turned sixteen, a group of friends gave me the confectionary and candy cookbook from Time Life's *The Good Cook* cookbook series. My mother already owned several issues of the series but this one was all mine and I cherished it like a treasure. One recipe from the book I still remember is for

CHOCOLATE TRUFFLES

In a sauce pan, heat 1 cup of cream and 5 tablespoons of butter until they begin to simmer. Break 8 ounces of best quality dark chocolate into pieces and place it into a mixing bowl. Pour the hot cream over the chocolate and gently stir until the chocolate is completely melted. Do not beat any air into the mixture. Chill it for an hour or until set. Sift 2 cups of unsweetened cocoa powder into a deep dish. Working in batches, spoon little nuggets of the chocolate mixture onto the cocoa powder. Roll them in the cocoa powder to cover before rolling them into balls in the palms of your hands and rolling them once more in the cocoa power. This is the simplest way to make truffles as long as the weather and your hands are cold. For flavored truffles, infuse the hot cream and butter for 10 minutes with an aromatic such as mint leaves, orange or lemon zest, fresh ginger, crushed coffee beans, cloves, cinnamon, or chili flakes before briefly reheating it and pouring it through a strainer over the chocolate. Instead of cocoa powder, the truffles can also be rolled in confectioner's sugar or finely ground, toasted nuts.

This too is a truffle recipe, but a more elaborate one, for

TEA TRUFFLES

Steep the grated zest of 1 orange and 1 heaped tablespoon Earl Grey tea in 1 ½ cups of boiling water for 5 minutes. Strain and pour 1 cup of it into a metal bowl (discard the rest). Add 21 ounces of best quality dark chocolate in pieces and place the bowl over a pot with simmering water. When the chocolate is halfway melted, take the bowl off the steam and stir until the rest of the chocolate is fully melted. Mash 1 stick of softened butter with 1 cup of confectioner's sugar and add 4 egg yolks, one at a time, stirring until fully combined, careful to not beat any air into it. Add the slightly cooled chocolate mixture, stir and chill for an hour or until set. Drop little nuggets of it onto a deep dish with 2 cups of sifted non-sweetened cocoa powder, roll them in the cocoa until they are fully, lightly covered, keeping them in uneven, organic shapes. Chill them to harden but serve them at room temperature.

The French buy chocolate truffles only from chocolatiers, but perhaps you will agree with me that making them by hand at least every now and then offers a different kind of satisfaction well worth considering.

An excellent frozen dessert is made with orange juice instead of milk or cream. This is an idea I came up with when a client asked for a dairy-free frozen dessert.

ORANGE SHERBET

Heat 3 cups of fresh-squeezed orange juice in a saucepan set over low heat. Beat 6 egg yolks with 1 cup of sugar until a soft ribbon forms, temper them with 1 cup of the hot juice and return the mixture to the rest of the juice in the pan. Cook over low heat while stirring until it coats the back of a spoon. Pour the cream through a fine-mesh sieve. Chill thoroughly and freeze in an ice cream maker.

And here is another recipe for a frozen dessert, the easiest in my entire repertoire:

LEMON GELATO

In a blender, mix 1 quart of cultured buttermilk and one jar of lemon curd. Chill thoroughly before pouring it into an ice cream maker to churn it into a smooth gelato.

Here are four recipes, interesting at least for the history attached to them. To begin with one adapted from *The Alice B. Toklas Cookbook*, where it was attributed to Frederich, one of the many cooks employed by Miss Toklas and Gertrude Stein in their legendary Paris home. It has a famous name and is rather legendary itself.

SACHER TORTE

No one who has visited Vienna and taken a seat at the famous Café Sacher has not at least considered ordering a slice of this most famous of Austrian Torten.

For modern tastes it is perhaps not as rich or luscious as one might expect. But it is extremely sophisticated precisely because of its perfect balance, for which excellent apricot jam is at least as important as good chocolate.

Cream ½ cup plus 2 tablespoons of butter with 1 cup of sugar into which you have rubbed the grated peel of 1 lemon. Add 6 egg yolks, one at the time, beating vigorously to incorporate them into the butter. Stir 4.5 ounces melted, slightly cooled dark chocolate into the mix. Fold in the beaten whites of 6 eggs and ⅓ cup of flour, ¼ cup of potato starch and 2 tablespoons of unsweetened Dutch cocoa powder. Butter and flour a flat cake pan and bake for 40 minutes in a 325° oven. Leave the cake in the pan to cool down, then carefully unmold it. Brush the cake twice with strained apricot jam and, once the jam is set, glaze it with chocolate icing.

Frederich did not specify how to make a chocolate glaze, but the reader may use my recipe for cooked chocolate glaze I have given in the recipe for *Prinzregententorte*, in Chapter II.

The original recipe for *Sacher Torte* is in fact a secret as the house of Sacher claims, and the *Café Sacher Cookbook*, published not until 1975, went as far as introducing a purposely altered recipe that guaranteed less satisfying results than the original recipe by simply, cunningly, adding more flour to the batter and cutting back on chocolate and butter. But Frederich's recipe is likely the original handed down as it were to him by Frau Sacher herself when he used to work under her employ. So it has been possible for those in the know to make a real Sacher Torte since 1954, the year *The Alice B. Toklas Cookbook* was first published.

The following dessert was a favorite of the late Jean-Claude Baker, the charmingly flamboyant, late owner of *Chez Joséphine* in Times Square, named so in honor of his mother, Joséphine Baker. He once asked me to prepare this Nordic German dessert for him so he could make his restaurant's *chef de cuisine* taste and perhaps copy it.

ROTE GRÜTZE
(German Red Berry Compote)

Into a large saucepan, pour 1 ½ cups of non-sweetened cranberry, black currant or cherry juice. Add 2 wide strips of orange zest and one split vanilla bean, the seeds scraped out and added as well, and ¼ cup of sugar. Bring the liquid to a simmer. Dissolve 6 tablespoons of cornstarch in ½ cup of cold juice and stir it into the hot liquid. When it begins to thicken, add 6 cups of mixed berries – cored and quartered strawberries, blueberries, raspberries, blackberries and pitted cherries – and bring the liquid once more to a simmer. Add more sugar to taste and transfer the *Grütze* to a bowl. Cover and chill thoroughly. Remove orange zest and vanilla bean and serve in individual glass bowls with plain, liquid – neither whipped nor sweetened – heavy cream on the side.

If non-sweetened juice cannot be found, use 1 cup of juice and ½ cup of Pinot Noir.

The actor Stanley Tucci, who is reportedly obsessed with cooking, created in 1996 in the film *Big Night* a *playdoyer* for cooking as a noble art form, but only after the Danish movie director Gabriel Axel had made an even more powerful case for it in his 1987 film adaptation of Karen Blixen's novel, *Babette's Feast*.

STANLEY TUCCI'S TIMPANO

An extra large charlotte mold is oiled and lined with fresh pasta dough and tightly filled with alternating layers of precooked ziti pasta, marinara sauce, chopped salami, meatballs, hardboiled eggs, chopped Provolone, grated Romano cheese, and beaten eggs. Everything is sealed with fresh pasta dough, baked for a good hour, unmolded and cut like a cake.

And here is proof that the master is greater than the follower.

CAILLES EN SARCOPHAGES
(Coffined quail)

This is one of the dishes served in the festive meal prepared by chef Babette in *Babette's Feast*, played by Stéphane Audran.

Martine: Babette! Oh, that was really a very good dinner. Everybody thought it was a very good dinner.
Babette: I used to be the head chef at the Café Anglais.
Martine: We shall all remember this evening when you're back in Paris.
Babette: I am not going back to Paris.
Martine: You are not going back to Paris?
Babette: There is no one waiting for me. They are all dead. And I have no money.
Martine: No money? But the 10,000 francs?
Babette: All spent.
Martine: 10,000 francs?
Babette: Dinner for twelve at the Café Anglais cost 10,000 francs.
Philippa: But dear Babette, you should not have given all you owed to us.
Babette: It was not just for you.
Martine: Now you will be poor the rest of your life!
Babette: An artist is never poor.
Philippa: Did you prepare that sort of dinner at the Café Anglais?
Babette: Yes, I was able to make them happy when I gave my very best. Papin knew that.
Philippa: Achille Papin?
Babette: Yes. He said: Throughout the world sounds one long cry from the heart of the artist: Give me the chance to do my very best."

It is a recipe for life that is exquisitely and devastatingly romantic. Why its message of generosity has been neglected in favor of a doctrine of combative competitiveness in the food world I have never understood.

The recipe on how to make the "coffined quail" is the following.

Cut out 6 rounds of frozen puff pastry dough (preferably from a top brand that uses real butter), about 5 inches wide. Press a smaller ring of 3.5 inches onto each of them to create a centered indent. Brush them with egg wash, pierce the inner circle with a fork at various intervals and bake them on parchment-paper-lined sheet pans for 20 minutes in 400° F oven, until golden. Lift off the top of the inner rounds and reserve them as the lids. Scrape out the flaky center of the baked bottoms to create nests. Season 6 boned quails inside out with salt and pepper and stuff each of them with a slice of *cooked* foie gras and a couple of black truffle slices. Truss the quails and sear them in a mixture of butter and oil on all sides in a heavy skillet. Pour off most of the fat and deglaze the pan with ½ cup of Cognac. Set the Cognac aflame by tipping the pan towards the gas flame. When the flames have died down, transfer the quails onto an aluminum foil-lined baking dish, preheated in a 400° F oven. Roast them for 15 minutes, turning them once. To the skillet, add 2 tablespoons of butter, 3 finely chopped shallots and 2 dozen halved black morels, diligently cleaned and rinsed. Sauté them until they begin to brown, then deglaze the pan juices with ½ cup of white wine and ½ cup of chicken stock. Simmer for a minute before adding ½ cup of heavy cream. Reduce until thickened and season with salt and pepper. Place pastry nests on warmed plates, set quails, strings removed, into them, spoon sauce and morels over them. Top each quail with a pastry cap and garnish with chopped parsley or chervil.

VIII
FOOD IN GERMANY
BEFORE I CAME
TO NEW YORK

W HEN WE MOVED FROM PARIS to Munich, in 1977, one of the things that troubled me was the question of where I would now find French *pâtisseries*. Would the German *Konditoreien* have *éclairs au café, milles feuilles, croissants* and *pains au chocolat*? A thorough survey of the city's pastry shops informed me that none of the above could be found of acceptable quality. My mother argued that some of the baked goods were good – cheese cakes and poppy seed cakes and pretzels, for example. Surely, said I, I could try to make these French pastries myself. Not, said my mother, in my kitchen.

In those years we travelled back to France at least twice a year, always returning with staples that could not be found in Germany at the time – Dijon mustard, salted French butter, tarragon vinegar. These added variety to my mother's dinner parties, much to the delight and envy of her German friends whose culinary repertoire still harked back to the German food their own mothers had made. Consolingly, there was the increasing influence of Italy as Germans were discovering the pleasures of traveling south. Driving across the alps, they found the best Italian food. It gave them a sense of life and color, of the exotic.

If the food they tried on the Adriatic or in Tuscany was unlike anything they had ever had before, German food could be very good in its own way, with its unrivalled sausages and roast meats and *Mehlspeisen.**

Herr Sepp, the father of a boy I had befriended in primary school, once invited our family for dinner and there I ate for the first time, with suppressed excitement and bewilderment, *Insalata Caprese*. It is rather commonplace now but at the time, fresh basil, *Mozzarella di Buffalo*, extra virgin olive oil and balsamic vinegar were an absolute novelty to Germans. When done right, it is still a treat to be served

INSALATA CAPRESE

Slice ripe summer tomatoes and *Mozzarella di Buffalo* into thick slices. Rinse basil leaves and pad them dry with paper towels, careful not to bruise them. Arrange tomatoes, Mozzarella and basil in alternating layers on a platter. Serve at room temperature – never chilled – with small carafes of balsamic vinegar and best quality extra virgin olive oil on the side, as well

---

* Flour and egg-based sweet dishes, served warm and as a main course on meatless days.

as a good pepper mill and a small wooden bowl with flaky sea salt. According to an Italian acquaintance, the true connoisseur omits the balsamic.

Of course, the most famous dish made with basil is

PESTO ALLA GENOVESE

Fill a food processor with 3 handfuls of fresh basil leaves, a handful of stemmed Italian parsley, 1 teaspoon of coarse sea salt, ¼ cup of European (rather than the more affordable but less flavorful Chinese) pine nuts, ground white pepper to taste and a handful of ground Parmesan. Pulse until processed to a paste. With the machine running, add about 3 tablespoons olive oil, not more. Fill the paste into a glass jar, pressing down to remove any air pockets, and top it with enough olive oil to just cover its surface. Refrigerate and use up within one week.

Pesto is, of course, an herb and nut paste that is supposed to include garlic. But chopped, diced or mashed raw garlic quickly develops sulfur, giving off an unpleasantly pungent odor and sharp flavor. Therefore, I don't add the garlic until the last moment, when I use the pesto. It tastes better that way. Mixing a tablespoon of Greek, "live" yogurt into the pesto before storing it away helps it maintain a bright green color.

No one in those days in Germany thought of making pesto from scratch. Everybody simply conveniently bought it ready-made in a jar. I never tasted freshly made pesto until I moved to New York. Finding large bunches of fresh basil for as little as two dollars even in the city's ordinary supermarkets was a revelation. Back in Germany, fresh basil had been all but impossible to come by. Occasionally it was available at Italian specialty stores, packed in sawdust and rolled up in layers of red tissue paper. I never really liked the taste of imported jarred pesto, acidic as it was due to the citric acid manufacturers must add to their product to prevent fermentation. Growing basil in the garden was not an option, the German climate is simply not suitable for it. In any case, Germans prefer their pasta with creamy sauces. So that nearly every pasta sauce that was experimented with ended up having heavy cream added to it, including pesto.

My mother had upon our return to Germany started to work full-time as a teacher again. On weekdays we fared not so lavishly at lunchtime when all of us got home after school at about the same time, at first when my brother and I were still in primary school and later when we were enrolled at the *Gymnasium*, German high school. At my mother's behest, we still ate nearly every meal together, and usually the food was homemade. She went through great pains to plan ahead and only rarely relied on the modern commodity of frozen foods. Usually, the next day's lunch meal would be decided upon and set up in the evening, and whoever got home first midday the next day would be in charge of putting the finishing touches to it, so that the others who, quite starved, came home a bit later would find a ready meal – tortellini, cheese-filled crêpes, meat patties, fish with rice or mashed potatoes were not unusual. She often asked us what we wanted to eat, and I often requested her

BAKED ENDIVES WITH HAM AND CHEESE

Stem and wash 4 endives, cut them lengthwise in half (quarter them if they are very thick) and cook them in well-salted, simmering water for about 5 minutes. When they are fork tender, transfer them to an ice bath and then onto a \paper towel-lined plate to fully drain them. Reserve 1 cup of the cooking liquid. In a saucepan, melt 2 tablespoons of butter over a low flame. Whisk 1 heaped tablespoon of flour into it. Gradually add 1½ cups of milk, whisking continuously. Simmer for 5 minutes, scraping the bottom with a heat-resistant spatula to prevent the sauce from scorching. When the *béchamel* gets as thick as custard, add some of the reserved cooking liquid, a quarter cup at a time – it should have the consistency of a thick sauce. Season the *béchamel* with salt, finely ground white pepper, grated nutmeg and a pinch of sugar. Wrap each piece of endive in a thin slice of Swiss cheese and a slice of top quality cooked ham – *Jambon de Paris* or *Prosciutto Cotto* are best. Align the wrapped endives in a buttered baking dish and pour the *Bbchamel* over them. Scatter 2 tablespoons of bread crumbs and 1 cup of grated Swiss cheese over the endives. The prepared dish may now be stored in the refrigerator for a night if needed. Bake the dish at 375° F for about 30 minutes, until bubbly and browned. Serve with steamed potatoes, skinned and showered with chopped fresh parsley. This dish is easy to prepare ahead of time. It can also be made with the white and light green parts of leeks or quartered fennel bulbs.

A year after our move to Munich, a French family we had befriended when we lived in Paris announced they were coming to visit. They had never been to Germany before, so my parents acted as their tour guide. After a day of walks around midtown and a visit to the Old Pinakothek to see Rubens' *Rape of the Daughters of Leucippus*, we had supper at the historic *Hofbräuhaus*, one of the most renowned beer halls in all of Germany. Of the typically Bavarian supper I only remember the pork roast with potato dumplings and the waitresses, Rubenesque young women in traditional *Dirndl* dresses. My father explained in French to our guests that the waitresses all came from small Bavarian villages and spoke the requisite Bavarian dialect. At that, the waitress who was serving us looked up and said in French, *Pas moi, moi je suis française.* Here is the recipe for how to make

KARTOFFELKNÖDEL HALB UND HALB
(Bavarian Potato Dumpling)

Cut several slices of white Pullman bread into small cubes and fry them in a skillet with a bit of salted butter until golden and crunchy. Peel and cook 1 pound of russet potatoes in well-salted water until tender, drain them and push them through a ricer into a large bowl, leaving them to steam off. Peel 1 pound of Yukon Gold potatoes, line another large bowl with a kitchen towel, and grate the raw potatoes directly, using the fine setting of a box grater set. Gather the ends of the towel and squeeze as much liquid from the shredded potatoes as possible. Discard the liquid and add the raw potatoes to the still warm, cooked ones. Add one egg, season with salt and kneed it lightly, adding potato starch by the teaspoon if it is too sticky. Working with floured hands, shape the dough into 8-10 balls, filling each with a tablespoon of croutons. Carefully drop them into a large pot of simmering, salted water and cook them over medium heat for about 15 minutes. Do not let the water come to a rolling boil. Turn the heat off and cover the pot once the dumplings are floating on top. They are ready to eat after another 5 minutes. Serve with Bavarian-style pork roast, a recipe of which can be found in Chapter XII. A hearty meal for a cold day.

Once, in the fall, my family was invited to the *Oktoberfest* where we had the privilege of enjoying unlimited free rides, courtesy of the insurance company the husband of one of my mother's colleagues was working for. The beer "tents" were really huge banquet halls with acoustics that made a pandemonium of the brass music and the thousands or was it only hundreds of voices. It was more the drunk tourists than the locals who made this demoniacal noise. No wonder my mother had always thought of the *Oktoberfest* as a barbaric thing, primitive and possibly dangerous. A carnal meal of rotisserie chicken and quart-size beer mugs was served in a manner appropriate to the surroundings. I was feeling sick from all the rides and asked if I might have some herbal tea.

Sometimes on weekends we went to visit my grandmothers Oma and Nona in Lower Bavaria, where the food was uniformly good, with Nona's food always being superlative. Her house and dining room were elegantly furnished with antique furniture, the first Louis XV fauteuil I ever sat in. The dining room table was set with bone China, hand-painted with the very traditional so-called "blue onion" motif — made famous by the house of *Meissen* that began manufacturing it in the Eighteenth Century. My grandmother was a hostess in the tradition of the Dual Monarchy of Austria and Hungary though she was born in the Czech Republic. It is unnecessary to say that her elegant cooking was not German at all but influenced by the rich culinary traditions of Austria, Eastern Europe and Italy, and therefore a recipe of one of her specialties has no place here. The temptation however is too great. This is the way to prepare

NONA'S SCHLUTZKRAPFEN
(Tyrolian Spinach Ravioli)

In a food processor, blend 1 cup of flour with 1 cup of rye flour until combined. With the machine running, add 3 eggs beaten with ¼ cup of warm water and process until the dough comes together in a ball. Wrap it into cellophane and chill it for at least one hour.

Thoroughly rinse 1 bunch of spinach, pinch off the stems (use them in a salad or smoothie) and blanch the leaves in rapidly boiling, salted water for barely 1 minute. Drain and instantly transfer them to an ice bath. Drain again, gather the leaves into a ball and squeeze them until quite dry. Loosen up the bundle, drop the leaves into a food processor and add ½ cup of Ricotta, a couple tablespoons of shredded Gruyère or Comté, a small ball of fresh Mozzarella cut into cubes, a quarter white onion, diced, and 1 crushed clove of garlic, as well as salt, white pepper and grated nutmeg. Pulse and process everything to a paste. Add more salt if necessary, it should be fairly salty. Transfer it into a bowl.

Working in batches, roll out the dough by hand as thin as possible (or use a pasta rolling machine), cut it into 3-inch squares, brush the edges with water, place a dollop of filling into the center of each square and fold over the edges to form a triangle, pressing down at the edges to seal them, or use a special ravioli tray to fill the pasta. Dust the *Schlutzkrapfen* with flour and lay them side by side, not touching, on a sheet pan lined with a flour-dusted dish towel. Chill them until ready to use (freeze them if you are not going to cook them that same day). Drop them into boiling, well-salted water and cook them for 1 more minute once they rise to the top. In the meantime, melt 1 tablespoon of butter per person in a large skillet. Squeeze the brine from a small handful of crunchy barrel sauerkraut, reserving the liquid, and lightly brown it in the butter, adding some caraway seeds. Using a slotted spoon, transfer the cooked *Schlutzkrapfen* into the skillet. Add a handful of thinly cut chives and the sauerkraut brine, cook for a minute, carefully tossing the pasta to fully coat it with the butter and transfer it to a serving platter.

Once around Christmas in the early Eighties to our surprise and delight we received a letter from a distant relative of my father who lived in Dresden in the so-called German Democratic Republic, behind the Iron Curtain. She had been given permission to visit the West – after years of petitions and paper work. It was the most bittersweet of meetings. Of all the *Stollen* I have tasted, it is strange to remark that the one she brought as a gift from Dresden, the place where this most famous of holiday cakes originated, was the least delicious.

In the center of Munich was an elegantly flamboyant restaurant named Roy that I would never have had the opportunity to dine at had it not been for an invitation by the father of my friend Vanessa, at the occasion of her sixteenth birthday. The décor was very gay and the waiters were very gay and it was managed by a man who was very gay indeed. The cooking was beyond compare, neither careless nor cocky, as men's cooking can be, but extraordinary and refined. I did not have a similarly magnificent dining experience again until many years later, when Filip Noterdaeme and I were treated to a dinner at Jean-Georges, courtesy of a group of men I had been cooking for all summer. We were to go to the opera afterwards and the staff packed us a box of chocolates and *mignardises* that were the best intermission snack there ever was. It would be a pleasure to be able to expect something approaching it when ordering a little bite to eat at a cabaret. Has food in nightclubs – the few that still exist in New York City – improved? It has not at the opera, it is incredibly bad, almost as bad as at Grand Central Station. Do they cook these meals in the microwaves of the staff cafeteria?

One day in Munich there was a strange incident at the weekly gym class I was attending with a friend from my school. The hardened old coach whose calves were littered with varicose veins had, week after week, attempted to teach us routines for the balance beam, the pommel horse, the parallel, the uneven bars and the still rings. So far, so good, but when he began to express sentimental feelings for Germany before the war and mused about what would have happened if the Germans had won the war, my friend and I became frightened and quite agitated. I thought of my father, who had in his own youth been an accomplished gymnast and had unwittingly assumed I might become one, too. Had he not said he would fetch us at the end of the class. So I called him and said we would like to leave now. He said he would come and collect us outside, which he did in our very French Citroën car. It was a short drive home, where we had a comforting dinner of

KAISERSCHMARR'N
(A mess worthy of a Kaiser)

Marinate a handful of raisins in a splash of rum. Separate 3 eggs and beat the yolks with 2 tablespoons sugar and the scraped seeds of ½ vanilla bean until they form a soft ribbon. Stirring swiftly without overworking the dough, mix 2 cups of milk and 3 tablespoons of melted butter into the yolks before adding 2 cups of flour, sieved with 1 teaspoon of baking soda. Sprinkle the drained raisins over the batter. Beat the 3 egg whites and 1 pinch of salt to a soft peak and fold them into the dough. Heat a deep, non-stick skillet over a medium low flame and add 2 tablespoons of butter. Once it has melted, pour the entire batter over it. Cook for several minutes, shaking the pan occasionally, until the pancake begins to brown. Flip it to cook the other side (it does not matter if it breaks into pieces as you do this.) Once the pancake is cooked through and lightly browned on both sides, carefully tear it into bite-size pieces, using two forks, not spoons. Do not squish the pieces or they will get rubbery. Sprinkle the pieces with 2 tablespoons of sugar and toss them in the pan over a medium flame until the sugar is dissolved and the *Schmarr'n* is lightly caramelized on all sides. Transfer it to a warm platter, dust it with confectioner's sugar and serve with plum compote or apple sauce.

If this rustic dish is fit for a *Kaiser*, one should not look down on it if it is served in a burgher's home.

In the winter, the best way to forget the bitter cold was to go ice skating or skiing. With Nona and her husband owning an apartment in Bad Hofgastein, an Austrian skiing resort, we often took advantage of their offer to let us stay there for extended periods of time. On our way, we usually made a stopover in Salzburg where we had coffee at Café Tomaselli, with its endless varieties of cakes and tortes, redolent of a distant past. In Bad Hofgastein, feasting continued. There is no disparity between Austria's culinary sophistication and the country's century-old connection to Italy, Hungary and Bohemia. The cuisine is so refined yet simple that it takes a seasoned cook to recognize its subtle qualities. There are soups, dumplings, noodle dishes, boiled beef with delicate condiments, stews, salads and of course desserts, each one better than the former. It helps that they have a relaxed attitude about it. A dish, Nona once said, will always taste of the mood of the cook who prepared it.

Once, on our way to Bad Hofgastein, we stopped at Nona's house in Lower Bavaria for lunch. As always at her house we ate extremely well. During lunch, Nona's husband, my step-grandfather, entertained us with a joke about a good German consul needing in his employ a German chauffeur; an English butler; a French maid; a Chinese gardener; and a Japanese chef, whereas a bad consul would naturally have a French chauffeur, a Chinese butler, a German maid, a Japanese gardener and an English chef. My mother was filled with disdain about this joke which she found to be in very bad taste but his cheery, *Tell me, Ulla, you'd rather have the chef be a Frenchman, wouldn't you*, put her completely at her ease so that the two got on fairly well after that.

In Bad Hofgastein we frequently lunched in full skiing gear at one of the multiple inns that dotted the edges of slopes. The most popular menu item for young skiers was the *Germknödel*, a steamed, prune-lekvar-stuffed dumpling. The adults would be drinking copious amounts of *Glühwein*, mulled wine spiked with rum, and all too frequently joked about the most important skiing technique being the *Einkehrschwung*, a pun on the classic skier's 180° turn that suggests it will swiftly lead you to the nearest pub*.

---

* *Einkehren* in German means to turn in one leg to make a turn but also to visit a restaurant or pub

Was the rich food and heavy drink suitable for a day of physical exercise, was the food in the Austrian alps better than on the Bavarian side of them? It was easy to decide. Nowadays there is less of a difference.

In those days, my mother always made a point of buying local specialties to take home to Munich. There was Tarragon mustard, Austrian pastry flour, soft as fine coral sand, and air-dried, pre-cut croutons, ready to be pan-fried in butter.

In the town of Hofgastein we had lunch at a hidden little café where I ate one last time before crossing the border to Germany

GERMKNÖDEL
(Sweet Yeast Dumplings)

Grind ½ cup of poppy seeds into a fine powder and mix it with 1 cup of confectioner's sugar. If you do not have the special, hand-cranked poppy seed grinder, grind the seeds in batches in an electric coffee grinder, meticulously cleaned beforehand to remove any traces of coffee beans (add some regular sugar to the seeds before grinding them and pulse until the seeds are ground, careful to not over-process them lest they turn into an oily paste).

To make the dough for the dumplings, carefully place 2 eggs into a bowl with warm water to temper them. Into the bowl of a stand mixer equipped with a dough hook, scoop 2 cups of flour with 1 tablespoon of dry yeast and a pinch of salt. Warm up ⅓ cup of milk and break the tempered eggs into it, beating the mixture until homogenous. With the machine running on low, add the mixture to the flour along with with 2 tablespoons of sugar and, if desired, a few drops of orange flower water or bergamot essence. Turn the machine up to medium speed and add 6 tablespoons of softened butter, one at a time, adding the next piece only when the former has been fully incorporated. Let the machine continue to work the dough until it is elastic and detaches from the bowl of the stand mixer. This can be of course done by hand and is not as labor-intensive as it sounds.

Cover the dough and let it rest in a warm place for at least two hours, until doubled in volume. Punch it down and divide it into six equal portions. Shape each portion into a ball, flatten it, place a tablespoon of firm prune *lekvar* or prune jam (not to be confused with *plum* jam which is not an acceptable substitute), fold the dough over it, seal it well and shape it once again into a ball. Line a sheet pan with a clean dish towel, dust it with flour and place the dumplings onto it, spaced apart so they have room to expand. Cover with another towel and let the dumplings rest in a moderately warm spot for another hour. *Germknödel* are traditionally cooked in a special steamer but for the home kitchen, it is best to cook them as follows: Pour enough water into a deep frying skillet with a tight-fitting lid (or a Dutch oven) to just cover its bottom, add 2 tablespoons of neutral oil and ½ teaspoon of salt. Bring it to a simmer. Carefully place the dumplings, sealed side down, into the liquid, leaving enough room between them to expand as they cook. Cover and bring the liquid once again to a full boil before turning the heat down to medium low. Cook for 20 minutes without lifting the lid. By then, all the water should have evaporated and the bottom of the dumplings should have a thin, golden and pleasantly salty crust. To serve, place a dumpling each on warm dessert plates, pour 2-3 tablespoons of melted butter over each and douse them generously with the poppy seed sugar.

This dish was the *Mehlspeise* I desired most in my childhood. It was all the more special because it was available only at a certain time and in a certain place.

In Munich I loved strolling around the Viktualienmarket on Saturdays, not realizing that I would rarely see again such dream-like, slightly grumpy perfection. How with such excellence, variety and abundance could one not be inspired to creative cooking? The farmer's markets of New York City are certainly not outdoing themselves in the way their wares are handled or presented. Can one be excited about haphazard heaps of bruised lettuces and herbs and over-sized, over-fertilized root vegetables? Never. One must show more respect for the primary ingredient, even at the marketplace.

One of the things one could not buy anywhere even in those long-ago days and had no recourse but make from scratch was elderflower syrup. Stored in bottles it would keep for several months and was pure ambrosia.

When I was nineteen, my parents moved to Barcelona and I moved into a little flat in one of Munich's cozy central neighborhoods. It was conveniently close to the city's Academy of Fine Arts were I had been admitted to study interior design. The flat had large glass sliding doors that gave onto a grey cement balcony I painting Richard Meier white. It was a very pleasant, compact and modern place. The kitchen, though no larger than a walk-in closet, had all I needed to cook for a large number of people with fair ease. Those were my first days of happy housekeeping and home entertaining. I frequently hosted dinner parties. The neighborhood had several excellent bakeries, a well-sorted small supermarket, a greengrocer and Italian, Greek and Turkish delis where I could find specialty ingredients like imported olives and pickled peppers, Greek yogurt, feta cheese and freshly made *taramasalata*, so different from the kind sold in jars in the United States.

German culture at the time did not view being a chef as a viable option for educated people. It was a divided world. The home kitchen was a woman's domain and the restaurant kitchen a hidden men's world that no one wanted to know much about. It seemed that there was something unsavory about it. My mother would every now and then buy a food magazine, usually when there was a special edition advertising a new diet for weight loss. I was very fond of Time Life's *The Good Cook* series, its step-by step photographs with copper pans, marble counters and wooden cutting boards and masculine hands demonstrating technique. The aesthetic was resolutely modern. I learned more about cooking from the few volumes my mother possessed than from any other cookbook. It was not until years later via Luke Barr's *Provence 1970* that I found out more about Richard Olney, the openly gay American expat who had edited the entire Time Life series and whose role in the shaping of modern American cuisine has continuously been overlooked. It was the beginning of my research that eventually prompted me to write a series of essays about gay men and food which I titled "The Joy of Gay Cooking" and was published by Slate Magazine, an online journal. What would Olney, who passed away in 1999, think of the current madness surrounding the food world? And what role would he play in it?

In my early childhood, whenever I had been asked what I wanted to become later in my life, I had always answered, a painter, a dancer and a cook. The puzzled reactions had always been the least enthusiastic in regards to the latter of the three. A young man wearing an apron was regarded as being a mere step away from cross-dressing.

Then perceptions of the culinary world began to change. In Munich, it began with Eckart Witzigmann. It was he who first introduced the Germans to *nouvelle cuisine*, and his restaurant, Aubergine, was the first in all of Germany to be awarded three stars from the prestigious Guide Michelin. It was frequented by connoisseurs from all over the world and by Munich's *Schickeria* but continued to be derided by conservatives and locals. The restaurant's exclusivity, forbidding prices and unorthodox menus, so different from anything *Münchners* had ever seen or tasted provoked admiration and derision, envy and desire. In short, Aubergine was the talk of the town. My mother and I once chanced upon a television documentary that juxtaposed the orchestrated madness of Witzigmann's overstaffed and hectic kitchen with the elegant formality of the dining room. Years later in New York, a French chef who had as a young apprentice worked for Witzigmann told me, *He used to drive us mad because he wanted everything made on the spot and did not let us prepare anything ahead of time.* I still regret that I have never been able to eat at the Aubergine. The story goes that a police squad stormed Witzigmann's home one early morning and arrested him for possession of drugs, and before long, he had lost his license and had a dramatic fall from grace. At the time my mother and I were watching the documentary, Witzigmann was still a celebrated star chef. When the film was over, my mother suggested with a gleeful glint in her eyes, *Go and impress him with one of your creations, he might hire you as his apprentice.*

My mother had a very modern way of preparing veal cutlets, so very different from the traditional German version. She made it like this and conspiringly called it

OUR SECRET SCHNITZEL

Pound veal cutlets until very thin and season them with salt, white pepper and a bit of powered ginger. Fill a pressure cooker with a couple of inches of water, the juice of one halved lemon as well as the lemon half. Brush the flat steaming insert with oil and lay out the cutlets in it. Close the lid tight and cook the meat over high flame for 10 minutes. Serve drizzled with a tiny bit of melted butter and a light green salad.

My mother said that, cooked this way, the cutlets were more tender than cooked any other way. She loved that it was also a low-calorie dish. It was an argument I could have dispensed with. As she never had much time for cooking on weekdays and constantly struggled with losing some imaginary weight she said she had gained, it was a perfect solution for her. After lunch she was desperate for a quiet moment by herself, smoking a cigarette and reading the papers. This was perhaps her favorite moment of the day.

Here is how Bavarians like to prepare a

WIENER SCHNITZEL

Butterfly ¾ inch thick slices of pork loin (the classic Austrian version calls for top round of veal) and pound them into thin cutlets of about ⅛ inch thickness. To do this, place each butterflied slice between sheets of wax paper and pound it with a round, flat meat tenderizer. It should at least double in size. Season the cutlets with salt and pepper and coat them first in flour, shaking off the excess, then in beaten eggs, and finally in fine bread crumbs, pressing lightly to make them adhere to the egg. Pour enough neutral-tasting oil – never canola – into a large frying pan so that the Schnitzel will float in it and heat it to 350° F. Pan-fry each Schnitzel for about two minutes. Do not flip it but rather shake the pan so the hot oil can wash over the top and fry it this way. This will make the top coating cook and puff up as desired. When it is golden brown, carefully lift it out with a spatula and transfer it onto a paper towel-lined plate to drain off any excess oil. Serve with lemon wedges and potato salad. There are people who like it a lot.

In late 1989, a group of friends and I drove to Berlin so we could witness the historic fall of the Berlin Wall. By the time we got there, East Berliners were pouring into the West. Patrols of the East German police were still standing guard across the border, confused and defensive, watching the people celebrate. We made our way to the East sector of the city. It was a ghost town. Everyone, it seemed, had left. One of the patrols came up to us and roughly asked what we were doing here. We want to take a look at the past, I said. Everything is going to change now. That's possible, he said, but once you rich Westeners are coming over here you are going to just buy everything and we will have no place to go. But it's you coming over to our side, I muttered. He waved us away.

In West Berlin cooking had not developed much in the twenty or so years before the fall of the wall. More attention was given to alternative lifestyles and individual freedom, the sector having been for decades an island of resilience and nonconformity in a sea of hostility. Turkish *Döner* – spit-roasted layers of veal slices, broiled, shaved, and served on a pita pocket with shredded cabbage, sliced onions, diced cucumber and garlicky yogurt sauce was still the only interesting meal to be found among the ubiquitous sausages with ketchup and curry, herring salads with mayonnaise and of course *Buletten*, German meat patties, so different from American burgers.

This is the way to make *Buletten*, which in Bavaria are called

FLEISCHPFLANZERL*

Finely chop 1 onion and cook it in a frying pan with one tablespoon of butter and one crushed clove of garlic until

---

* The word *Fleischpflanzerl*, oddly, signifies a little plant made of meat, whereas the Prussian name for the same thing signifies, literally, small bullets. A good sign as any for the two region's cultural differences.

*"In my early childhood, whenever I had been asked what I wanted
to become later in my life, I had always answered, a painter,
a dancer and a cook."*

translucent and lightly golden. Cut off and discard the crusts of 6 slices of stale white bread, tear the bread into pieces and soak them in milk. In a mixing bowl, kneed together 1½ pounds of ground meat (any variety or combination of beef, veal and pork, not too lean), the bread, squeezed dry, 1 egg, the onions, a tablespoon of mustard, salt, pepper and finely chopped fresh or crushed dried thyme.* Cook a teaspoon of it in a frying pan to taste the seasoning, the mixture should not be bland. Wet your hands with cold water and shape the mixture into flattened balls, about the size of a clementine. Roll them in flour and cook them in a frying pan set over medium heat with a couple tablespoons neutral oil and a tablespoon butter. Fry them on both sides until golden brown, transfer them to a baking dish and finish cooking them in a 375° F oven for about 10 minutes.

Here is the recipe for what is often served with them,

PARSLEY'D CARROTS

Peel 6 large carrots and cut them on the bias into irregular diamonds, about the size of garlic cloves. Add them into a medium-size pot with a bit of water, a peeled and julienned small knob of fresh ginger (or a pinch of powdered ginger) and cook, covered, over medium heat for about 5 minutes or until they are tender. Add 1 tablespoon butter, a dash of brown sugar and a handful of chopped parsley. Cook for 5 more minutes, stirring now and then, until caramelized and shiny. Season with salt and pepper. This is a particular favorite with children.

At a fashionable vegetarian restaurant in Munich I ate for the first time whole-grain tempeh, and thought it was interesting. It was served fried to a crisp with a peanut sauce on the side but not at all oily, I gratefully noticed. Tempeh is rather bland on its own and requires frying and a deft sauce to make it come to life.

Whenever Nona and her husband came to town they always invited

---

* Instead of buying dried thyme, which rarely delivers what it ought to, wash and tumble-dry a bunch of fresh thyme, lay it out on a parchment paper-lined sheet pan. Place it in a warm spot or an oven equipped with a pilot light. After 2-4 days, when the thyme is completely dry, strip the leaves off the branches and store them in an airtight glass container.

us to a lavish dinner at Munich's only Cantonese restaurant – diced chicken with water chestnuts and sugar snap peas, sweet-and-sour pork, crispy pan-fried and seasoned egg noodles with vegetables and fried bananas with ice cream for dessert. The pan-fried noodles were my favorite dish and to my great disappointment, I have never ever found a Chinese restaurant in New York City that made them the same way.

Close to the *Viktualienmarkt* was a café that served freshly made *Schmalznudeln*, Bavarian yeast donuts, fried in clarified butter, very popular as a warm pick-me-up in the early morning hours after a night out on the town. Another popular thing to do was to have brunch on Sundays at a café in the borough of Neuhausen, where the menu consisted entirely of the most perfectly assembled platters of cheeses and hams, and where *café au lait* had replaced the henceforth more popular cappuccino. Conversation was lively and extended as long as possible to avoid going home to work on one's studies.

And then the family of a dear friend invited me to dine at Munich's first sushi restaurant, and I tasted for the first time a California roll. I knew fresh crab meat from having often eaten it in France and usually thought its flavor exquisite (I liked it with homemade mayonnaise). And now I was told that these pressed sticks with orange coloring on one side were crab meat, too. Surely it was unlike the meat of the crabs I used to catch at low tide in Brittany and Normandy on countless summer vacations.

Then the time had come for me to leave Germany, to leave Europe, to move to New York City and change my life. Above everything I wanted to become an entertainer, and leaving my conventional life behind was thrilling.

It was not until many years later that I realized that growing up in a safe and loving home in both France and Germany had given me the considerable inner strength that nothing and no one could ever take away from me.

IX
DISHES FROM MY
CHILDHOOD IN FRANCE

T HESE DISHES ADDED VARIETY to my mother's culinary repertoire when we lived in Paris in the Seventies. They would no longer be considered novel or even modern, nor have they the benefit of being called beneficial, which, as defined by Filip Noterdaeme's older brother, is something that is good for your health until someone claims it is not. On the contrary, they are most of them exceedingly rich in the way of a bygone era, which is the way revivals are created – that is, everybody grows up eating them and then one person remembering them recreates them, intent to reclaim the past. Even dipping a soft miniature cake baked in the shape of a shell into a cup of herbal tea can do this. Then everybody tries to imitate that. It is a pleasure for us, perhaps for the tea.

It is, of course, understood that there are always those who rush in and obstinately insist on authenticity, on one specific ingredient here and a precise measurement there. This, a matter too frequently of lack of imagination, is not arguable. It is a pleasure to retire before such a fact.

For the preparation of these dishes, no special skills or what professional chefs call technique is required. Those used in these recipes can be acquired by trial and error in the process. To commence then at the beginning.

I. COLD HORS D'OEUVRE

MELON BALLS WITH PROSCIUTTO

The best melons are those from Cavaillon. Cut one in half, scoop out the seeds and carve as many balls as you can from the halves, using a melon baller. Sprinkle them with coarsely ground black pepper. Remove the strip of fat off the thinnest slices of *Prosciutto di Parma* or *San Daniele* you can get, tear each slice lengthwise in half and wrap each strip around a melon ball, securing it with a small wooden pick. Serve on a round platter with a halved lemon in the center for the used picks. An alternate version of this idea is made with fresh Bosc pear segments and thinly sliced *Bresaola*.

ROAST BEEF WHEELS

Turn red bell peppers over a gas flame or grill until their skins are browned and blistered all over (or roast them in a 450° F oven). Instantly pack them into a paper bag, fold up the bag and let the peppers rest in it so the steam can loosen their skins further. Once they are cool enough to handle, strip or rub off their charred skins, split the peppers (catch any juices and use them for something else, like a salad dressing) and cut them into narrow strips. Cut thin slices of cold roast beef into long strips and roll each piece around a rinsed anchovy and a strip of red pepper, securing each pinwheel with a small wooden pick. Serve on round platters with a halved lemon in the center for the used picks.

SALMON ROLL-UPS

Peel and split a hothouse cucumber lengthwise, remove the seeds with a teaspoon, split the halves once more lengthwise and cut them into bite-size pieces. Sprinkle them with salt and finely grated lemon peel and refrigerate them, covered, for a good hour. Cut thin slices of smoked salmon into wide strips, wrap one strip around each cucumber piece, affixing the salmon with a wooden pick and dip the roll-ups into finely chopped dill. Serve on silver trays with a halved lemon in the center for the used picks.

GRAPES AND BLUE CHEESE

In a food processor, pulse roasted pistachios to a course powder. Do not over-process the nuts or they will turn oily. Pour the nut-meal into a bowl and add into the processor equal amounts of butter and *Roquefort*. Process until creamy and homogenous. Chill the mixture lightly. Pluck red grapes from their stems and, working with cold hands, cover each grape in cheese mixture, shape it into a ball and roll it in the ground pistachios. Arrange them on a platter to appear like a cluster of grapes on a vine, adding a little leafy branch at the top to complete the image. Not for the impatient cook nor for faint-of-heart eaters.

TAPENADE CANAPÉS

In a food processor, purée 2 cups of pitted, Moroccan-style, oil-cured black olives, 1 tablespoon of Dijon mustard, 6 rinsed anchovy filets, and 1 tablespoon of drained capers into a thick paste. Cut off the crusts of thinly sliced white Pullman bread, spread them with the paste, top them with a thin slice of Gruyère and cut the slices into triangles. Garnish each triangle with a sliver of pink radish.

DEVILED EGGS

Hard-boil 8 eggs according to the instructions given in Chapter VI, in the recipe for *Assiette à la Broodthaers*. Peel the cooled eggs under running water, careful to not rip off any of the egg white. Cut them in half and gingerly squeeze out the egg yolk halves. In a food processor, churn the yolks with 3 tablespoons of best quality, preferably homemade mayonnaise, a teaspoon of Dijon mustard, salt, white pepper and a pinch of cayenne pepper. Pipe or spoon the paste back into the egg white's cavity and garnish with finely sliced chives.

II. HOT HORS D'OEUVRE

PIEROGI (I)

Finely chop 1 large yellow onion and sauté it with a bit of butter in a frying pan until translucent but not brown. Add 2 pounds of ground chuck beef and cook it, stirring frequently, until the meat is barely cooked and still soft. Transfer into a bowl lined with a triple layer of paper towels and refrigerate until cool. Remove the paper towels which will have soaked up much of the residue fat and assertively season the meat with salt, pepper, fresh, chopped thyme leaves, finely diced pickles and a heaped tablespoon of Dijon mustard. Lay out one of two large sheets of store-bought puff pastry on a floured surface. Using a 2-inch cookie cutter, lightly mark as many rounds as will fit the sheet, brush the entire surface with water and place a little heap of meat farce into the center of each marked round. Roll out the second sheet of puff pastry so as to be slightly larger than the first and carefully place it over the first layer. Press the dough down around each mound of filling, using your fingertips. Cut out the *pierogis* with the cookie cutter and transfer them onto parchment-paper-lined cookie sheets. Brush them with an egg wash made of 2 egg yolks lightly beaten with two tablespoon of water, poke a little hole into each of them and chill them in the freezer for 30 minutes before baking them in a 400° F oven until puffed and golden brown, about 20 minutes. Serve warm.

These were a favorite at the receptions my parents routinely gave at the end of my or my brother's annual birthday parties, when our little friends' parents would come to pick up their children and the adults would have a party of their own before departing.

PIEROGI (II)

Thoroughly rinse 6 bunches of spinach and remove any thick stems. Drop the spinach into a large pot of rapidly boiling water and blanch it for just a minute. Drain and immediately transfer the hot spinach into an ice bath. Once it is cool, drain it once more, transfer the leaves onto a clean dish towel, gather the corners of the towel and, twisting it, squeeze as much water as possible from the spinach. Chop it finely and season it with salt, white pepper, nutmeg, and a pinch of cayenne pepper. Add several handfuls of finely diced firm feta cheese. Proceed as with *Pierogi (I)*, above.

COUGÈRES

In a sauce pan, bring 1 cup of water, 1 ½ teaspoons salt and 1 stick of butter to a boil. Add in one go 1 cup of flour and swiftly stir work it into the liquid with a wooden spoon until it comes together in a ball. Cook it for another minute before transferring it into a stand mixer with a paddle attachment. Churn on a low setting until it is no longer steaming before adding 3 eggs, one at a time, adding the next egg only after the former egg is completely incorporated into the dough. Check the consistency of the dough. If it does not fall off the spoon in a pointed tip, add one more egg white and, if necessary,

the yolk as well. Stir about a ¾ cup of finely grated Comté
into the dough and season it with a pinch of paprika. Chill
the dough thoroughly before spooning little nugget-shaped
mounds of it onto parchment paper-lined sheet pans, leaving
a good inch of space between each of them. Brush them with
a lightly beaten egg and sprinkle them with a bit of grated
Comté and perhaps a few caraway seeds. Bake them in a 425°
F oven for 10 minutes before lowering the oven temperature
to 375° F and baking them for about 10 more minutes, until
golden brown and crusty. Serve warm.

BACON-WRAPPED DATES

Remove the pits and stems of the plumpest, softest *Medjool*
dates you can find. If they are very large, split them in half.
Wrap each date (or halved date) with a very thin strip of cured
or smoked bacon or speck, choosing strips that are not too
fatty. Affix the bacon with small wooden picks and sprinkle the
dates with coarse black pepper. Place them onto parchment
paper-lined sheet pans and bake them in a 375° F oven until
crisped. Transfer them onto a paper-towel lined plate to soak
up some of their fat before placing them onto serving platters,
along with a halved lemon for the used wooden picks.

The same hors d'oeuvre can be prepared with pitted dried prunes,
which ought to be soaked for at least 30 minutes in black tea first.

CHEESE STICKS

Into a mixing bowl, finely grate ½ pound of Gruyere. Toss
the cheese with 1 cup of flour, 1 teaspoon of baking powder,
1 teaspoon of salt and 1 teaspoon of paprika. Add 1 stick of
butter, cut into pieces, and 2 egg yolks, and work everything by
hand into a pliable dough. Shape it into a ball, flatten it, wrap
it in cellophane and chill it for a good hour. Roll it out on a
flour-dusted surface and brush it with an egg yolk beaten with
2 tablespoons of water. Using a fluted pastry wheel cutter, cut
the dough into strips, about ½ inch wide and 5 inches long.
Sprinkle them with caraway or fennel seeds before transferring
the strips onto parchment paper-lined sheet pans. Bake them
at 350° F until golden brown.

III. SOUP

This is the soup we were served for lunch nearly every day as a first course at my *école maternelle*, French kindergarten. I remember once peeking through the cellar windows of the kitchen in the kindergarten's basement and seeing a Rubenesque woman clad in chef's whites plunge a giant immersion blender into a large stock pot.

POTAGE DE LÉGUMES
(Vegetable Soup)

Peel and dice equal amounts of mealy potatoes (like Idaho or russet), carrots, and the white and light green parts of well-rinsed leeks as well as half their volume each of onion, celery stalks and turnip. Place all vegetables into a large pot and cover them with water. Add a bay leaf and a sprig of fresh thyme and bring the water to a simmer. When all vegetables are softened, remove the herbs and purée the soup with an immersion blender, adding more water if necessary to give it the consistency of a pleasantly thick but not heavy soup. Season with salt and pepper and stir about a tablespoon of butter per quart into it. Serve hot with sliced bread.

LENTIL SOUP

Finely dice 1 yellow onion, 1 carrot and 2 celery stalks and sauté them with a bit of olive oil in a Dutch oven until fragrant. Add 1 ½ cups of *lentilles du Puy*, 1 smoked ham hock, 1 bay leaf, a couple of twigs of fresh thyme and 4 cups of water. Bring it to a simmer and cook over a medium flame until the lentils are tender. Remove the bay lea and the thyme sprigs (the leaves will have fallen off into the soup) and the ham hock and, using an immersion blender, purée the soup only partly to keep it chunky. Strip any meat off the ham hock, dice it and return it to the soup. Season the soup with salt and pepper and a soupçon of red wine vinegar and serve garnished with chopped French parsley and toasted country bread on the side. For a more filling version, heat some cooked sausages, whole or sliced, in the puréed soup, but do not let the soup come to a boil again. This is a robust dish for a lunch in the winter.

SOUPE DE POISSON

In a Dutch oven, heat 2 tablespoons of olive oil and add 4 cleaned, halved soft shell crabs and 1 scaled and gutted red snapper or other lean fish, cut into chunks (remove the gills and tail end but include the head.) Sauté for a few minutes before adding 1 diced carrot, 1 sliced leek, 1 chopped stalk of celery, half of a diced onion and half of a diced fennel bulb. Sauté everything until fragrant before deglazing with a shot of anise-flavored spirit like Pernod or Pastis (or white vermouth) and 1 glass dry white wine. Add 1 tablespoon of tomato paste, a pinch of cayenne pepper, several strands of saffron, a bay leaf and a twig of fresh thyme. Add enough water to barely cover the solids and simmer the stew gently for 30 minutes. Remove the bay leaf, thyme sprig, fish eye balls and large fish bones such as the jaw and backbone and, working in batches, blend the soup to a puree before passing it through a fine-mesh sieve, discarding any leftover solids. Season with salt and pepper and serve hot with a dollop of mayonnaise seasoned with *Harissa* (Moroccan spiced chili paste,) toasted slices of baguette and whole peeled garlic cloves for rubbing the bread.

This is a childhood favorite, irredeemably linked to summer vacations in both Southern France as well as Brittany. Adding fresh wild fennel blossoms gives the soup an irresistible anise flavor.

SORREL VELOUTÉ

In a Dutch oven, sauté 1 diced onion in 2 tablespoons of butter until translucent. Add 2 good handfuls of rinsed fresh sorrel, thick stems and leaf-veins removed. Stir well and add 2 peeled and diced Idaho potatoes and 1 quart of water. Bring it to a simmer. When the potato cubes are tender, purée the soup with an immersion blender, season it with salt and white pepper and add ½ cup of heavy cream. Do not bring the soup to a simmer again. Serve hot with butter-roasted croutons.

IV. FISH AND SEAFOOD

CRUSTACÉS MAYONNAISE

One of the seasonal pleasures of spending summers by the sea was hunting for crabs and shrimp, armed with little nets and hooks. My older brother and I were always proud of our catch and my mother always discreetly supplemented it with more crustaceans from a local seafood store. Favorites were pink shrimp, velvet crabs and spider crabs and real prawns, none of which are commonly available in the United States. The closest are Maine shrimp, spotted prawn, Dungeoness crab, and King crab. Boil them in salted water seasoned with a bay leaf, a few pepper corns and a couple of cloves. Cooking times depend on size. Shrimp are done once they float to the top, larger crustaceans with thick shells must be cooked for about 10 minutes per pound. Remove them from the water as soon as they are done. Chill them thoroughly and serve them with nutcrackers, stainless steel seafood picks and

HOMEMADE MAYONNAISE

Start with at least 2 if not 3 egg yolks from the freshest, pasture-raised eggs you can find short of visiting a chicken farm. They must be room temperature: submerge the eggs in warm water for a few minutes to temper them before cracking them open. Reserve the egg whites, they can be beaten to a firm peak later and folded into the mayonnaise for a lighter *mayonnaise mousseline*, or used for something else such as a meringues, a light cookie batter or for clarifying stock. Slide the yolks into a mixing bowl, add a heaped teaspoon of Dijon mustard and stir well. Add drop by drop ¼ cup of cold-pressed sunflower oil, constantly whisking. When it commences to stiffen and emulsify, add 1 more cup oil in a steady thin stream, never letting up on the quick stirring or whisking motion. By the end, the mayonnaise will be quite firm. Dissolve a generous pinch of salt and powdered white pepper in the juice of one lemon or a couple tablespoons of good white wine vinegar and stir the mixture into the mayonnaise. Taste the result and add more salt if necessary.

Mayonnaise can more easily be made in a stand mixer with a whisk attachment but never in a blender or food processor.

COLD FISH WITH MAYONNAISE

Choose a white-fleshed, lean fish like striped bass or halibut. If using a whole fish, chose a medium size, rinse and pat it it dry, season the cavity with salt and pepper and stuff it with fennel fronds, parsley stems or dill weeds and perhaps a sliced clove of garlic. Rub the entire fish with a bit of olive oil and season it with salt and white pepper. If using filets, season them in the same manner and layer them atop the above-mentioned herbs. Bake the fish enclosed in folded parchment paper in a 350° F oven until just about done. Baking times will depend on the size of the fish or filets, anything between 10 and 30 minutes. Do not overcook it. To test for doneness, pierce the fish in its thickest part with a toothpick. If the flesh offers no resistance, the fish is done. Remove it from the oven, pour off any pan juices and reserve them. When the fish is cold enough to handle, carefully filet it and arrange it on a platter, or simply transfer the cooked filets onto it. Cover and chill. Carefully spoon the reserved, gelatinous liquid over the filets (warm it slightly if it has set, it will get liquid again). If you wish, you may arrange leaves of fresh tarragon on the fish in a decorative pattern before doing so. Serve with homemade mayonnaise.

In both my *école maternelle* and my French primary school, seafood was served for lunch on Fridays and it was inevitably one of two dishes, the first one being cod filets in white sauce served with rice (which I loathed) and the second, way more popular one being fried fish sticks served with mashed potatoes. This is the way to make

BREADED FISH FILETS

Choose a firm-cooking, rather plain fish like cod. Cut filets into pieces no larger than half the palm of a hand, season them with salt and pepper, dip them first into flour, then beaten eggs and finally bread crumbs. Fry them on both sides in a mix of neutral-tasting oil and butter until browned and crusty and serve them with a lemon wedge and buttery mashed potatoes, sprinkled with chopped parsley.

This was a festive first course at many a dinner party hosted by my parents in our Paris apartment. If we as children were seated along with the adults, my mother would prepare a separate first course for us, also in a shell – usually a nest of tomato-sauce-dressed spaghetti, showered with melted cheese and baked in the oven along with the scallops until browned and deliciously crisp.

COQUILLES SAINT JAQUES GRATINÉES
(Baked Scallops)

You will need one large scallop per person including the roe plus one scallop shell per person. To serve 6, sauté 3 diced shallots in two tablespoons of butter until translucent, add a teaspoon of tomato paste and the rinsed roe. If diver scallops with their own roe are not available, use regular large scallops and substitute sea urchin roe. Cook until the roe is plump, deglaze with a splash of Cognac, tip the pan towards to gas flame to set the alcohol on fire and burn it off, dust everything with 1 tablespoon of flour, stir and add 2 cups of milk. Bring to a simmer and cook for a few minutes before puréeing it in a blender to a smooth, thick sauce. Season it with salt and white pepper. Place one scallop (remove the tough muscle tendon on the side) into each shell and spoon 2 tablespoons of cooled sauce over them. Sprinkle with a mix of salted bread crumbs and chopped parsley and top with a few gratings of cold butter. Bake at 400° F for about 15 minutes, until browned and bubbly.

TRUITE AU BLEU

Americans are still squeamish about being served whole fish on the bone and less than apt at fileting it properly on their plate. It is a skill well worth acquiring, the reward being that fish cooked whole is always more succulent and flavorful. Because of its friendly size, trout is a good way to start.

Truite au bleu can only be made with live trout as only their quickly dissipating layer of protective gel guarantees the blue color that gives the dish its name. If murder in the kitchen is not an option, one may still cook trout as described below, buying the fish already gutted and cleaned from a fish monger, but the dish should then be aptly named *truite au gris*, no longer blue but grey.

Prepare a *court bouillon*, a light poaching stock, out of ½ bottle of dry white wine, 1 quart of water, 1 quartered onion, a sliced peeled carrot, 2 sliced stems of celery, a few sprigs of parsley and a bay leaf, and 1 teaspoon of whole white pepper corns. Simmer for 30 minutes, strain, season with salt and let it completely cool down. Knock out each live trout by hitting them on the head with a mallet. Clean them out but do not wipe them down. Lay them side by side in a fish poacher. Bring 1 cup of white wine vinegar to a boil and pour it over the bodies. Now add the cooled court bouillon and bring everything to a light simmer. The trout ought to be done after 10 minutes. Serve with lemon wedges and melted butter, peeled salt-water boiled potatoes (peeled before, not after boiling), garnished with chopped parsley.

TRUITE AMANDINE

Coarsely crush sliced almonds and mix them with an equal amount of fine bread crumbs. Season boned and skinned trout filets with salt and white pepper and dip them first in flour, then a beaten egg and finally in the almond and bread crumb mixture. In a non-stick frying pan, heat enough flavorless oil to cover its surface and carefully lower the fish filets into it. Now add a couple of tablespoons of butter and pan-fry the fish on both sides. Serve with a lemon wedge.

SOLE À L'ORANGE

Season skinned grey sole filets with salt and white pepper. Melt a bit of butter in a non-stick frying pan and lower the filets into it. Cook over medium heat until almost opaque. Pour some freshly squeezed and strained orange juice over them, a couple of tablespoons per serving, and scatter one tablespoon of cold butter per two servings over it. Cover then pan and cook for a couple more minutes, shaking the pan occasionally, until the fish is cooked through and the butter and juices are combined. Serve the filets with the sauce spooned over them.

RAIE AU BEURRE NOIR
(Skate Wings with Browned Butter Sauce)

Season 2 skate wings with salt and white pepper and coat them lightly in flour. In a non-stick frying pan, heat a tablespoon of butter with two tablespoons of oil and lower the wings into the pan. Fry them on both sides until golden brown, transfer them to a platter and place it in a 375° F oven for another 10 minutes or until a wooden pick inserted into its thickest part meets no resistance. Meanwhile, pour out the oil from the pan and deglaze the brown bits with a splash of dry white wine or dry vermouth and 2 tablespoons of drained capers. Add 3 tablespoons of butter and cook until the butter solids have caramelized before adding some chopped parsley and cooking it for another minute, adding a splash of water if it gets too dry. Serve the ray wings with the sauce spooned over them.

LOUP DE MER AU COURT BOUILLON
(Poached Mediterranean Seabass)

Fill a fish poacher halfway with water, add half a bottle of dry white wine, a couple of bay leaves, several carrot slices, half an onion, a few white peppercorns, 2 cloves, and couple of lemon slices and bring it to a simmer. Place 1 whole cleaned, large European sea bass into it and keep the temperature low enough to never let the liquid go beyond a very low simmer. Cooking times vary, count about 5 minutes per pound. Serve the fish whole, with the most classic of French sauces,

BEURRE BLANC

Finely chop 6 large shallots, transfer them to a medium sauce pan and add enough dry white wine until they are barely covered. Add a bit of ground white pepper and simmer the shallots over a medium low flame until they are completely translucent and soft, about 10 minutes (there ought to be a few tablespoons of liquid left on the bottom of the pan.) Set the pan over a very low flame and incorporate 8 tablespoon of cold salted butter, one at a time, whisking constantly. Pour into a preheated sauce boat and serve immediately.

V. STARCHES

GNOCCHI ALLA PARIGINA

These are not to be confused with *Gnocchi alla Romana* described in Chapter VII, nor do they have anything in common with potato-based gnocchi from the same chapter – or any of the more idiosyncratic variations made with Ricotta, pumpkin purée or chestnut flour. They are named after the French capital for the simple reason that the required dough, *pâte à choux*, puff paste, is a French invention. Hence, one may be inclined to think of this dish as an Italian appropriation of a French invention, a rare exception to the rule, which is the exact reverse.

Bring 1 cup of milk and 6 tablespoons of butter to a simmer. Add 1 cup of flour all at once and vigorously work it into the liquid until it comes together in a ball. Cook it for another minute while stirring and transfer it to a mixing bowl. Churn it with a wooden spoon until it is no longer releasing hot steam. Gradually add 4 eggs, one at a time, beating the dough each time until the mass is homogenous and shiny (you can do this in a stand mixer equipped with a paddle attachment, beating the dough at low medium speed.)

Add ½ cup of finely ground – never shredded – Parmesan cheese and season it with salt, white pepper and nutmeg or mace. Chill the dough for a good hour, during which you prepare the *béchamel* sauce. Melt 2 tablespoons of butter in a medium size saucepan. Away from the flame, stir 2 leveled tablespoons of flour into the butter. Return the pot to the flame and gradually (to avoid lumps) whisk 2 cups of milk into the base. Bring the sauce to a simmer, turn down the heat and cook it for a few minutes, using a spatula to scrape the bottom of the pot to prevent it from scorching. It should have the consistency of a light sauce that coats the back of a wooden spoon; add more milk if it gets too thick. Season it with salt and white pepper. Grease an oval baking dish with an ample amount of softened butter and scatter quenelles-shaped portions of the puff paste into it, no larger than an medium-size apricot and a good inch apart from each other. Carefully spoon the room-temperature *béchamel* sauce over the quenelles, scatter a good cup of finely ground Parmesan over them and bake for 30 minutes in a 425° F oven until risen, bubbly and lightly browned. Serve immediately.

POMMES DAUPHINES

Prepare a *pâte à choux* as you would for *Gnocchi alla Parigina*, described above. Peel and boil 4 large russet potatoes until tender. Push them through a ricer. Combine them with the *pâte à choux* – the amount of each should be about equal. Season the dough assertively with salt, white pepper and a hint of nutmeg and chill it until firm enough to hold its shape. Spoon portions of the dough, the size of lychees, onto a shallow dish with sifted flour and shake the pan to cover them with flour before rolling them into balls. Place them on a floured tray and freeze them if you are not going to fry them immediately. Deep-fry them in peanut oil heated to 360° F until puffed up and golden brown. Keep them warm in a moderate oven until ready to serve.

GRATIN DAUPHINOIS

Peel and rinse 6-8 large Yukon Gold or other firm-cooking potatoes. Using a mandolin or Benriner, slice them as thinly as possible. Layer the slices in an overlaying pattern into a buttered baking dish, seasoning each layer with salt and pepper, adding some thin slices of yellow onion as well as some fresh thyme leaves and a bit of shredded Gruyère in between layers. Top everything off with a bit more grated Gruyère and pour enough homemade warmed beef stock over the potatoes to cover them halfway. If stock is not an option, you may use milk. Cream, often used nowadays, is too rich in my opinion. Dot the potatoes with a few pieces of butter, cover the dish with aluminum foil and bake it at 375° F for 45 minutes. Uncover and continue baking the gratin until the potatoes are softened and the crust is brown and bubbly.

VI. POULTRY AND MEATS

POULET À LA MOUTARDE

Into a baking dish, add a couple of peeled and cubed potatoes, several whole garlic cloves, 4 quartered shallots and 2 carrots, cut into chunks. Season the vegetables with salt, pepper and fresh thyme, drizzle them with a bit of olive oil and toss them well until fully coated with oil. Rinse and pat dry a whole chicken, season it inside out with salt and pepper and slather it inside out with plentiful Dijon mustard. Tuck in the wingtips, place it breast -side up on top of the vegetables, shower it with chopped fresh thyme and black pepper, shave some cold butter over it and roast for a good hour in a 375° F oven, until browned and crusty, basting it with white wine a couple of times in the last 15 minutes.

ESCALOPE AUX CHAMPIGNONS À LA CRÈME
(Veal Cutlets with Mushrooms and Cream)

Preheat the oven to 200° F. Season two portion-sized veal cutlets, pounded to a ⅛ inch thickness, with salt and pan-fry them in two tablespoons of very hot oil for about two minutes on each side until nicely browned. Transfer them to a platter and place it in the warm oven. To the pan add 2 chopped shallots. Shake the pan so that their juiced deglaze the brown bits. When they begin to caramelize, add 4 thinly sliced button mushrooms. Once these have broken down and begin to caramelize, deglaze the pan with a splash of white wine. Cook for a good minute before adding about ½ cup of cream. Stir and simmer until it has become a thick sauce. Season it with salt and white pepper and perhaps a few chopped tarragon or parsley leaves. Pour the sauce over the veal cutlets and serve them with steamed Basmati rice, roasted potatoes or even fresh egg noodles.

BLANQUETTE DE VEAU
(Veal Stew)

Cut up two pounds of veal shoulder into large chunks, rinse them well in cold water, fill them into a Dutch oven, cover them with cold water and bring it to a simmer, skimming off any rising foam. Add 1 peeled carrot cut into large chunks; 1 thickly sliced leek, white and light green part only; half an onion spiked with 3 cloves; a bay leaf; a few sprigs each of fresh thyme and parsley; 1 teaspoon of white peppercorns; and a teaspoon of salt. Cover and simmer over very low heat for up to two hours, or until the meat is exceedingly tender. Set a colander over a bowl and ladle the stew it. Wipe out the pot, and melt 3 tablespoons of butter in it. Add 1 tablespoon of flour, whisk until smooth and, whisking constantly, add 3 cups of the strained broth. Simmer until thickened and add 1 cup of heavy cream, the juice of one half of a lemon and salt, white pepper and grated nutmeg to taste. Temper 3 egg yolks with a bit of the hot sauce before adding them to the sauce.

Return the chunks of veal to the sauce, as well as handful of peeled and cooked pearl onions, about 6 quartered and cooked mushrooms and a handful of large green olives (with their pits – do not use pitted olives.) Do not bring the sauce to a simmer again. Garnish with chopped parsley or tarragon and serve with plain long grain rice.

GIGOT D'AGNEAU ROTÎ
(Roasted Leg of Lamb)

Trim off most of the fat of a bone-in leg of lamb. Using a paring knife, make small deep incisions on all sides and push peeled and halved garlic cloves into them. Brush the leg on all sides with olive oil and season it with salt, coarsely ground black pepper and crushed dried thyme leaves. I am rather fond of my mother's method of spreading a couple tablespoons of Dijon mustard over the leg of lamb as well, it lends it a robust flavor. Place it on a rack and let it rest at room temperature for an hour before searing it under the broiler for 5 minutes on each side. Adjust the oven temperature to 325° F, cover the leg loosely with aluminum foil and roast it for another good hour. Remove the foil and roast it until an instant thermometer inserted into the thickest part of the meat reads 135° F. This may take up to another 30 minutes or so. Remove it from the oven and let it rest for at least 15 minutes before carving it. Once the meat is carved and laid out on a warmed platter, place the roasting pan over a high flame and deglaze it with some red wine, adding 2 tablespoons of butter when it has all but evaporated, shaking the pan until the butter is incorporated. Drizzle the sauce over the meat. Serve with

SAUCE BÉARNAISE

Chop 6 shallots into fairly fine dice and slide them into a sauce pan. Never chop onions or shallots with a machine, it makes them release too much water and sulfur, spoiling their sweet flavor. Add several sprigs of fresh tarragon and enough white wine vinegar to cover. Bring the liquid to a simmer, making sure that the tarragon is fully submerged. Simmer until the shallots are very soft and translucent and all but about a scant half cup of the liquid remains. Take it off the flame and cover it. When cooled down, remove the tarragon sprigs, beat two egg yolks and two tablespoons of cold water into the mixture and set the pan over a low flame. Gently warm it up while stirring. It should never come to a simmer. When it is hot, incorporate up to 6 tablespoons of cold salted butter into the mixture, one tablespoon at a time, stirring swiftly. Pour the sauce into a preheated *saucière* or bowl and serve immediately.

LAMB-STUFFED ZUCCHINI

Cut off the stems and ends of 8 zucchini, cut the zucchini in half and hollow them out with an apple corer. Dice 1 Spanish onion and sauté it in a frying pan with 2 tablespoons of olive oil until softened. Transfer it to a mixing bowl and add 2 slices of stale white bread, crusts removed and soaked in cold milk; 2 pounds of lean, ground lamb, and one egg. Mix well and season assertively with salt, pepper, fresh thyme, paprika and cumin. Pipe the mixture into the zucchini halves. Press any leftover meat filling into the bottom of a pie dish and stick the zucchini halves onto it – vertically, like columns. Drizzle them with olive oil and roast them in a 375° F oven for about 45 minutes.

POIVRONS FARCIS
(Stuffed Bell Peppers)

Pre-cook 4 whole red bell peppers in salted boiling water for 3 minutes (keep them submerged in the water by weighing them down with a plate). Drop them into ice water to cool them down, then slice off and reserve the top. Removed the core and seeds. Dice 1 yellow onion and 2 cloves of garlic and sauté both in 2 tablespoons of olive oil until translucent. Add 1 pound of ground beef and sauté it until lightly browned. Deglaze with 2 tablespoons of red wine vinegar and add 1 cup of tomato puree and ¼ cup of Basmati rice. Simmer for a few minutes, adding a splash of water or wine if it gets too dry, and season with salt, pepper, paprika, fresh thyme and a pinch of cinnamon. Fill the mixture into the bell peppers and cover each of them with their tops. Put 4 thick onions slices into an oiled baking dish, place a bell pepper on each slice, drizzle them with a bit of white wine and olive oil and bake them at 375° F for 40 minutes.

VII. VEGETABLES

COOKED CUCUMBERS

Peel, split and seed 3 hothouse cucumbers. Split the halves once again lengthwise and cut them into little chunks. Melt 1 tablespoon of butter in a saucepan and add the cucumber chunks. Cook for a few minutes, stirring now and then, until they are translucent. Lower the flame and season with salt and pepper. In a bowl, mix 1 egg yolk with ½ cup of heavy cream. Add the liquid from the pot to the mixture to temper the yolk and pour the sauce over the hot cucumbers. Warm it gently, shaking the pan, but do not bring the sauce to a simmer or it will curdle. Season with a bit of lemon juice just before serving.

HARICOTS VERTS

Cut off the beans' little stems but not the tips. To do this most efficiently, take a small handful of them at a time, align the beans into a tight bundle, all facing the same direction, and cut off the stems in one go. Blanch them in heavily salted water for a couple of minutes, more if using regular string beans. They should no longer taste raw yet still have a snap to them. Immediately transfer them to an ice bath to preserve their vibrant green color. Strain them once they are cool. Melt a bit of butter in a medium-size pot, add a couple of thinly sliced shallots or garlic cloves, gently frying them until translucent. Add some finely chopped fresh savory and the blanched haricots. Toss lightly and cover the pot for a couple of minutes to heat the beans from the rising steam. Season with salt and pepper and serve.

GRATIN DE CHOU-FLEUR
(Baked Cauliflower)

Remove the leaves and core of a whole cauliflower and break it up into large florets. Cut them in half or quarter them, according to size. Blanch the florets in boiling salted water with an added splash of white vinegar for 2 minutes before transferring them into an ice bath. Once the florets are cool, drain them and place them on a dishcloth or paper-towel-lined tray to drain off any excess water. In a sauce pan, melt 3 tablespoons of butter, whisk 3 tablespoons of flour into it before adding 1 ½ cups of milk. Cook for several minutes while stirring, until thickened. Season with salt, pepper and nutmeg. Add 1 cup of grated Gruyère and stir well. Once the sauce has cooled down a bit, add 2 egg yolks. Spread out the cauliflower florets in a butter baking dish, pour the sauce over them, scatter a little extra grated Gruyère on top and bake in a 375° F oven for about 15 minutes, until bubbly and golden brown (pass it under the broiler for an extra brown top).

SAUTÉED SWISS CHARD

Trim the stems of one large bunch of Swiss chard and, running a knife along the stems's sides towards the tip, cut off the leafy greens. Slice the leafy greens into wide strips, rinse them well and tumble them dry like salad leaves. Cut the stems into bite size pieces and rinse them well. In a sauté pan, melt 2 tablespoons of butter and add 2 chopped cloves of garlic. Add the drained stems once the garlic is fragrant and begins to soften. Cook the stems over medium heat until they are translucent and tender. Add the greens, stir, cover and cook for another minute. Season with salt, white pepper and nutmeg, add a splash of cream, bring to a quick simmer and serve.

VIII. SIMPLE EVERYDAY MEALS

GALETTE COMPLÈTE

In France, there are essentially two variants of pancakes: *crêpes*, made with milk and eggs, traditionally used for sweet fillings only, and *galettes*, made with nothing but buckwheat flour and water, for savory fillings. The most popular *galette* variation is called *complète* because its filling has virtually everything: ham, cheese, and an egg.

French buckwheat flour, called *blé noir*, is neither as grainy nor as dark as American buckwheat flour. Its flavor is also incomparably more subtle, possibly because it is milled from buckwheat groats that have been hulled. Making *galettes* with American buckwheat flour will therefore yield a coarser pancake. I have had satisfactory results by sifting the buckwheat flour through a fine mesh sieve to rid it of any coarse particles and blending it with some bread flour to mellow its rather assertive flavor.

Slowly stir 2 cups of cold water into ¾ cups of sifted buckwheat flour mixed with ¾ cups of unleavened bread flour. Add 1 teaspoon of salt and a pinch of white pepper. Let the dough rest for at least one hour, if not overnight. Heat a cast iron *crêpe* pan and brush it with some oil. Make a test *galette* first: ladle a scant half cup of dough into the hot pan and either spread it out with the special T-shaped wooden crêpe tool or quickly tilt the pan this and that way until the entire surface of the pan is covered with a thin, blistery layer of dough. If the dough is too thick, add more water to it. Once the dough has solidified, flip the *galette* and cook it for just a minute on the other side before flipping it once more. Crack open an egg and drop it directly onto the galette. Scatter a handful of shredded *Gruyère* over it. When the egg begins to set and the cheese begins to melt, add one thin slice of cooked ham over it and fold the galette into a trapezoid. Leave it in the hot pan for another few moments to make sure the egg white is set and serve. The yolk should still be runny.

CROQUE MONSIEUR ET CROQUE MADAME

Make a *béchamel* sauce: In a sauce pan, melt 2 tablespoons of butter, add 2 tablespoons of flour and whisk vigorously. Gradually add 1 ½ cups of milk, constantly whisking. Bring to a simmer, and cook it for a couple of minutes while stirring it with spatula, scraping the bottom to prevent the sauce from scorching. Season the *béchamel* assertively with salt, white pepper and a pinch of nutmeg, pour it into a bowl and set it aside to cool down. Cut off the crusts of an even number of slices of best quality white Pullman bread. Spread some cold *béchamel* onto half of them. Onto each of those slices, add 1 slice of Gruyère, cut to fit, a thin slice of the best quality cooked ham you can find, folded over to fit the bread, and a second slice of cheese. Spread a bit of Dijon mustard onto the remaining slices and assemble the sandwiches. Press them lightly and spread some softened butter onto their top. Melt a bit of butter in a frying pan and place the sandwiches into it, buttered side up. Brown them lightly on both sides, transfer them onto a parchment paper-lined sheet pan, top them with a bit of more *béchamel* and grated cheese and briefly place them under the broiler, just long enough until the topping is browned and bubbly. Served this way, this sandwich is called a *Croque Monsieur.*

A *Croque Madame* is the same warm sandwich but topped with a fried egg, sprinkled with flaky sea salt and coarsely ground black pepper.

QUICHE LORRAINE

This ancient savory tarte is the base for countless newfangled versions that rarely measure up to the original. The two most common mistakes are the use of puff pastry as a base and the addition of cheese, which is optional to some but heresy to purists. I have been known to occasionally commit this heresy.

To make a *pâte brisée*, pulse 1 ¼ cups of flour, 1 teaspoon of salt and 1 stick of cold butter, cut into pieces, in a food processor until the mixture resembles coarse-meal. Transfer it to a mixing bowl, scatter 3 tablespoons of ice-cold water over it, toss it lightly before swiftly pressing it into a ball, adding more water by the teaspoon if necessary but being careful to not overwork the dough: it should remain flaky and not become elastic. Flatten the ball into a thick disk, wrap it in cellophane or wax paper and chill it for at least 30 minutes. Roll it out ⅛ inch thin and line a greased and floured fluted tart pan with it, pinching off the excess. Lightly dust it with flour and place it in the freezer for 10 minutes while the oven is heating up to 350° F. Meanwhile cut ½ pound of smoked slab bacon into ½-inch cubes and gently panfry them. Do not let them go past a very light browning stage. Remove them from the pan with a slotted spoon and set them on a plate lined with several layers of paper towels. Cover the tart shell with an oversized round piece of parchment paper and scatter 2 cups of dried chickpeas over it to prevent the dough from rising. Par-bake the tart shell for 10 minutes, remove the paper and weights and bake it for another 5 minutes, until the crust is completely opaque but not browned. Break up 6 whole eggs and slowly stir 1 cup of cream into them. Do not beat the mixture; it must not be frothy. Season it with coarsely ground black pepper, nutmeg and very little salt, (the bacon is adding quite a bit of salt as is). Scatter the bacon cubes into the tart shell and pour the egg mixture over it. Bake the quiche for 30-40 minutes, until golden brown and set. It is best served warm. Prepare it at least once without cheese before deciding for yourself if breaking the rule and adding it is as good an idea as it appears to be.

IX. SALADS

ARTICHAUTS À LA VINAIGRETTE

Prepare one artichoke per person. Trim off each artichoke's stem so they can be placed upright on a plate. Loosen the petals of each artichoke a bit so they cook more evenly. Do not bother trimming the pointed tips of the petals as some cookbooks advise us to; it is superfluous practice. Cook artichokes in salted water aromatized with the juice and halves of one lemon until tender when pierced with a knife, 20 to 30 minutes. Removing the "choke," the tight inner layer of hay before serving the artichoke is a bit precious (we never did in our family) but will be appreciated by all: loosen up the layered leaves without detaching them and reach into the center of each artichoke with a spoon to scoop out the choke. Serve with little bowls of emulsified vinaigrette for dipping. To make the vinaigrette, whisk a tablespoon of Dijon mustard into a mix of lemon juice and white wine vinegar seasoned with salt, honey and finely ground white pepper. Continue whisking while gradually adding olive oil, two to three times the volume of the base. Some like adding crushed garlic.

This is a salad the mother of a school friend put together with durable pantry items on the evening we arrived back at the family's Versailles villa after an eventful two weeks I had spent with them as their guest in Mougins, near Cannes.

TUNA AND CORN SALAD

Hard-boil 8 eggs according to the instructions given in Chapter VI, in the recipe for *Assiette à la Broodthaers*. When they are cold enough to handle, peel the eggs and keep them submerged in cold water. In a mixing bowl, whisk 1 tablespoon of Dijon mustard, 3-4 tablespoons of red wine vinegar, salt and pepper and ¼ cup of sunflower seed oil until emulsified. Add 1 large can of drained sweet corn kernels, 1 can of drained, water-packed tuna, half a red onion, diced, and toss well. Garnish with the hard-boiled eggs, cut into quarters. My friend's mother served it with nothing but sliced baguette.

SALADE D'ENDIVE

Arrange the leaves of 4 endives in a floral pattern on a round platter. Scatter 2 diced pears, crumbled Roquefort cheese and walnut halves over them and drizzle everything with a light vinaigrette. Garnish with chopped parsley and serve.

RICE SALAD

Boil 1 ½ cups of long grains rice in a large pot of salted water until done and drain, running a bit of cold water over it to prevent it from cooking any further. Drain well and transfer into a large mixing bowl. Add 1 diced red bell pepper, 3 seeded and diced sun-ripened tomatoes, a few drained capers, a handful of raisins, some pitted and halved oil-cured Moroccan-style black olives, half a diced red onion, and some chopped French parsley. Dress with a mustard vinaigrette, toss well and macerate for at least one hour before serving.

CÉLERI RÉMOULADE

Cut a large celeriac in half and carve off the skin and any dark spots. Shred it by hand or with the help of a food processor. In a mixing bowl, add 1 tablespoon of Dijon mustard, 1 tablespoon of honey, 2 tablespoons of mayonnaise, ¼ cup of sour cream or yogurt, the juice of half a lemon, a good pinch of curry powder, and salt and pepper. Mix well and add the celeriac. Garnish with 1 Granny Smith apple, cut into thin julienne and tossed with the juice of half a lemon, and serve.

MÂCHE SALAD

Rinse mâche florets well and tumble them dry. Toss them with thinly sliced shallots, toasted pine nuts and halved red grapes.

Dress the salad with a light vinaigrette made with Champagne vinegar, salt, honey, coarse black pepper, and walnut oil.

MOROCCAN ORANGE SALAD

Carve the peel and pith off 4 oranges and cut the fruit crosswise into thick slices. Arrange them on a platter and drizzle them with 2 tablespoons of *Harissa* or *Sambal Oelek*, diluted with 2 tablespoons of white wine vinegar. Scatter a few red onion rings and pitted oil-cured Moroccan olives over them, sprinkle with chopped parsley and torn mint leaves.

X. DESSERTS

ÉCLAIRS

Bring ½ cup of water, ½ cup of milk, a generous pinch of salt and 4 tablespoons of butter to a boil. Add ¾ cup of flour all at once and vigorously work the flour into the liquid with a wooden spoon until a ball forms. Cook it for another minute while stirring and transfer it to the mixing bowl of a stand mixer with a paddle attachment. Mix on low speed for a couple of minutes until the dough does not release any more hot steam, then add 3 to 4 eggs, one at a time, beating the dough each time until the mass is homogenous and shiny. You may only need half of the fourth egg to get the right consistency – the paste must not be too soft lest it won't hold its shape. Fill the cooled dough into a pastry bag with a large round tip and pipe logs of about 6 inches onto parchment-paper lined baking sheets. Brush them lightly with one egg, beaten with a bit of water and a pinch of salt (use the leftover half egg if you have one). Bake them for 10 minutes at 400° F before lowering the oven temperature to 325° F and baking them for another 25 minutes, until they are completely dry and bronze-colored. Using a pastry tip, make two holes into their bottoms for later filling.

To make the classic *crème pâtissière* filling, gently heat 2 cups of milk, a pinch of salt, ¼ cup of sugar, the scraped seeds of one vanilla bean and the split bean pod in a sauce pan until simmering. Turn of the heat, cover and let it steep

* A Javanese, vinegar-based hot chili and garlic sauce.

for 10 minutes before removing the vanilla bean, scraping any loosened seeds into the milk (rinse and dry the bean pod and store it for another use such as flavoring a compote.) In a mixing bowl, lightly beat 4 egg yolks with ¼ cup of sugar, 2 tablespoons of flour and 3 tablespoons of cornstarch. Temper the egg mixture with a bit of the hot milk before adding it to the pot setting it over medium heat. Cook while constantly whisking until thickened and then for another two minutes, scraping the bottom to prevent it from burning. Pour the cream into a bowl and beat 2 tablespoons cold butter, one at a time, into it. To make coffee éclairs, sprinkle 1 tablespoon of gelatin powder over a double shot of cold espresso, wait for it to "bloom" and then add it to the warm cream, stirring until it has dissolved. Or use Grand Marnier or Cointreau or even Triple Sec or rum instead of the coffee. To make chocolate éclairs, substitute ¼ cup of dark chocolate chips or 2 ounces of dark chocolate for the butter in the pastry cream. For vanilla or chocolate éclairs, bloom the gelatin in 3 tablespoons of water. Pour the finished pastry cream into a pie dish, press a sheet of cellophane directly onto it and refrigerate it until cold. Once again, beat the cream vigorously to aerate it, then fill it into a pastry bag. Pipe it into the éclairs (via the poked holes on the bottom) and refrigerate them.

Dip the top of the stuffed éclairs into a glaze made of 2 cups of confectioner's sugar mixed with 2 tablespoons milk, 2 tablespoons of melted butter and either 1 tablespoon of Grand Marnier or rum or for vanilla éclairs, or 1 tablespoon espresso (or a few drops coffee essence) for coffee éclairs. For chocolate éclairs, it is best to use the very fine cooked chocolate glaze given in the recipe for *Prinzregententorte* in Chapter II.

This was the *dessert de rigueur* my mother served at large dinner parties. To the cook's relief, it tastes best when prepared one day ahead of time.

CHARLOTTE DIPLOMATE

In a sauce pan, gently heat 2 cups of red currant jelly until barely liquefied and just warm. Pour it over 2 cups of fresh raspberries. Stir and refrigerate immediately. Line the bottom of a classic charlotte mold or tall trifle bowl with ladyfingers dipped into a mix of dry white wine and Kirsch. Next, tightly line the walls of the mold with vertical rows of dipped ladyfingers, cutting some of them into triangles to create a completely enclosed wall. Spread a couple of tablespoons of the berry and jelly mix onto the bottom layer of ladyfingers and top this with a layer of dipped ladyfingers. Continue until your reach the very top of the mold, finishing with a layer of ladyfingers. Cover the charlotte with cellophane and press a flat plate onto it, weighing it down with something heavy to compress the charlotte. Refrigerate it for several hours or overnight. Invert it onto a platter and serve with a classic

CRÈME ANGLAISE

Scrape the seeds out of a split vanilla bean and, using your fingertips, work them into ½ cup of white sugar. Place the split bean into a saucepan, add a pinch of salt, 1 tablespoon of sugar, 1½ cups of milk and ½ cup of heavy cream. Gently bring the mix to a simmer. Fish out the vanilla bean and scrape any remaining seeds into the milk. Rinse and dry the bean pod halves and store them for another use. Beat the vanilla sugar with 8 egg yolks until a soft ribbon forms. Add 1 tablespoon of cornstarch and two tablespoons of cold milk. Slowly add a cup of the scalding hot milk and cream to the egg mixture, constantly stirring. Pour the mix back into the saucepan and heat it slowly while constantly stirring, scraping the bottom to prevent it from scorching. When it begins to simmer, cook it for just a few more seconds and pour it through a fine mesh sieve into a bowl. Place a paper towel (to absorb the steam) and a large plate over the bowl to prevent a skin from forming as it cools down (stir it now and then in the first half hour. Do not chill it until it has reached room temperature. When it is time to serve the dessert, spoon a bit of *crème anglaise* around the inverted charlotte and serve the rest of it in a bowl.

CHARLOTTE AUX POIRES

Following the same principle as for a *charlotte diplomate*, make a charlotte layered with ladyfingers, sliced canned pears and vanilla crème patissière, using the recipe given above for éclairs. Use the syrup of the canned pears to dip the ladyfingers into.

Serve inverted on a platter surrounded by a raspberry coulis, made by cooking 2 cups of fresh or frozen raspberries with 1 cup of raspberry jelly, ¼ cup of water and ¼ cup of sugar for 5 minutes before passing it through a sieve.

CHARLOTTE AU CHOCOLAT

A third version calls for filling a charlotte with *mousse au chocolat*, a recipe thereof can be found in Chapter IV. Dip the ladyfingers into strong cold coffee spiked with a splash or rum or orange liquor. Serve inverted as usual, with a *crème anglaise* as described above or garnished with whipped cream.

TARTE TATIN

It has of late become rather common to make this famous signature cake of the venerable sisters Tatin with puff pastry – largely out of the convenience of it being available ready-made in the frozen section of nearly every supermarket. Do not pay it any heed and make it the traditional way, with a *pâte brisée*, a simple short crust, using the recipe included in the instructions on how to make a quiche *lorraine*, further above.

Peel 5-7 large apples of a firm cooking variety like Crispin, Mutsu, Honeycrisp, or even Golden Delicious. Cutting vertically around the core, slice each apple into 3 sections. Sprinkle these with the juice of one lemon to prevent them from turning brown. Turn the oven to 400° F. Melt 3 tablespoons of butter in a cast iron skillet. Add 1 cup of sugar and tilt the pan until its surface is covered wit sugar. When it has melted and turns amber, add the apple sections, one at time, carefully arranging them in a tightly overlapping pattern. Cook the apples for about 20 minutes on medium high, shaking the skillet every now and then to prevent them from sticking to the bottom of the pan but careful to not disturb their alignment. Roll out the pastry dough into a round disc, slightly larger than the skillet. Roll it around the rolling pin and carefully unroll it over the apples, tucking in the overlap. Brush it with cream, sprinkle it with raw sugar, pierce the dough in several spots with a fork to let any steam escape and place the skillet into the hot oven. Bake the upside down *tarte* until the crust is golden brown, about 30 minutes. Let it rest for a few minutes before placing a

flat, round serving platter over the skillet and, holding the two firmly together, swiftly flip the *tarte* around to invert it onto the platter. Serving this *tarte* with vanilla ice cream would be overkill, but offering some mildly sweetened, whipped crème fraiche on the side would not be a crime.

TARTE AUX PRUNES
(French Plum Tart)

I had this tart every day during the extended summer vacation I once spent as the guest of a French family in Mougins. The grandmother who presided over every meal, served on a terrace overlooking a beautiful garden with a kidney-shaped pool and a fruit orchard, made the tart each morning, using the exquisite little round, peach-colered plums from her garden, known stateside as cherry plums and hard to find. *Mirabelles* or *Reines Claudes* (Greengage plums) would make a fine substitute if they were available. What distinguishes this tart from others is that the small round stone fruit is halved, pitted, and laid on the pastry shell skin-side up, resulting in pleasantly caramelized orbs of wrinkled skins with succulent, pleasantly tart fruit pulp beneath. For this tart, a *pâte sucrée crust*, similar to a *pâte brisée* but lightly sweetened and less flaky so as to hold its shape and not crumble under the oozing juices of the fruit, is best.

Swiftly work 1 stick of cold butter into 1 cup plus 2 tablespoons of flour mixed with 2 tablespoons of sugar and 4 tablespoons of ground almonds. When the mixture looks like coarse meal, add an egg yolk beaten with 2 tablespoons of cream and quickly work everything into a ball. Flatten it, wrap it in cellophane or wax paper and chill it for at least 30 minutes. Grease and flour a fluted tart pan, roll out the dough and line the pan with it. Pierce it in several parts with a fork and place it in the freezer for 20 minutes. Cut cherry plums, *Mirabelles* or *Reines Claudes* in half, remove the pits and align the fruit in circles on the tart shell, as tight as possible. Sprinkle with sugar and a few flakes of butter and bake in a 350° F oven for about 40 minutes or until the crust and fruit are lightly browned. I don't recall being served anything with it, nor do I recall feeling the need for anything else but a second or third piece, which I, being a guest of the house, regretfully never dared to ask for.

In lieu of the special European heirloom plums described above, a slightly altered version can be made in America with so-called "Italian plums" or prunes, really Damson plums, an eye-shaped variety that is in season on the East coast in the early fall. Or else, use common round plums.

PLUM TART

Proceed as above up to the short freezing of the dough-lined tart shell. For this variation, the crust must be "blind baked." To do this, dust it with flour, cover it with a round piece of parchment paper, large enough to stick up the sides, and weigh it down with 2 cups of dried chickpeas or pie weights. Bake at 350° F for about 12 minutes. Carefully remove the paper and pie weights. If the dough is still shiny, return it once more to the oven for a few minutes but not long enough for it to take on any color.

Cut Italian plums lengthwise into quarters and arrange them in the tart shell, skin side down, in an overlapping circular pattern. If using round plums, cut them in half, remove the small pit and cut the halves in slices as you would an apple. Bake the tart for 35 minutes before spooning a bit of heated and strained apricot jam mixed with a little bit of rum over the fruit and baking it for another 10 minutes, until the crust is golden brown and the juices bubbly. Serve at room temperature with whipped, barely sweetened heavy cream.

For an even more luscious version, line the par-baked pastry shell with a round piece of marzipan, rolled out between layers of wax paper or cellophane, before adding the plums.

Use any leftover scraps of pastry dough to make what I call

COOKIE BREAK

Assemble any pastry dough scraps into a ball, flatten it into a disc and roll it out. Transfer it as is onto a parchment paper-lined sheet pan, brush it with a lightly beaten egg or cream (or milk) and sprinkle it generously with raw sugar and a few anise or fennel seeds. Bake in a 350° F oven until golden brown, about 15-20 minutes, and break it into uneven pieces. Pile them onto a platter. No one passing by will resist them and they are usually gone long before dinner time.

CHOUQUETTES

These unassuming "little cabbages" are sold by the pound in every good French *pâtisserie*. They are delicious and intriguingly simple to make. In fact, they are the puff paste equivalent to the above-mentioned cookie break – an excellent way to use up surplus puff paste from an éclair project.

Fill puff paste, prepared according to directions in the recipe for éclairs, above, into a pastry bag and pipe little round mounds the size of walnuts onto a parchment -paper lined sheet pan. Brush them with egg wash and sprinkle them with sugar clusters. Bake them for 10 minutes at 400° F before lowering the oven temperature to 325° F and baking them for another 20 minutes, until they are bronze-colored. Filling them with cream would be a game changer but also spoil the notion that they are not much more than crust and air and that one can thus eat as many as one's heart desires.

FLAN PÂTISSIER

Pour 3 cups of milk and 1 cup of heavy cream into a sauce pan and add ½ cup of sugar, a pinch of salt, the scraped seeds of one split vanilla bean as well as the pod. Bring to a simmer over medium heat, take it off the flame, cover and steep for 10 minutes. In a mixing bowl, beat 4 egg yolks and 2 whole eggs with ½ cup of sugar to a soft ribbon before adding a scant cup of cornstarch. Remove the vanilla bean pod from the milk, scraping out its insides once more to get a maximum of seeds into the milk. Reheat it briefly before tempering the egg mixture with some of it and mixing it with the hot milk. Cook until thickened while constantly stirring. Press the custard through a fine mesh sieve into a mixing bowl, add a shot of spiced rum and stir until it is no longer steaming. Press a sheet of cellophane directly over the custard and refrigerate it until cold.

Butter a 9-inch spring form and line it, bottom and sides, with a sheet of store-bought puff pastry, pressing well on the sides and cutting off the excess. Pierce it all over with a fork and place it in the freezer for 30 minutes. Cover it with an oversize round piece of parchment paper and pour 3 cups of dried chickpeas or pie weights onto the parchment, lining them up against the sides lest the dough slides down during the par-baking. Bake the shell for 25 minutes in a 375° F oven. The crust should be no longer shiny but not browned yet. Once it has cooled down a bit, carefully remove the paper and beans (you can reuse them many times). Let the crust cool down before filling it.

Briefly stir the cold custard once more to homogenize it and pour it into the par-baked pastry shell. Smoothen its surface and bake it for 45 minutes at 375° F before briefly placing it under the broiler to brown its surface. Serve cold.

FAR BRETON

Scatter a splash of rum over a dozen pitted dried prunes and toss them well. Place 1 tablespoon butter into a rectangular glass or stoneware baking dish and place it in the oven. Turn the oven to 325° F. In a sauce pan, gently heat 1 quart of milk. In a mixing bowl, beat 6 eggs with 1 cup of sugar and 1 teaspoon of salt to a soft ribbon before incorporating, bit by bit, 2 cups of flour, stirring slowly. Pour the hot milk over the mixture while stirring. Remove the baking dish from the oven, spread the melted butter around with a pastry brush and pour the batter over it. Scatter the prunes over the dough, shave a couple of tablespoons of salted butter over it and bake the *far* for 90 minutes or until set and darkly caramelized.

CROISSANTS AUX AMANDES

This is a French classic that is still largely misunderstood in America, where a forceful eagerness to impress and succeed has turned this unpretentious and ingenious way to make use of stale croissants into something rather precious yet less satisfying than the original. Here is the way it is still done in France.

Make an almond cream by beating 2 sticks of softened butter with 1 ⅓ cups of sugar until fluffy before adding 2 ½ cups of ground almonds. Beating vigorously, add 5 eggs, on at a time. Incorporate a scant ½ cup of flour into the mix as well as ¼ cup of rum. Do not overwork the dough at this point or it will break. Take several stale croissants and cut them in half as you would a roll for a sandwich. Bring 2 cups of water, 1 cup of sugar and a splash of rum or Grand Marnier to a boil. Quickly dip the bottom halves of the croissants all the way into the hot syrup and line them up on a baking sheet lined with parchment paper. Spread some almond cream onto the bottoms and cover them with the tops equally dipped into the syrup. Spread an additional 2 tablespoons of almond cream over each piece, scatter some sliced almonds over them and bake them at 350° F for about 15 minutes or until golden brown. Dust with confectioner's sugar.

BABA AU RHUM

In the bowl of a stand mixer, combine ½ cup of warm milk, 2 eggs, the zest of 1 lemon and 1 orange, 4 tablespoons of fresh orange juice, 2 tablespoons of sugar and a pinch of salt. With the dough hook attached and the machine running on low speed, Gradually add 1 ⅔ cups of flour and let the machine work the dough until it is no longer sticky. With the machine still running, gradually add 4 tablespoons of softened butter and continue working the dough until it is shiny. Fill it into 6-8 buttered and floured popover molds – filling them halfway only. Cover them and let them rise until doubled in volume, about 30 minutes. Meanwhile, make the syrup. Pour 2 cups of water and 1 cup of sugar into a sauce pan, add several strips of lemon and orange peel, the scraped seeds and the split pod of 1 vanilla bean and 4 pieces of star anise. Bring the syrup to a simmer and cook it for 3 minutes. Cool it slightly before adding ½ cup of spiced rum. Bake the risen *babas* in a 350° F oven for 20-25 minutes until golden brown. Let them cool down completely before un-molding them and submerging them in the cooled syrup for one minute. Set them in a shallow bowl, ladle a bit more syrup over them and brush the tops with lightly warmed apricot, quince or rose jelly. Refrigerate until ready to serve.

CRÊPES AU CHOCOLAT

Pour 2 cups of flour and a good pinch of salt into a mixing bowl, add 3 eggs into the center and gradually incorporate them into the flour. Still stirring, gradually add 2 cups of milk to the flour and egg base. Stir until homogenous but do not overwork the dough. Add more milk if the dough is not liquid enough to pour. If the dough is lumpy, pass it through a fine-mesh sieve. Add 2 tablespoons of melted butter and let the dough rest in the refrigerator for at last 30 minutes. Heat a non-stick *crêpe* pan and pour just enough dough into it to cover its surface as you tilt the pan every which way. Cook it over medium high heat until lightly browned before flipping it and cooking it for just a few seconds on the other side before flipping it once more. Lower the heat and place 1 ½ tablespoons of softened salted butter on the *crêpe*, spreading it around with a spatula as it melts. Dust it with a heaped tablespoon of instant chocolate powder – it will melt into the butter and form a chocolate sauce. Sprinkle a bit of flaky seas salt over the chocolate, fold the *crêpe* over twice and serve immediately.

For an even richer version, spread a mashed ripe banana over the chocolate sauce before folding the crêpe over.

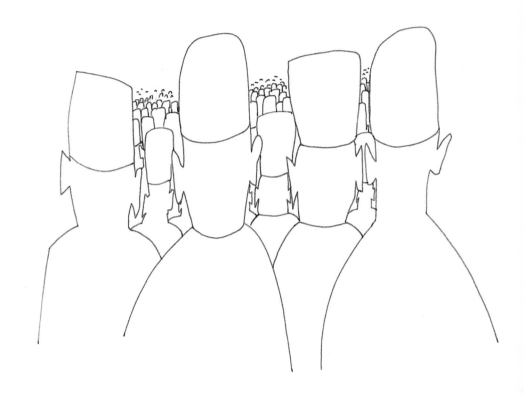

X
SERVING AND BEING
SERVED IN
NEW YORK CITY

CERTAINLY, I HAVE SERVED MANY more meals than I have been served. Certainly, of those I was served, too many were unsatisfactory, and those I served myself are too numerous to recall. My experience of both serving and being served in New York date from 1992 and during these twenty-five years the entire culinary world of New York and America has changed radically. My participation in this development was marginal, even if I was in many ways ahead of the curve – that is, without being aware of it. But my early experiences in the restaurant and the catering world both as an insider and outsider are perhaps not uninteresting.

The first restaurant I went to in New York City during my first visit in 1992 was a pleasant experience. A friend took *me* to a small, sunny and cheerful Italian restaurant in Brooklyn Heights, where I ate my first Caesar salad. When I moved here just a few months later, I had to find a way to make a living. When I asked fellow students at my dance school how one went about finding work, they told me that it was easiest and most convenient to wait tables, and the important thing to tell the hiring manager was that I was experienced. I inquired about work in a café that had just opened a few blocks from my home, a furnished sublet on the Upper West Side I had completely redecorated to my taste before doing anything else. The café was owned by an Israeli businessman who had made his fortune in the garment industry and become enamored with the idea of opening a café in the old European tradition. It would therefore be a pleasant place to work in, or so I assumed. So I was hired. I started working the next day and the owner, proud and smiling, assured me that the cakes that I would be serving were of excellent quality. When I inspected them closer I must have looked suspicious, and he sheepishly confessed that none of them were homemade but instead came from an industrial bakery that supplied virtually every café restaurant in New York City in those days. He was not as embarrassed as I was indignant. If the cakes weren't homemade surely the kitchen would at least know how to provide a good meal. The first meal I had there was inedible – commencing with the salad. Obviously the chef in charge had not the slightest instinct for cooking. I wondered if perhaps I should not rather propose to become their chef but after peeking into the kitchen and seeing the state she was in, and learning how little chefs earned in this country, I immediately dismissed the thought.

Shortly after I began working at the café, the owner arranged for his nephew to act as the café's manager. The young man had just absolved his military service in Israel and was anxious, inexperienced and without any clue about how to run a restaurant. It was touching to witness how he tried to make up for his ignorance. He had a misplaced sense of urgency and was always getting very much involved with everything that went on in the dining room albeit without ever being effective or helpful. I remember very well one of his blunders: one of my customers had ordered a pasta dish with shrimp and the chef had then admitted to me that he had forgotten to tell me that he had run out of shrimp. The nephew, overhearing our conversation, jumped up and, to both our surprise, announced heroically that he was going to go get some and stormed out of the restaurant before we could say anything. Unmoved, I politely asked the customer to order something else, which he did. When the manager returned 20 minutes later, out of breath and triumphantly handing me a little tin can of baby shrimp preserved in water, I explained that the problem had long been solved. At this, he all but lost his temper. Do you know, he exclaimed, how far I had to run to find this and how much I had to pay for it. The other waiters and I concluded that as a manager he was utterly dispensable.

I had not planned to work at the café for very long but ended up staying there for almost a year. Perhaps it was out of convenience. One day I thanked the owner and said I was moving on to something else. It was a blow to them. I had been a popular waiter and reliable employee, and a cheerful presence in their chaotic establishment, which closed not long after I left.

An acquaintance from dance school told me that I ought to apply with a big catering company that was hiring new waitstaff for the busy holiday season. Restaurant Associates was a very large catering company, with all the typical characteristics and limitations. The company was very corporate, ambitious and rigid, and the food was generally unimaginative, either perfunctory or simply disappointing. I suffered from the carelessness with which it was frequently handled. The company had exclusive catering accounts in most of the city's major museums and concert venues. Despite there always being a surplus of banquet food the staff had to content itself with inedible staff meals and stoically watch as the banquets' leftovers were haphazardly thrown into the garbage, which ultimately convinced me to once more look for a better employer. A fellow waiter told me that in any case there were many other caterers I could apply to work for, having already purchased the prerequisite cater waiter's uniform – a tuxedo, white button-down shirt, black tie and sensible black shoes. I was delighted, as I had considered going back to restaurant work. He told me that he would be happy to make an introduction with Glorious Food if I was interested. With more grins and winks he said he was rather sure I would be hired, being young and handsome – at twenty-three such things had to be taken advantage of. To thank him, a cocked eyebrow and pursed lips were suitable.

Little by little, as I settled into my new life, I began to explore the city's better restaurants whose threshold I had previously not dared to cross. It was my slightly raised income from catering that afforded me this opportunity. I could not help noticing all around a strange service system that left me wondering about its sense and sensibility. Surely more could be accomplished with better training and more grace than I was obliged to observe. First, one was shown to one's table by a hostess who oddly was also the one handing you the menu. This seemed her only task for the evening, a rare feat. It was accomplished with such little decorum that it made me wonder why it was necessary to put someone in charge of it in the first place. Invariably, there was little grace involved in the next steps as well. Someone who was usually ignorant of the English language would hurriedly fill one's glass with water without prompting and someone else would slam a basket of bread on the table. Eventually a waiter with a very earnest demeanor would introduce himself by name, advertise the ordering of pre-dinner cocktails, announce the daily specials and return just a minute later to take one's order. Sometimes a sommelier would come to discuss a suitable wine. The waiter would bring the drinks but not the food, which was brought by yet another server. Eating at one's leisure would be all but impossible: as soon as one would put one's fork down, the plate would to my horror be whisked away by yet another server, even if other people at the table were still eating. Throughout all this, someone or other would repeatedly stop by the table and hurriedly ask, How is everything. In other words, the intrusions never ceased. The check would arrive sometimes without prompting, and after the horror of realizing that the tax was not included in the prices on the menu one had to do the math to figure out the proper amount for tipping the waiter even if one had seen less of him than of the multitude of others involved in the service. By the time one left, one felt more exhausted than one might if one had prepared the meal oneself.

New York was at the time still a culinary backwater. Whenever I followed up on a good restaurant review and went to dine at the establishment, I could not help remarking that evidently everything tastes good on paper and that focusing on restaurants and their ups and downs to a high degree was a bore. I believed then and now that what mattered was that everyone should first learn the basics of home cooking. How,

I wondered, could so many people accept such low standards on a daily basis while agreeing to pay such inflated prices for it. I supposed that most people simply had no references since they had grown up eating processed food. When I asked anyone what kind of food they had been eating growing up, the common answer was, TV dinners. Generally, there was at the time little interest in learning more about food preparation. It would have been considered precious. Anyone who was neither a professional chef nor a housewife simply did not cook. All this changed during the course of the Nineties, when the Food Network turned cooking into entertainment for the broad masses. It was a mixed blessing, bringing a great amount of energy to the field, most of it veering into the wrong direction of combative competition and aggressive entrepreneurialism.

However good food could be found – the word foodie had not been coined yet – in Chinese, Japanese, Indian, Middle Eastern and Latin American specialty stores and markets, and of course restaurants that served such cuisines. Eating at those places was, in those years before the internet facilitated and trivialized research, the only way to figure out how to possibly use indigenous ingredients I had never seen, much less tasted. In short it was an adventure, and what it lacked in decorum it made up in flavors, textures and combinations that never ceased to puzzle me. Some of them took some getting used to. Cilantro and Sichuan peppercorns in particular, at first tasting, were flavors I was so puzzled by that I did not know what to think of them. Not until a day or so later did it occur to me that I had actually liked them and that I could not wait to experiment with them in my own kitchen.

A friend recommended a Chinese Cuban restaurant that had become an Upper West Side institution. It was suitably affordable and somewhat similar to a restaurant in Chelsea I had been taken to during my first visit to New York, a year earlier, when I was still going through a vegetarian phase for reasons that shall not be explained in these pages. I had been advised to order yellow rice with black beans and when it was brought to the table I had been horrified, simply horrified, by the look of it. However I found the combination to be winsome, even if the place could not be called clean by any standard and the service was rather brusque. It was in fact so brusque as to be amusing. One quickly learned to adjust.

Everybody was excited about the farmer's market on Union Square. I remained more impressed with the food markets of Chinatown, Koreatown and the Lower East Side. I found them to be much more interesting since they were carrying things I had never seen or cooked with before. Once on Union Square I was offered a taste of artisanal cheese from Wisconsin. Soon, the cheese monger explained proudly, our cheeses will be better than those French ones. To be casual I said, perhaps in a few centuries. But, he said, you will never find such great Cheddar in France.

When I commenced to work for Glorious Food, I was asked to take part in a training session where all new applicants were shown how to properly set a table and do what was confusingly referred to as "French service" and what in France is called *service à l'anglaise*. When I got home after the training I felt confident that I would enjoy working for the company. Their owner, Sean Driscoll, had style and grace and a sense of humor. I freelanced for his company for several years.

It was through the catering world that I witnessed a side of New York City that was closer to what one imagined the city to be than what it really was. In other words, the catering world dealt in illusions. It did not take too long to see through it all because one was by definition part of the illusion and had to learn its inner workings. Once, when I was still working for Restaurant Associates, I was sent to help out at a cocktail reception on the top floor of the Sony Building. Seeing the nightly view of Manhattan's skyline for the first time from high above, I could not help feeling that I had arrived somewhere. It was then that the "captain" (that is what headwaiters are called in the catering industry) took me very firmly by the arm and led me into a corner where he explained that the view was for guests only.

In addition to Glorious Food, I also signed up with Feast and Fêtes, the catering company of Daniel Boulud, the famous French chef. Hard-working and driven, his boundless energy and ambition would have been frightening had it not been for the permanent twinkle of mischief in his sharp eyes. With his short and agile body he would march through his kitchen with the authority and furrowed brows of a war general. In his brusque way, he questioned his French sous-chefs and always made last minute changes that threw them into a loop. Putting my French to use, I always offered to help. More charmed than annoyed, they let me. Many of them had come to New York for a non-paid *stage* and were constantly overworked and homesick or upset about being in New York yet never getting to see any of it. I asked them many questions, and one very popular hors d'oeuvre they told me how to make was

SALSIFY CRISPS

Peel several fresh salsify and immediately submerge them in ice water acidulated with the juice of half a lemon to prevent them from blackening. Drop the peeled salsify into a pot of boiling, salted water seasoned with the juice of the other lemon half and cook them until they are knife-tender, for about 7 minutes. Transfer them to a bowl with ice water. Drain and pad them dry and wrap each root into a thin slice of Prosciutto. For each root, brush a leaf of store-bought phyllo pastry with melted butter and sprinkle it with a tablespoon of finely ground Parmesan before rolling it tightly around it. Place the rolls seam-side down on a parchment-paper-lined sheet pan, brush them once more with butter and bake them in a 400° F oven until crisp and golden, about 5 minutes. Slice them into 1-inch pieces and serve them warm. When salsify are not in season, white or even green asparagus can be substituted.

They were delicate and tasty and made evident Daniel Boulud's talent. Almost everything coming out of Feast and Fêtes's kitchen was exceptionally good. As the company offered me a good amount of work, I got to taste every single dish from its repertoire. I learned a lot simply from watching the chefs at work. The company certainly had luck in hiring well-trained chefs, though it had weaknesses in other ways. I realized that if the food had not been as good as it was, I would have never considered working for them. One of the most requested main courses from the company's repertoire was

ROASTED RACK OF LAMB

Trim off most of the fat of one or several racks of lamb, carving out the fat and meat in between the rib bones and removing the thick flab of fat covering the tenderloin. Rub the meat with olive oil and season it with salt and black pepper. Mash several cloves of garlic and add finely chopped fresh thyme, rosemary, some lemon juice and olive oil to make a thick paste. Sear the racks on all sides until lightly browned, brush them with the paste and roast them in a 425° F oven for 10 to 15 minutes, until medium rare. Cover them with aluminum foil and wait 5 minutes before cutting the racks into individual chops, slicing through the rib joints. Serve with

DEMIGLACE

Nothing will improve a meat course as much as a real demiglace. The traditional method, made with veal bones, is all but impractical to make at home but I developed my own, simplified and flexible version that suits any roasted meats. As a matter of fact, I have been known to serve it even with seared tuna filets, with much success. I have become so fond of it I resolved to simply call it *Liquid Gold.*

Coat 3 pounds of chicken backs, necks or cut-up wings and 4-6 halved shallots (with their skins) with a couple tablespoons of grape-seed oil, scatter everything on a parchment paper-lined sheet pan and roast it in a 400° F oven until dark golden brown, about 25 minutes. Meanwhile, fill a large stock pot with water and bring it to a simmer. Slide the browned chicken parts and shallots into it, along with the parchment paper. Submerge the parchment paper in the water until any brown bits stuck to it have dissolved into the water. Remove the paper, invert a small plate into the pot to keep the chicken parts fully submerged and simmer the stock over a low flame for one hour, skimming off any fat. Remove the plate and add two handfuls of loosely cut up vegetables – peeled carrots, celery stalks, fennel bulb, yellow onion, as well as few aromatics of your choice – bay leaf, cinnamon stick, pepper corns, star anise – tied into a piece of cheese cloth or a teabag. Once again lower an inverted plate (clean) into the pot to keep all solids submerged in the water and simmer the stock for another hour, skimming of any foam. Don't ever let it ever come to a rolling boil. Add water if necessary to keep all solids submerged. Strain the liquid through a fine mesh sieve into a bowl, discard all solids and let the stock cool down to room temperature. Pour it back it into the cleaned stockpot and add 1 bottle of simple Merlot or Cabernet Sauvignon and 6 lightly beaten egg whites with their crushed egg shells, whisking briefly to combine. Slowly bring the stock to a simmer. Do not touch it and never let it come to a rolling boil. When the egg white has solidified to a floating raft, skim out most of it with a strainer before gently pouring the clarified liquid through a sieve lined with a damp *mousseline* cloth or a paper towel – never a cheese cloth – into a large sauce pan. Bring it to a simmer and reduce it to the consistency of a thin syrup. Season it with salt and, just before serving it, whisk cold butter, one tablespoon at a time and no more than 2 tablespoons per cup of demiglace, into it, until emulsified.

The less enjoyable part of working for the company was that it was so disorganized and that Jean-Christophe, the cofounder and director of operations, always tried to cut back on costs by not renting as much equipment as needed for a smooth event. This meant that the wait staff had to always compensate and work under less than favorable conditions, and all of that merely for the sake of marginally cutting down on expenses. He continued to run the company successfully but not without the staff having to continuously make up for his shortcomings. To make light of it, we used to among ourselves refer to him as Jean Pissed-Off.

After three years had passed, I began to fear that catering might become a permanency. I gave myself another year to find a way out of it. It must be acknowledged that the perks that come with the territory are addictive to some who get stuck in the seductive loop of working in temporary festive setups that give one the illusion of participating in a glamorous lifestyle.

During that time, I graciously agreed to occasionally work for Nancy, a resourceful single mother who ran her small catering company out of a rather run-down building in Dumbo in Brooklyn. This was long before the neighborhood became a gentrified hub for trust fund babies and well-heeled millennials. I was at first uncertain if she was not a little mad, and she was equally certain that I could be convinced to work for her full-time as a manager. Nancy was cheerful and had the smile of a flower maiden. She dressed smartly and was a survivor. At the end of our first meeting, I agreed to observe her business for a week to figure out what I could possibly do for her. It was then that she told me that I should, if it suited me, come along as she made the rounds inside an office building in midtown where she peddled lunch boxes prepared in her kitchen. In a flash her despair and some of her resolve became apparent. She did not have enough clients. I did join her on one of these trips and helped her sell her little plastic containers of soup and wrapped sandwiches, saw the slightly embarrassed expressions on the secretaries' faces, the indignant looks of the security staff in the lobby and the nervous flicker in her own eyes as she fidgeted with bills and coins to give back the exact change. On the way over the Brooklyn Bridge, driving in her rusty mini van, we were stopped by a patrol car. The cop asked her if she didn't know that commercial traffic was not allowed on the bridge. She was very engaging and in her charming way managed to dissuade him from giving her a ticket. It was uncanny, and impressively so. It was impossible to not marvel at her insistently positive attitude.

I was becoming acquainted simultaneously with Nancy and her food. *Show me what you cook and I'll tell you who you are.* She was the first I ever saw make pita chips. She was frugal by necessity and her menus were exactly what her clients asked for. When she was hired to prepare a banquet for the headquarters of a Scottish bank she served *haggis*, and they were satisfied. They were even more pleased, as well they should, when she served them a Scottish dessert known as

RASPBERRY CRANACHAN

Spread out 1 cup of rolled oats on a parchment paper-lined sheet pan, spray them with an oil spray and sprinkle 2 tablespoons of raw sugar over them. Toast them in a 350° F oven until light golden and crisp. Stir 1 cup of *fromage blanc* or farmer's cheese with 4 tablespoons of whisky and ¼ cup of honey until smooth. Whip 2 cups of cream to a soft peak and fold it into the farmer's cheese. Fold in the oats. Alternating layers, fill the mixture and 1 quart of fresh raspberries into individual serving glasses. Garnish each serving with a mint leaf, dipped into whisky and sugar.

It remains one of the most old-fashioned desserts I have ever tasted. But could it make me forget my horror of *haggis*?

I was commencing to feel that working for Nancy was possibly more precarious than the acquired taste of sheep offal. I didn't know if I could handle it. When the banquet for the Scottish bank was over, she asked me to accompany her two kitchen assistants and the headwaiter as they drove the mini van back to Dumbo. It was late when we pulled up to the building. The two assistants, strangely embarrassed, asked me to please enter the building ahead of them, they were too afraid of the rats. Just as I unlocked the door, I heard hurried scuttling noises. Of the three of us, the only one who had the presence of mind of finding the light switch was the headwaiter. He marched into the kitchen with the equipment and told the assistants to store the perishables in the refrigerator and he would explain all. It was a bare and plausible story.

Ten years ago Nancy had worked as a line cook at an elegant French restaurant. It was at that time that the French chef had his first fully automatic ice cream maker installed in the restaurant's kitchen. He was evidently very excited about it and kept trying out new flavors, once asking her to taste it right out of his hand. It is not that he wasn't well behaved, to him there was nothing unusual or disorderly about eating ice cream right out of one's hand. A year later she got pregnant and, not being able to work the usual long restaurant hours as a single mother, had to reorient herself. She rented the little house in Dumbo that had once belonged to a manufacturer of pickles and jams and started a small catering business.

She did not find many clients then and commenced selling lunch boxes to office workers. After several years of this she had no money to properly maintain the building or pay an exterminator. Always at night, her kitchen would be invaded by vermin that came through the many holes in the walls and floors.

I told the headwaiter that I liked Nancy, as we had been speaking of her, but that I would not return to work for her. The next day I called her and explained that I had decided against accepting her offer. Nothing was said on either side of the decrepit building in Dumbo or her sad lunch sales expeditions. We parted ways in the most amiable fashion. I went back to working for less troubled, more established caterers. But to this day I sometimes prepare my own version of Nancy's

PITA CHIPS

Take 6 round, pocket-style pita and warm them up in a 350° F oven for just a few minutes. This makes splitting them easier. Cut them in half, split them open, cut each split half into 3 segments and transfer them into a large mixing bowl. In a cup, dissolve a teaspoon of salt in ½ cup of warm water. Whisk ¼ cup of olive oil into the water and sprinkle the mixture over the pita wedges, tossing them lightly until coated. In a mortar, pound ½ cup of dried Greek oregano into a fine powder and sprinkle it over the wedges. Spread them out on a parchment paper-lined sheet pan and bake them at 400° F until they are crisp and lightly browned, about 8 minutes. I like to serve these with

TAHINI DIP

In a small sauce pan, fry 4 lightly crushed, peeled garlic cloves in ¼ cup of olive oil until lightly browned. Tip the pan to fully submerge the garlic in oil and prevent it from burning. Add a teaspoon of chili flakes, immediately take the pan off the fire and submerge its bottom in cold water to lower the oil temperature and prevent the chili flakes from burning. Pour 1 cup scalding hot water into a blender, add 1 cup of tahini, the grated zest and juice of 1 lemon plus salt to taste and process until creamy. Add more water if it seems too thick. With the machine running, add the oil and garlic and blend until emulsified. Transfer it to a serving bowl, drizzle a bit of olive oil over it and dust it with paprika powder.

Once, I found myself working at a very large and sumptuous holiday party that took over most of the Public Library on 42nd Street. With so many guests and so many waiters wearing tuxedos, it was all but impossible to tell who was who. After a few hours, it became pretty apparent to myself and a friendly co-worker that the party was pretty much running well all by itself and that our presence was more or less superfluous. We decided to take a break from serving drinks on the ground floor and retreated to the second floor, where we enjoyed a chat amidst the crowd, pretending to be guests and to no one's surprise or objection sipping Champagne. We had a lovely time, blending in perfectly with the other guests, and did not get caught.

The dessert buffet set up on the third floor was very opulent. The pastry chefs, exhausted but proud, said they had prepared over fifty different kinds of cakes, tarts, tortes, cakes, mousses in porcelain cups and assorted *mignardises* and cookies, but the guests were at this point more interested in dancing, drinking and smoking. Here is one example of the many desserts that were left untouched all evening and that the pastry chef encouraged me to take home:

PEAR AND CARAMEL TART

Peel, quarter and core 3 pears, simmer them until tender in a syrup made of 2 cups of water, ½ cup of sugar and 1 vanilla bean, seeds scraped out and reserved. Lift the pear quarters out of the syrup and transfer them to a colander to drain and cool, reserving the poaching liquid.

In a food processor, pulse 1¼ cups of flour, ¼ cup of cocoa powder, ¼ cup of confectioner's sugar, a pinch each of salt and ground clove with 1 cut-up stick of cold butter into coarse meal. With the machine running, add 1 egg yolk beaten with 3 tablespoons of cream and process until the dough comes together in a ball. Flatten it into a disc, wrap it in cellophane and refrigerate if for an hour before rolling it out on a floured surface and lining a buttered and floured fluted tart shell with it. Dust it with flour and place it in the freezer for 15 minutes. Press an oversize round piece of parchment paper over it, spread 1 cup of baking weights or dried chickpeas onto it and bake it in a 325° F oven for 15 minutes. Remove the paper and weights and bake the tart shell for another 5 minutes, until it is completely done.

"Catering is a seductive loop of working in temporary festive setups that give one the illusion of participating in a glamorous lifestyle."

Strain the poaching liquid, add the reserved vanilla seeds and simmer it until reduced to half s cup. Add 1 ½ cups of heavy cream, heat the mixture gently, and lower 3 tea bags of Earl Grey tea into it. Steep for 5 minutes before removing the tea bags, squeezing all liquid from them into the cream. Bring it once again to a simmer. Beat 4 egg yolks with 2 tablespoons of cornstarch, temper the mixture with some of the hot cream before adding it to the pot. Cook it gently over low heat until it covers the back of a wooden spoon. Add one package of powdered flavorless gelatin, bloomed in 2 tablespoons of cold water or pear liquor. Stir the custard until it is no longer steaming hot.

Line the bottom of the cooled tart shell with a thin layer of marzipan, rolled out between sheets of cellophane. Cut the pears into wedges and arrange them on the marzipan. Gently pour the custard over it. The pears should be completely covered. Refrigerate the tart for several hours.

In a sauce pan, bring 1 cup of heavy cream, 1 cup of brown sugar and the reserved vanilla seeds to a boil and simmer it until reduced to a thick syrup. Transfer to a bowl and stir by hand until it is no longer hot before carefully glazing the tart with it, finishing it with a touch of flaky sea salt. This dessert is even better than it looks.

This was another and equally delicious dessert no one touched that evening and that I had too much of:

GRAND MARNIER SOUFFLÉ

In a sauce pan, heat 2 cups of milk with a pinch of salt, ½ cup of sugar and the scraped seeds and split pod of one vanilla bean. Beat 4 egg yolks with ½ cup of flour and 2 tablespoons of cornstarch until smooth. Remove the bean pod from the milk, temper the yolks with a bit of the hot milk before adding them to the pot. Cook while stirring until thickened. Take the pot off the stove. Whisk 4 egg whites to a firm peak while gradually adding ¾ cups of sugar. Continue beating until stiff and shiny. Whisk ¼ cup of Grand Marnier into the hot pastry cream. Stir until no longer steaming hot, then fold in the egg whites, one third of their mass at a time. Butter the bottom and sides of 12 individual soufflé dishes and dust them with sugar. Fill the dishes to two thirds with the mixture, flatten their tops and bake them at 475° F for about about 8 minutes, until risen and lightly browned. Dust them with confectioner's sugar and serve them immediately with a raspberry sauce, a recipe for which can be found in Chapter IX. It may not look perfect each time but it will always taste good.

Here is one of the many classic French desserts that were almost always included in dessert buffets:

CRÈME BRULÉE

Split a vanilla bean lengthwise, scrape out the seeds and rub them into ¼ cup of sugar. Stir it into 5 large, lightly beaten egg yolks. Do not beat any air into them. In a saucepan, bring 1 cup of heavy cream and ½ cup of milk to a simmer with a strip of lemon peel, a strip of orange peel and maybe 2 pieces of star anise. Temper the yolks with a bit of the hot liquid before pouring the rest of it over them, stirring gently. Strain the mixture through a fine mesh sieve and pour it into 4 ramekins, placed in a baking dish filled halfway with hot water. Cover them loosely with foil and them bake in a 325° F oven until barely set, about 30 minutes. Cool them completely before covering each of them with a heaped tablespoon of caster sugar. Spread out the sugar with the back of a spoon for an even layer and use a blow torch to caramelize the sugar. Alternately, place the ramekins under the broiler until the sugar has caramelized into a crackly layer.

And one more classic dessert recipe, for

APPLE CHARLOTTE

Marinate ½ cup of dark raisins with a splash of rum for at least 10 minutes. Peel and core 5 Golden Delicious apples, cut them up into eights and sauté them in a skillet with 3 tablespoons butter and 3 tablespoons sugar until wilted and lightly browned. Add the raisins, a pinch each of cinnamon and ground allspice, the juice and grated zest of 1 lemon and 3 tablespoons of orange jam. Line the bottom and sides of a buttered charlotte mold with parchment paper. Brush 8 slices of brioche, crusts removed, with melted butter and line the bottom and sides of the charlotte mold with them, trimming the slices as necessary. Fill the cooled apple mixture into the mold, cover it completely with one layer of buttered brioche slices and press on it lightly to condense it. Cover with foil, transfer to a baking dish filled halfway with hot water and bake in a 350° F oven for about one hour, until the apples are softened and caramel-colored. Remove the foil and bake the charlotte for another 5 minutes, until the top is golden brown and crusty. Place a plate into the mold add a weight to compress the *charlotte*. Refrigerate for a couple of hours and gently reheat it before serving. Trim off the crusts if necessary and invert the charlotte onto a round platter. Serve topped with *crème anglaise* or, as I remember serving once at the Met Costume Ball catered by Glorious Food,

CANDY CANE STICK ICE CREAM

Place 6 mint candy sticks into a ziplock bag and coarsely crush them with a meat tenderizer or rolling pin. In a saucepan, bring 2 cups of half and half to a simmer. Temper 6 egg yolks, lightly beaten with ½ cup of sugar, with some of the hot liquid before adding them to the pot. Add 1 tablespoon of the candy cane powder and cook over a low flame while continuously stirring until it covers the back of a wooden spoon. Strain the cream and chill completely. Churn it in an ice cream maker until it has the consistency of soft serve ice cream. Swiftly fold in the rest of the candy cane powder, transfer into pre-chilled containers and store in the freezer.

The presence of countless celebrities at the Met Costume Ball at the Metropolitan Museum was entertaining. Then the inevitable occurred. Madonna appeared. When she made her entrance, the room began to spin out of control. For the entire evening her name was on everybody's lips. News of her being there spread even into the kitchen and the chefs were desperate to catch a glimpse of her. For the rest of the evening, everybody and everyone went out of his or her way to pass by her table. She seemed to be quite aware and unconcerned that this should be so. I felt as if I had been locked into a beehive with everyone circling around the queen in a mad dance.

After this rather disturbing experience no event no matter how spectacular or who happened to be in attendance fazed me. Experience taught me that it was all a show, and it was repetitive. Then, one hot day in late July, I was booked to work at a very large children's event at the Central Park Zoo. On my arrival at noon I was told that there would be several food stations serving peanut butter and jelly sandwiches, hot dogs, mini hamburgers, cotton candy, ice cream, and chocolate chip cookies and all other sorts of junk food and would I please beware of the many clowns, acrobats and all sorts of animators that would provide the entertainment. By the time the five hundred children arrived, my tuxedo was soaked in sweat from setting up tables and carrying trays of food. Our request to be permitted to work without a jacket was met with indifference. Later when the screaming and yelling of the overexcited children was made all the more oppressive by the resigned silence of their nannies as the event wore on longer than expected, I felt a surge of anger that for a moment completely transformed me. I became a madly deranged person and felt I had no choice but to either aggressively start to throw things or leave at once. I was saved by a song the disc jockey put on in that instant: Frank Sinatra's classic recording of *The Summer Wind*. Hearing the music, I was miraculously able to calm down.

The reasons I did not wish to work as a waiter any longer, confirmed by the view of those who'd been at it forever, were manifold. It was a lifestyle that gave one the false sense of having a life when it was but an illusion of one party after another that never amounted to anything other than having to do the clean up next. One got to eat good food, but it wasn't satisfying. I was booked a lot but that did not flatter me, it bored me. One booker demanded priority over all other bookers. I could not agree to let her have that. One late fall I decided to go visit my family in Germany. I had not been there in a while. One week before my departure the booker called and asked me to work for an important client on Thanksgiving. She said only the best waiters would do and that it would pay double. It was necessary to make clear to her that I was not going to cancel my trip, not even for her. She hung up on me and called back a minute later in tears, sobbing that it was a cruel thing to do to her. She was not used to waiters turning down offers for jobs that paid twice the usual amount. I went to Germany.

One season I put it in my head that I could start my own cookie company, making and selling the kind of cookies I knew from my childhood and the likes of which could not be found anywhere in New York. It was a rather laborious and uneconomical undertaking to bake, fill, decoratively package and hand-deliver the little gift boxes filled with eight varieties of *Plätzchen*, as they are called in Germany. It took a while for me to understand that if I ever wanted to make a profit, I would have to hire and underpay others to do the labor for me. After three months of tirelessly doing everything on my own, I told myself that I was just not a capitalist, that I had not moved to New York City to become a manufacturer or entrepreneur and that it was time to stop this nonsense, which I did.

Then Rosalie, a resolute woman from Louisiana who ran a little catering company out of her apartment in Prospect Park inquired about me. I told her that I was not interested in working as a waiter any longer, and she proposed to hire me as her kitchen assistant. The wage was just a little lower than a waiter's wage and she was very pleased with my work. She was entirely self-trained and very proud of her decorating skills for wedding cakes. I was amused by her ingenious idea to stuff large quantities of washed spinach or lettuce leaves into a pillow case with a zipper before placing it into her washing machine that she would then turn on to the spinning cycle. It was a very convenient and efficient way to tumble dry any large quantities of leafy greens. I was less pleased with her insistence of using commercial cake mixes for her tiered wedding cakes. These, she said, produced the most reliable results. In any case, she added, chuckling, no one could tell the difference and everyone was always pleased with her cakes. It had come to her being pleased with her food if the clients were pleased. She was not versed in classical cuisine and her style of food was old-fashioned American cookery, so I was not surprised when one of her most requested hors d'oeuvres was

PECAN-CRUSTED CHICKEN SKEWERS

In a food processor, pulse a chunk of softened mild blue cheese with about the same amount of sour cream until smooth. Transfer into a mixing bowl and add enough buttermilk until it has reached the consistency of a light dipping sauce. Season with crushed celery seeds, grated lemon peel, salt and black pepper.

Take several boneless skinless chicken thighs, remove all veins and tendons and membranes that run through them and split them into three or four strips each. Season them with salt, roll them in flour, dip them in lightly beaten egg whites, and finally press them into a bed of chopped pecans until fully coated. Chill them thoroughly. In the meantime, soak wooden skewers in water to prevent them from scorching later. In a sauce pan, bring the contents of a whole bottle of vinegar-based (not oil-based) hot sauce and one stick of butter to a simmer. Cook it for 10 minutes, then transfer it to a wide metal bowl. Rinse the sauce pan, add 2 inches of water and bring it a simmer, setting the bowl over it to keep the sauce warm.

Stick the chicken pieces onto the skewers, line them up on a parchment paper-lined sheet pan and bake them at 400° F for about 12 minutes, until lightly browned and cooked through. Place the chicken skewers into the bowl and repeatedly spoon the sauce over the chicken before transferring them to a papertowel-lined platter to drain off excess sauce. Serve with the blue cheese dip in a bowl for dipping, garnished with chopped light green celery leaves.

This is a very filling and savory hors d'oeuvre, but be warned that it has nothing do do with so-called Buffalo wings.

Having been exposed to the techniques and dishes of so many more or less talented cooks and chefs, with my usual ease I updated my own cooking standards and incorporated each lesson into my own practice – which came very handy when I became a private chef. I had never planned this. Back in Munich, the owner of the Italian restaurant where I was working part-time to pay for dance classes had offered me to become a partner if I took over the kitchen, but I had turned down the offer, having already decided to leave Germany and move to New York. It is a feeble joke that even though I moved to New York to pursue a career outside of the kitchen I still ended up in it, and one might add that moving to London had been another option I had briefly considered until I was offered a free ticket to New York. It was one of the many opportunities that would change my life forever.

One day in late autumn, the Feast and Fêtes booker sent me to work at a dinner party to be held at the Dakota building on 72nd Street. Everybody always spoke with reverence about that building. The apartment was one of the more diminutive ones. The host was celebrating his fortieth birthday with a big party. He had invited many more guest that could reasonably fit around the dining tables set up in every room of the apartment which had been cleared of all other furniture. The chefs were frantic. It would be all but impossible to execute the company's signature *service à l'assiette*, the style of plating every single course in the manner done in restaurants but rarely in catering, in the apartment's tiny galley kitchen. To make matters worse, Daniel Boulud himself was going to be among the guests. The cooks always got very anxious when he came to any of the parties because they knew that he liked to change everything about their set-up in the last minute. He did this by instinct, not necessarily to improve the working conditions of his sous-chefs or heighten the quality of the food, but to assert his leading position. And so he did that evening, too. When the waiters brought the first course, a wild mushroom risotto, to the table of honor, he took a brief look at the plates and with one swift motion sent them all back to the kitchen, following in their wake. I do not recall what exactly he did there, but in any case the first course was brought out again 5 minutes later, this time to his full satisfaction, accentuated by a round of applause. The suggestiveness of his action alone was such that later, the host claimed that chef Boulud had made his cooks prepare the entire first course all over again from scratch – as if that were possible in five minutes. A mushroom risotto – any risotto – is a fairly time-consuming dish to prepare. Here is how I make it.

WILD MUSHROOM RISOTTO

Clean two pounds of mixed mushrooms and slice off their stems. In a stock pot, heat 2 tablespoons of olive oil and add the mushroom stems, a quartered onion, 1 chopped celery stalk a few sprigs of fresh thyme. Stir-fry the vegetables until fragrant before adding 2 quarts of water and 6 cut-up chicken wings or 3 halved chicken backs. Invert a small plate into the pot to keep all solids fully submerged and simmer the broth over a low flame for one hour, skimming off any foam and fat. Strain it through a fine mesh sieve, discard solids and and return the broth to the cleaned stock pot, set over a low flame to keep it warm.

Thinly slice the mushroom heads and panfry them in three batches with 1 tablespoon of olive oil per batch until brown and crisp. Season them with salt and pepper.

In a Dutch oven, melt two tablespoons butter and add two finely chopped shallots, one mashed garlic clove and one diced medium-size yellow onion. Sauté until translucent before adding 1 ½ cups of Carnaroli rice. Stir-fry the rice until fragrant and shiny. Add 1 cup of white wine, stir and simmer until halfway evaporated. Add 2 cups of the mushroom broth, stir, bring to a simmer, cover and cook over a small flame for 10 minutes. Shake the pan and add another cup of stock, turn the heat to medium and cook while stirring until most of the liquid is absorbed. Continue this way until the rice has the desired consistency – al dente and suspended in a creamy emulsion. Season it with salt, freshly ground pepper and a splash of vinegar sherry. Fold in a couple tablespoons of softened butter (or ½ cup of heavy cream, whipped to a soft peak) and 2 tablespoons of freshly ground Parmesan cheese. Scoop the risotto into preheated shallow dining plates and top each portion with a generous heap of the pan-fried mushrooms, briefly reheated in a non-stick frying pan, and chopped parsley.

And here is a very popular main course often served by Feast and Fêtes and the simplest to prepare ahead of time and reheat when needed. This is my adaptation of it.

BRAISED SHORT RIBS

Ask your butcher for *English-cut* short ribs, cut from the meatiest ribs. Carve the meat off the bones in one chunk, slicing it off as close to the bone as possible. The advantage of doing this before braising the ribs is that, while the bones might slip off easily once the meat is cooked, you will be left with an unsightly flab of skin clinging to the meat.

Pour a bottle of a decent but inexpensive Cabernet Sauvignon into a large sauce pan and place it over medium heat. When it is hot, light it with a match. There will be only a faint flame dancing on its surface for a short time. Burning off the alcohol prevents the wine from turning the stew bitter.

Cut each slab of rib meat into three large chunks, place them into a bowl and toss them until coated with a couple tablespoons of neutral-tasting oil, coarsely ground black pepper and salt to taste. Brown the meat and the bones in batches in a heated Dutch oven without any additional fat, deglazing the pot with a bit of water in between batches, saving the glaze in a bowl and rinsing out the pot before browning the next batch. After the final batch, remove the meat but instead of deglazing the pot simply add skinned, quartered shallots, a few peeled garlic cloves and a couple of carrots, cut into irregular chunks, and a bit of salt. Set over medium high heat, the vegetables will sweat and deglaze the brown bits on the bottom. Now add the meat and bones, a couple of bay leaves and a few sprigs of fresh thyme, folded into a rolled-up dark green leek leaf and tied into a bundle. Pour the hot wine over it and bring everything to a light simmer. The meat should be at least halfway covered but not completely submerged (add water or homemade chicken stock if necessary.) Cut out a round piece of parchment paper that will fit into the pot to cover up the stew, cut out a hole in its center to let any steam escape, place it directly onto the meat, cover the pot with its lid and place it in a 300° F oven. Braise the meat for about 3 hours. The meat should by then be very tender and easily fall apart. Remove the parchment paper, lift out the meat chunks with tongs, place them in a bowl and immediately cover it with a plate to keep it moist. Strain the sauce into a bowl, discard the bones and press on the vegetables to extract as much juice as possible. Pour the sauce back into the pot and bring it to a simmer. Skim off any rising fat and reduce it until thick and syrupy. Season with salt to taste and return the meat chunks to the sauce. Spooning the warm sauce over the meat, careful to not break up the pieces. Do not bring to a boil again. This is a delicious and much lighter version than you will ever be served in a restaurant.

When I first tasted Boulud's short ribs in the early Nineties, it was considered quite *de rigueur* to serve this lowly cut of meat at an elegant event. Arguably, it was this humble yet complex homey dish that started a movement in New York City dining that was eventually taken up by a new generation of chefs and became known as *nose to tail* eating, all very amusing, although I still prefer root to flower eating.

The dinner at the Dakota was a long and elaborate one with many toasts and speeches for the host. The spectacular finale of the evening was an exclusive cabaret performance by Miss Julie Wilson. Her work was not very well known outside of New York but cabaret aficionados thought of her as the eminent doyenne of that rarified world. I sometimes thought that she ought to have had a career on Broadway but it appeared that no one of influence in the Broadway world had championed her. She arrived at the Dakota on time but the guests were still eating. She was asked to wait in the unheated, cold office behind the dining room. That was indeed a humiliating experience that taught me a lot of about the comedy and misery of being a cabaret performer. I brought her a blanket and a cup of warm tea. She declined to eat any food. It was then that we commenced our tacit but thoroughly enjoyable friendship.

Years later, she sometimes came to see my cabaret shows. Once, after a show in a downtown club, I invited her for a late night snack at a charming Italian wine bar around the corner of the club. There, we shared a platter of assembled paninis.

PANINI I
(Prosciutto di Parma, Onion Confit, Fontina)

Toss 2 diced Vidalia onions into a baking dish, add 3 tablespoons of olive oil, 1 tablespoon of brown sugar and few sprigs of fresh thyme, place a piece of parchment paper directly onto the onions, cover the dish with aluminum foil and bake them a 325° F for a good hour, checking periodically. The onions should be lightly caramelized and very soft. Season them with salt and coarsely crushed peppercorns.

Italian-style white bread with a thin crust and a light texture is most suitable for these Italian-style pressed sandwiches. Build a sandwich out of two bread slices, lightly brushed with olive oil, a tablespoon of the onion confit, a thin slice of Prosciutto, fat completely removed and folded to fit the bread slice, and a slice of Fontina cheese, cut to size. Press the sandwich in a hot panini press or pan-fry it in a hot griddle pan, weighed down by a small cast iron pan or a brick wrapped in aluminum foil (flip the panini once to brown it on both sides). Cut the *panino* diagonally in two and serve with a few *Niçoise* olives on the side.

PANINI II
(Gorgonzola, Pear and Bresaola)

Build a sandwich out of two bread slices, lightly brushed with olive oil and filled with *Gorgonzola* cheese, a few thin slices of Bosc pear drizzled with a bit of chestnut honey, and 2 thin slices of *Bresaola*. Proceed as with *Panini I* and serve with a few roasted and salted hazelnuts on the side.

PANINI III
(Basil Pesto, Pepperonata, and Pecorino Sardo)

To make the pepperonata, dice 2 red bell peppers, 2 yellow bell peppers and 1 Spanish onion, transfer all to a baking dish, add a splash of olive oil and a bit or red wine vinegar, 1 tablespoon of brown sugar and few sprigs of fresh oregano and roast the peppers in a 350° F oven for about 30 minutes, until lightly browned. Season with salt and ground white pepper. Build a sandwich out of two bread slices, lightly spread with basil pesto (a recipe for which can be found in Chapter VIII), a spoon of pepperonata and two thin slices of *pecorino sardo*. Proceed as with *Panini I* and serve with a couple of cherry tomatoes on the side.

---

* Dry-cured beef

All the condiments for the panini can be prepared ahead of time, but the paninis must be assembled and griddled in the last moment. It does not take a long time and they are always more than the sum of their parts. Both the cabaret club and the wine bar have since then closed.

A week after the party at the Dakota, the caterer's booker called me and said the host, a well-connected media executive, had inquired about a capable young waiter who could regularly come and work with his own private chef whenever he was having a dinner party. Would I be interested. I said I was.

That winter, uneventful in most ways, the executive's assistant would frequently book me to serve dinner at his parties at the Dakota. Pedro, the executive's private chef, was a handsome young man from Venezuela and usually quite hyper from a long and lonely day of cooking by the time I arrived to set the table. When he saw me for the first time, he flashed a wide grin and seemed pleased. During that first day we worked together, he would not keep his hands off me, which was very amusing. Stealthily making out with the cook between serving courses was something I had never done before.

After this first day, he was often in a bad mood, which made him impatient and morose. He had a wild temper and his working pace was frantic. He would loudly toss around his pots and pans, which made the host cringe. He would have made even more noise if the kitchen had not been right behind the dining room, but his food was always refined and understated and stylishly presented. He once served a

CELERIAC SOUP

Peel and dice 1 celeriac and 3 shallots. In a Dutch oven, melt 2 tablespoons of butter and gently cook the shallots in it until they are translucent. Add the celeriac, sauté briefly until lightly caramelized and deglaze with homemade chicken stock, enough to barely cover. Add a branch of fresh thyme and 1 peeled and diced Granny Smith apple. Simmer until the celeriac is tender. Remove the thyme sprig and purée the soup in batches in a blender. Strain it through a fine-mesh sieve and season it with salt, white pepper and nutmeg. Heat gently before serving, do not let it come to a boil again. Just before serving, add a tablespoon of sherry vinegar. Serve garnished with a small dollop of heavy cream – whipped to a soft peak with a pinch of salt and nutmeg – as well as some chopped parsley and, if available, a few very thin shaved slices of fresh, peeled chestnut.

Pedro was not very well versed in making desserts or baked goods. He said he had no patience for it. One evening he had me serve a very professional-looking cheese cake. Did you make that cake, I asked. When he answered that he had, I noticed behind the garbage can a folded golden cardboard box from a well-known pastry shop. Are you sure, I provocatively continued. At once, he flashed an infectious grin and, chuckling, said, Don't tell. I can teach you some desserts, I said. Ah yes, he said, perhaps one day.

SOUFFLÉ-STYLE CHEESECAKE

Chop and melt 5 ounces of French or Belgian white chocolate (or a scant cup of white chocolate chips) in a bowl set over simmering water. Beat 4 egg yolks with 4 tablespoons sugar and the scraped seeds of 1 vanilla bean to a soft ribbon. Whisk one package (8 ounces) of softened Neufchâtel cream cheese into it and fold in the white chocolate. Beat 4 egg whites to a firm peak, adding a pinch of salt, and fold them into the mixture, one third at a time. Brush the bottom and sides of a 7-inch spring form with butter and line the sides only with a 6-inch wide ribbon of parchment-paper to add some height to it. Wrap the bottom and sides of the spring form with a large sheet of aluminum foil to prevent water from seeping into the cake. Pour the mousse into the form and tap it lightly against the kitchen counter to pop any large air bubbles and ensure an even rise. Place it inside a baking dish filled halfway with hot water and bake it for 10 minutes at 350° F before turning the heat down to 325° F and baking it for another 25 minutes. Turn the oven off and leave the cake in it for another 15 minutes. Remove the spring form's ring once the cheesecake has cooled down but do not refrigerate it. Serve with fresh strawberries or sliced kiwis. This is a very elegant yet understated dessert.

Pedro was always restless and talked of one day going off to Paris or Italy. He was at the time cooking full-time for a male couple downtown and only cooked once a week for the executive. He seemed rather bored by the former and annoyed by the latter. It made me think of how strange it would be to cook for the same two people almost every day, to play such an intimate part of their private lives while remaining strictly an employee. Little did I know that this was quite literally what I would soon do myself.

One day in the spring the executive told me that he had bought and renovated a large mansion in the Hamptons and that he wanted me to come to his office to discuss an idea. It was evident he wanted to make me a job offer for the summer. I was apprehensive, I had heard strange stories of young men being hired as pool boys, and of how their boring jobs were all about rearranging the lawn furniture and looking pretty while putting out towels and watering the plants.

I arrived at the executive's office rather uptight. He began by captivatingly saying: "Wouldn't you love to spend your summer weekends in a beautiful house in the Hamptons" –along those lines. I would have my own room in the guesthouse and all I would have to do is serve him and his friends casual breakfasts, lunches and dinners. I was quite certain I was not interested. Will Pedro be there, I asked. No, he said, you would be in charge of getting prepared foods from a local store and simply serve that. With a neat smile, he added, There will be a Housekeeper to help you. It was then that I made a serendipitous counteroffer. Why don't you, I said, let me do the cooking. Then I will be the chef and the housekeeper can do the serving.

Of course there was no way of knowing if I was up to the task. I had not done any professional cooking since the few months I had worked in the kitchen of the Italian restaurant in Munich. My own cooking had always been spontaneous but this would require a lot of planning ahead. In my naive way I told myself that as long as I managed to make the food delicious it would be quite a nice opportunity.

It wasn't that simple. I soon discovered that cooking for a group of male executives from New York City was challenging in many more ways than I could have imagined. There were eight of them. All of them were either alpha-males and overachievers, which made them controlling, or they were users, which made them demanding, or they were bored and could become annoying, or they were on a diet and had very particular demands. Of the lot, one of them, an investment banker, was the most amiable, patient and friendly, and he would eventually become my most important and reliable employer. He was seeing someone at the time who was dishonest and only cared about being spoiled by him. He kept making demands. One day the executive staged an intervention. The result was that the young man was banned not just from the house but also the investment banker's life, who naturally went through a desolate period until he met someone new. His new partner was well mannered and kind. They got along very well and eventually became husband and husband. Later, they became the fathers of two lively children.

During my first season in the Hamptons, I cooked French dishes and Italian dishes and Spanish dishes and German dishes, and to perfection, but objected to serving a combination of them in one meal. It was my correct sense of balance that wouldn't let me do it. The men disagreed with me, they thought I was being uptight. Eventually I learned to laugh at their American insouciance. And presented them with Mexican, Thai, Vietnamese, Danish, Swedish, Chinese, Malaysian or Greek lunches and dinners. It was suspiciously a plot to bring more variety to my cooking while maintaining some integrity within each menu. In the course of time the men came to embrace my approach as it gave them for each meal the opportunity to travel to a different place without ever leaving the comfort of the Hamptons. They thought I was delightfully entertaining.

The executive was pleased to have a European young man attend to him and his guests too were pleased. More and more of them arrived. It became difficult to deal with all of them at once. The executive always told them not to worry, there would always be enough food. And with that he ignored my concerns and plea for some help. I produced my improvised style of cooking all through the summer. Unlike regular chefs used to the rigidity of restaurant work, I was flexible and did not mind working in an open kitchen where every move I made was exposed to all (this was long before open restaurant kitchens became fashionable). Whenever I saw unexpected guests arrive in the driveway, I cursed under my breath and, having learned from experience, automatically doubled the volume of whatever I was preparing for the next meal.

For the very first meal I ever cooked for them, having arrived a mere few hours before dinner time, I improvised a simple a dinner of grilled sausages with a balsamic glaze, sautéed broccoli rabe and roasted potatoes, and a dessert of grilled peaches. I had never grilled fruit before, but it seemed an interesting idea. This is the way I made them.

GRILLED PEACHES

Take tree-ripe but firm peaches, cut them in half, remove the pits, brush the cut side with olive oil, place them on a clean, medium hot grill and cook them for a few minutes, until they have grill marks and are slightly softened.

Crack open the peach pits with a hammer and remove the "almond." Peel the almonds and lightly crack them to release their bitter almond flavor. Make a syrup by boiling ½ cup of sugar and 1 cup of water with the cracked peach almonds. Cook it for a few minutes, until reduced by half, and strain. Serve the peaches drizzled with the syrup.

I had to be resourceful. In the refrigerator I found a half-empty bottle

THE ART OF GAY COOKING

of Champagne that had been opened during the cocktail hour and not been finished. I would improvise a Zabaglione with the Champagne. While the men were still eating their main course, I whipped up the concoction. It was a light and sophisticated condiment for the grilled peaches, and a good way to show off my skills.

CHAMPAGNE ZABAGLIONE

In a large stainless steel or copper bowl, lightly beat 2 eggs, 4 egg yolks and 1 heaped tablespoon of sugar before adding 2 glasses of Champagne. Set the bowl over a pot of simmering water and whisk to a warm soft ribbon. Serve immediately.

I made this first dessert in a haste, but later in the season, whenever I had the time, I prepared some baked desserts. For example,

PEACH CROSTATA

In a food processor, pulse 1 ¼ cups of flour, ½ cup of sugar, 2 heaped tablespoons of coarse polenta, a pinch of salt and ½ stick of cold butter into coarse meal. With the machine running, add 1 lightly beaten egg. Process until the dough comes together in a ball. Flatten it to a disc, wrap it in cellophane and refrigerate it for 30 minutes. Slice 8-10 sun-ripened peaches into eights. Toss them into a bowl and add 2 tablespoons of sugar, the grated zest and juice of 1 Meyer lemon (or regular lemon), 1 heaped tablespoon of cornstarch and 2 tablespoons of coarsely chopped fresh rosemary. On a floured surface, roll out the dough to a round disc about 12 inches wide. Transfer it onto a large piece of parchment and pierce it all over with a fork. Roll out ½ cup of marzipan to a disc of 10 inches and place it on its center. Pile the peaches over the marzipan and fold over one inch of the dough all around the *crostata*, crimping the edges. Brush the edges of the dough with egg white or cream, sprinkle them with raw sugar and slide the parchment paper with the crostata onto a sheet pan. Bake in a 375° F oven for about 45 minutes, until bubbly and lightly browned. Serve at room temperature.

Or a

RHUBARB COBBLER

Strip the thin red skin off 5 or 6 stalks of rinsed rhubarb and slice them against the grain, a quarter inch thick. Toss the pieces with a few juliennes of orange peel, the juice of half the orange, 2 heaped tablespoons of sugar and 1 tablespoon of cornstarch and transfer them to a rectangular baking dish. Mix 1 ½ cups of flour with ¾ cup of sugar and the scraped seeds of 1 vanilla bean and rub 1 ½ sliced sticks of cold butter into it with your fingertips until you have a crumble. Scatter the crumble loosely over the rhubarb and bake it in a 350° F oven until lightly browned and bubbly, for about 35 minutes. Serve warm or at room temperature with basic vanilla ice cream.

I never announced my menus to the guests or the hosts unless prompted, preferring to let the food to speak for itself.

After a long and laborious summer during which I gained a good amount of experience I felt confident that I could find work as a private chef in the city. There was no way I would go back to being a cater waiter. The executive's way of thanking me was to recommend my services to some friends of his. The investment banker thought I deserved a present and sent me a full set of professional chef's knives. On one of the last dinners I was to cook at the Hamptons house the executive introduced me to a male couple, an orchestra conductor and his medical doctor boyfriend. They were already employing a full-time chef in the city but had enjoyed the dinner a great deal and wondered if I could not possibly be an improvement over him. A few days later, they invited me to their townhouse in the West Village for a long conversation. It was rather uncomfortable that they were willing to let go their current chef so they could hire me. Would I be interested? They assured me that their current chef would easily find work elsewhere and that I could start immediately. Years later I found out that he had indeed ended up as a prep chef for a new television station that featured a cooking show that was beginning to get very popular at the time called *Emeril Live*. In any case, I took a chance, accepted the couple's offer and became not only an entertaining and lively presence in their household but their favorite chef of all time. The doctor was usually out all day but the conductor liked to have lunch at home and during those lunches he and I often had long conversations.

During that period, New York's cabaret scene was beginning to show interest in my work and it was finally possible for me to perform more regularly on my free evenings. The conductor and the doctor once even came to one of my shows and the conductor told me that he was considering introducing me to influential people who could help my career as a singer but that he would then risk losing me as his chef. It made me wonder how under these circumstances I would ever possibly have a performing career but what else could I say than, Of course, I understand. The subject was never brought up again. I took great pains to please his palate every day and produce a large variety of ever-changing meals. The conductor thought that everything I cooked was first rate but the doctor demanded a diet that excluded a long list of ingredients he did not like or that he claimed he was allergic to. These included all kinds of fish, seafood, and mushrooms, as well as most vegetables other than tomatoes and bell peppers. What he liked more than anything was my

STUFFED TURKEY

The turkey is small, weighing no more than 6 pounds. On the day before serving it, it is rinsed and patted dry. Season the cavity only with ample amounts of kosher salt, set it on a platter and leave it uncovered overnight in the refrigerator for the skin to dry. Place the giblets and neck into a sauce pan, add 3 cups of water and bring it to a simmer, skimming of any rising foam. Once the water is clear, add a bay leaf, a sprig of thyme, a cracked clove of garlic, ½ stalk of celery and some black peppercorns. Simmer for 20 more minutes. Strain and store in the refrigerator. Cut off the crusts of half a loaf of sourdough country bread and tear the crumb into pieces. Scatter them on a sheet pan, place it in the oven and let them dry up overnight. Results are best if your oven is slightly warmed by a pilot light.

The next day, make the stuffing. In a frying pan set over a medium flame, break up the forcemeat squeezed from 4 Italian-style, sweet pork sausages. When the meat begins to release its fat, add 4 chopped shallots and mix them with the meat. Once the meat and shallots begin to brown, add 2 finely diced celery stalks and a handfull of chopped sage leaves. Cook for a few more minutes and transfer onto a platter lined with a triple layer of paper towels (to soak up the fat).

Transfer the fried sausage meat into a large mixing bowl and add the dried bread pieces. In a blender, mix 2 eggs with ½ pound of cleaned chicken livers to a smooth puree and pour it over the stuffing. Mix well, adding the reserved turkey stock,

¼ cup at a time, until the consistency of the stuffing is heavy and wet but still holding its shape. Season it with salt, pepper, nutmeg and a touch of powdered chili pepper. To check the seasoning, cook a small amount in a frying pan and taste it; it should be quite savory. Add more salt and pepper if necessary.

Dry out the turkey's cavity with paper towels and fill it to two thirds with stuffing. Fill any leftover stuffing into a casserole and bake it separately. Wrap the turkey wingtips with oil-sprayed aluminum foil, brush the entire bird with melted butter and season it with generously with salt and pepper. Set it into a roasting rack, atop a bed of thick onion slices and celery stalks over which you pour two glasses of white wine and roast it in a 400° F oven until the skin is golden and crisp and juices running out of the thigh joint when pierced are no longer pink, a bit longer than 2 hours. Do not baste it but remove the aluminum foil from the wing tips after one hour. Spoon out the stuffing before carving the bird according to tradition, with the stuffing on the side and the panjuices strained and lightly reduced, fat spooned off and replaced with a piece of butter that is whisked into it just before serving.

The doctor said it was the best turkey he had ever had. He told me that his mother had, for as long as he could remember, made a big to-do about her annual Thanksgiving turkey, getting up in the middle of the night to put it into the oven and basting it every hour for 6 hours or so, and that every year the bird had been dry and tasteless. Another homey dish he frequently requested was

CHICKEN POT PIE

Pour 1 ½ cups of flour into a large mixing bowl, add 1 teaspoon of salt and cut 4 tablespoons of cold butter and 4 tablespoons of well-chilled lard into it with two knives or a pastry cutter. Sprinkle with ¼ cup of ice water and swiftly kneed everything into a ball, adding more water if necessary but careful to not over-moisten or over-work the dough. Flatten the ball into a disc, wrap it in cellophane and chill it for at least 30 minutes.

Strip the meat off 1 whole roasted chicken – you may opt to buy a fully cooked rotisserie chicken from a reliable place. Shred the meat into coarse chunks. Place all the bones and skin into a sauce pan, cover them with water, add a chunk of onion, a chopped celery stalk, a sprig of parsley, a piece of carrot and a sliced knob of ginger and simmer everything for 30 minutes. Strain it through a fine-mesh sieve and discard the solids.

In a sauce pan, melt 3 tablespoons of butter. Add 2 tablespoons of flour, mix the two into a paste and gradually add 1 cup of milk and 1 cup of the chicken stock. Simmer for several minutes before pouring it into a mixing bowl and covering it with plate set over a paper towel to soak up the steam and prevent condensation water from dripping back into the sauce.

Peel 2 cups of white pearl onions and cook them for 5 minutes in 2 cups of simmering milk seasoned with salt and a bit of nutmeg. Peel 2-3 carrots and cut them on the bias into irregular, thumbnail-size diamond shapes. Blanch them in boiling salted water for 1 minute.

When the white sauce has reached room temperature, season it with white pepper and salt and add 1 cup of briefly rinsed frozen peas, the chicken meat, a handful of cubed, best quality cooked ham, the blanched carrots and cooked pearl onions, plus a few small leaves of fresh tarragon. Fill the mixture into individual soufflé ramekins or a pie dish, roll out the dough, cut it out to size and cover the ramekins or pie dish with it, tucking in the overlap, piercing it in several places with a fork and brushing it with an egg yolk diluted with a bit of water. Set the pies on a parchment-paper-lined sheet pan and bake them in a 350° F oven for about 40 minutes, until the crust is golden and flaky. Serve warm.

At the time I had just begun to work for the couple the conductor decided that he ought to learn German. When he hired an Austrian woman to come once a week and teach him German conversation over lunch, I made a point of always preparing Austrian or German food for his lessons. I made *Wiener Schnitzel* with potato salad, *Tafelspitz* (boiled tri-tip) with an egg-and-chive chive sauce and a tart apple sauce to which a bit of fresh grated horseradish had been added. Another week, I made *Semmelknödel* (bread dumplings) with creamy mushrooms. Once, I served venison stew with red cabbage, another time a savory strudel, filled with sauerkraut and speck, spiced with paprika and baked under a layer of sour cream. Once, on a warm summer day, I served them a light supper of open-faced sandwiches with smoked trout, dill and cucumber.

Then, there were the dinner parties, usually small affairs with four or six invited guests, served at the beautifully rustic wooden dining table in the eat-in kitchen that gave out to the garden in the backyard. One day, the conductor told me that both Stephen Sondheim and Joel Grey were to be among the six guests. He was very proud to have them both come to dinner but during the cocktail hour in the living room, Stephen Sondheim took him aside and told him in no uncertain terms that he did not care for Joel Grey. The conductor came into the kitchen and explained the delicate situation. He was quite worked up about it. We decided to seat the two men at opposite ends of the table. Sondheim talked about the current lack of talent on Broadway, of his undying admiration for Barbra Streisand, and how his musicals were really operas, and Joel Grey talked about his work as a photographer. I served a light Mediterranean-style three-course dinner and the two guests of honor successfully avoided each other all evening. They did not even look at each other. It was ludicrous.

Because of the necessity to bring variety to my daily menus I had no choice but to continuously learn about different cuisines and cook according to them, eager to not ever repeat any dish. It was an accomplishment of which I was quite proud. It made things more interesting not just for them but for myself.

However there was one incident where things turned out differently.

In the spring, the couple travelled to India for a week to visit a friend who had started a foundation that built hospitals in the northern part of the country. He had been the couple's houseguest in the fall and once told me that he had made his fortune with the sale of a Van Gogh painting he had found in a garbage can on a little side street in Soho. It wasn't a believable story but given my position it would have been extremely unseemly to challenge it. The conductor and the doctor had agreed to sponsor a red ambulance and also bought a new set of red suitcases for their trip. When the couple returned, they had many stories to tell of the vegetarian Indian food they had eaten all week and how interesting that had been and perhaps one ought to continue eating that way. The next day, I went to several specialty markets in the city and brought back sour mango powder and bitter melons and a whole array of Indian spices I had never used before. That evening when the couple came home for their dinner, they were shocked to find the smells of Indian food permeating the entire house. It was a most unfortunate misunderstanding on my part. They were in fact quite fed up with Indian food and explained that what they had meant was that they were merely considering to become *vegetarians*. Whereupon the couple left to eat out at their favorite Italian restaurant.

I usually did not work for them on weekends unless they had a dinner party. However during the summer months, I cooked for them seven days a week as they requested my services in their summer house in the Hamptons. One day the conductor asked me if I would agree to prepare an elegant benefit dinner for four dozen people he was going to host out there. What is the occasion, I asked. He explained that since his involvement in politics he had become rather fond of Bill Clinton who had just ended his presidency and of Hillary Clinton who was a supporter of the gay community and now running for U.S. Senator in New York. Was she perhaps going to eventually run for president. And perhaps after her presidency their daughter Chelsea would become senator or governor somewhere and so on ad infinitum. Telling the Secret Service what I was going to serve would be futile, so I told them I would improvise on the day of the dinner. No, they said, we must know ahead of time because there may be allergies or other problems. It seemed to me a useless effort since the market might in the days leading up to the event not have what I needed to execute my intended menu. But the former President and First Lady were so pleased with the way it all turned out that word got out to the Secret Service agents who promptly began to show up in the kitchen during the long dinner service, one hungry pair at a time, in what seemed like an endless succession of male couples in dark suits. Then it was time for a photo op with the Clintons.

After two years of working full-time for the couple I felt that it was time for me to move on and focus more on performing. I gave them my notice one day in late spring, promising to stay on for the rest of the summer or until they found a suitable replacement. Having grown rather fond of my food on their plates and my presence in their lives they were, in a word, offended. They were used to firing chefs, not to have them leave on their own behalf. When I bid them farewell and thanked them for the opportunity they had given me, the gesture was not returned. It was their personal assistant who went through great lengths to persuade the conductor to write me the customary recommendation letter. It arrived in the mail several weeks later, and rather complimentary it was. I have never had any need for it.

Once more it became necessary to find part-time work, and it was difficult at first. But one day, I ran into the investment banker from the first summer house I had ever cooked in. He said he'd planned to reach out to me and that he would call me. I wondered if he might make me the kind of offer I was looking for. When he called, he said he was about to move into his newly acquired, fully renovated townhouse and to my astonishment it was just across the street from the conductor's house. After telling me that he was looking for a chef who would cook for him just once a week, I accepted instantly. To be sure the wage I asked for was more than double the humiliatingly diminutive wage I had earned when I was cooking for him and the other men at the executive's Hamptons mansion. We agreed that I would cook for him whenever he was entertaining guests and that I would have a free hand in creating the menus. Do you have any preferences, I said to him. To which he answered, Anything, Daniel, you feel like making, as long as it is light and crispy.

So I became the only person who ever cooked in the investment banker's beautifully appointed modern kitchen, though rarely more than once a week. To be sure he had a large extended family, and they were all living in New Jersey and frequently visiting. Their presence was a constant – it became a guessing game when they would invite themselves over again. There were several privileges I had with him; I gradually came to understand their value. He was very generous – there would be no limit to what equipment I was allowed to buy for his kitchen. I saw his and his boyfriend's easy-going American approachableness – there would be a very friendly rapport between us. I became, as they liked to say, family. We got on excellent terms with each other. They even allowed me and Filip Noterdaeme to spend days on end in their summer house when no one else was staying there.

As their chef I was neither pretentious nor fussy but understated and understanding of their requests for light cuisine. I cooked anything they asked me to, but I would not (indeed I refused to) step in front of the guests and announce the menu, for the simple reason that I saw my role in the kitchen and not in the dining room. It was the one thing I asked them to do. It was little enough to do in return for the thoughtful simplicity I applied to everything I did for them. For example, I frequently made for them and their guests

HALIBUT STEAKS EN PAPILLOTE

Rub two ½ inch-thick halibut steaks with olive oil, season them on both sides with salt and white pepper and sprinkle them with coarsely crushed fennel seeds. Using a mandoline, cut 1 fennel bulb, 1 lemon and two plum tomatoes into very thin slices. Place a large sheet of parchment paper over a baking dish, scatter the fennel and lemon slices on its center and place the halibut filets on it. Arrange the tomato slices on the filets and season them with salt and pepper. Drizzle the steaks with very little olive oil, fold the parchment paper over them, leaving a pocket of air and tucking the ends under. Bake at 400° F for about 15 minutes or until the thickest part of the fish is easily pierced with a wooden pick.

The investment banker was reliable. He was forethoughtful, felt amused by my temperament and met all unexpected situations with a calm demeanor. His one ambition was to get the last tenant in his townhouse to move out so he could turn it once again into a single-family home. The only obstacle was rent-control, for the woman had been living in her apartment for several decades. He would frequently say that she should accept his offer to move her to another apartment so he could finally live as comfortably as he wanted to. He did not understand that such stubbornness as old ladies have could not be swayed.

While I flourished so happily under the freedom and financial stability afforded to me by my contract with the investment banker other endeavors weren't always so fortunate. My cabaret performances in spite of my efforts were not leading to the show business career I had imagined. It was not a time period when appreciation of the cabaret art form was highly developed. Filip Noterdaeme once remarked that the only places that still booked performers were restaurants who wanted to sell more of their bad food and they did not even pay the artists well. I was often forced to use the money I earned as a chef to pay my musicians. There was no pleasure in having been foretold that this would happen when I had started out. Filip Noterdaeme bravely decided that he would direct my next show. He had never directed a show before but he felt that he, having seen the one-man shows of Eartha Kitt and Rosemary Clooney, Peggy Lee, the incomparable Hildegarde, Shirley Horn as well as Joey Arias and Justin V. Bond and Kenny Mellman in the early Kiki and Herb days, could make a difference. They had taught him what the art of cabaret was. Through a few recommendations, I was able to book my new show in a well-respected cabaret. I was very excited, things would change from now on. I would build up a following and perform in better and bigger venues to fashionable society as New York City surely still harbored. I was not pleased when I arrived at the club one evening and was told by the owner that I could not expect my show to go on that night unless I had more people in the audience. He glossed over my stupefaction and said that in any case I would need at least 20 paying people in the audience. I had called the box office earlier to ask about reservations. The reservationist, having misunderstood my name, had assured me that the show was sold out.

There was a phone call from a curator named Limor Tomer, and the invitation I received was as warm as it could possibly be. I was booked to perform a show of German cabaret songs in the Café of the newly opened Neue Galerie Museum, and with some luck I found in Todd Almond the perfect pianist to hire. There I sang to a well-healed Upper East side crowd and ended up performing a new show every season for the next eight years. Sold-out shows and excellent references opened the doors for bookings at cabaret events in art museums across the country.

Still, it was necessary to continue to support myself as a part-time chef, and I had a growing number of clients. One very popular first course in my repertoire was

RICOTTA-FILLED RAVIOLI WITH SAGE BUTTER

Make a batch of fresh pasta dough in a food processor by adding 4 lightly beaten eggs to 2 cups of flour and 1 cup of semolina flour with the motor running. Add a bit of water if necessary and process until the ingredients come together in a soft ball. Wrap the dough in cellophane and let it rest for at least 30 minutes. In a mixing bowl, season 1 cup of drained Ricotta – sheep's milk Ricotta is best – with salt, white pepper and the grated zest of 1 Meyer lemon or ½ lemon and ½ Clementine. Working in batches, roll out the pasta dough with a pasta machine or a rolling pin and, using a ravioli tray or a pastry cutter, fill it with the Ricotta mix and cut it accordingly. Boil the ravioli in salted water until al dente. Melt 1 tablespoon of butter per person in a frying pan and fry several fresh sage leaves in it before adding the drained ravioli along with a bit of pasta water. Toss until fully coated with the butter emulsion and serve with coarsely ground black pepper and finely ground – never grated – Parmesan.

This is of course the most basic filling for ravioli. I also make a version filled with sautéed and diced mushrooms, served with a sauce made of chicken *demiglace*, butter and sherry. Sometimes I add chestnut flour to the dough and fill the ravioli with puréed squash, dressing them with melted butter, red chili flakes, Parmesan and crushed, toasted ginger snaps.

Festivals invited me to perform in Munich, Vienna, Zurich, Cologne and Berlin, where to my surprise it was usually the lesbians in the audience who took the liveliest interest in my style of performing. I would sing in German, French and English and was treated more like an American than an expat. I was not pleased when a critic in Berlin wrote how surprising it was to see a show full of heartfelt sentiment that had come from America, of all places. To this day I have refused to return to Berlin.

Meanwhile in New York more and more cabaret performers began to include German and French songs in their act; I hoped that audiences would detect which artists truly inhabited the songs and who put them on like an ill-fitting costume. In hopes of making their act more continental, many of these performers would come to see my shows, and later I would hear that they were adopting my repertoire, with the usual American eagerness. I would do my best to feel amused by it. To me, they still remained as American as

APPLE PIE

Cut 1 stick of cold butter into 1 ¼ cups of flour mixed with a good pinch of salt and a teaspoon of baking powder. Scatter 3-4 tablespoons of ice-cold water over the mix, toss everything like a salad before swiftly gathering it and pressing it together. Shape the dough into a disc without overworking it, wrap it in cellophane and chill it for one hour. Peel, core and slice 4-6 tart apples. Toss them into a hot pan with a splash of water (to prevent them from burning), a tablespoon of sugar and 4 whole cloves (or a pinch of ground cloves.) Cook them for just a few minutes, until they barely begin to look translucent, and immediately transfer them into a shallow bowl to cool off. Drizzle them with the juice of half of a lemon and carefully toss them until they are no longer steaming. Grease and flour a glass pie dish, roll out the dough and line the dish with it, crimping the edges. Pierce it with a fork in several places and place it in the freezer for 10 minutes.

Rub the scraped seeds of 1 vanilla bean into ½ teaspoon of sugar, add 1 cup of flour and cut ½ stick of cold butter into it, rubbing the mixture between your fingers to from loose *streusel* (crumbs.) Scoop the cooled apples into the pie shell in one mound, scatter the streusel over them and bake the pie at 375° F for about 50 minutes or more. The pie is done when is it bubbly and the bottom crust is no longer shiny but light golden and opaque – lift the dish, holding it up with oven mitts – to look from below.

The pre-cooking of the apples and the streusel make this effectively a Germanic adaptation of the American classic.

Meanwhile I continued to prepare sophisticated dinners for my growing number of clients in Manhattan, but one of the most frequent requests I heard was for

ADULT CHOCOLATE CHIP COOKIES

Cream one stick of softened butter with 1 scant cup of dark brown sugar, the seeds scraped out of 1 vanilla bean and 2 tablespoons of Bourbon. Add 1 egg and beat until combined. Into this mix, swiftly work 1 ¼ cups of flour, a good pinch of salt, 1 teaspoon baking powder, 1 cup of extra dark chocolate chips and 1 cup of coarsely chopped pecans. Chill the dough for 1 hour. Line two sheet pans with parchment paper and spoon dollops of dough, the size of a walnut, onto them, an inch apart. Flatten them lightly with wet fingers and sprinkle them with a few grains coarse sea salt. Bake them in a 350° F oven for about 12 minutes, until lightly browned at the edges.

After a good dozen years of balancing cooking and performing and working closely with Filip Noterdaeme on the Homeless Museum of Art, I became worried. I realized I did not know how much longer I could sustain this kind of lifestyle. I became preoccupied with questions regarding talent, ambition, mediocrity, success and failure, none of which I had any definite answers for. I became restless and more and more absorbed in trying to understand something I could not fathom. One day I announced I needed to leave for a while, I needed to be by myself. I would go to my parent's house on the island in Brittany and take some time off to write. I bought my ticket, and Filip Noterdaeme threw me a farewell party at our home on the day before I was leaving. I told everyone that I was going to work on a culinary memoir and everybody was interested. Filip Noterdaeme and I wrote to each other every day while I was away and when I returned a month later I had a first draft of the book in my luggage.

After that I found it much easier to accept the improvised, marginal nature of our lives where it was all about living for the moment and for each other. The seasons came and went, with the first half of the summers spent cooking in the Hamptons and the second on vacation on the island with Filip Noterdaeme. Having made my peace with myself, I adapted to the thought that I would always be a bohemian artist and live freely. The dreaded sense of feeling like a mere servant had disappeared.

XI

FOOD IN THE HAMPTONS
DURING THE SUMMER

I N THE BEGINNING, like fish out of water, I was gasping for air. Working as an in-house chef is intense. The Hamptons are famous for being a playground for the rich and I did not quite understand to what degree their sense of entitlement would impact my work until a couple of weeks into my first season there. The fee I was paid per weekend was even less than what I would have earned as a cater waiter in the city, but by the time I realized how taxing the job was, it was too late to negotiate a raise. Shopping for groceries and fresh produce was not a problem for I was given a credit card for all expenses. There was no limit to my budget. What was lacking was a consensus about what the executive had described as casual family-style meals. The executive had invited three friends to spend the summer at the house – not for free, they had to buy what was called "summer shares" – and since they were all four of them either dating someone or looking for someone to date there were usually four couples staying at the house. It appeared that all of them were accustomed to the kind of service that is common in restaurants, hotels and holiday resorts. Had they not understood that these places employed a large staff of invisible cooks, dishwashers, waiters and maids to make everything appear seamless? On the first evening, I improvised a welcoming supper within just a couple of hours. I set the table and announced that dinner was ready. Great, they said. They eagerly sat down. I brought the platters of food to the table and took a seat along with everybody else. Unfolding their napkins the men just sat and waited to be served, looking slightly indignant. The fact that I had sat down with them was evidently not what they had expected. Casual family style dinner was apparently not the same here as it had been at my grandmother's house, where the housekeeper and cook had always sat at table with the family. I got up, took the platters one by one and diligently served everyone. I never sat down with them at the same table again, not once. I had understood where my place was.

The next morning, the executive took me to the Barefoot Contessa food shop. He wanted me to sample its fare – chicken salads, tuna salads, bean salads, mashed potatoes and marinated roasted vegetables. I instantly recognized it for what it was: an overpriced approximation of simple classic dishes that might have been outstanding had any of it been prepared with proper care and attention to detail. Later, I was waiting in line at the nice butcher store across the street, long since closed. Suddenly a young woman started acting up about wanting to be served immediately. The butcher exclaimed that she would have to wait for her turn like everybody else. At that, she instantly broke into tears and accused him of being rude. Apparently, this was the way she had been taught to conduct business. When it was my turn I asked him for an entire filet of beef. He carefully trimmed it and tied it into a perfect roast. He also offered me a few shin bones for making stock. The sum I paid was astronomical, but it was the only place in town where one could get meat of decent quality and he knew it. The filet became the pièce de résistance of that day's lunch, the first of many I would serve at the house, roasted and served at room temperature, sliced and simply dressed with a black olive tapenade.

FILET OF BEEF WITH BLACK OLIVE TAPENADE

Remove the pits of 2 cups of Moroccan-style cured black olives. Transfer them to a food processor and add about 8 rinsed anchovy filets, 2 tablespoons of drained capers, 1 teaspoon of Dijon mustard and 4 roasted garlic cloves*. With the machine running, add about ¼ cup of olive oil and process until emulsified to a thick paste.

Brush a trimmed and tied filet of beef with olive oil and season it all over with salt, coarsely ground black pepper and finely chopped fresh thyme. Place it on a rack set over a sheet pan filled with water and roast it in a 425° F oven for 15 minutes, turning it once after 8 minutes. Lower the temperature to 350° F and roast for another 15 minutes or until an instant thermometer inserted in its thickest part reads 120° F. Let it rest for at least 15 minutes on the rack before removing the strings.

Thinly slice one large red onion, toss the slices into a bowl and season them with a fair sprinkling of sea salt and a bit of red wine vinegar

Thinly slice the filet mignon and arrange the slices on a platter, spreading a bit of tapenade between each layer. Scatter the onions all over the meat. Garnish with finely chopped parsley and, if available, some lavender blossoms. Serve with grilled slices of country bread and leaves of Romaine lettuce, laced with freshly squeezed lemon juice and a few drops of

* Slice off the top of one or several whole heads of garlic, brush it with olive oil, wrap it in aluminum foil and roast it at 350° F for 45 minutes. Squeeze the softened gloves out of the skins and use as directed or mash them with a bit of salt and olive oil into a paste that can be filled in a jar, topped with a bit of olive oil and stored in the refrigerator. Use up within a week.

olive oil. This makes a lovely supper in warm weather. When there is no time to make a roast, store-bought, sliced roast beef is a handy alternative.

The men were constantly hungry and passed through the kitchen like sheep grazing their way through a meadow. They never stopped eating. When I had to admit that I did not have a driver's license a car service was arranged to take me to the markets for the time being – until the arrival of the housekeeper who was set to move in the next week and whose duties would include helping me with the shopping. The driver picked me up in the morning and drove me to the different markets. Traffic was bad and there was little time to waste. The kitchen at the house had two large refrigerators but even so there was never enough space to store all the perishable goods I returned with. It occurred to me that I could keep the boxes of oranges, vegetables and dozens of lettuces in the wine cellar. Homemade chocolate chip cookies and biscotti were stored away in a secret place so they would not be found and consumed before I planned on serving them, but in hunting for them late at night the men always found them anyway. Later I gave up on hiding them, but when they complained about having gained weight I reminded them that they would not do as badly if it weren't for their extracurricular indulgences.

After the filet and salad a simple dessert of dark chocolate sorbet and biscotti was served. Cooking meat, chicken or fish on the outdoor gas grill was the quickest and most efficient way to prepare either but might easily become monotonous, not just to those it was served to but to the cook. I had already made up my mind to never prepare the same dish the same way more than once. At the very least, I would offer variations of a theme. One version of grilled steak was

GRILLED SKIRT STEAK WITH SPICY GOAT CHEESE

Cut a whole skirt steak into 3-inch segments and transfer the pieces into a bowl. Pour just enough olive oil over them to coat them thinly and season them with kosher salt, Spanish smoked paprika and finely crushed celery seeds or chopped thyme. Toss until fully coated, liberally massaging the spices into the meat and let the flavors develop for at least one hour.

Remove the seeds from several canned, Adobo-preserved chipotle peppers and coarsely mash the peppers with a fork before adding a softened log of mild goat cheese and a good tablespoon of wildflower honey. Season with salt to taste. Do not refrigerate it so it remains soft.

Grill the steaks on a medium hot grill on both sides, flipping them twice, to desired doneness. Beware that the thin end pieces will cook faster but also taste best when lightly charred and crunchy. Serve three pieces of meat per person, garnished with a dollop of the spiced goat cheese and sprinkled with toasted salted pumpkin seeds, thinly sliced scallions and chopped cilantro. This goes very well with roasted acorn squash.

Needless to say, the whipped goat cheese was too spicy for some, so I quickly made an herb sauce from Argentina called *Chimichurri* for them. I picked a big handful of parsley from the herb garden, chopped it very finely and added just a pinch of chili flakes, crushed fresh garlic, salt, a couple tablespoons of red wine vinegar and a touch of olive oil. It is a simple and delicious condiment. I sometimes make a variation of it with cilantro and lime juice which is even more fragrant.

The live-in housekeeper the executive had hired via an agency was scheduled to arrive on Saturday afternoon on the second weekend of the season. The men were sitting on the terrace, sipping cappuccinos and espressos made with the executive's favorite new gadget, a fully automated espresso machine, something that was not as common then in home kitchens as it is now. They were all dressed in a style that was becoming fashionable at the time and was later often referred to as "the nerd look": Prada shorts with striped belts, tucked-in short-sleeved button-down shirts, and Gucci soft suede loafers worn without socks. There was lively talk of plans for the rest of the weekend – which cocktail parties to attend, when to make an appearance at the gay beach, and whom they ought to invite over for lunch, an afternoon dip into the pool, or dinner. I had just set out a very simple

CITRUS-FLAVORED POUND CAKE

Rub the finely grated zest of 1 orange and 1 lemon into ¾ cups of sugar. Squeeze the juice of the orange and lemon into a glass. Using a wooden spoon, incorporate 5 tablespoons of softened butter into the sugar and beat it lightly to a creamy consistency, adding 3 tablespoons of fragrant olive oil along the way. Add 3 eggs, one by one. The eggs must not be cold;

submerge them for a few minutes in a bowl of warm water if they are. Sift 1 ¼ cups of flour and 1 teaspoon of baking powder over the mix and swiftly fold it into it. Now add the citrus juice and finally fold in ½ cup of coarse polenta. Pour the dough into a parchment-paper-lined – the paper greased and floured – loaf pan and shower it generously with raw sugar. Bake at 350° F for about 50 minutes or until cake tester comes out clean. Un-mold immediately and set on a wire rack to cool. Serve with clotted cream or whipped cream cheese and raspberry jam.

The garden was beautifully landscaped, facing a pond. The executive was very proud of it and of how it had been all done just in time for the season. We had seen, on the day of our arrival, the last missing pieces of instant turf being rolled out on the lawn by a group of exhausted Mexican gardeners. Suddenly, a moving truck pulled up to the garage and a tall and busty young woman with a big mop of dark curly hair climbed out of the passenger's seat, smiling shyly at the group of immobile men who eyed her apprehensively. "That's her," said the executive and got up to greet her. The other men remained seated and watched as the driver opened the trunk, revealing several large duffel bags, a mahogany armoire and an oversized pink teddy bear. The men winced at the sight of it. That was all. It haunted them that she had already committed the crime of bad taste. Changes would have to be implemented.

Lucia was from Brazil. An agency that specialized in the placement of domestic workers had recommended her, believing that she would be just right for a household of gay men. She had previously worked for one – a middle-aged businessman and father of three children who had just come out of the closet and lived in Atlanta. Although they were indeed gay, the men at the Hamptons house were nothing like the easy-going, tall and tan and young and lovely boys of Ipanema – or Atlanta. They expected her to live to serve. The next morning, she stepped into the kitchen to find the men already having breakfast and waiting for her. Well, good morning, they said, slightly peeved that she had gotten up later than they. She was wearing a long, tight-fitting, sleeveless black dress and rhinestone-encrusted sandals. Listen, the executive said, we want you to be comfortable, so why don't you and I go shopping this afternoon to get you a new outfit. Lucia had no choice but to consent and the men's mood improved a little. They figured that, once she was wearing proper servant's attire, in a short while she would know her place and eagerly clean their bathrooms, wash their laundry and scrub the floors. It was rather distressing to observe how it dawned on her what she had gotten herself into. That afternoon, any hopes Lucia might be allowed to be herself were shattered. The executive took her to a mall in Bridgehampton. He swiftly picked for her a pair of white sneakers, white tennis socks, kaki shorts, and white polo shirts. Her shapely hourglass figure was completely obscured by the square-cut new garments that made her look like a toddler, and she looked forlorn and broken. It was a heavy blow to her. Things were about to get worse.

Her probation days dragged on. Each of the men constantly called upon her to do something. But no one had more demands than the executive, who had put it in his head that he would properly train her. He traversed the rooms running his index along the surfaces to check for dust, asked her to make the beds in the six bedrooms and change the sheets in the master suite each day, to clean each of the seven bathrooms

*"It haunted the men that the new housekeeper had
already committed the crime of bad taste."*

every morning, sweep the porch, bring fresh towels to the pool, wash and iron his and everybody else's personal laundry, vacuum every room and polish his sports car. His need for meticulous order and cleanliness was impossible to fulfill. However he loved nothing more than starting his day with a civilized breakfast so something home-baked was in order. One morning, he was very pleased when I serve him warm

CURRANT SCONES

Mix 2 cups of flour with 1 teaspoon of salt and 1 teaspoon of baking powder. Slice 1 stick cold butter into it, kneed the butter into the flour with your fingertips until the mixture resembles coarse meal, then add ½ cup of dried currants and ¾ cups of buttermilk. Toss everything lightly at first to evenly moisten the flour and then carefully knead the dough very briefly until it barely holds together. Do not to overwork the dough or it will become gummy. On a floured surface, shape it into a log and flatten it. Brush it with a bit of cream or egg yolk mixed with a little water, sprinkle with anise or fennel seeds and a generous amount of raw sugar. Cut the log into irregular triangles and bake them on a parchment paper-lined baking sheet at 375° F until golden brown, about 25 minutes. These are best eaten warm, right out of the oven.

The scones cried for clotted cream and orange jam. So did the executive. Lucia became a bundle of nerves. The executive kept her at his beck and call. Later that morning he took me aside and asked me, Do you think she is going to make it? Where can one find a good housekeeper these days? I tried to explain that there was only so much one person could do in one day. He did not think my advice was justified. She can rest during the week, he said.

There were still workers and painters doing final touch-ups in the house. On their last day, a cleaning crew arrived to do away with the last bits of work dust and paint stains on the window panes and wooden floors. Among them was a tiny, energetic woman who seemed quite a bit more driven than the rest. That evening, the executive confidently announced to the other men, I have found ourselves a cleaning machine. The next week, Lucia was let go and replaced by the woman from the cleaning crew. Her name was Martha. She and I became good friends. I heard nothing more of Lucia until months later when she called me and told me that the executive had never paid her agency and that she had found a new job.

The news about a young chef serving delicious food at the summer house spread fast among the men's social circles. The executive and the men kept inviting more and more people to come by and join them for brunch, lunch, and dinner. Many more dropped by uninvited around mealtimes as if by coincidence. One early afternoon the telephone rang and the executive took the call in the kitchen. Someone was inviting him and the other men to come and have dinner at their house. He answered that he would be enchanted to see them. He then nonchalantly added, why don't you and your friends rather come here, we have our chef Daniel at our service. So a dozen more people would be coming for dinner that day. How to expand the menu to accommodate that number of people in such a short time was my problem. Martha and I would hurriedly drive into town and stop at several shops. She, barely four feet tall, looked rather diminutive in the large American car and her driving style, which she had acquired in the winding little streets of Bogota, provoked mayhem on the road. The other drivers cursed her out and I cursed, too. In spite of the stress of having to constantly accommodate more guests than expected, I was delighted to do nothing but cook every day and to try out things in the kitchen I had never done before. It was pleasurably exciting to put together new menus every day. This was the extravagant Greek lunch menu the men sat down to one Sunday:

TZAZIKI

EGGPLANT DIP

TARAMASALATA

GRIDDLED PITA

GRILLED MARINATED ZUCCHINI WITH MINT

STUFFED GRAPE LEAVES

SPINACH PIE

GREEK SALAD

GRILLED OCTOPUS WITH CHARRED LEMON

GRILLED ARTICHOKE HEARTS WITH AVGOLEMONO SAUCE

PISTACHIO BAKLAVA

HONEY-FLAVORED YOGURT GELATO

WITH POMEGRANATE SEEDS

One of the guests asked me for the recipe for my

TARAMASALATA

Soak 4 slices of stale white bread, crusts removed, in milk until softened. Squeeze out most of the milk and add them into a food processor with 3 heaped tablespoons of *Tarama*, Greek salt-cured cured carp roe as well as a quarter of a white onion, chopped, and the juice of half a lemon. To give it the traditional pink color, add a few drops of red beet juice by finely grating a small piece of raw red beet over a sieve set over the roe and pressing a spoon against the gratings to extract the juice. Process into a fine paste and transfer into a mixing bowl. Gradually whisk about ½ cup of mild olive oil into it until fully emulsified. Chill until ready to serve with

GRIDDLED PITA

Kneed 3 cups of flour, 2 teaspoons of salt, 1 packet (or 2 teaspoons) granulated yeast, about 2 tablespoons of olive oil and 1 ¼ cups of tepid water into a smooth dough, by hand or in a stand mixer with a dough hook attachment. If available, ¼ cup of chickpea flour can be added for flavor (add a bit more water if you do.) Cover the dough and store in a warm place for several hours or until it has doubled in size. Kneed the dough once more and divide it into 10 pieces. Roll each portion into a ball and flatten in into a thin disc no thicker than ¼ inch. Dust the discs with flour and let them rise once more. Cook them on a heated, lightly greased griddle or cast iron pan, turning them twice. Spray a bit of water onto their tops as they cook, the steam with facilitate the pita to blow up for the typical pocket-shape.

Perhaps I was a little mad to make pita breads from scratch. No one would have minded store-bought pita. But I did it on my own behalf, using this opportunity to find out what it would feel like to make virtually everything I served from scratch – long before this kind of activity became a popular obsession with those who advertise all their doings on social media. Many guests liked to come into the kitchen and chat with me and watch me as I rushed against time. Television cooking shows were not yet shown twenty-four hours a day. But I didn't need any cameras, I had a live audience.

Listening to the men's conversations was a lesson in itself. They had a great deal to say about their newest technical gadgets, three-star hotels they had stayed at during recent trips to London, Copenhagen or Paris, which airlines had the most comfortable business class and which New York restaurants the best-looking waiters. Regarding food, I learned that they considered a meal without chicken, fish or meat incomplete. This was at the time typical of all Americans and particularly of the urban gay male. One of them, always the first in line for the lunch buffet, frequently asked me, What's the protein today, and no one considered it bad manners. Professing to avoid what they refer to as "carbs" and sugar is also characteristic of Americans, although they perhaps crave either of the two more than anything else and can truly never get enough of them. They have, however, the unpardonable habit of not finishing what is on their plate. This is all the more perplexing as they also have a habit of helping themselves to seconds. Some of the men were so pleased with my food that they indulged more than was perhaps good for them. One of them once remarked that he was gaining too much weight and that he needed to go on a diet. Eat, drink, and be merry, I said. Ah, if only one had the discipline to indulge with measure. One wondered how he went about his meals in the city, on his work days. I expressed that perhaps, since eating homemade food was apparently not part of his *mode de vie*, some blame ought to be attributed to his habit of eating out or ordering in every night. He winced, glanced at the buffet and promised to be more disciplined.

The Greek lunch was the beginning of my decision to henceforth base every meal I served at the house on a different cuisine of the world, an idea that had come to me gradually and made cooking more of an adventure. During the week – which I partially spent in the city to recover and rest – I perused the markets and food stores of Chinatown, Little Italy, Curry Hill, Koreatown, the Lower East Side and Spanish Harlem. Did I know how to use any of the exotic ingredients I found there? This was long before the internet made looking up any recipe an easy task. I would have to find out on my own. Naturally this made it all the more exciting. I would come up with my own solutions. Every Friday morning, I would board the first train to East Hampton with a cooler full of specialty ingredients. I used to call it the slave train because it was filled with domestic workers who, like me, were on their way to work. Martha would always pick me up at the station. Driving to several different nearby shops and markets, we were like a tornado rushing through the aisles, hurriedly piling up groceries in baskets and shopping carts. Was it ever enough? To my consternation it never was. Too soon to be sure we would have to return to the stores for more, for there was always the next meal for even more guests who seemed to arrive at the house in hungry packs. The phone kept ringing and even though there was a phone in every room of the house it was I whom everyone expected to pick it up and take messages. No one who came for lunch ever brought a gift but dinner guests brought, without exception, either a bottle of Champagne or a scented candle. Hardly anyone ever drank or asked for Champagne but it was nonetheless a popular if generic gift: unlike choosing a bottle of wine which requires a certain degree of connoisseurship that no one in this particular social circle had, a bottle of Champagne was a safe choice and unquestionable status symbol. Over the summer, the Champagne bottles piled up in the cellar and the scented candles piled up in the closet under the staircase, many of them still gift-wrapped. At some point, I counted seventeen bottles of Champagne and thirty-nine scented candles in all sizes, shapes and scents. Then one Sunday evening, just as everyone was getting ready to drive or fly back to the city, the executive graciously invited me to stay at the house. Make yourself at home and enjoy a few days at the beach, he said. It sounded rather enticing. But I was to find out that the Hamptons were a playground on weekends and a maintenance factory on weekdays. The next morning, I woke up from the sound of several leaf blowers. An entire army of Mexican gardeners and landscapers had descended on the property. Inside the main house, the housekeeper was already frantically vacuuming and shouting directions in Spanish at the Ecuadorian cleaning lady the executive had eventually agreed to hire part-time to assist her. The whistling of the two washing machines' tumbling cycles was reverberating through the air, interspersed by staccato ringtones coming from the two laundry driers and three dishwashers. It was infernal. I took one of the bicycles and went for a ride. It was not encouraging that the entire region was buzzing with workers and the noise of countless, oversized lawn mowers and pick-up trucks. At a Columbian deli in Amagansett that no white Americans ever stepped into I bought myself a savory late breakfast.

PAN DE BONO
(Colombian Cheese Buns)

In a food processor, pulse 2 cups of yucca flour, 2 tablespoons of white Masarepa*, 1 teaspoon of baking powder, 1 teaspoon of salt, 2 heaped tablespoons of sugar, 1 medium-size Mozzarella, cut into cubes, and ½ cup of mild feta cheese until roughly combined. Add 1 egg and process

---

* Precooked white or yellow cornmeal. Instant polenta is an acceptable substitute but do not use regular cornmeal or Mexican *Masa Harina*.

into a smooth, pliable dough that holds its shape. Add more yucca starch if it seems too soft. Divide it into 12 portions and roll each portion into a ball, using white cornmeal to prevent it from sticking. Sprinkle them with flaky sea salt and bake them on a parchment-paper-lined sheet pan in a 375° F oven until puffed up and golden brown, about 20 minutes. These are best served warm. Colombians like them dipped into hot chocolate.

A slightly different version of these buns is known in Brazil as *pão de queijo*. The yucca flour is the key ingredient. Neither of these are well known in the United States yet but with more and more people affecting a gluten intolerance, they are bound to become popular as a bread alternative. Here is another one.

AREPAS DE CHOCLO
(Colombian Sweet Corn Griddle Cakes)

Shave off the kernels of 3 ears of sweet corn into a food processor and pulse them to a coarse mush. Transfer it to a mixing bowl and add 1 cup of yellow Masarepa, ¼ cup of rice flour, ¼ cup of raw sugar, 1 small, shredded firm Mozzarella, a good pinch of salt and 1 teaspoon of warm milk in which you have melted 2 tablespoons of butter. Combine everything and let it rest for 10 minutes. The dough should have the consistency of a thick pancake batter – add more milk if it is too thick. Make pancakes as you would with any other batter. You can stack two pancakes on top of each other with a slice of Mozzarella between them and cook them a bit longer until the cheese is melted, flipping them once. A bit of hot sauce may be served on the side. This is a delicious midday meal.

The convenient corn creamer I started to use years later to make these arepas was a chance purchase in a store in Chinatown one day when I was looking around for special steaming baskets for making wontons. Two dozen creamed ears of corn, cooked simply with butter for a few minutes, will yield an original first course for about eight people.

In the village of East Hampton the old shops were slowly being pushed out by rent hikes and promptly replaced by luxury fashion boutiques, overpriced restaurants with subpar fare, and real estate offices. Was I aware that this was but a taste of what would soon happen in the city? By the train station, I saw dozens of Mexican day workers in ragged clothes sitting on the balustrades, waiting to be picked up for menial cash jobs. They were willing to do anything, from mowing lawns to pruning shrubs and bushes or washing dishes. I returned to the house. There, the housekeeper was taking a break, grumbling that there was no leftover chicken for her rice and beans.

Suddenly, the contractor arrived with two painters. Hastily, rugs were rolled up as the painters readied themselves to repaint one of the living rooms a different shade of beige. Sofas and armchairs were quickly covered with plastic planes but there was not enough time to to gather and put away all the hand-blown decorative glass vases lined up on a sideboard. Meanwhile in the guest rooms on the second floor an interior decorator was installing the new window shades the executive had ordered. They did not look noticeably different from the old ones but everyone later commented that they were an important improvement.

When an engineer arrived a little later to fix the house's entertainment system I was no longer amused. The men's need for constant background music cannot be debated here, but a partial list of the satellite music stations that they insisted on playing all day long is offered as a curiosity. Hits from the 60s, Hits from the 70s, Hits from the 80s, Oldies but Goldies, Easy Listening, Showtunes, Showstoppers, Hard Rock Café, Country and Western, Rhythm 'n Blues, Top Ten Hits, Madonnarama, Glam Rock, Karaoke Central. I had made it a habit of always turning down the volume in the kitchen. Naturally the executive kept turning it up again every time he came into the kitchen, and I would promptly turn it down again once he'd left.

After several hours of this kind of maintenance mayhem, I asked Martha to kindly drive me to the train station. On the train back to the city, I heaved a sigh of relief.

After my first season in the Hamptons ended, I was hired by the conductor and his medical doctor partner. Two years later, I left the couple and cooking in the Hamptons during the summer season became once again a lucrative seasonal occupation. One house I ended up cooking in quite frequently was very famous not only throughout the Hamptons but throughout the United States, particularly because it had a rather piquant family connection to the late Jackie Kennedy Onassis. The house was called Grey Gardens. Of course, Jackie O. had never lived in it but I liked to think that she, prone as she allegedly was to periodically going on fruit fasts, might have enjoyed what I always made for breakfast on Saturdays and Sundays no matter which house I was cooking in.

FRUIT MACÉDOINE

Peel and dice any combination of papaya, mango, apple, pear, pineapple, kiwi, and melon. Plums, apricots and peaches may also be used as long as they are firm. The dice should be no larger and preferably smaller than the size of a raspberry. Do not mix the variety; rather, place the dice in layers into a glass bowl, one kind of fruit at a time. That way, the flavors of each fruit will remain distinct and their shape more pristine. If using apples, pears or peaches, lace them with a bit of lemon juice to prevent oxidation. The last layer should consist of berries – diced strawberries, whole raspberries, blackberries or blueberries. Dig the serving spoon all the way to the bottom of the bowl so that when serving the *macédoine*, every portion gets a taste of each fruit. This refreshing salad is better than the sum of its parts.

Grey Gardens was no longer in the bad state it had been in when the Maysles Brothers had filmed their engrossing documentary about poor Little Edie and her mother who were then living in it in squalor in the company of countless stray cats. The house had however once again acquired an inordinately bohemian patina. It had been renovated some twenty years earlier by its new owners, Washington Post executive editor Ben Bradlee and his journalist wife Sally Quinn. Since the couple only used the house in August they rented it out for the rest of the year, and in those years, one of my clients, an investment banker with a lovely interior decorator wife and three kids, gaily rented it.

Miss Quinn was apparently adamant about not allowing her tenants to make any changes to the interior, dated as it was. The kitchen in particular proved to me that Washington insiders consider the culinary arts a waste of time. The crystal and porcelain were mismatched and chipped, as was the flatware that made one think of a yard sale. The linen was stained and the pots and pans were cheap and damaged. There was nothing to do but cope and make the best of the situation amidst the once again decomposing Grey Gardens chaos, so radically different from the meticulously micromanaged gay men's households I had gotten used to and that suited my own need for cleanliness and order so much more.

As the years went by, working under all kinds of conditions became easier and more enjoyable, except for the time of the 2003 East Coast power outage. I was at the time cooking once again for the executive, who had rented out his mansion for the month of August and arranged to rent a charming, old-fashioned little house, next to the imposing East Hampton Golf Club and conveniently close to the beach. He had insisted on having it completely redecorated for the month. His faithful assistant had all but cleared the little house of all its furnishings and replaced everything with vintage modernist furniture and art work. He did however not replace the electric stove and so, when the power went out on August 14, there was no choice but to cook every meal on the little charcoal barbecue on the terrace. It was on that occasion that I learned how to make

GRILLED LOBSTER WITH HERBED BUTTER

Rinse 2 handfuls of mixed aromatic *fines herbes* (parsley, dill, basil, cilantro, chervil, sorrel, chervil, even spinach, but *not* rosemary, oregano or thyme), tumble them dry and roll them up in several sheets of paper towel to blot off any remaining water. Pick the leaves off the stems and chop them finely.

In a mortar, pound 1 clove of garlic with a teaspoon of coarse sea salt until you have a paste, add ½ pound of cold butter, cut into pieces, the chopped herbs, finely ground white pepper, a pinch of anise seeds, and a dash of anise liquor (like Sambuca or Pastis) or dry vermouth. Work the herbs into the butter with the pestle and transfer the herbed butter into a bowl.

Place medium-size live lobsters, one per person, in a tub filled with cold tab water and leave them in it for a good thirty minutes – it will sedate them. Heat a charcoal grill with the lid on, place a sheet pan on it and fill it with water. When the water is simmering, place the lobsters on it, replace the lid on the grill and precook them for 5 minutes – or until their color has noticeably changed to red. Immediately submerge them fully in ice water for a moment. Lightly crack the claws with a mallet and split the lobster bodies lengthwise in half, cutting through their heads (this is easier done if you place them belly-up on your cutting board). Place the halved bodies, flesh side down, on the medium-hot, well-oiled grill and cook for less than a minute before flipping them. Baste the tail meat with softened herbed butter and grill the lobsters for another 5 minutes, until the meat is opaque. Serve in the shell, with melted herbed butter for dipping, and sliced baguette, warmed on the grill.

With intensive experience I gradually became more playful in the kitchen. I no longer limited my repertoire to classic dishes from around the world, I began to experiment. Spontaneity became my motto. It was a protracted, indeed a perpetual game. A combination of fish and fresh fruit might be toothsome. A few fresh chilies, freshly squeezed citrus juices or minced ginger could brighten the flavor of a dish. I rarely consulted cookbooks. But oddly the world around me began to show an increasing interest in them. Many clients began to accumulate them on their coffee tables even though it was extremely unlikely that they would ever take it upon themselves to put them to use and actually cook a meal – too daunting, too complicated, too messy. They were quite satisfied to continue to merely watch the occasional cooking show on TV and eat out or order in rather than to actually do any of the cooking themselves. Some had the unfortunate habit of telling me about cooking shows they liked or a cookbook they found interesting – even if they did not understand the least about it. While most of these books were overproduced and useless to me, one tome by Jean-Georges Vongerichten, *Cooking at Home with a Four-Star Chef,* was a true inspiration, teaching me much in the way of cooking with a light hand. This is my adaptation of his recipe for a

CAPER RAISIN SAUCE

Empty the content of one small jar of *nonpareil* capers into a saucepan, add ½ cup of golden raisins and enough water to cover them and simmer everything over low heat for about 10 minutes. Transfer to a blender and purée. If you want, you can whisk a bit of cold butter into the warm sauce before serving it, but no more than 2 tablespoons.

Chef Jean-Georges serves this sauce with pan-seared sea scallops and roasted cauliflower but I find it also quite suitable for a simple

STEAMED STRIPED BASS

Cut a striped bass filet into portions and season it with salt only. Fill a large pot that fits a flat-bottomed steaming basket (metal or bamboo) with 2 inches of water and add a scant combination of aromatics such as juniper berries, fennel seeds, bay leaves, parsley, fennel or cilantro stems, lemon slices, a splash of white vermouth or tequila. Simmer the liquid for a few minutes, until fragrant. If using a stainless steel steaming basket, spray it with oil. If using a bamboo basket, line it with a round piece of parchment paper, perforated in several spots, or even a couple of lettuce or cabbage leaves. Arrange the filets in the basket without overlapping, place the basket into the pot, close the lid and steam the filets until they are opaque and a wooden pick pierces their thickest part without resistance, for 5 to 10 minutes or more, depending on the size of the filets. Spoon a tiny amount of olive or even mustard oil over the warm fish and serve it with the caper (or any other) sauce on the side.

One day a houseguest told me he had in his possession a copy of the first edition of *Mastering the Art of French Cooking*, the famous cookbook written by Julia Child, the matronly Washington insider who with the aid of television became America's most beloved authority on French cookery. My mother had learned how to cook French food from French cookbooks, notably Françoise Bernard's *Les Recettes Faciles*. I used to wonder what the French would think of *Mastering the Art of French Cooking*. It is of course a book for total beginners, unlike Madame Bernard's which naturally expected its adult readers to have some prior knowledge and experience. Miss Child's recipes are exhausting to read and unnecessarily complicated. Take for instance her recipe for a basic omelet that runs for seven pages, whereas Bernard's *Les Recettes Faciles*, translated below, instructs the reader to do the following.

OMELETTE CLASSIQUE

You should own a good quality, heavy-bottomed frying pan that you use almost exclusively for making omelets. Keep it very clean, even the smallest food particle or crust will definitely make the omelet stick to the pan.

In a mixing bowl, lightly beat 7 eggs, seasoned with salt and pepper. Gently heat 2 tablespoons of oil in the frying pan to lukewarm. Incorporate the oil into the eggs. Replace the pan (without rinsing) over high heat. Once it is very hot, pour the eggs into it and cook them for 3 to 4 minutes. Mix with a fork to cook it all the way through. As soon as it is a bit dry on the sides but still creamy at the center, fold it over and invert it onto a warmed platter.

If the omelet gets stuck the pan, the pan was either not clean or not hot enough. The omelet's texture will be dry if you add any other liquid than oil to the batter or omit the mixing part during the cooking process.

By the spring of 2004 cooking had become my second nature. My eighth Hamptons season was about to begin and I was looking for some diversion that would take my mind off all kitchen matters on my free days. A year earlier a friend had given Filip Noterdaeme and I an old accordion, which I had stored away in the little den high up in the gable of our attic apartment. This friend knew that I often hired accordionists to accompany me when I was booked in cabarets that did not have a piano. From time to time, I had thought about learning how to play the accordion. The idea of accompanying myself on an instrument and to not have to split the meager fees I earned for these shows cheered me up. Perhaps this was the right moment. The den was hard to reach without a ladder which was all the way down in the basement but that did not deter me – I placed a bar stool on the dresser below the den and stepped onto it to get the accordion down. Once I had retrieved it, the heavy accordion made me lose my balance and I fell all the way down to the floor, onto my right wrist. Fearing the worst, I left a note for Filip Noterdaeme, written uneasily with my left hand, and rushed to the emergency room. There, I was made to wait for several hours before I was being told that my right wrist was indeed broken and that I would need surgery. Blessedly, Filip Noterdaeme arrived just in time to take me home. The painkillers I had been given by the nurse, something I had no experience with, were a knock-out.

After my operation a week later, my right hand looked rather useless, held fast in an awkward crooked angle by a metal fixator that had been screwed into my bones and extended from my forearm to my hand. I was worried that I would lose my summer job. Would the men who had hired me accept a one-handed chef? The head of the household said they would and surprisingly they did and even hired a very eager French houseboy who assisted me in the kitchen as best as he could. I used to joke that, together, we were cooking with three left hands. Occasionally one of the men would come into the kitchen and chat with me while I was trying to peel and cut up vegetables, my left hand slowly becoming more adept at stirring, chopping and slicing. The food processor and the blender became my favorite tools that season, a welcome relief from the usual handiwork required to create a satisfying home-cooked meal. I turned everything I could think of into soups, emulsions, dips and purées. The men were gracious and patient and did not complain. The Mexican butcher at the store was overcome with pity when he saw my temporarily crippled hand and gave me his mother's recipe for an easy

GUACAMOLE

In a food processor, pulse one third of a large white onion, peeled and roughly chopped, 1 sliced jalapeño with perhaps some but not all of its seeds and membranes (whence its heat stems from) removed according to preference, salt to taste and a handful of fresh cilantro – leaves and stems – until roughly blended. Add 2 ripe, sliced avocados and pulse everything into a chunky dip. Serve immediately with corn chips.

After my hand was healed again, I resolved to rather mash the avocados with a pastry cutter and folding the processed onion paste into them. Everyone agrees that this is the best guacamole to be had.

GAZPACHO

In a blender, liquify chunks of peeled hothouse cucumber, sun-ripe tomatoes, red and green bell pepper, white onion and just enough watermelon to add a bit of sweetness to make up for what is lacking in most tomatoes available in America. This detail is an idea I came up with by sheer instinct, long before "watermelon *gazpacho*" became fashionable, perhaps because I had known the taste of *gazpacho* in Spain where it is made with sweet and fragrant, sun-ripened tomatoes, more delicious than any I have ever found in America.. Add a few chunks of stale white country bread, crusts removed, and blend once again until smooth and creamy. Season with red wine vinegar, salt and white pepper and pass it through a fine mesh sieve to remove any seeds and bits of tomato and bell pepper skin. Chill thoroughly and serve in chilled soup bowls, garnished with a few drops of olive oil and a sprig of cilantro.

Traditionally, little bowls with finely diced cucumber, tomato, green, yellow and red bell pepper and toasted croutons are served on the side. I might have even included separate dishes of diced green mango, pickled watermelon pith and perhaps some diced avocado, however because of my handicap the gazpacho was served plain at this time.

The fixator stayed on for the whole summer. When it finally came off, my right hand was weak and I had to regularly do very tedious rehabilitation exercises, working with a physical therapist who it turned out had once been Filip Noterdaeme's and my current landlord's girlfriend. When she found out that he was now owning the building in which he had been just a tenant back then, she deeply regretted her fate. Imagine, she said, If I had not broken up with him, I would now be on easy street and a landlady and would not have to teach you these exercises. She also assured me that my right hand would regain its dexterity. It eventually did, but I never used it to learn how to play the accordion. I had lost interest.

Before the summer was over, one event created some happy diversion. *Rouge*, a burlesque show I was frequently performing with in those years, had been invited to perform for one night at the Town Hall of East Hampton. My clients gave me the night off. Discretion was thrown to the winds and several of them came to see the show. I was the only male member of the cast and had been cast to sing *La Vie en Rose*. I performed with a rhinestone-encrusted pink ribbon decoratively tied around my disfigured wrist. Before the show, the producer informed us that our presence at a big garden party in nearby Springs had been requested later that night. Almost immediately after taking our bows we were whisked to the address in a white stretch limousine. There, we made quite an impression on the over two hundred guests in attendance. The burlesque dancers were still wearing their show costumes and the male guests were following them around like hungry dogs. Some of the female guests were not amused.

The next evening, after another day of cooking breakfast, lunch and dinner, I took the train back to the city. During the trip, a young man, dressed in torn cargo jeans and a leather jacket and nervously pacing up and down the aisle struck up a flirtatious conversation with me. Grinning sheepishly, he told me that he was straight but making this trip to the city to perform a strip routine at "Amateur Night" at the Gaiety, a notorious gay burlesque in Times Square. It was going to be his first trial at being a stripper. That explained everything – he was flirting with me to get into character.

The Hamptons were in those years becoming even more exclusive. The executive announced excitedly that a billionaire from South Africa had made him an offer he could not refuse to buy his house. To the great regret of the other men, he accepted the offer, sold him the house and bought a smaller house instead. Not too long before, he and his friends had wondered aloud why there weren't any young men coming out to the Hamptons any more like they themselves used to when they were younger. Well, I had thought to myself, they simply can't afford it any longer, and it is you and your kind who drove up the prices. I was only partially right. Now, a new generation of rich people was beginning to invade the Hamptons. The area became completely gentrified. So the boys of Wall Street, Madison Avenue,

Silicon Valley, and the inflated world of modern art and real estate quietly bought up old houses, out-pricing long-established Long Island families and driving the immigrant service-industry workers further away from the popular South Fork. It was the same old story.

On July Fourth, one of my clients liked to organize a party on the lawn of his new house overlooking Three-Mile Harbor. There were going to be celebratory fireworks across the water. American flags were flying from every building and countless anchored boats on the bay. Everybody was very excited. They were not the first fireworks I had ever seen, in fact I believe that once you have seen one set of them you have seen them all. I had requisitioned a kitchen assistant and several waiters from the city — since food would have to be served, it might as well be me preparing it rather than an over-charging Hamptons caterer. The guests cheered at the fireworks and ogled the attractive waiters. They couldn't keep their eyes of them. Finally they turned to the picnic-style buffet, which I had been working on for two days. No need to make too much dessert, the host had said, I will order mini cupcakes with little American flags. This was my menu:

VIETNAMESE SUMMER ROLLS WITH SHRIMP
AND TAMARIND DIPPING SAUCE

CHICKEN BANH MI
COLE SLAW WITH GREEN MANGO, SCALLIONS
AND CASHEWS
SWEET AND SOUR CELLOPHANE NOODLE SALAD

PANDAN-FLAVORED EGG CUSTARD

The neighbors had all been invited as well so they would not complain about the noise from the party. The store-bought cupcakes did not taste like they had been made with real butter although it said so on the printed packaging.

This is the way I prepared

CHICKEN BANH MI
(Vietnamese-style Sandwiches)

Using a mandolin with an attached shredder, cut peeled carrots and daikon radishes into thin long strands, fill them into Mason jars and pour over them a warmed mix of equal parts rice vinegar and water, seasoned with sugar and salt. Close with a lid and refrigerate. This is best made a day ahead of time.

Clean boneless, skinless chicken thighs well, careful to remove any pieces of cartilage as well as the thick vein that runs through them. Put them into a large mixing bowl, add just enough peanut oil to coat them with a thin film. Season them generously with salt, black pepper, a dash of sugar and a fair amount of *achiote* (or paprika) powder. Toss well and refrigerate for several hours or overnight.

Prepare the trimmings: thinly sliced hothouse cucumbers and jalapenos, rinsed and tumble-dried cilantro sprigs and a bowl of mayonnaise mixed with a bit of finely diced pickled ginger and *Sambal Oelek** to taste.

Grill or panfry the chicken thighs on both sides until done and slice them not too thinly across the grain. Spray oval French rolls with water and crisp them in the oven, about 5 minutes at 375° F. Slice them open and fill them with sliced chicken, drizzled with a bit of spicy mayonnaise and topped with a handful of drained pickled carrot and daikon strips, a few slices of cucumber and jalapeno and a sprig of cilantro. Serve the sandwiches wrapped halfway in a piece of parchment paper.

The spicy mayonnaise is also an excellent condiment for breaded or cornmeal-dusted, pan-fried flounder or fluke.

The next weekend I was back at Grey Gardens. When I arrived with the usual dozen large shopping bags of fresh groceries, I found the kitchen in a terrible state. The entire family and several guests had been staying at the house for the whole week without either a chef or a maid at their service. The refrigerator was full of old leftover takeout food and the laundry room was overflowing with bed sheets, children's and adult's clothes next to piles of wet beach towels. I was fuming. It took me several hours to get the kitchen back to my working standards. I had to completely empty and clean out the refrigerator to make room for my freshly bought groceries. For lunch I decided to prepare as a first course a dish I had made up on the spot. The family was about to sit down to eat when we heard voices calling out in the parlor. It was a couple of their friends dropping in. The host and hostess got up to greet them. One of them was a young architect who was very engaging. It was a casual lunch indeed and conversation was lively. The architect had come to talk to the host about his project of building a subterranean public park on the Lower East Side of Manhattan

* Oriental chili and garlic paste

that he hoped would have the same kind of success the High Line was already having in Chelsea on the West Side. However what effect would it have on the neighborhood, I wondered. We think it will add value to it, he said, but first we need sponsors. I thought about the history of the Lower East Side as a working class neighborhood and the strange change Chelsea had seen since the High Line had opened. The architect seemed oblivious to any skepticism. It was a groundbreaking public park he wanted to build.

The improvised dish was a fitting first course for the extensible lunch. It was a tongue-in-cheek adaptation of the classic "Caesar salad" and alluded to everything the terrible Roman Emperor Nero was known for – namely, setting Rome on fire.

Later, I learned that Caesar salad is supposed to have been invented in California in the Twenties by an Italian-American restaurateur named Caesar Cardini. It therefore has nothing to do at all with the Roman Emperor Julius Caesar. But I still continue to this day to call my creation

NERO SALAD

Cut several hearts of Romaine lettuce lengthwise in half, drizzle them with very little olive oil and place them on a clean, medium hot charcoal grill. Cook them just briefly, turning them once, until lightly charred on the edges but altogether barely wilted. Season the hearts lightly with salt and arrange them on a platter. For the dressing, poach 2 eggs in simmering water for 2 minutes and transfer them to a blender. Add 6 anchovy filets, 2 tablespoons of capers, a few pickled green peppercorns, the zest and juice of 1 lemon and ¼ cup of white wine vinegar. Blend until smooth and pour into a mixing bowl. Little by little, whisk ½ cup of olive oil into the mixture until the dressing is emulsified and creamy* Scatter a scant amount of the dressing over the charred lettuce and top it with just a little *shredded pecorino di Romano*. This is the only instance I ever use Pecorino shredded, not ground, to prevent it from dissolving in the dressing. Serve with thick grilled slices of olive oil-brushed country bread.

After three years of renting Grey Gardens, the family decided that it had had enough of the social scene of the Hamptons and began to look for a less crowded place to spend their summers at. They settled on a

---

* It is best to do this last step by hand as processing olive oil in an electric blender oxidizes the oil, making it bitter.

beautiful old mansion on the shore of Bellport, overlooking the bay and distant Fire Island. The owner was a friend of theirs and a writer. One of the books she had been a co-writer for was *Every Step You Take*, the autobiography of Jock Soto, the legendary New York City Ballet principal. There was a copy of it in my guest-room, and reading it prompted me to reach out to Jock. We had briefly met some years earlier but I had not known what I now learned through his book: that he was a passionate cook. We became friends and years later, when Filip Noterdaeme and I got married, he insisted to host a wedding dinner party for us at his and his husband Luis Fuentes' loft in Williamsburg. I had always declined requests to cook for weddings. So many gay and lesbian couples were getting married in those days but I had, as soon as the courts in New York State had legalized gay marriage, announced to all my clients that I was not prepared to deal with two grooms and two mothers-in-law at the same time. For my own wedding party however I insisted that I would at least make the cake.

Jock and Luis asked us to make a guest list. Who would we like to invite. We wanted to have our friends Broadway legend Tommy Tune and downtown legend Joey Arias and singer and radio show host Julian Fleisher and filmmaker Scott McGehee with their partners or dates and some more friends, but not more than sixteen altogether. Everybody accepted the invitation. It was a very romantic dinner. Filip Noterdaeme and I wore white, and I got to make my own cake and eat it, too.

WEDDING CAKE

A day in advance bake 2 batches of cake layers, using 2 different recipes.

For the first batch, beat 6 eggs and a ¾ cup of sugar to a soft ribbon. Fold in ½ cup of flour and ½ cup of potato starch, sifted together with 1 teaspoon of baking powder. Divide the dough into two 9-inch ring molds, lined with parchment paper and greased and floured, and bake them in a 325° F oven for about 40 minutes, until a cake tester comes out clean.

For the second batch, flavor 1 ¼ cups of sugar with the finely grated zest of 1 orange. Add 7 egg yolks and beat them and the sugar to a soft ribbon. Add the juice of 1 orange and 1 tablespoon vanilla essence and stir to combine. Gradually add 2 ½ cups of ground almonds and 4 tablespoons of melted butter. Beat 7 egg whites and a pinch of salt to a firm peak and gently fold them into the almond base, one third at a time. Divide the dough into two 9-inch ring molds, lined with parchment paper and greased and floured, and bake in a 350° F oven for about 30 minutes, until a cake tester comes out clean.

Unmold all 4 cake layers when they are no longer warm and wrap them tightly in cellophane without but do not yet remove the parchment paper that clings to them.

Prepare the

ORANGE BUTTER CREAM

Pour 4 cups of fresh-squeezed orange juice through a fine-mesh sieve and gently heat it in a non-reactive sauce pan. Beat 8 egg yolks with ½ cup of sugar and stir into them ¼ cup of flour and ⅓ cup of cornstarch, sifted together, until smooth. Temper the mix with a bit of hot juice before pouring it into the sauce pan. Gently bring it to a simmer while constantly stirring. Cook for a minute until thickened, strain it through a fine-mesh sieve into a bowl and cover it with a plate set over a paper towel to absorb any rising steam. Once the cream has reached room temperature, place it in the refrigerator.

The next day, gently heat 2 cups of apricot jam with 1/4 cup of orange liquor and strain it through a fine-mesh sieve. Bring ½ cup of sugar and ½ cup of water to a boil. When it turns syrupy, take it off the fire and add ¼ cup of rum. Beat 2 sticks of softened butter until very creamy. Gradually add the orange pastry cream, at first just one tablespoon at a time, beating until fully combined before adding more.

Assemble the cake. Carefully pull the parchment paper off the 4 cakes and cut each cake horizontally in two. Starting with an almond cake, stack the layers in an alternating pattern, brushing them first with syrup, then spreading a bit of apricot jam on them and finally adding buttercream, spreading it to a ¼-inch thickness. After the final layer has been added, brush the top and sides of the cake with apricot jam and refrigerate it for an hour before covering the whole cake, top and sides, with a large sheet of rolled-out marzipan. Press the marzipan against the sides and cut off any overlap. Glaze the marzipan with a sugar glaze made of 4 cups of confectioner's sugar beaten to a soft ribbon with a splash of white rum and about ½ cup of milk. Once the glaze has set, kneed some red or pink food coloring (or some red juice squeezed from shredded red beet) into an extra batch of marzipan, roll it out to a ribbon and wrap it around the bottom of the cake, covering the seam with a bow made of the scraps of the pink marzipan. The cake must be kept refrigerated but tastes best served at room temperature.

After several summers devoted to working in the Hamptons while Filip Noterdaeme, on summer break from his diverse teaching jobs, had no choice but to remain in the stiflingly hot city, I decided that we owed it to ourselves as inveterate Europeans to take an annual European-style summer vacation. I told my clients that I would no longer be available for work during the month of August. But, said the mother of one of them, what are they going to do without you. They are going to finally have a chance to go on a diet, I said.

*"For my own wedding party, however, I insisted that
I would at least make the cake."*

XII
RECIPES FROM FRIENDS

BREAKFAST

Stacy Switzer, *Kansas City, Missouri*
GERMAN PANCAKES

Stir 1 pack of dry yeast and a pinch of sugar into 1 cup of warm water. When it begins to foam, combine it with ½ cup of sugar, 2 ½ teaspoons of flour, 1 teaspoon of salt and enough water to make a smooth runny dough. Cover and refrigerate overnight. In the morning, add 4 beaten eggs and 1 tablespoon of melted butter. Fry pancakes in hot buttered iron pan and serve them immediately with jam.

Lisa Jarnot, *Queens, New York*
FOUR-FOOD GROUP GLUTEN-FREE PANCAKES
FOR FUSSY KIDS

In a blender, process 2 chicken eggs (or 6 quail eggs) with one peeled, quartered and cored apple (or one banana) and a tablespoon of peanut or almond butter until smooth. Stir in a handful of shredded carrots, a handful of shredded zucchini, a pinch of salt, a pinch of cinnamon, a cup of rice flour and a handful of flax seeds. Add enough almond or rice milk (or – if you want the added health benefits of gelatin colloid and amino acids – homemade chicken stock, preferably made with a stewing hen and cooked for several hours) to make a batter.

    Fry in batches with butter, ghee, or coconut oil.

Cathleen Chaffee, *Detroit, Michigan*
GRANDMA NORMIE'S IRISH SODA BREAD

In a mixing bowl combine 4 cups of flour with ½ teaspoon of salt, ¼ cup of sugar, 1 ½ teaspoons of baking soda and 2 teaspoons of baking powder. Cut 6 tablespoons of cold butter into the flour mix, from a well in the center and add 1 ¼ cups of buttermilk and 1 egg. Stir well with a fork before adding a generous ½ cup of raisins. Kneed the dough well, divide it in half and form each portion into a flattened ball. Cut a cross on top of each ball to keep the fairies away. Brush with melted butter, dust with cinnamon sugar and bake for 40-45 minutes on a parchment-paper lined sheet pan at 375° F.

Jason Dottley, *Miami, Florida*
AVOCADO TOAST

This is my current breakfast obsession.

Find a perfectly ripe avocado and dice one per person into a bowl. Add a sprinkle of sea salt. Squeeze half a lemon into the bowl and use a fork to mash the avocado, stirring in a few big drops of extra virgin olive oil. Chill for 30 minutes in the refrigerator. Toast your favorite bread. I prefer a thick, hearty whole grain bread, but sourdough is also a wonderful choice. Spread the avocado mixture onto the toast while the toast is hot. Finish with coarse ground sea salt and a squirt of lemon juice.

Marko Gnann, *New York City*
QUAINT SECOND BREAKFAST

This was a favorite in my childhood years in West Berlin. Choose very ripe strawberries, wash and quarter them and macerate them in a bowl for a good hour, dusted with a generous amount of sugar. Add enough cold milk to submerge them at least by half and serve with a slice of pumpernickel bread, spread with salted butter.

APPETIZERS

David Bruson, *New York City*
CHICKEN LIVER PATÉ

Chop one medium onion and caramelize in sauté pan with ¼ stick of butter. Once the onion is nicely browned, remove it to a plate. In same pan, add another ¼ stick of butter and 1 pound of cleaned chicken livers. Sauté livers over medium heat until cooked through. Set aside and let cool. In the meantime, very finely chop ¼ cup of fresh parsley.

Once the livers have cooled, add them to a food processor with the caramelized onions, fresh parsley, and 8 ounces Neufchâtel or American cream cheese. Process until fully incorporated and smooth. Salt and Pepper to taste. Syphon off mixture into ramekins and fill to the top of each. Cover with plastic wrap and chill to solidify.

Serve chilled or room temperature with toasted baguette slices.

Donald Lanziero, *New York City*
SHRIMP FROM THE DEVIL PRIEST

Preheat the broiler. In a 12-inch sauté pan, heat 1/4 extra virgin oil over medium heat. Add 6 thinly sliced cloves of garlic and 4 seeded and thinly sliced jalapenos and cook until softened, about 3 minutes. Add 1 tablespoon red pepper flakes, 2 cups of tomato sauce and 1 cup of dry white wine and bring to a boil. Lower the heat and simmer for 4 minutes. Season with salt to taste. Lay 20 large peeled shrimp, split down the back and deveined, in the sauce and simmer until just cooked through, 4 to 6 minutes. Meanwhile, place 4 slices of rustic country bread on a baking sheet and toast them under the broiler, turning once. Place a slice of toasted bread in the center of each of 4 plates, top with 5 shrimp per toast and spoon the sauce over them. Sprinkle with 2 tablespoons fresh marjoram leaves and ¼ cup of toasted bread crumbs. Drizzle with a bit of olive oil and serve.

Anastassia Tabolina, *Queens, New York*
SELEDKA POD SHUBOI
(Herring Under A Fur Coat)

Plan ahead. The cooked vegetables must be completely cooled down when you assemble the dish and the dish itself must be refrigerated for at least 6 hours before being served.

Put 4 Yukon Gold or other firm-cooking potatoes, 3 large carrots and 2 large beets into a large pot, cover them with water and bring it to a simmer. Remove each vegetable when fork tender, first the carrots, then the potatoes, then the beets. When they are cool, peel and separately shred them. Rinse 4 oil-packed *Matjes* herring filets and soak them in cold milk for an hour. Rinse again, pat them dry and dice them. Chop one medium-size red onion, transfer it into a bowl and cover with boiling water. Drain out the liquid after 5 minutes and add the onions to the herring, mixing well. Boil 3 eggs for 10 minutes, chill them in an ice bath, peel them and set them aside. Dress the potatoes with salt, celery seed and very little mayonnaise, the carrots with a bit of lemon juice, salt and pepper, the beets with salt, pepper and a dash of sugar.

Place a large ring form (bottom removed) on a round platter (or small ring forms on individual serving plates) and press the potato mixture into it in an even layer. Top it with the herring mix, followed by the carrots and finally the beets, gently pressing down each layer with a glass before adding the next. As a final layer, spread some thick sour cream over it (mayonnaise is more traditional but there is no right or wrong). Refrigerate for 6 hours. Just before serving, finely grate the boiled eggs and sprinkle an even layer over the cream. Season with salt and black pepper and garnish with a bit of chopped dill. Remove the ring and serve with toasted pumpernickel bread.

Alain Mousnier, *Paris, France*
PATÉ DE THON

This is a recipe from my mother Maryse that brings back early memories of summers by the ocean and the season's first catch of tuna. The original was a bit mysterious because it was very vague in terms of measuring. For my mother, who owned no precise kitchen scale to measure the amount of nutmeg or five-spice she used, it was always an instinctual handling of the utensils that mattered. As to the "glass" of white wine, it would have been one of those Duralex wine glasses, the kind whose bottom reveals your age as you empty it. This is what my mother has passed on to me: a basic instruction and lots of feeling. It's a recipe for bliss, best savored an hour out of the oven, still warm, bay leaves removed, spread on a slice of bread and eaten in the disarray of the kitchen. Simply unforgettable.

Pass 2 pounds each of fresh tuna and leaf lard through a meat grinder. Add 2 crushed cloves of garlic, a large chopped yellow onion, previously cooked until soft in some olive oil, and season with salt to taste as well as a generous amount of freshly grated nutmeg, black pepper, crushed thyme leaves and five-spice. Mix well and fill into a high, earthenware baking dish. Shape the top into a dome and cover it with fresh bay leaves, lightly pressed into the mixture. Gently pour a glass of white wine over the mix and bake the terrine for an hour at 375° F. Pour a shot glass of Cognac over it and bake for another half hour at 325°F.

A PIZZA AND A SAVORY TART

Penny Arcade, *New York City*
PIZZA RUSTICA CHIENA A LA PICERNESA
(a la Agatina Pierri Parisi è Antoinetta Parisi Ventura)

When I was a child, certain foods were only made and eaten on certain holidays. This *Pizza Rustica Chiena* (filled) was made only at Easter, usually on the Thursday before Good Friday, and eaten only on Easter and *Pasquetta*, the Monday that follows Easter Sunday.

In a bowl, mix 4 cups of all-purpose flour, ¼ teaspoon dry active yeast, 2 teaspoons salt and ¼ teaspoon sugar. Make a well and pour in 1 ½ cups of warmed water (use bottled water as the chlorine in tab water retards yeast growth) and 2 tablespoons extra virgin olive oil and mix together. Work the dough just until everything is thoroughly mixed and slightly sticky. Cover with a cloth and let rise for 14 hours, or until doubled in size. Punch it down and let it rise once more before using. In a pinch, you can buy pre-made pizza dough.

Cut ¼ pound of cooked ham, ¼ pound of *Soppresata*, ¼ pound of *Salsiccia Picernese* (Italian hard salami) and ½ pound of Mozzarella into cubes. In a mixing bowl, beat 8 eggs with ¼ teaspoon of fresh black pepper and fold ¼ pound of grated Pecorino and 1 pound of whole milk fresh Ricotta. Add the cubed meats and cheese plus ½ cup of chopped Italian parsley, ¼ cup of slivered sundries tomatoes and 3 tablespoons of finely chopped fresh garlic. Mix until thoroughly combined.

Divide the dough in two sections, reserving a small piece for the traditional cross decoration, and roll them out. Grease a 10-inch spring form pan or a 13x15 inch pan, line it with one half of the dough and pour in the egg mixture. Cover with the other half of the dough, tucking in the ends to form a closed pie. Shape a cross out of the bit of extra dough and place it in the center of the pie. Brush everything with one lightly beaten egg, make a three-point slash around the crust for steam to escape and bake at 325° F for 1 hour and 15 minutes. Allow to cool completely before serving.

Jason Fox, *Brooklyn, New York*
RUSTIC TOMATO TART

Measure out 1 ¼ cups of flour, and add ⅔ of it to a food processor. Cut 1 ¼ sticks of unsalted butter into quarter pats and lay them on top of flour in food processor. After 20-30 short pulses, the dough forms a ball and no loose flour remains. Add the remaining flour and pulse 5-7 short times. Dump dough into bowl and add 3 tablespoons of cold water. Mix gently until incorporated. Shape dough into round disc, wrap, and refrigerate for approximately 2 hours.

Slice 2 beefsteak tomatoes into ¼-inch slices. Sprinkle both sides of the slices with salt and lay them on a (clean) kitchen towel-lined tray to sweat and drain for 30 minutes. Do the same with approximately ¾ cup of cherry tomatoes, sliced in half. Gently press a paper towel on the tomatoes to soak up as much excess liquid as possible.

Roll out the dough on a piece of parchment paper and transfer parchment paper to a sheet pan. Spread a thin layer of goat cheese on pie dough, leaving about 2 inches on all sides. Arrange the sliced beefsteak tomatoes on top of the cheese and scatter the cherry tomatoes over them. Top with ground pepper, crumbled feta cheese, and fresh basil and/or thyme.

Fold the edges of the dough over the filling to form a border, careful not to tear the dough. Brush the edges with egg white and bake the tart at 400° F F for approximately 45 minutes, or until the crust and feta have sufficiently browned.

SALADS

Kim David Smith, *New York City*
TUNA SALAD

In a large mixing bowl, toss together 2 tins of canned tuna (in water, not oil), drained, 3 tablespoons store -bought hummus, 1 ½ teaspoon of lime juice, ¼ teaspoon of wasabi powder, 1 finely chopped scallion, ¼ chopped jalapeño, ½ stalk diced celery or ¼ finely chopped Granny Smith apple. Season with salt and ground pepper to taste. Serve on mixed spring greens with slices of apple and occasionally a drizzle of olive oil and some balsamic vinegar.

Peter Glebo, *New York City*
ORIENTAL COLE SLAW

Shred 1 head red cabbage. Lightly brown 4 ounces of sliced almonds and ¼ cup of sesame seeds in 1 ½ tablespoons of margarine. Chop 1 bunch green onions. Set everything aside separately until ready to serve. Mix ¾ cups of oil, 6 tablespoons of rice vinegar, 1 tablespoon of sugar, 1 teaspoon of salt. Toss everything together and add 2 packs of chicken-flavored ramen noodles, crushed. Serve immediately.

Alfredo Taylor-White, *New York City*
SPICY PICKLED CUCUMBER SALAD

In a bowl, mix 2 medium sized cucumbers (peeled and thinly sliced in bias or rounds), 1 medium sized onion (peeled, thinly sliced and slivered), 1 teaspoon of green or red chilies (thinly sliced, with or without seeds), ¼ cup of white vinegar, 1 tablespoon of sugar, 1 teaspoon of salt and ½ teaspoon of white pepper. Let it sit overnight, covered in refrigerator. Variations can be made with herbs (dill, tarragon, thyme, cilantro etc.) Chilies can be omitted or replaced with a favorite hot sauce.

Zach Udko, *New York City*
CAESAR SALAD WITH TOFU CROUTONS

Growing up in Los Angeles in the 1980s, some of my fondest dining memories involve tableside Caesar salad service. I loved the theatrical flair of handsome overdressed waiters mincing and swirling the freshest ingredients in big wooden bowls before tossing my salad. Nowadays, few endeavors are more futile than attempting to find a satisfying Caesar dressing on a supermarket shelf.

In a blender, process the drained, oil-packed anchovy fillets of one tin can, ¼ cup of red wine vinegar, the juice of half a lemon, 2 cloves of garlic, a heaping tablespoon of mayonnaise, a tablespoon of Dijon mustard, and a teaspoon of Worcestershire sauce until creamy. Scrape it into a bowl and whisk in ¼ cup of extra virgin olive oil. Season with flaky sea salt and black pepper to taste.

Cut extra-firm tofu into cubes, toss them into a bowl and season them with olive oil, minced garlic, finely grated Parmesan cheese, crushed red pepper flakes, salt and black pepper. Spread them out on a parchment paper-lined sheet pan and bake at 400° F for approximately 20 minutes or until crispy, turning the pieces once or twice.

Once they are cool, transfer them to a bowl. Add chopped, crisp hearts of romaine lettuce, ½ cup of freshly grated Parmesan cheese and as much dressing as needed. Toss and serve immediately.

Cathay Che, *Brooklyn, New York*
QUINOA SALAD

Cook 2 cups of quinoa in chicken broth. Once cooled, dress it with a fancy store-bought Mexican Salsa and mix into it some roasted corn, crumbled

Cojita cheese and toasted pumpkin seeds. Serve over baby arugula leaves. Sometimes I add shrimp sautéed in garlic chili oil

Eddy Malave, *Queens, New York*
DAKKOS SALAD

Fill cold water into a mixing bowl and add a couple handfuls Paximadia chunks (dried Greek barley bread.) Give them a brief soaking then quickly drain out the water. Sort of a "run through" so to speak … Add tomatoes, sliced if low on time or crushed if you are in a Zen mode (the traditional Greek way is to use crushed tomatoes to help soak the hard bread more), crumbled or cubed feta cheese, capers, dried oregano, a few raw spinach leaves and a generous amount of of olive oil. Mix all together and let it breathe.

I like to serve this with side dishes of large, lightly dressed butter beans or eggplant cooked in olive oil.

Birgit Rathsmann, *Brooklyn, New York*
GADO GADO

Indonesia has always absorbed and synthesized the influences of many cultures. *Gado Gado* is a salad that combines vegetables from Europe, Asia and the Americas and uses Indonesian seasonings to unify all these disparate elements.

Blanch and drain a good handful of string beans, cut in half. Blanch 2 sliced carrots. Boil 1 large potato until tender, peel and set aside. Cut a large piece of tofu into cubes and fry them in neutral oil until crisp. Boil 2 eggs for 8 minutes, chill them in ice water and peel them. Have at the ready 1 cup of crunchy bean sprouts, head of cabbage, shredded (variation: steamed but still crunchy cauliflower), ½ sliced cucumber, 1 ripe tomato, and crispy fried shallots.

Crush 1 sliced red chili and 1 garlic clove in a mortar. Add paste to a blender with 1 tablespoon dark brown sugar, ½ teaspoon salt, 1 cup of coconut milk, 1 teaspoon oriental shrimp paste, 4 tablespoons peanut butter and 1 teaspoon tamarind paste. Blend and cook the sauce with a piece of lemon peel over low heat for 10 minutes, until it has thickened and darkened. Remove the lemon peel.

Arrange all vegetables on a large round serving dish: shredded cabbage on bottom, topped by a layer of string beans, carrots, sliced potato, cucumber slices and bean sprouts. Scatter the tofu cubes over the bean sprouts, decorate the circumference of the serving dish with alternate egg and tomato slices. Drizzle the warm peanut sauce over the vegetables and sprinkle everything with crispy shallots. *Gado Gado* should be served at room temperature, and the vegetables should be crunchy

SOUPS AND STEWS

Joachim Bartholomae, *Hamburg, Germany*
BUTCH TEA

It takes some time to prepare this clear *consommé* and you'll have to be willing to splurge and be wasteful. On the other hand, this is a perfect recipe for clumsy blokes since everything that goes into the pot will end up in the trash.

First, make the *bouillon*. Take a good pound of prime rib – and I do mean prime rib. Anything else would be just a filler. Further, 2 split knucklebones, 2 carrots, 1 leek, a chunk of celeriac and 5 crushed peppercorns. You may also add some potato peels, a twig of fresh rosemary and a couple of tablespoons of *Grünkern**. Put all that into a stock pot, cover it with about 3 quarts of water and simmer it gently for 2 hours. Pour the bouillon through a fine-mesh sieve, discard everything but the meat and chill the broth and meat together in the refrigerator, preferably overnight. The next morning, there will be a white, hardened layer of fat on top of the broth. Remove that with a slotted spoon. You can throw the fat away or use it for frying potatoes. Married and monogamous homosexuals may opt to use it for a distinctly different kind of gay activity. Bring the broth once more to a simmer. The prime rib is now no longer useful for this dish (it's quite delicious served cold, thinly sliced, with some horseradish cream on the side, but that's another story).

Now on to the second step: Mix 7 ounces of ground sirloin with 1 teaspoon of salt and 2 egg whites and chill it in the freezer for half an hour before adding it to the cold bouillon. Bring it to a simmer and cook it gently for one hour, stirring frequently to prevent the mass from sticking to the bottom. At this time the soup will look quite disgusting and smell somewhat funky but don't fret: after 1 hour, you can pour it through a fine-mesh sieve set over a clean pot and discard the greyish mess. If you've done everything right, you will now have a deeply golden consommé. You might want to add a little more salt but very cautious to not over-season it.

Fairies like this brew piping hot, sipped from dainty espresso-cups, pinky duly lifted. Butch queens gulp it down from a mug, chilled, as a morning remedy for hangovers.

---

* Smoked green wheat kernels. Closest alternative in the States would be *frekkeh*.

Sidney Long, *Newport, Rhode Island*
WHITE BEAN SOUP

Put two cans of organic cannellini beans, rinsed, into a large soup pot, add water, a big yellow beet, peeled and diced, and a couple of tablespoons of miso paste. The trick is to add just enough miso to give the soup flavor but not enough to be able to identify it as the flavoring agent. You can add whatever vegetable is at hand for flavor and looks. Keep at a low boil for twenty minutes or until the beet is done and served it up with a warm baguette and a cucumber salad.

Phoebe Legere, *New York City*
SOUPE POIREAU-CÉLERI LEGERE

How to be beautiful, happy, rich and thin: Eat this soup every day for one week. Peel off the outer skin of 4 leeks. Cut off the root and cut the leeks in sections. Cook for 15 minutes in boiling water. Rinse and cut the 8 celery stalks into sections. Rinse and chop 2 stalks of parsley. Mix everything together. Look in the mirror. Smile warmly and say, "I love you darling!"

Add 2 tablespoons vegan crème fraîche. Velvetize in a blender. C'est prêt! Optional: tiny pinch of curry powder.

Shien Lee, *Brooklyn, New York*
TAIWANESE CHICKEN SOUP

Soak 1 ounce dried shiitake mushrooms in 3 cups of boiling water for 20 minutes. Use a bowl or a smaller pot to keep the mushrooms submerged in the water. While the mushrooms are soaking, mix 2 tablespoon of soy sauce, 2 teaspoons of sugar, a pinch of salt and 2 teaspoons of cornstarch in a large bowl. Make sure there are no cornstarch lumps. To this, add 1 ½ pounds of chicken thighs, with skin and bones, and a 1-inch piece of fresh ginger, peeled and thinly sliced. Toss to coat with the marinade and set aside.

When the mushrooms have softened, remove them from the water, saving the soaking liquid, and thinly slice them. Put everything plus a few Chinese dried jujubes and goji berries and a dash of Chinese rice wine into a pot, add soaking liquid and enough water to cover, bring to a light simmer, and cook covered for 25 minutes. Serve hot.

Abi Maryan, *New York City*
POTATO GARLIC LEEK SOUP

Smash 10 peeled garlic cloves, sweat in butter with 1 chopped onion 3 fat leeks, white and light green parts only, washed and sliced until soft. Add 2 peeled and cubed starchy potatoes. Cover with water until 2 inches above vegetables. Cook until potatoes are soft. Purée in blender. Add salt, pepper and heavy cream to taste. Best served with sourdough bread and butter and a sturdy, full bodied red from Southern France.

Julie Atlas Muz, *New York City*
POLISH LASKOVSKA PICKLE SOUP

This is my grandfather's and my mother's pickle soup recipe. It ROCKS!

Make a chicken or a beef stock (from SCRATCH.) Boil a whole chicken, 1 leek, 1 bunch of celery, a very large carrot in a big pot of water with a lot of salt for an hour or so. Let cool, allow the chicken to cool in the stock (it's more juicy that way.) Remove and discard the celery and leeks. Remove the chicken, shred the meat and discard the bones and skin. Remove the carrot and chop it. Bring 2 quarts of the homemade stock to a boil and add 2-4 good, peeled and quartered potatoes. When they are boiling, add at least 5 grated sour dill pickles (the more the better.) Add shredded chicken and chopped carrot and some pickle juice to taste. You should be able to really taste the pickles. When the potatoes are almost cooked through, ladle some hot broth into a bowl and mix it with sour cream. Add the diluted sour cream mixture into the soup.

I find that the soup is better the next day. It just gets more delicious. Make A LOT of it if you can. Enjoy.

Sergej Isakov, *Queens, New York*
KOVURMA
(Uzbek Meat Stew)

Peel and slice 3 onions, panfry them in a Dutch oven with some oil until translucent, then add 1 sliced fresh hot chili pepper, a pinch of cinnamon and a pinch of black cumin. Stir and fry for until the onion is lightly browned, then add 3 cups of peeled tomatoes and bring everything to a simmer. Cook for about 20 minutes. Season with salt and black pepper and keep warm.

Peel 2 pounds of potatoes and cut them into cubes. Season them with salt and deep-fry them in hot oil until golden brown. Transfer them to a sheet pan lined with paper towels to drain off the extra oil, season them with salt while still hot and set them aside.

Cut one pound of leg of lamb into small pieces, season them with salt and fry them in the same oil until browned. Transfer the meat to a sheet pan lined with paper towels to drain off the extra oil. Season it black pepper before adding it along with the potatoes to the tomato sauce. Stir and serve with chopped dill and scallions.

Nicole Renaud, *New York City*
KHARCHO
(Georgian Lamb Neck Soup)

My friend Yuri Lemeshev taught me how to make this traditional peasant's soup years ago. Unlike the *soupes* and *potages* I grew up eating in France where soup is served as a warm appetizer, this is a full meal all by itself – a perfect, comforting dinner choice for one of those freezing New York City winter days.

In a large stockpot, bring 2 quarts of water to a boil. Meanwhile, in a separate pot, heat 3 tablespoons of olive oil and add 2 pounds of lamb neck (on the bone, cut into chunks) and 4 minced cloves of garlic. Brown the meat and bones on all sides and transfer all to the boiling water (add more water if necessary, the meat should be fully submerged.) Add some salt and cook at a slow boil for 30 minutes, skimming off any foam that rises to the surface. Add half a celery root (diced), 1 finely sliced large carrot, 2 finely chopped onions, ½ cup of uncooked rice, ½ cup of finely chopped walnuts, ⅓ cup of dried cherries and a large handful of freshly chopped cilantro. Season the broth with a good pinch each of paprika, dried thyme and sage, freshly ground black pepper, and a couple of bay leaves. Cook for 15 minutes at a slow boil, then reduce to a simmer and cook for 50 more minutes. Adjust the seasoning and spice the soup with a few drops of Tabasco and the juice of one lemon before serving, garnished with finely chopped parsley or mint.

Madeleine Edwards Kemble, *New York City*
4 FAMILY MEAL
(French Onion Soup with Oxtail)

Whenever I was in charge of preparing the family meal for the kitchen staff at Prune Restaurant (where I used to work as a chef) I followed an elaborate pattern. I first talked to Chef and the other cooks to think of the theme that would ground the day's family meal. Next, I scoured the walk-in refrigerator for produce that either wouldn't be used or begged to be used up. There frequently was a tinge of disappointment due the lack of readily available proteins but I always found a renewed sense of resourcefulness and pride in knowing that I could create a wonderful meal for ten people at the drop of a hat while saving the restaurant extra expenses. The theme of the day might have been *French Bistro* and the theme of my life is that I love soup. Finding out that the bone-in braised oxtail special of the day wouldn't get plated with any of the bone was like hitting the jackpot.

Caramelize some white onions while preparing your *mise en place* for service. Once they have reached slow-cooked golden perfection, turn up the heat a little bit and add a decent amount of sherry vinegar, and a dash of both Worcestershire and fish sauce. Make sure a heaping spoonful of roasted and puréed garlic freshly made for evening service somehow finds its way into this family meal mix. Also add a sprig of thyme. Use the canned beef stock that the bar only uses for brunch, there is always a quart somewhere lying around. Add the bone scraps, find the meaty ones if you can. Cover with water but don't drown out all the goodness. Season. Simmer the soup while you hustle to set up your station in the upstairs kitchen. Grill some scallions greens that were scrap from another project. Chop and add these to the soup to bulk it up a little and to give it a nice char flavor to offset and deepen the tanginess of the sherry vinegar. Remember that there was some extra Swiss cheese from the "Monte Cristo" sandwiches in the family bin and hope that nobody else has gotten to it yet. Grab some of the staling peasant bread that we save to make bread crumbs. Transfer soup to large flat Dutch oven that fits in the salamander. Pick what meat you can from the bones. Float some crispy bread to sop your soup. Cover with Swiss cheese in what feels like a gluttonous rampage. Place the pot in the Salamander or under a broiler and broil until the cheese is melted and bubbly and crisp and screaming to be eaten. Note that the server who brought in a $10 kale salad from an expensive health food bar down the street has decided to save it for later. Smile for a second to yourself – but don't smile too long: dinner service starts in fifteen minutes.

Christopher Baldovino, *Miami, Florida*
BIG VEGAN POT

Sautee chopped garlic and white onions until very caramelized, then add lentils, soybeans, corn, diced carrots, celery and squash (preferably butternut, but any would work). Add vegetable stock and one bunch of sage and simmer. Season with salt and pepper and check for doneness after 45 minutes.

The beauty of this dish is the consistency the squash adds to the dish.

EGG DISHES

Noah Fecks, *Brooklyn, New York*
BREAD OMELETTE

In a bowl, whisk together 2 large eggs, 1 tablespoon of water or milk, salt and pepper to taste and, if available, a teaspoon of snipped chives, fresh minced rosemary leaves, or even a tablespoon of minced spinach or kale, and set aside.

In an omelette pan, heat one tablespoon of good olive oil with one teaspoon of unsalted butter over medium high heat. Once the butter has melted and the oil is shimmering add stale bread that has been cut coarsely into one inch or larger cubes (French or Italian bread is best, but any stale bread will do. You're looking for a big generous handful of bread cubes).

Toss the bread to completely coat it with the oil and butter mixture and panfry it until golden, turning frequently to toast it on all sides, taking care not to burn the bread.

Pour the egg mixture over the bread and allow the eggs to cook, enrobing the toasted bread. Proceed as you would with any omelette preparation, or stir with a fork to make a "scramble."

Serve in a bowl and garnish with shaved hard cheese or Sriracha sauce.

Daniel Nardicio, *New York City*
NELLY FRITTATA

I love a frittata – the ease with which you can make one and even the sound of it: frit-ta-ta. It's a veritable tap dance in your mouth. If gay guys are eating it, I call it my Nelly Fritatta.

This is a very popular dish I often make for breakfast at my summer house in Fire Island. I like to use a cast-iron skillet because it really looks beautiful when you pull it out of the oven and it's just a golden cheesy goodness and the contrast of the yellow of farm fresh eggs with the coal black skillet makes for a sexy visual presentation.

Turn the oven to 375° F. Peel 5 garlic cloves, roll them in olive oil and pop them in the oven on a piece of aluminum foil to roast them a bit while it is preheating. Take some cold leftovers, anything you have around or like – diced leftover meat from a roast chicken, steamed broccoli rabe or shaved grilled corn, but don't use anything that will leak water as it cooks or you'll end up with a juicy mess – and sauté them in a cast iron skillet with 2 tablespoons butter. Take the pan off the flame to cool slightly to prevent the eggs from frying as they hit the pan. Blend one dozen farm fresh Grade A large eggs on high with 3 teaspoons milk plus salt to taste and maybe one peeled raw garlic clove (unless you're planning on kissing someone or have a big social engagement that afternoon). Pour the egg mixture into the cast iron pan, toss the pre-roasted garlic cloves into it and sprinkle the mixture with ½ to 1 cup of grated cheese (I like smoked Gouda or a good grated Parmesan), garnish with fresh basil or thin tomato slices (previously drained on a paper towel for at least 10 minutes) or just liberal amounts of black pepper. Then bake in the middle shelf for approximately 25 minutes, or until a knife pulls out clean. The last 10 minutes are important – no one likes a rubbery Nelly Frittata.

Enjoy with a sexy boy – or nine! Like with the classic porcelain baby in a *New Orleans King Cake* for Mardi Gras, it's good luck if you get a garlic clove.

Pejk Malinovski, *New York City*
EGG IN A CUP

I had two great-grandmothers, Omi and Fräuli. Well, Omi was my *real* great-grandmother, Fräuli was in fact the nanny who came along when Omi fled Vienna in 1938, right after the *Anschluss*. She didn't have to come, she wasn't Jewish, but she always put the children first. Fräuli was a kind of angel, a kind angel, with mild blue eyes and strong arms. She took care of three generations of my family, my grandmother, my mother and my brother and me, she never had "a life of her own." After spending the war years in Sweden, Fräuli and Omi lived together in a small apartment in Copenhagen, from 1945 to their death in 1992. Whenever I see pictures of Gertrude Stein and Alice B. Toklas, I think of Omi and Fräuli, for that's what they looked like and that's how they lived. They did everything together, except having sex (I think!?).

My brother and I spent a lot of time with them: they had seen so much, they told good stories. And whenever we walked in the door, Fräuli would make us *egg in cup*, a perfect little power snack for kids on the go. She would soft boil an egg, cube a slice of buttered rye bread and mash it all up with salt and pepper. The butter would melt from the warm egg and it was all mushy and delicious.

I still make egg in a cup for myself and whenever I do I feel Fräuli's love again and I honor her selfless spirit, her German songs, her gentle hands, the soft flappy skin under her arms, the hard stubbles on her chin, which I got to shave when she was very old and her sight had gone, her refined melancholy – the last remnant of the Austro-Hungarian empire.

David Berger, *Queens, New York*
TORTILLA DE PATATAS
(As taught to me by Clara De La Peña)

Peel and coarsely chop 1 large Spanish onion. Wash, peel and very finely slice 1 large russet potato. Heat an 8-inch frying pan (regular or non-stick) on a low-medium flame, add about 2 cups of olive oil (or enough to cover the vegetables). Scatter first the onion, then the potatoes into the oil, and cook everything until the potato starts to crumble and the onions are lightly caramelized. Place a strainer over a mixing bowl and pour the entire content of the pan into it. Allow the oil to fully drain (10 minutes or so). Season the potato mixture with salt and cracked black pepper (optional). Crack 6 large eggs into a mixing bowl and beat them lightly. Fold the seasoned, still warm potato/onion mixture into the beaten eggs.

Wipe out the pan, heat it over a medium flame and add a couple of tablespoons of the infused oil. Increase the flame to high and pour the egg potato mixture into the pan. Shake the pan as it cooks to prevent sticking. Once a crust has formed, cover the pan with a large plate and boldly flip the mixture onto it in one swooped motion. You don't want to flip too soon, or it'll be too wet to hold together, but at the same time, you don't want to flip too late and risk the egg burning itself onto the pan, which will leave half of your crust behind when you flip. Once flipped, jiggle the pan slightly to allow the tortilla to sit fully on the plate. Lift off the pan, wipe it out, replace it on the burner, flame on high, and add another 1-2 tablespoons of the oil. Now slide the half-cooked tortilla back into the pan and cook the second side, shaking the pan to prevent sticking. When done, invert it once again onto a large plate. Serve warm or cold. My personal preference is to cook it just long enough so that the tortilla is still creamy inside. Store the excess oil in a jar, to be used for the next tortilla event.

Evee Lynn, *New York City*
"LOST" EGGS IN MUSTARD SAUCE

In a sauce pan, melt 4 tablespoons butter. Add 2 tablespoons flour and stir until combined. Gradually while whisking constantly, add 2 cups of beef broth and 1 cup of milk. Add a bay leaf, bring to a simmer and cook, constantly stirring, for 15 minutes. Season it with salt, pepper, a dash of allspice, and 3 tablespoons mustard. Boil 6 eggs for 7 minutes, submerge them in cold water until cold enough to handle, peel them and add them to the sauce. Serve warm with boiled potatoes and a green salad.

PASTA

Alex Kristofcak, *Brooklyn, New York*
PAPPARDELLE
WITH FRIED SAGE AND SAUSAGES

Start out by setting a large pot of water with 1 teaspoon of salt and a squirt of oil on high heat. Prepare the sauce: heat up 2 tablespoons of oil in a medium skillet over medium high heat. When the oil is hot, fry a couple of sage leaves in it for about 30 seconds. Remove the leaves and set them aside. Empty the contents of 2 fresh hot sausages into the same skillet, break up the meat into smaller chunks with a spatula and brown them, stirring continuously, for 5 minutes. Turn the heat down to medium and cook for another 5 minutes before transferring the sausage meat onto a plate. Add 2 tablespoons of butter to the skillet and turn the heat up to medium-high. Add 1 tablespoon of all-purpose flour and whisk it into the butter. After a paste forms, pour in ½ cup of whole milk, a couple of tablespoons at a time, whisk vigorously to dissolve any lumps. Turn off the heat and stir 4 tablespoons of finely ground Parmesan cheese into the white sauce. The pot of water should be boiling now – add 1 pound of pasta. Fresh *pappardelle* would be ideal, but dry pasta will work just fine. Fresh pasta cooks within just a few a minutes; if using dry pasta, drain it 1-2 minutes before the recommended cooking time to ensure a nice al dente consistency. Reserve 1 cup of cooking liquid and drain the rest. Return the pasta to the pot and add the cheese sauce. Stir, adding a bit of cooking liquid as needed to create a nicely creamy but not overly runny sauce that covers the pasta. Stir in the sausage meat and divide onto 2-3 plates. Garnish with the fried sage, freshly grated Parmesan, Maldon salt and fresh ground pepper.

Lena Imamura, *New York City*
VEGETARIAN PASTA (FOR 2 OR 3)

Slice 1 yellow pepper, 1 orange pepper (sliced the long way) 4 portobello mushroom caps into long strips. Dice 2 zucchini, mince 4 cloves of garlic.

Boil a pot of water (enough for pasta to swim), add salt and 1 pack of spinach linguini. Cook them to taste, drain, drizzle with olive oil and cover. Take a large frying pan, add enough olive oil to stir fry the vegetables. Once oil is hot, add half the minced garlic and the zucchinis and stir. When zucchinis start turning soft but not browning, add peppers and portobello mushrooms and stir. Add second half of minced garlic, a pinch of salt & pepper, a shake of curry powder, turmeric and cajun spice, not a lot, just enough for flavor. Add pasta to the mix, stir all together until mixed (no heat necessary). Serve sprinkled with Parmesan cheese.

Georgia Krantz, Portland, Oregon

LINGUINE WITH TOMATOES, BASIL AND BRIE

My mother made this for us when I was growing up. We all thought it was deliriously delicious and I continue to make it to this day. The original recipe she passed on to me is full of her tiny, occasionally indecipherable notes – decisions about necessary alterations. She changed all the proportions of the ingredients in thick black ink, making the original numbers illegible. She also wrote "No!" over "linguine," preferring "a spaghetti form." I like thin linguine, so I marked "thin" next to "linguine." Another note is about basil tasting too raw when it wasn't cut fine enough.

At least 2 hours before serving, cut 5 ripe large tomatoes into ½-inch cubes and toss them into a bowl with 1¼ pound of Brie cheese, rind removed, torn into irregular pieces, a good handful basil leaves, rinsed, patted dry and cut into juliennes, 4 garlic cloves, peeled and finely minced, and 1 ¼ cup best-quality olive oil. Season with 1 teaspoon salt and 1 teaspoon freshly ground black pepper and set aside, covered, at room temperature.

Bring 6 quarts of water to a boil in a large pot. Add 1 tablespoon olive oil and 1 teaspoon salt. Add 1 ¾ pounds thin linguine and cook them until they're al dente. Drain pasta and immediately toss with the tomato combo. Serve at once, passing the pepper mill. Serves 6.

Fatima El Shibli, Brooklyn, New York

RIGATONI WITH EGGPLANT SAUCE

Heat avocado oil in a saucepan (I don't use olive in high heat) and sauté one whole eggplant diced in small cubes. The eggplant will absorb the oil and if you like you can add a little water or vegetable stock to prevent it from sticking at first. Make sure you "over" cook the eggplant really well, so it's nice and soft. Add 3-4 cloves of crushed garlic after about 6 min as well as some salt and ground cumin. Once the eggplant is soft, add 1 -2 tablespoons tomato paste to it, a little paprika and some chili powder (not hot, the dark kind). Add your favorite tomato sauce. I like Marinara or roasted garlic in a jar. Best of course is to make your own. Stir and let simmer for at least 6-7 minutes. Add a healthy amount of parsley, a little lemon juice, and 1-2 tablespoons of capers.

In the meantime, cook rigatoni until al dente, drain, transfer into a large bowl, pour the sauce over it and garnish with sliced scallions and some extra virgin olive oil drizzled on top. Voila!

David Lamarche, *New York City*
SOBA NOODLES WITH TAHINI DRESSING
(Inspired by macrobiotic cuisine to please my partner Jonathon)

Boil soba noodles as you would any pasta, but as they are cooking, keep adding cold water whenever the pot comes again to another boil. When they are done (slightly more than al dente), rinse them in hot water, and toss them with a little sesame oil before mixing with the dressing.

Mix ¼ cup of tahini with 2 tablespoons of shoyu or soy sauce and add whisk to a creamy consistency with a few tablespoons of olive oil. Add 4 tablespoons of chopped parsley and 4 pitted and quartered umeboshi* plums. Add dressing to soba noodles. Mix well and serve warm. You can also add steamed vegetables or chicken to this dish.

Damian Barr, *Brighton, England*
LOBSTER MAC AND CHEESE

A perfectly decadent pasta meal for these end times. I use 2 whole, cooked medium-sized lobsters (preferably from cold water) per batch. Each batch serves six people (or four sybarites).

Split the lobsters in half, pull out the tail meat and crack the knuckles and claws to remove their meat, careful to keep 2 claws as intact as possible for the garnish. Slice the meat into chunks, setting aside any "bitty" bits. Reserve any red coral and mash it with a fork into 2 tablespoons butter you are going to use to make your roux; it gives it a nice and salty umami base and a pleasing pink color. Melt the roux butter in a sauce pan and whisk 1 heaped tablespoon flour into it. Gradually, stirring all the while, add about 2 cups of full fat milk. Cook it for several minutes. Add equal parts Emmental, Gruyère and mild Cheddar – as much as it will take – and a splash of Riesling or Cognac (previously heated and flambé'd) to "cut"

---

* Pickled Japanese plums

the cheese. Season with salt and a tiny bit of smoked sweet paprika to taste. Stir into this the 'bitty' bits of lobster meat.

Cook macaroni in salted water until al dente. Drain them and layer them with the lobster meat in a buttered baking dish. Pour cheese sauce over the whole thing. Grate more cheese over the top and bake in a 375° F oven until golden brown and bubbly, about 30 minutes.

While it is cooking whoosh 2 claws through the dishwasher so they are nice and clean. Then rinse them well so they don't smell of detergent and use as spectacular garnish when taking your lobster mac and cheese to table. You can gild the claws with gold leaf if you want to go all out and give the whole thing an air of ancient Rome.

RICE DISHES

Lukas Volger, *New York City*
FRIED RICE FOR ONE

Fried rice is one of the few things I use a non-stick pan for; a well-seasoned cast-iron skillet works, too, but you'll have to scrub it.

Heat a splash of neutral oil in a medium-skillet set over medium-high heat. Add a small handful of thinly sliced onion strips and cook, stirring, until softened but retaining a little crunch. Stir in a minced clove of garlic and 1 teaspoon of grated fresh ginger, cook 'til fragrant, then 1 ½ cups of leftover cooked rice. Sprinkle with a pinch of sugar and a pinch of salt. Stir constantly, until heated through and the grains glisten; this will take a few minutes. Clear a little space in the middle of the pan and pour in 2 teaspoons soy sauce and a few drops toasted sesame oil, allowing it to bubble and caramelize, then stir it into the rice. Add ½ cup of leftover cooked vegetables (sweet potato, broccoli, cauliflower, roasted carrots, etc.), the vegetables and a handful leafy greens (spinach, chard, kale, etc.) and stir until heated through and the greens are wilted. Finish with 1 sliced scallion and some minced chive. Scoop it onto a plate. Top with a fried egg and a dollop of yogurt combined with a bit of sambal or chili paste

Rich Benjamin, *Brooklyn, New York*
DIRTY RICE

Soak 2 cups of dried red kidney beans overnight in cold water and boil them until tender. Drain them and reserve the cooking water. In a Dutch oven, heat about ⅓ cup canola oil and add the beans along with 4 peeled and crushed cloves of garlic, 1 chopped shallot, ¼ teaspoon of powdered cloves, ¼ teaspoon of onion powder, ¾ teaspoon of Adobo seasoning plus salt and pepper to taste, 1 tablespoon of chopped parsley, a sprig of thyme and 1 bay leaf. Sauté until fragrant, then add 5 cups of the cooking water (if there is not enough bean water, add regular water to make 5 ½ cups of liquid), Add 3 cups of long-grain rice, bring everything to a simmer and stir once. Cover the pot tightly with foil wrap and a lid, turn heat to lowest setting and cook for 30 minutes. Check rice consistency. For softer rice, add water, if not cover for another 5-10 minutes until rice is tender to taste. Fluff gently with a fork and serve with grilled pork chops or tenderloins.

Antoine Lefebvre, *Paris, France*
OYAKODON
(Japanese Rice Bowl)

Oyako means "family" in Japanese, and *Don* means "bowl." This dish with chicken and egg is in fact a family in a bowl.

Begin by preparing your teriyaki sauce: In a sauce pan, mix ½ cup of soy sauce, ⅓ cup of Mirin (sweet rice wine) and 1 tablespoon of sugar. Bring to a boil and cook for a couple minutes. Set aside.

Cook the rice in the Japanese fashion: Rinse the rice in plentiful cold water until water runs clear, then cook it in a rice cooker or boil it accordingly, using 1 ½ cups of water per cup of rice.

Debone the chicken legs and cut them into bite-size pieces. Stir-fry them in flavor-neutral oil with a few slices of onion, lacing it with teriyaki sauce as you cook it. Once the chicken and onions are browned, cover them with Dashi broth and simmer for 5 minutes. Beat 5 eggs and slowly pour them over the mix. Make sure that there is still some broth on the bottom of the pan or the eggs will fry. Cover and cook just long enough for the egg to barely set. Ladle rice into bowls and scoop chicken and egg mixture over it. Drizzle with teriyaki sauce and garnish with sliced scallions and cut–up strips of *Nori* (toasted seaweed sheets). *Itadakimass* (Bon Appétit)!

Daniel Bartholomew, *Waterloo, Ontario*
TRINIDADIAN STEWED CHICKEN
AND PEAS WITH RICE

In a medium-size pot, heat ½ tablespoon of oil, add ½ cup of chopped onions, 1 can of pigeon peas, rinsed, 2 sprigs of West Indian thyme, fry until fragrant and add 1 tablespoon of "browning" (a burnt caramel-based coloring agent commonly used in the Caribbean) or dark brown sugar and salt to taste. Add 2 cups of rice and cook the rice slowly while stirring with a fork, adding hot water in small increments.

Season 8 pieces of chicken with salt, ½ teaspoon black pepper and ½ teaspoon Jamaican jerk seasoning and marinate it for 30 minutes in a mix of 1 finely chopped Spanish onion, ¼ bunch chopped cilantro, 1 large knob of finely grated ginger and 3 cloves of mashed garlic. In a Dutch oven, heat 1 tablespoon oil. Add 1 tablespoon sugar, cook it until it browns and begins to smoke, then add the chicken pieces (scrape off the marinade before adding them). Brown them on all sides before add the remaining seasonings and about a cup of hot water, mixed with a tablespoon of ketchup to taste. Cover and cook over a medium flame for about 20 minutes or until the chicken is tender. Season with a bit of vinegar to taste. Serve with the rice and enjoy.

COUSCOUS

Jonah Bokaer & Tsvi Bokaer, *Brooklyn, New York*
COUSCOUS WITH SQUASH AND FAVA BEANS
(Traditional Tunisian family recipe)

Go with your gut feeling in regards to seasoning and measurements, but always start with small amounts and add as you go, "to taste."

If using dried favas, plan ahead and soak them overnight in cold water.

Fresh green favas can be plucked and skinned the day you're serving the dish.

Canned favas (sold as "*foul*" in Middle Eastern grocery stores) are also okay.

Cook soaked favas in salted water, adding coriander & olive oil to taste, until tender as they spill out of their shells.

Fill the desired amount of couscous into a large mixing bowl, sprinkle with 1 ¼ teaspoon of salt per pound and add about a quarter cup of oil per pound. Pour boiling hot water over grain until water is ½ inch over the wet grain. Mix vigorously for a while, cover tight with a plate or a lid and spread a kitchen towel over it all and set aside. The grain will steam and do its thing – absorption – all by itself.

Rinse and clean green zucchini, yellow squash, green cabbage, stalks of celery and large tomatoes; peel and quarter several cloves of garlic. Cut the vegetables into bite-size chunks: circles and half circles for green zucchini, rectangles for yellow squash, large triangles for cabbage, tomatoes in large chunks.

Break up the couscous grain that has turned into a solid mass by scraping and stirring it with large wooden spoon – or do it by hand, Tunisian–style. When the grain is loose & fluffy, taste it and add some olive and salt if needed – you'll know if the grain is too dry or too "tame."

Pour a generous amount of olive oil into the bottom of a pot, add garlic, bay leaves, ground and coarse coriander seeds – to taste, but at least 1 tablespoon – and stir until golden and fragrant. Add the vegetables and stir, adding salt & cracked black pepper, with a sprinkle of hot pepper flakes. Toss well, over a high flame, until all vegetables "catch" the ingredients' flavors, then add the shelled favas and the broth they were cooked in, enough to cover everything by ½ inch. If using fresh favas, add them as is, plus some water. If using canned beans, add them with their canning juice. Simmer and taste until it is the way you like it and until you "recognize" the taste – vegetables should be tender but not too soft. Adjust the seasoning with more coriander, salt or olive oil. Serve over couscous, with lemon wedges and a good sprinkle of chopped feta cheese. Have fun and be daring in life, and art. Thus couscous will taste as it should, with trust & patience.

FISH AND SEAFOOD

Tobias Larsson, *New York City*
GRAVLAX

Cut 1 large center-cut piece of salmon in half. Mix ¾ cup of kosher salt and 1 cup pf sugar with one bunch of washed, drained and roughly chopped dill. Place one half of the salmon on a large piece of cellophane, cover it with the mixture, and place the other half over it (the "meat side" facing each other and skin out). Wrap the cellophane around it, place it in a baking dish and, if possible, weigh it down with something heavy. Refrigerate for 48 hours, turning it every 12 hours. Wipe away all the drained liquid and serve with a sauce made of 1 cup of crème fraîche, 1 jar of caviar or other fish roe, ½ diced yellow onion, lightly buttered toast, chopped dill and sliced lemon.

Yolanda Luzarraga, *Queens, New York*
CEVICHE DE CAMARONES ECUATORIANO

Combine 1 ½ cups of thinly sliced onion and ½ cup of fresh lime juice and salt in a small bowl. Set aside and stir occasionally.

Season 1 ½ pounds of peeled and de-veined medium-size shrimp with salt and black pepper. Heat a non-stick skillet over medium heat, spray it a bit of oil and cook the shrimp in it for 3-4 minutes, until pink, turning them frequently. Transfer them to a platter and place them it the refrigerator for 10 minutes to cool.

Stir together 2 cups of diced tomatoes, ¾ cup of fresh orange juice, ⅓ cup of tomato ketchup, ¼ cup of chopped cilantro, 2 tablespoons of extra virgin olive oil and 1 tablespoon of mustard. Add onion mixture and shrimp; toss together to combine and enjoy.

Edmund White, *New York City*
MONKFISH IN SAFFRON BUTTER

Melt a half stick (4 tablespoons) of salted butter, add 1 chopped shallot, 1 tablespoon of chopped preserved lemon, a few strands of saffron. When the butter has melted and is bubbling but not browned, add 1 pound of monkfish in small pieces, the size of your palm. After 6 minutes, flip the fish and cook 4 more minutes. Add parsley and serve with rice in the cooking juice.

Edwin Outwater & Tom Ho, *Chicago, Illinois*
VIETNAMESE-STYLE FISH EN PAPILLOTE

This meal combines Edwin's California cuisine tendencies with some of Tom's favorite Vietnamese flavors. This evolved over several years, very gradually, and we prepare it often. It's our home cooking.

First, heat up some fragrant, cooked jasmine rice. Then dice up some leeks and/or scallions, garlic, Thai red chili, ginger and Shiitake mushrooms. Then brush a whitefish (could be anything from cod to halibut depending on mood/budget) with some caramel sauce from Charles Phan's *The Slanted Door Cookbook* (cook 1 pound of palm sugar, ¾ cup of water, and juice of ½ lemon to a dark caramel, carefully add 1 ¼ cup of fish sauce (it will splatter), stir until caramel is dissolved, cool and store in a glass jar, it lasts for a month once you make it!), oyster sauce, a drop of Mirin rice wine. Sprinkle with salt and pepper. Then cover the fish with the diced veggies, wrap it in parchment the traditional way and put it in the oven at 375 degrees for 18 minutes or so. Serve over rice.

Josh Balog, *New York City*
SIMPLE, YET ELEGANT SEAFOOD DINNER

This is my special go-to menu when I'm entertaining ladies at home.

Sometimes two to three gals at the same time.

First course, a watercress salad with micro greens, shaved fennel and sliced orange. Keep it simple and light on the dressing. Olive oil, squeezed lemon, salt and pepper.

Second course, pan-seared Branzino filets over sautéed Spinach. The secret: Always start to sear the Branzino with the skin side down. Two to three minutes or until the skin is lightly golden. When you flip the Branzino over, you can peel the skin right off. It makes for a clean crisp presentation.

Dessert: creme brûlée – I torch it myself, the girls love it! And of course, a nice after dinner joint on the balcony.

CHICKEN AND A DUCK

Zoila Baigorria, *New York City*
AJI DE GALLINA
(Peruvian Chicken Stew)

Place one whole chicken breast in a pot, cover it with cold water, add salt, a carrot and a celery stalk, and bring to a simmer. When the chicken is cooked through, strain 3 cups of the liquid into a blender and blend it with 7 slices of toasted white bread. Shred the cooled chicken into pieces and dice the carrot and celery. Heat 3 tablespoons of vegetable oil in a casserole and add 4 minced garlic cloves and 2 chopped onions. When lightly browned, add 1 cup of finely chopped *Aji Amarillo* peppers (or 2 tablespoons of jarred *Aji Amarillo* paste) and half a teaspoon of turmeric and stir -fry for a few minutes. Add the thickened broth and 1 can of evaporated milk and bring to a light simmer. When the sauce has thickened, add the shredded chicken, the carrot and celery, season with salt and pepper and serve over rice, with sides of boiled peeled potatoes and sliced hard-boiled eggs.

Trac Vu, *New York City*
VIETNAMESE CHICKEN

This is the classic Viet way of cooking a chicken. You can eat it as is, or you can use it as an ingredient for a multitude of dishes. I show you how to make a succulent poached chicken, and the rest is up to you.

Fill a large pot with water and bring it to a vigorous boil. Drop in 1 whole chicken. Bring the water back to a simmer, and continue to simmer for fifteen short minutes. Make sure chicken is still wholly submerged in simmering by weighing it down with a plate and adding boiling water if necessary. After 15 minutes, turn off the gas, cover the pot tightly, and let sit for 45 minutes more. Remove from water.

Door #1: Ceremonial Chicken

Slice chicken into bite size, making sure every piece has some skin. Arrange attractively on a large plate, and sprinkle with julienned kaffir lime leaves. Serve with a dipping sauce made of 6 tablespoons of freshly squeezed lime juice, 3 teaspoons of salt and 1 ½ teaspoons of fine white pepper. Serve with rice.

Door #2: Broth

Boil the broth down to a quarter of its volume with generous amount of chive and scallions and a few red pepper flakes. Add a little bit of fish sauce and/or shrimp paste. Pour broth on rice noodle, or rice, or leave for sipping, and go back to Door #1 for chicken to go with it.

Door #3: Hue Chicken Salad

Shred chicken into long, thin strands. Gently massage 3 teaspoons of ground black pepper, 6 teaspoons of kosher salt or to taste, 6 teaspoons of sugar and 1 cup of freshly squeezed lime juice into the chicken. Fold in 3 small yellow onions, sliced paper-thin and rinsed, 6 Thai bird chilies or 1 Serrano chili, chopped, 5 cups of loosely packed *rau ram* (Vietnamese Cilantro) leaves or mint leaves and 3 teaspoons of vegetable oil.

Julian Fleisher, *New York City*
CHICKEN FOR A WEEKEND

This is the dish I like to prepare on weekends spent in my country house in the Catskills during the cold months of the year. It's the first thing I do when arriving, even before making a fire in the chimney. By the time the house is warm and cozy, the chicken is ready to eat.

Take a large Bundt cake pan, cover the hole of the central tube with aluminum foil and fill the bottom with cut up root vegetables, tossed with some olive oil, rosemary and thyme, and seasoned with salt and pepper. Wash and pat dry a whole chicken, season the cavity with salt and pepper and invert it over the tube, wings facing upwards. Brush it with olive oil or softened butter and sprinkle the skin aggressively with kosher salt. Roast at 425° F for about an hour. The chicken juices drip over the vegetables, basting them as they roast.

I extend this dish into the weekend by making sandwiches with the breast meat and soup with the bones.

Wayne Koestenbaum, *New York City*
CHICKEN WITH HOISIN SAUCE

I got this recipe from a precious source, *Mrs. Chiang's Szechwan Cook Book,* by Ellen Schrecker (with John Schrecker), originally published in 1976. In this dish, hoisin sauce, which is, unfortunately, mostly sugar, plays the starring role. The shiny brown-purple substance tastes like plum sauce and comes in jars. For years at a time, I lose my appetite for hoisin, but then, suddenly, the yearning for its unctuousness – its ability to cloak meat with an absolving envelope of tightly-clinging syrup – returns.

Chop ginger and garlic. You could use 2 cloves of garlic, or 1, or 3. I use one. Skin the ginger before chopping; I like to use more ginger than garlic. Also chop some scallions into 1- or 2-inch lengths, and slice the white bottoms of the scallions into smaller slivers. Over the years I have developed a very detailed and pleasurable relationship to the ritual of subdividing scallions.

Wash boneless chicken breasts, one pound, or more, but not too much more, lest you crowd the pan. Dry the chicken breasts with paper towels. Chop the chicken in 1 inch pieces, or larger, if you wish. Aim to make the pieces a uniform size, but don't worry if their proportions vary.

Put the chicken pieces into a bowl, and add 3 tablespoons of soy sauce, a teaspoon of sesame oil, and a tablespoon of sherry. Stir. Let this concoction sit around for 10 minutes or longer.

In a wok or a big pan, pour in some peanut oil. When the oil is hot, throw in the scallions, and press them into the pan while stir -frying them. Work up a bit of caramelization, or at least satisfy yourself that the scallions will cook through and not be too crunchy (unless you like them al dente). Then throw in the ginger and garlic and let them sizzle. After thirty seconds, maybe forty-five, add as much hoisin sauce as you can bear. A tablespoon is the minimum. Mrs. Chiang recommends 2 tablespoons.

Stir-fry for fifteen seconds to unite the hoisin sauce with the items already at play in the pan.

Stir the chicken in its marinade, and if the contents of the bowl seem too dry, add a tablespoon of water. Then, spoon the chicken and its marinade into the hot pan. Stir-fry the pieces – with loose, nonchalant gestures – into and around the goodies already in the pan, to make sure that the chicken has a chance to befriend all the hot materials (the *soffrito*). Rotate and toss the pieces of chicken to see that all of their sides get touched by heat and adequately moistened. If the pan looks dry, add more soy sauce. And if you get impatient, cover the pan for 10 seconds, and then uncover it, and keep selectively covering the pan to induce brief interludes of steaming, which, if allowed to go overboard, will ruin the texture of the meat. However, steaming (when performed judiciously) speeds up the process and helps ensure that the fatter pieces of chicken receive adequate heat.

Test to see if the chicken is adequately cooked by slicing into one of the plumpest pieces, and make sure the meat no longer has a pink interior.

When done, slide everything onto a dish or plate, and serve with rice.

Start making the rice *before* you start making the chicken.

You'll probably want to serve the chicken with a vegetable; and so, before you cook the chicken, prepare a salad of asparagus by steaming or boiling the asparagus (chopped, on the bias, into 1- or 2-inch pieces) and then dressing them in soy sauce, sesame oil, hot pepper oil, rice wine vinegar, and, if you're ambitious, roasted ground Szechwan pepper.

Or, one minute before you're finished stir-frying the chicken, you could add the pre-boiled or pre-steamed asparagus pieces (undressed) to the pan, and spoon in a little more hoisin sauce if you're worried that the asparagus's presence will denude the dish of its full portion of sweet grease.

Serves two.

Bill Palant, *New York City*
CHICKEN WITH ARTICHOKE HEARTS

Mix a few tablespoons flour with salt, ground pepper, and garlic salt to taste. Press 4 boneless chicken breasts into the flour, shake off excess flour and brown them on both sides in 4 tablespoons of olive oil. Transfer browned chicken breasts into a casserole dish. In the same pan, sauté ½ pound of sliced button mushrooms, 1 bunch of scallions, and chopped onions, if desired. Spoon the mix over the chicken breasts. In the same pan, simmer 1 cup of dry white wine and 1 cup of chicken broth with

1 large can artichoke hearts, drained and quartered. Cover and simmer until tender. Add black olives, cherry tomatoes and sliced red bell pepper. Spoon mixture over the chicken breast and roast uncovered for 20-25 minutes at 350° F.

Sprinkle with chopped parsley and serve.

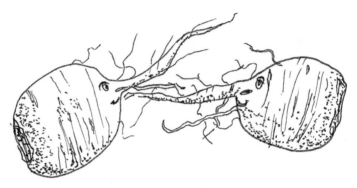

Tommy Tune, *New York City*
KING RANCH CHICKEN
(A Texas favorite)

Combine 10 ounces of cream of chicken soup, 10 ounces cream of mushroom soup, 10 ounces of canned tomatoes and 2 cups of chicken broth. Cut 12 corn tortillas into pieces and toss them with 3 cups of cooked chicken, cut into bite-size pieces, 1 large chopped onion, and chopped green chilies to taste. Grease a 3-quart casserole, layer of the mixture into it, pour half the soup mixture over it, repeat layers of the two and add 2 cups of grated Cheddar cheese on top. Bake at 350° F for 45 to 60 minutes.

Serves 8.

Barbara Häusler, *Munich, Germany*
COQ AU RIESLING

In a frying pan, sauté 1 pound of mushrooms, halved or quartered according to size, in a bit of flavor-neutral oil until all completely dry and nicely browned. Deglaze with the juice of 1 lemon, cook until the lemon juice has evaporated, season with salt and black pepper and set aside.

In a Dutch oven, melt a tablespoon butter and fry 3 thick slices of bacon, cut into dice, in it until crisp. Transfer to a plate lined with some paper towels to drain off the fat. Pour out most of the fat from the pan and add 1 pound of chicken necks, backs or cut-up wings. Brown the pieces well before deglazing with 2 cups of chicken broth. Simmer for 10 minutes, strain the stock and set aside. Discard the chicken pieces.

Wipe out the pan, add a bit of oil and brown 4 chicken legs (cut into separate drum sticks and thighs and seasoned with salt and pepper) on all sides. Transfer the chicken pieces to a pan, cover and keep warm in a 300° F oven. Melt a tablespoon of butter in the pan, add 5 chopped shallots, 2 sliced carrots and a teaspoon sugar and sauté gently until lightly caramelized. Dust with a heaped tablespoon of flour and sauté for a few minutes before adding 1 glass of very dry Riesling. Once it has come to a simmer, add reserved stock, 1 cup heavy cream, a crushed clove of garlic (optional), and a little bundle of fresh parsley, thyme, rosemary and bay leaf, tied with a string or stuffed into a loose tea bag. Bring to a simmer and reduce until lightly thickened. Pile the chicken pieces over it, cover and cook over medium low heat for about 25 minutes. Transfer the chicken pieces to the same pan used before, cover and keep it warm in the oven. Discard the herb bundle, add a splash of Cognac or Noilly Prat Vermouth to the sauce. Simmer until the sauce has reached the right consistency, adding more cream or chicken broth if necessary. Season with salt, pepper and a pinch of Cayenne to taste, plus a bit of lemon juice before adding the bacon and mushrooms. Cover and keep warm until ready to serve.

Transfer the chicken pieces to a platter and ladle the sauce over them. I like to serve this with Tagliatelle pasta.

Sherry Vine, *New York City*
CHICKEN SOUVLAKI AT SHERRY'S

I am very good at reheating coffee in the microwave, but here is how I prepare Chicken Souvlaki: Pick up phone. Ask Siri to call *Greek Kitchen*. Order delicious food for delivery. Pay delivery person. Eat on bed while watching *Game of Thrones*.

Gordon Ross, *Hout Bay, South Africa*
CHICKEN CURRY

In a frying pan, gently sauté a chopped 1-inch block of fresh ginger and a chopped clove of garlic in a bit of oil before adding 4 large free-range boneless chicken breasts, seasoned with salt and pepper, to the pan. Brown them lightly on both sides and transfer them to a casserole. Add 2 chopped medium-size onions to the pan and stir-fry them until they are translucent. Add 2-3 heaped teaspoons medium-hot curry powder, 1 teaspoon paprika (preferably Hungarian), 1 teaspoon ground cinnamon and 1 heaped tablespoon plain flour to soak up all the juices, followed by a 14 ounce tin of chopped Italian tomatoes, a 14 ounce tin of unsweetened coconut crème and 1 pint of chicken stock. Add the chicken stock gradually, stirring all the while. Scraping the base of the frying pan with a wooden spoon to get all the flavorsome paste dissolved into the sauce. Cook the sauce medium heat until it thickens a bit, season it with salt and pour it over the chicken breasts. Cover and finish cooking the chicken in a medium-hot oven until done, about 30 minutes at 325° F. Serve with boiled rice, mango chutney and finely sliced cucumber in plain yoghurt.

Douglas Ladnier, *Los Angeles, California*
ROAST CHICKEN DINNER

Preheat oven to 450° F. Cut 1 onion into large slices and scatter them into a roasting pan. Rinse 1 whole chicken, remove any innards (neck, organs, etc.) and place it on top of the onions, breasts facing up. Cut 1 orange in half and squeeze a bit of juice from each half on top of and around the chicken. put both halves inside the chicken, one facing up, one facing down.

Slice 4-6 potatoes thinly (not much thicker than potato chips, do not peel them) and place them all around the chicken to fill up the rest of the empty space in the pan. Scatter some chopped garlic over the potatoes and pour ¼ cup olive oil on top of the chicken and potatoes. Sprinkle everything with plenty of salt and pepper, a generous amount of chopped fresh rosemary (or use bottled rosemary pieces) and a little cinnamon (not too much of it, it is for mild flavor). Roast for 1 hour without touching it. After 1 hour, use a baster or a soup ladle to get the juices from the bottom of the pan and pour it over the top of the chicken and all of the potatoes three times, every 10 minutes for the next half hour.

After 1 hour and fifteen minutes of cook time (total) add green vegetables on top of potatoes (asparagus or broccoli) and include them in the final two bastings. After 1 hour and 30 minutes of total cook time, your whole meal is ready. remove from oven and let cool for a few minutes before you carve the chicken. Carefully carve out the breasts and then cut the legs and thighs off together to serve. Potatoes and chicken skin should be browned and crispy and delicious. This is the best chicken dinner ever!!!

SAUCES

Sidney Long, *Newport, Rhode Island*
SAUCE FOR EVERYTHING

Stir 1 tablespoon of sugar into 2 tablespoons rice vinegar. Heat in a small saucepan until it forms a light syrup. Cool slightly and serve over everything!

Recipe doesn't make much syrup so one could increase proportions as desired.

PORK

Emily Gould, *Brooklyn, New York*
ORANGE-FLAVORED PORK CHOPS

Place a big pot of salted water on the stove. While it heats, submerge 1.5-2 pounds of pork chops (shoulder or rib) in a marinade of one 16-ounce bottle of orange juice (cheap kind is a -ok!), the juice of 2 lemons, salt, and 2 cloves of chopped garlic. Peel and cut up 4 potatoes and add them to the water.

Wash and roughly chop 1 bunch greens (kale or mustard). Sautée 2 chopped cloves of garlic with 3 tablespoons of olive oil in a pot with a heavy bottom. When it starts to smell good, remove a spoonful of the oil and set aside for the potatoes. To the remainder, add the greens and sautée 'til tender (eat one to find out). Salt to taste.

When the potatoes are easily pierced by a fork/starting to fall apart, after about 20 minutes, drain them, return them to the pot, add a splash of milk, a chunk of butter and reserved garlic oil and mash with potato masher or wooden spoon. Salt to taste but be careful since you already salted the water.

Back to the chops! Put some oil in the cast-iron pan and preheat it to medium-high. Drain the chops and blot them dry with paper towels, then sprinkle on a little more salt. When the pan is HOT, sear them on both sides. Don't move them around as they cook. If the chops are really thick, you can sear them then stick them in a 350° F oven to cook the rest of the way. If they're thin, they will cook really quickly – they'll only need a few minutes on each side. Cut into one to see if it's done – you want it to be hot on the inside and not at all pink.

Pile it all up on a plate! Yum!

Christopher Baldovino, *Miami, Florida*
PORK MEDAILLONS WITH CARROT PURÉE

Marinate pork loin medallions in maple syrup, grated ginger, lime juice, crushed garlic, salt & pepper for a minimum of 4 hours, much longer for better results. Sear pork in hot skillet. Reduce marinade, emulsify it in a blender with a piece of butter and pour over seared medallions.

Sautee garlic and onions until caramelized and brown, set some aside for garnish, then add chopped carrots and chicken stock. Boil until carrots are overcooked. Purée but not until completely smooth, season with salt and pepper.

The same marinade can be used for grilled salmon, substituting orange, tangerine or blood orange for the lime. The texture of the salmon marinated in citrus and then grilled is so lovely. As a side: crispy roasted julienned carrots and parsnips.

Mira Evnine, *Brooklyn, New York*
SHORT RIBS IN MOLE VERDE

Place 12 -16 separated spare pork ribs into a large pot. Add 2 teaspoons salt, 1 teaspoon black peppercorns, 1 garlic clove, ½ large white onion, 1 Mexican bay leaf and enough water to cover the meat by about 2 inches. Bring to a gentle simmer and cook over medium high heat for about 40 minutes, stirring intermittently and skimming off any rising foam. Scoop out the ribs and transfer them to a bowl. Strain the broth and reserve it.

Remove the husks of 1 ½ pounds of tomatillos, rinse them and place them along with 2-3 Serrano chilies (or 3-4 jalapeños) into a sauce pan. Cover them with water and cook them over medium heat until the tomatillos lighten in color, about 10 minutes. Strain, cut off and discard the chilies' stems and transfer the chilies and tomatillos to a blender. Add 1 bunch of rinsed cilantro (leaves and stems), 2 cloves of garlic, ½ cup of white onion in chunks and 1 cup reserved pork broth. Puree until smooth. Working in batches, brown the ribs with a little canola oil in a Dutch oven set over medium high heat. After browning the last batch, remove the ribs from the pot and pour the mole into it, refrying it for 1 minute. Stir in the remaining pork broth and bring it to a simmer. Season with salt to taste. Add 3 sliced Mexican zucchini and ½ pound trimmed green beans and cook over medium heat for 10-15 minutes, until the vegetables are almost cooked through. Add the ribs, stir and cook for just a few more minutes to reheat the meat. Garnish with cilantro sprigs and serve with warm corn tortillas and, if desired, a side of rice and beans.

Klaus Pohl, *Vienna and New York*
SCHWEINSBRATEN
(Bavarian Pork Roast with Bread Dumplings and Red Cabbage)

Take a 5 pounds of pork shoulder roast with its rind and carve a grid into the rind. Wrap the roast in kitchen towels soaked in dark beer and cure it overnight. Cut some incisions into the roast and push whole peeled garlic cloves into them. Also wedge a few garlic cloves under the rind. Season the roast aggressively with salt. Into a large Dutch oven that fits the roast, place about 1 pound of bones (preferably pork feet and neck or ox tail), add 1 large sliced onion, 2 sliced carrots, a thick slice of celery root, 1 sliced parsnip, 1 sliced leek, a handful of crusty chunks of stale sourdough bread, 1 small onion spiked with a cloves, a few strips of lemon peel and a couple slices of fresh ginger. Place the roast on top, rind facing up, pour 1 cup water and 2 cups dark beer over it, season the rind once again with salt and pepper, cover with the lid and place in the cold oven. Turn it to 500° F and roast for 1 hour before basting it with more beer every fifteen minutes. After another hour, remove the lid, season the rind once again with salt and roast for another 20 minutes or more, until the rind is golden brown and crusty. Do not fret – remove the meat from the pot and let it rest on a carving board. Add 2 cups of meat stock to the pot and simmer everything for fifteen minutes before passing it through a fine-mesh sieve. Remove the bones and mash up the cooked vegetables separately, Serve the roast surrounded by a handful of dried prunes and apricots with the mashed vegetables and the sauce on the side. Some like to gnaw on the bones, offer those on a separate platter. Serve with

BLAUKRAUT

In a large heavy pot, brown a few thin slices of bacon with some goose or duck fat before adding 1 medium-size head of shredded red cabbage, an inch of water, a few tablespoons of raspberry jam, a few raisins and cloves. Cover with apple slices and simmer on low heat for 2 hours.

Also

BREAD DUMPLINGS
Semmelknödel

Tear up a stale loaf of white bread – or several Kaiser rolls. Place the bread into a large mixing bowl and knead cold milk into them until you have the consistency of a chunky dough that holds its shape. Add chopped parsley, 3 egg yolks, salt and pepper, and shape the dough into 6 balls. Brown a handful of diced bacon with coarsely crushed pepper corns, a few raisins and diced dried apricots. Make an indent into the dumplings, spoon some of the mix into the cavity, seal them assiduously and sensually roll them once again into plump balls. Drop them into quietly simmering salty water. Turn the flame down to low. They are done 5 minutes after they have floated to the top, about 20 minutes total.

BEEF

Janine Lai, *Brooklyn, New York*
BRAISED OXTAIL

Toss 3 pounds of oxtail pieces, 1 large onion, quartered, 1 bunch scallions, thinly sliced, 5 cloves of garlic, minced, 1 knob of fresh ginger, minced, 1 scotch bonnet or habañero pepper, seeded and chopped, ¼ cup of soy sauce, 2 sprig fresh thyme, 1 teaspoon of salt and 1 teaspoon of ground black pepper in a covered container or Ziplock bag if you want to marinate it overnight (optional). Brown the oxtail pieces in batches in a large skillet on high with some vegetable oil for roughly 10 minutes. Once browned, place the oxtail and other ingredients in a heavy pot with a tight-fitting lid, add 2 cups of water and braise in a 275° F oven for 6 hours or until very tender. Add a can drained fava beans and 1 teaspoon of ground allspice, and a slurry of 2 tablespoons of cornstarch mixed with ¼ cup of cold water and mix well. Adjust the seasoning, adding more salt to taste, bring to a simmer and place once again in a 250° F oven for another hour or so.

I like to serve this over cheesy white corn grits with a handful of baby arugula.

Jock Soto, *New Mexico*
GRILLED SKIRT STEAK WITH ARUGULA*

This recipe is incredibly easy and perfect for entertaining a crowd, but keep in mind that a successful dinner party is as much about the personalities one mixes as it is about the edible ingredients one combines. I once made this dish for a dinner I gave in honor of Johnny Reinhold, the famous Jewelry designer. I also invited several male dancers from New York City Ballet and, as a surprise guest, Debbie Harry. After dinner all the ballet boys decided to take off their shirts for a spontaneous finale. Everyone

* Adapted from Jock Soto's memoir, *Every Step You Take* (Harper Collins 2011). Used with permission.

went away happy – well fed and well entertained. What more can a host hope for?

Marinade a 3 pounds of skirt steak in a mix of ½ cup of olive oil, ¼ cup of red wine vinegar, 5 finely chopped cloves of garlic, 2 tablespoons of chopped fresh rosemary, 1 teaspoon of salt and ½ teaspoon of pepper. Leave the meat to marinate overnight in the refrigerator, covered, or for at least 3 hours. Let it come to room temperature before the next step.

Get your grill very hot and sear the steak for about 3 minutes per side. Remove the meat from the heat and let is rest while you toss a couple of bunches of arugula salad, washed and tumbled dry, with a light vinaigrette of nothing but red wine vinegar, salt and pepper and olive oil. Slice the meat diagonally against the grain into strips and arrange them on a platter. I like to place the dressed arugula directly on top of the steak, right down the center.

You can vary this very simple recipe by adding *Sazon* (Puerto Rican seasoning salt), soy sauce, ground cumin, Worcestershire sauce, mustard or other surprise ingredients of your choosing to the marinade.

Tim Ranney, *New York City*
PEKING ROAST

With a sharp knife, cut slits into a 5-pound beef roast and insert slivers of garlic and onion into it. Put the meat into a bowl and slowly pour 1 cup vinegar (apple cider or white) over it; then add enough water to cover the meat. Cover with plastic wrap and refrigerate for 48 hours, turning the meat occasionally.

When you're ready to cook the meat, pour off the vinegar solution and pat the meat dry with a paper towel. Brown it well on all sides in some oil, in a heavy pot (a cast-iron Dutch oven is best).

Pour 2 cups brewed coffee over the meat and add 2 cups of beef or dark chicken stock. Cover and cook over very low heat for about 6 hours on top of the stove. You may need to add more liquid, so check the roast once in a while, making sure it doesn't cook dry. Add only a small amount of liquid at a time. Season it with salt or pepper about 20 minutes before serving.

Strain cooking liquids. Make a slurry with 2 tablespoons of cornstarch and stock or water. Add to strained cooking liquid. Add ½ cup half & half. Stir until desired consistency.

Serve with *spätzle* or mashed potatoes & sautéed red cabbage with caraway seeds.

Makes great sandwiches.

Rami Ramirez, *Queens, New York*
ROPA VIEJA
("Old Clothes," Cuban-style Flank Steak)

Place a 2 pounds of flank steak in a large pot cover it with cold water. Add 1 bay leaf, 1 large onion, cut in half, a couple of cracked garlic cloves, 1 carrot, peeled and cut into chunks, 1 celery stick in chunks, and a loose-leaf tea bag filled with a couple of cloves, peppercorns and allspice berries. Lower a plate into the pot to keep the meat and vegetables submerged and bring the water to a simmer, skimming off any rising foam. When the water is clear, reduce the heat to very low, cover and cook for at least 2 hours, until the meat is fork tender. Remove the meat and set it aside, covered. Strain and reserve the broth for another use. When the meat is cold enough to handle, shred it into strips and cut those into 2-inch long pieces.

In a Dutch oven, heat a couple tablespoons vegetable oil and sauté in it 1 large onion, thinly sliced, and 6 garlic cloves, chopped. When the onions begin to caramelize, add 1 green bell pepper, cut into thin strips. Stir and cook it for a few minutes, then add ½ cup dry white cooking wine. Cook until the alcohol has evaporated, then add 2 cups plain tomato puree. Stir and bring to a simmer. Season with salt to taste and add the shredded meat. Add a bit of the broth if the mixture is too dry. Cook gently for about 20 minutes. Check the seasoning, adding salt and pepper to taste. Before serving, stir in 1 jar of preserved red peppers, chopped. Serve with white rice, fried sweet plantains and a green salad, lightly dressed with lime juice, salt and pepper, chopped garlic, oregano, and olive oil.

A VEGETABLE SIDE DISH

Julie Johnson Staples, *Brooklyn, New York*
SAUTÉED CORN AND OKRA

Pick two handfuls of small okra pods, wash them, slice off their caps and cut them into ½-inch slices. Cut off the kernels of 4 ears of sweet corn and sauté them in a frying pan with a bit of olive oil. When the kernels begin to caramelize, add the okra along with a medium sweet onion, chopped, and sauté for just a few minutes. The okra should still be crunchy. Depending what I serve it with, I may toss in a few sweet small grape tomatoes, cut in half, for color. Season with salt and pepper and serve. This is excellent with fish.

DESSERTS

Tim Cusack, *New York City*
ALPHABET CITY BROWNIES

A bunch of *Cannabis sativa* should be chopped finely (or pulverized in a coffee grinder). Approximately ⅛ ounce will produce the desired result. Take 1½ sticks of unsalted butter and gently melt it in a small saucepan. To this add the first ingredient, reduce to low heat, and bring the mixture to a gentle simmer, stirring often to prevent scorching. Cook until the butter becomes an alarming greenish brown sludge, 30-40 minutes. Only then will it be ready. Remove from the heat and press though a mesh sieve, capturing the butter in a measuring cup. Return the cooked cannabis to the saucepan and reheat on a high flame. Deglaze with a good-quality dark rum, scraping up all of the brown bits with a spoon. Press the liquid once more through the sieve and into the same container as butter. Set aside. Prepare a packaged brownie mix according to instructions. Replace the oil called for on the box with the cannabis-infused butter. Chopped nuts and bittersweet chocolate can be added if desired. Bake as directed, but watch carefully, as these tend to set quickly and it is better for them to be slightly underdone. Let cool slightly and cut into generous-sized squares. Eat with care. One brownie is quite sufficient.

Rick Whitaker, *New York City*
CHERRY CLAFOUTIS

Heat the oven to 350° F. Smear some butter onto the bottom and sides of a big non-stick skillet. (Nine inches? That should do it.) Put some sugar in the skillet, shake it around, and throw out the leftover sugar. Cover the bottom of the skillet with pitted sour cherries. (I use Adro, from Hungary, sold in a glass jar; I drain them first.)

In a large bowl, beat 3 eggs until foamy. Add ⅓ cup of sugar and beat some more, until a little thick, a minute or two. Add ⅓ cup of flour. Beat some more, until smooth. Add 1 ½ cups of half & half (or ¾ cups of milk and ¾ cup of cream), a teaspoon of vanilla extract, and a pinch of salt. Beat to blend. Pour the batter over the cherries. Bake for about 25 minutes, until the eggs are set and the clafoutis has begun to brown. Let cool, then sprinkle with a little powdered sugar.

Bryan Lowder, *New York City*
BANANA PUDDING
WITH VANILLA-BEAN MOUSSE

Banana pudding is one of the South's calling cards. It's a treat that even a Yankee can enjoy.

In a saucepan, gently heat 2 cups of milk and ¼ cup of sugar. In a bowl, cream ½ cup of sugar and 3 tablespoons f cornstarch with 1 egg and 2 egg yolks (reserve the egg whites). Temper the mixture with a bit of the hot milk before adding it to the sauce pan and bringing it to simmer. Cook while stirring constantly until thickened. Remove the saucepan from the heat and whisk in 3 tablespoons of cold butter, one slice at a time, until the mixture is glossy and smooth. Add 1 teaspoon of vanilla extract and 1 tablespoon of banana liqueur. Transfer the pudding to a medium bowl, cover it with plastic wrap, cool it to room temperature, then refrigerate until chilled through, about 2 hours. Once the pudding has chilled, fold in 3 large or 4 medium ripe bananas, halved lengthwise and cut into ¼-inch slices. Whip 1 cup of heavy cream until frothy. Add 1 tablespoon of caster sugar and continue whipping until the cream forms firm peaks. Gently fold the whipped cream into the pudding until just combined. Refrigerate the pudding while you make the vanilla-bean mousse.

Whip 1 cup heavy cream with the whisk attachment of a stand mixer (or a handheld electric mixer) until frothy. Add ¼ cup the caster sugar and the scraped seeds of 1 vanilla bean and whip the cream to a soft peak. In a separate bowl, beat the 2 egg whites until foamy, add ¼ cup of caster sugar and beat to a firm peak. Gently fold the egg whites into the whipped cream.

Spread about two thirds of the pudding into a large glass dish. Top with an even layer of 25 to 30 Nilla Wafers (DO NOT be tempted by carpetbaggers from Whole Foods or the like – they are crude imitations), then add the remaining pudding. Spread the vanilla mousse evenly over the pudding. Roughly crumble a few more Nilla Wafers over the mousse. Cover with plastic wrap and refrigerate for at least 1 hour before serving. The pudding's texture will be best if served on the day of preparation, but refrigerating overnight is fine. (Due to the raw eggs in the mousse, do not keep leftovers longer than two days.)

Anny Jones, *New Hampshire*
ORANGE AND MARSALA JELLIES
(Adapted from *Good Things in England* by Florence White)

This is a very old Christmas recipe.

Peel off the zest of 1 large orange with a potato peeler & soak it for 1 hour in 5 ounces of sweet fine quality Italian (NOT American) Marsala. Cut the orange plus 2 more large oranges and one lemon in half. Squeeze the juice from all the fruit, being careful not the tear the peel of the 2 intact oranges and the lemon. Dissolve 3 ounces of sugar and ½ ounce of gelatin in 10 ounces of water, first leaving it to soak for a few minutes & then, very gently heating it and stirring until both sugar & gelatin are completely dissolved & the liquid is clear. Strain the Marsala and orange juice into a bowl, add the dissolved sweetened gelatin, and place it in the refrigerator to begin to set. Meanwhile, carefully remove all the leftover pulp from the 2 oranges and the lemon and prop them up on a bed of crumpled foil so they are level. When the jelly is just starting to set, pour it into the citrus cups. There will be some jelly left over that can be put in little cups or dishes. When the jellies are set, cut them in half with a very sharp knife & arrange with flowers & leaves on a striking plate. In France I have some deep green Wedgewood leaf plates that help this desert look particularly stunning.

For a children's version without alcohol simply substitute 5 fluid ounces of orange juice for the Marsala.

Lionel Casseroux, *New York City*
CRÈME RENVERSÉE MAMAN COLETTE

In a saucepan, melt down 10 sugar cubes (about ⅓ cup of sugar) and 3 tablespoons white vinegar and cook it to an amber caramel. Pour it into a 7-inch cake mold or ovenproof shallow round serving bowl and tip the mold in every direction to evenly spread out the caramel. Bring 4 cups milk to a simmer with 2 tablespoons alcohol-free vanilla essence and another 10 sugar cubes / ⅓ cup of sugar. In a mixing bowl, beat 6 whole eggs until homogenous and slowly add the hot milk. Pour the mixture over the caramel, set the mold into a baking dish, add enough hot water to surround it by an inch and bake at 375° F for 35 minutes, until a cake taster comes out dry. Cool and refrigerate for several hours. Invert onto a platter just before serving.

Monique Truong, *Brooklyn, New York*
BLUEBERRY "CLAFOUTIS"

This is my magic act dessert. It's incredibly simple and people often clap afterwards. *Clafloutis* is in quotation marks because this dish is more American than it is French.

Preheat oven to 350° F. In a medium bowl, combine ⅔ cups of flour, a scant ½ cup of sugar, 1½ teaspoons of baking powder, and ¼ of teaspoon kosher salt. Whisk in ⅔ cups of milk and ½ teaspoon of vanilla extract, until the batter is smooth.

Place 5 tablespoons salted butter into a 9- or 10-inch glass or ceramic pie dish and place in the hot oven until the butter has just melted. Take the dish out and pour the batter over the butter. Sprinkle 2 cups fresh blueberries, washed and patted dry on top of the batter. Do not mix or touch the batter and the berries; they will sort themselves out in the baking. Return the dish to the oven and bake for about 1 hour until nice and golden at the edges and the berries are bubbling. Spoon out while still hot or very warm. It's particularly nice when served with vanilla ice cream. If you make this ahead of time and serve it at room temperature, you'll be able to slice it like a cake.

CAKES AND COOKIES

Nicole Pleuler, *Hamburg, Germany*
APPLE MARZIPAN CAKE
(Orally transmitted by Christa Schmedes)

Swiftly work 300 grams of flour, 100 grams of sugar, 200 grams of softened butter and 1 egg into a pastry dough. Shape it into two even discs. Wrap them in cellophane and chill for at least 30 minutes.

Peel, halve and core 3-5 apples. Slice them thinly. Slice a 250 grams log of Marzipan into thin slices. Roll out a disc of dough and line a greased and floured tart pan with it. Arrange apple and marzipan slices on it in an alternating round pattern. Roll out the second disc of dough and cover the tart with it, pressing down the edge and piercing it with a fork in several spots. Brush it with egg wash and bake it for about 40 minutes at 350 ° F.

Hans R. Gallas, *San Francisco, California*
BLOOD ORANGE UPSIDE DOWN CAKE

The original upside down cake recipes, which date back to 1925, usually used pineapple, whose juice formed the tasty, caramel syrup, this cake's trademark. (The Dole Pineapple company had perfected the slicing of pineapple into perfect rings as early as 1911, making them very attractive on the bottom/top of these cakes!) This recipe uses a thinly sliced blood orange. Other fresh fruits work well too, including peaches, pears, apples, apricots or nectarines.

In a small sauce pan, melt ½ cup (1 stick) of butter. Add over low heat while gently stirring: 1 cup packed dark brown sugar and ½ teaspoon of cinnamon. Cook for a few minutes until smooth, caramel-like consistency.

Thinly slice 1 blood orange including the peel.

In a small bowl sift together: 1 cup of cake flour (1 cup of all-purpose flour may be used. Remove 2 tablespoons from the cup and replace with 2 tablespoons corn starch), 1 teaspoon of baking powder and a pinch of salt. In a small bowl, combine 4 egg yolks with 1 tablespoon melted butter and 1 teaspoon of vanilla essence. In a separate bowl, whip 4 egg whites to a firm peak, gradually add in 1 cup of sugar while continuously beating, then the yolk mixture. Fold in the flour, ¼ cup at a time.

Pour and spread "caramel" mixture into a 11 x 7 inch baking pan (or round or square 9-inch baking pan). Distribute orange slices over the mixture and cover with batter. Bake for about a half hour at 325° F. Cool for about 15 minutes, then carefully unmold it onto a plate or platter.

May be served slightly warm or completing cooled. Garnish with whipped cream or crème fraîche.

Shuki Cohen, *Queens, New York*
FLOURLESS LOW-SUGAR RAW VEGAN
CHOCOLATE CAKE

Grind 3 cups of raw almonds with their skin to a fine meal, mix in ½ cup of cocoa powder, 3 tablespoons of honey, 2 tablespoons of xylitol syrup, 2 teaspoons of vanilla extract and a pinch of salt. Mix and knead until pliable but not sticky. Press it evenly into a 10-inch cake ring. Put 4 cups of raw cashews into a large pot and add at least 3 times their volume in water. Bring to a boil, turn off the flame, cover and let it rest for 10 minutes. Strain the cashews and allow water to drip from strainer for 5 more minutes. Pulse these cashews in a food process for until finely ground and fluffy. Add 1 cup cocoa powder, 2 tablespoons of Stevia extract and ¾ teaspoon of salt. Bring 1 cup of almond milk to a boil on a medium flame. As soon as it starts to boil, add 2 tablespoons of Agar-Agar and stir until it dissolves completely. With the food processor running intermittently, add it slowly to the cashew mixture and whip it to a consistency of a heavy mousse, adding more almond milk if the mixture is too thick – but don't insist on achieving full-fledged fluffiness: No joy of veganism (or any other -ism) is complete without painful sacrifices. Pour the mousse on the crust and refrigerate it for 24 hours. Right before serving, whip on high speed and for at least 15 minutes a mixture of 70 gr of chocolate -flavored vegan protein powder and 1 cup of almond milk. The resulting soft whip can then be poured over the individual pieces of cake, but is not likely to be used like traditional icing – see above regarding necessary sacrifices.

Eli Jacobson, *New York City*
CAFÉ AU LAIT CHOCOLATE BANANA CAKE

Melt ½ cup of margarine and mix it with 1½ cups of graham cracker crumbs When the mixture is cool, fold in 1 cup of chocolate chips and ½ cup of chopped walnuts.

Cream ¾ cup of margarine with 1 ¾ cup of sugar and 3 eggs. Mix in 1 ¼ cup of mashed bananas and 1 teaspoon of vanilla. Gradually add 2 cups of flour mixed with ¾ cup of cocoa powder, 1 ½ teaspoons of baking powder, 1 teaspoon baking soda and ¾ teaspoon of salt, alternating it with ¾ cup of buttermilk. Divide the batter evenly in 2 greased and floured 9-inch cake pans, smoothing it out with a rubber spatula. Sprinkle the chocolate chip/graham cracker/walnut topping mixture evenly over the two cake batters and lightly press them into the mixture.

Bake in a 350° F oven for 32 to 35 minutes, until a cake tester comes out clean. Remove the pans from the oven and place them on wire racks to cool for 30 minutes. Unmold and invert them onto the wire rack.

Beat 1 ½ cups of chilled heavy cream until creamy before adding 1 tablespoon instant coffee and ⅓ cup of confectioner's sugar and beating it to a soft peak. Spread one half of the frosting onto one of the cake layers. Place the second layer over it and frost only the sides of the cake with the second half of the frosting. Just before serving, dust the top and sides of the cake with powdered sweetened cocoa.

Jeannine Bonamy, *Nantes, France*
GATEAU NANTAIS
(French Almond Cake)

Beat 3 eggs and ⅔ cup of sugar to a light foam. Add 1 ½ cups of almond flour and ⅓ cup of flour, whisking until there are no more lumps. Stir 1 stick of melted butter and a pinch of flaky sea salt into the mixture and pour the batter into two parchment-paper-lined 9-inch cake molds. Bake at 350° F until the cakes shrink from the sides. Once they are cooled down, unmold them, douse with rum and fill with apricot jam, passed through a sieve. Coat the sides and surface with more apricot jam and, once it has dried a bit, glaze with sugar glaze made of confectioner's sugar beaten with milk and a touch of rum.

Sarah Bodinson, *New York City*
SUGAR N' SPICE COOKIES
(Inherited from my Great Grandmother Rachel Kurz's)

Combine ⅔ cup of shortening with 1 cup of sugar, 1 egg, and ¼ cup of molasses. Add 2 cups of flour, 2 teaspoons of baking soda, ¼ teaspoon of salt, 1 teaspoon of cinnamon powder, ¾ teaspoon of ground cloves and ¾ teaspoon of ground ginger and kneed swiftly. Chill and roll out to ⅛-inch thickness. Cut out fluted rounds and place them on parchment-paper-lined sheet pans and bake at 375 ° F for 8 minutes. Dip them into powdered sugar when still warm to lightly coat them.

CANDY

Baseera Khan, *Brooklyn, New York*
GULAB JAMUN
(Fried Milk Balls)

Sift ½ cup fine sifted milk powder, 2 tablespoons of flour and 1 teaspoon of baking powder and mix it with 1 tablespoon of clarified butter 2 tablespoons of yogurt to a paste, adding a bit of warm milk if the dough is too dry. While the dough rests, bring 1 ½ cups of sugar with 2 cups of water, a pinch of cardamon powder, a few strands of saffron and a few drops of rose essence to a simmer and turn the flame down low. Shape the dough into little balls and deep-fry them at low/medium heat in vegetable oil. The oil can't be too hot because the balls have to cook all the way thru with a light golden outer shell. Give the syrup one more quick boil and add the fried jamun balls.

Let them soak in the syrup for 30 minutes before serving.

Robert Bear Karito, *Staten Island, New York*
HONEY "BEARMALLOWS"

For about 28 "bearmallows", sprinkle 4 envelopes (or 6 teaspoons) of unflavored gelatin over ½ cup of water in the bowl of a stand mixer outfitted with a whisk attachment. While it "blooms," line a 9 x 13 inch baking pan with parchment paper and sift granulated sugar over the paper.

In a heavy sauce pan fit with a candy thermometer, combine 2 cups of granulated sugar, 1 cup of good honey, the scraped seeds of 1 vanilla bean and ½ cup of water. Boil the mix over high heat until it reaches 240° F. Be sure to watch the syrup as it tends to boil over while cooking. Just softly agitate it with a wooden spoon if it is beginning to rise. With the stand mixer running, pour the syrup over the bloomed gelatin while the stand mixer is running. Beat for about 5 -7 minutes until the mix looks like stiff meringue. Immediately transfer it to the sugar coated pan, and cover with more sugar. Spread it out evenly, and let sit a few hours until completely set. Unmold, cut into squares and roll them in more sugar.

The success of this recipe relies completely on the quality of your honey. Try different types for different flavors. At the bear cave, we like to blowtorch our bearmallows and make them into s'mores with graham crackers and dark chocolate sprinkled with lots of sea salt.

TEA OR COCKTAIL TIME

Yanna Avis, *New York City*
HIGH TEA CUCUMBER SANDWICHES
(One of the most civilized luxuries, simple yet quite fiddly)

What's in a classic English cucumber sandwich? Not much: Pullman bread (old-fashioned white, no healthy seven-grains, please!) butter, cucumber, salt, pepper and a touch of dill, the subtlety of it all lying mostly in the cut of the cucumber.

Peel hothouse cucumber and slice very thinly with a truffle shaver. Lay the slices on kitchen or paper towels, sparkle a little salt on them and leave them for around 15 minutes. Cut away the crusts of the bread, slice and spread with butter, spread a layer of cucumber slices on half of the slices, season with a little pepper, a touch of fresh dill and cover them with the remaining buttered bread slices, pressing each sandwich firmly to hold them together (so they don't fall apart at the time of serving) and cut into triangles. Et voila! A disappearing art in sophisticated living.

Lauren Cerand, *New York City*
OLD ETONIAN

In a cocktail shaker filled with ice, shake 1 ½ ounces of gin, 1 ½ ounces of Lillet blanc, 2 dashes of orange bitters and 2 dashes of Crème de Noyaux. (This is no longer in common use, so we substitute Amarguinha, a Portuguese liqueur.)

Strain into a stemmed cocktail glass. Garnish with a twist of orange peel if convenient.

Erin McMonagle, *New York City*
FLOTUS COCKTAIL

A spin on the classic *Cuba Libre*, created to celebrate President Barack Obama's initiative to open up relations with Cuba, and honoring the First Lady's efforts to get Americans to eat their vegetables by using the artichoke liqueur Cynar.

Mix ½ ounce Cynar and 1 ½ ounce dark aged rum in a shaker with ice. Pour into a Collins glass filled to a third with crushed ice, add Coca Cola (preferably the Mexican kind made with sugar, not corn syrup) until glass is nearly full and top it off with seltzer. Garnish with an orange wedge or any fruit you feel like.

Karen Andersen, *Connecticut*
JAMAICAN SOURSOP JUICE

Soursop juice is traditionally served with Sunday dinner in most Jamaican households. I grew up making this drink and I am delighted that soursop has of late become a much sought-after exotic fruit. This drink is light and refreshing and has a multitude of nutritional and medicinal benefits.

Peel 1 small, ripe soursop, discard the skin and place the pulp in a bowl. Break into small pieces. Add water and squeeze pulp repeatedly. Use a stainer/sieve to pour juice into a jug, separating the juice from the pulp and seeds. Add the juice of up to 2 limes and sweeten juice to taste with sugar. Best served chilled or with some crushed ice.

TREASURES

Olga Mychajluk, *Toronto, Canada*
MUMMY-LOVES-SASKIA COMFORT FOOD

It didn't start out that way… I've been making this for a few years now and my daughter Saskia defies all kid expectations and takes this in a mason jar for her lunch.

In a bowl, mix 1 tin of fava beans, drained and rinsed, 1 bunch of spring onions, chopped, 2 cloves of garlic, crushed and minced, a generous handful of fresh cilantro, chopped coarsely. Season with salt, pepper, a pinch of dried sumac, a pinch of crushed hot chili flakes, lemon juice and olive oil.

Optional: sliced radish OR chopped red pepper OR halved cherry tomatoes – not all at once though. Cover and put in fridge. Tastes even better the next day. Serve with: day-old baguette slices fried in butter.

OLGA'S COMFORT FOOD

Double-toast 2 slices of actual rye bread – not that scary stuff that has molasses in it – to ensure they are properly crisp. Open a tin can of good sardines in oil and squash the sardines with a fork, skins, bones and all. Spread them onto the hot bread until they stick like a paté. Season with salt and pepper and spread a spoonful of smooth Dijon mustard on top. Sometimes I enjoy a crisp dill pickle on the side or slice of cucumber on top.

For some reason this tastes better when done standing at the counter and then consumed on the floor, in the hallway, leaning against the wall with a book in one hand, completely alone. If I'm feeling especially anti-social I will put a slice of an onion on top and have a glass of wine or beer with it – feeling rebellious in the middle of the day – if consuming good food can be considered rebellious.

Meow Meow, *No Fixed Address*
LE CROISSANT AU SÈCHE-CHEVEUX
(How to Improve a Room-Service Croissant)

When coming "home" to one's hotel room in a foreign city, after one's show, and it is that hour between the night and morning, and the hotel kitchen is closed, and all one can get from room service is a croissant which – *de temps en temps* – arrives with a flourish (and a large bill) but swathed in fürchterlich tight plastic, chilled and yet feucht – one simply must use the German for "moist" here, as it has all the lovely seepy sounds of a mysteriously sodden midnight pastry – do the following: Make a nest out of a dinner napkin, befitting of a fairy queen, or at least a tiny sparrow, free the croissant of its plastic sheath and place it in the fairy bower. Cover with rosy petals, or failing that, a second napkin. Failing that, hotel stationery (embossed side up), failing that – a pillow. Plug in the hair dryer from the bathroom or the second drawer down, and gently heat the croissant with the hottest air, turning it twice. Mind sudden bursts of crumbs. Then relish them. Eat in bed. On the chest of a lover. Let the lover lick your fingers clean afterwards.

Sleep well sated.

XIII
THE PRODUCE ON
THE ISLAND IN BRITTANY

FOR SIX SUCCESSIVE YEARS, during my adolescence, the little island in Brittany had been my joy, spending summer holidays there with my family and dreaming of returning there throughout the rest of the year. German summer holidays commenced in August with our trip across Europe that always included a stopover in Paris. The island, a way off the Atlantic coast and barely visible from the continent – the ferry takes over an hour to get there – benefitted from a mild climate. After several years of renting a place for the summer my family bought a property and built a very comfortable, modern house on it. Then I moved to the United States and did not return to the island for many years as working all summer had become an economic necessity. Once Filip Noterdaeme and I decided to take regular summer vacations, it took me a year to convince him to travel there and many more to make the island our permanent summer destination. Appreciation comes with time. During our first visit, he had had his allergy attacks and had refused to stay on the island, judging it, with the prejudice of an urbanite, to be a bore. I told him that for me, living out of a suitcase, sleeping in crowded little budget hotels and visiting countless museums and churches across Italy was not an option in the heat of summer. I need culture, was his weak reply. I said, What you need is a break from it and to learn how to just *be*. My allergies are indifferent to pop psychology, was his impatient reply to this. But they weren't. A few years later, we returned to the island and he became not just enthralled with island life but just as eager to return every year as I had always been.

As I mentioned, in the summer of 2006, we became the seasonal tenants of what had once been a fisherman's house in one of the island's little villages. We were enchanted with everything. After careful examination of the gardens – one in front of the house with a small terrace that caught the morning sun and the other a little courtyard in the back – it was to my great satisfaction that I discovered that zucchini and string beans had been planted in the back and were ripe for the taking. I also made out fresh thyme, rosemary and even sorrel. Several large bushes of lavender were teeming with busy bees. There was also a fig tree.

The kitchen had to be re-organized. The French are thrifty in the way they outfit their summer houses with castoffs from their main household. It took a bit of an effort to adapt it for my needs. A list of household items had to be made. Luckily most could be borrowed from my parents' new, recently acquired house. Over the years, we stored more and more household items in their house that we would come and get after our arrival and carry to our summer rental. This enabled us to travel light. The most important kitchen items were a chef's knife, a large wooden cutting board, a pepper mill, a citrus juicer, an espresso cooker, a milk frother, six sets of cutlery, place mats and several linen kitchen towels. After the kitchen of the fisherman's house had been turned upside down and cleaned inside out, the redecorating of the house commenced. The furniture had scarcely been rearranged, the framed posters and photographs taken off the walls and replaced with fragrant fig leaves from the garden, and any seashells or other tchotchkes crowding the shelves stashed away and out of sight when it was time to go grocery shopping.

There were two bakeries on the island, one in the harbor, owned by an ambitious husband and wife who mistreated their employees and never ceased believing they had invented the wood-burning oven, and the other in the village, run by a quiet and artistic fisherman's son who had learned ancient baking recipes from his mother and two grandmothers. The croissants we sampled from the former were not memorable; we became the latter's most faithful clients, buying our croissants from him every morning of our stay on the island.

On our way to and from the bakery, we always passed by a house and garden surrounded by an ancient stone wall. Behind the wall stood an heirloom plum tree, overloaded with the most delicious, tiniest of purple plums. It became a joke, me asking Filip Noterdame what he saw when he closed his eyes, and he answered, overripe plums begging to be plucked. That, I said, was not proper, and so stolen plums were changed to apricots from the market. He however insisted on climbing onto the wall to reach those plums, and since I was too nervous that he would get caught, I told him if he cared to take fruit without asking for permission he should do it when I was out of sight.

Going to the market later in the morning and buying heads of Batavia lettuce, cucumbers, heirloom tomatoes, radishes, zucchini, eggplant, peppers, onions, squashes, beets, carrots, leeks and potatoes was a delight. There was also locally made goat cheese and freshly caught seafood. But it was the foraging that thrilled me most. The gathering of wild blackberries, sloe berries, apples, figs, wild fennel fronds, and beach rocket made me feel like a gold digger about his nuggets. How could anything so precious be ignored. There is nothing that is comparable to it, as satisfactory or as thrilling, as picking the riches nature readily offers us.

Later when the time came to eat what we had foraged it never occurred to me to question what way to prepare it. Naturally the simplest, just to crush the blackberries with a bit of sugar and eat them with *fromage blanc*, serve the figs with a cheese course, make simple tarts or compotes with the apples (and the purloined plums), using the fennel to stuff whole fish and spicing up a salad with the peppery beach rocket. Later still, when the summer turned into fall and we felt ready for more substantial fare, I turned much of what we foraged into condiments to add variety to our daily menus.

It appeared that, with the exception of the blackberries, which grew everywhere around the island, no one seemed to be aware of the natural bounty around them and they continued going to the *supermarché* to buy herbs and fruit brought in from the continent or frozen convenience foods to feed their children. We were an exception, and not being French was just a part of it.

PISTOU À LA ROQUETTE
(*Arugula Pesto*)

Wash and tumble dry two handfuls of wild beach rocket or farmed baby arugula. Stuff it into a food processor with ½ cup of shelled walnuts and ½ teaspoon of salt. Pulse until coarsely chopped, then add ½ cup of ground Parmesan and process everything to a paste, adding no more than a couple tablespoons of olive oil. Store the pesto in an airtight glass container, pressed down and topped with just enough olive oil to cover. Use up within a week.

To serve, boil spaghetti in well-salted water until al dente. In a sauté pan, bring 1 tablespoon of pesto, a splash of heavy cream (optional, but only if using true wild beach rocket, to mellow its potent sharpness) and a few tablespoons of pasta water per serving to a simmer. Season with coarse black pepper and thinly sliced fresh garlic to taste. Add the pasta, toss and serve with extra grated – never shredded Parmesan on the side.

Here is what I did when we picked too many figs to eat.

FIG CHUTNEY

Wash a good quart of ripe figs. Carefully peel off and discard their skins. Quarter the skinned fruit and transfer it to a saucepan. Add ½ cup of water, ¼ cup of red wine vinegar, 1 bay leaf, 2 thinly sliced shallots, a few whole black peppercorns, a couple of cloves, a tablespoon of mustard seeds and 2 tablespoons of honey. Bring to a simmer and cook for about 15 minutes. Fill the chutney into a mason jar, screw the lid on tightly and let it cool down to room temperature before refrigerating it. Serve as a condiment for *patés*, cold cuts or cheese.

And here is a more complex dessert made with foraged wild blackberries and sloe berries.

GOAT CHEESE PANNA COTTA WITH BERRY COULIS

In a sauce pan, bring 2 cups of heavy cream, 1 cup of milk, ¼ cup of sugar, the scraped seeds of 1 vanilla bean as well as the split vanilla bean to a simmer, cover it with a lid and set it aside. If available, add 2 fresh fig tree leaves; they add an indelible aroma. After about 15 minutes, remove the fig leaves and vanilla pod (scrape the rest of its seeds into the milk, rinse it, dry and store it in a jar reserved for vanilla sugar). Into the warm cream, add 1 cup of very mild fresh goat cheese and ½ cup of sugar. Reheat gently while constantly stirring to dissolve the sugar and cheese in the cream. Do not let it come to a simmer again. Meanwhile, pour ¼ cup of cold water into a small bowl, sprinkle 1 tablespoon powdered flavorless gelatin over it and let it "bloom" for 1 minute. Pour the warm cream through a fine-mesh sieve into a mixing bowl and add the bloomed gelatin. Stir until it has completely dissolved and ladle the cream – about ½ cup per portion – into individual-serving glasses like wide Champagne *coupes* or tumblers. Chill until set.

In a sauce pan, bring 2 cups of blackberries, a handful of sloe berries (or, if unavailable, blueberries) and 1 cup of water to a simmer. Add ¼ cup of sugar and a cinnamon stick. Simmer until the fruit is broken down, add a splash of spiced rum, cover and let it come to room temperature. Remove the cinnamon stick, press the mixture through a fine-mesh sieve to remove seeds, pits and pieces of skin. It should have the consistency of thin puree. If it is too thin, simmer it once again until thickened; if it is too thick, add a bit of rum or water. You may need to add more sugar to taste. Once it has cooled to room temperature, pour about 3 tablespoons over each of the set panna cottas. Refrigerate and serve chilled.

If foraging was limited to a handful of ingredients, the farmers offered about thirty different kinds of vegetables every morning and the fishermen sold a large variety of seafood directly off their docked boats. There was no way of knowing ahead of time what the catch of the day might be. Back in 1983, on the evening of our arrival for the first summer my family and I ever spent on the island, friends had invited us to a welcoming dinner. The hostess had a perfect way of making

SARDINES MI-CRUES MARINÉES AU CITRON
(Semi-crudo of Lemon-marinated Sardines)

Beheading, gutting and boning raw sardines takes a bit of practice but is easily learned and perfected if you are not squeamish. The sardines must be absolutely fresh out of the sea. Instructions on how to clean, de-scale, gut and butterfly fresh sardines are given in Chapter II.

Squeeze the juice of 1 lemon per 6 sardines into a shallow dish. Lay the sardines into the lemon juice, skin side up, cover the dish with cellophane and refrigerate them for no more than 1 hour – if left to macerate longer, the sardines will be fully "cooked" by the acidity of the lemon. To finish, scatter a few thin red onion rings, sliced jalapeños (or other fresh hot chilies or, as a last resort, dried chili flakes), and chopped parsley over the sardines, drizzle them with olive oil and a sprinkle of flaky sea salt and serve with grilled or toasted slices of baguette.

Short of the acquired taste of fresh oysters, this is as good a lunch or appetizer as can be imagined to conjure the pure taste of the sea.

During our first summer on the island, Filip Noterdaeme, who abhorred picnics on the beach, established that he would have every meal at the house, eating at a properly set table in the garden. Our silver-plated 1950s WMF cutlery was my pride. I had bought it at a flea market in Berlin in 1991 and had left it in Munich when I moved to New York in 1993 and my parents had later brought it to the island for us to use. I ended up taking it back to New York but later, when Filip Noterdaeme and I got married, Cary Davis, one of my most faithful and generous clients In New York, gave us as a wedding gift an entire set of it for the summer house. Every meal we have with it becomes an elegant feast.

During our stay, I always preferred to eat lunch on the go as I spent most of my days biking around the little island, following the sun as I went from one beach to another, but Filip Noterdaeme insisted on returning home for lunch, which he, for once, delighted in preparing for himself, in peace.

FILIP NOTERDAEME'S FAVORITE LUNCH SANDWICH

Slice a 10-inch piece of baguette lengthwise in half, remove some of the crumb to make space for the filling, and toast it well. Spread the slices with a small amount of salted butter. Stuff them with vinegar-brined anchovies (not the usual, salt and oil-cured kind!), thin slices of cooked red beet, sliced *cornichons*, sliced red onion, green lettuce leaves and handpicked fresh herbs such as basil, cilantro or parsley. Season with ground pepper, press lightly and savor with a few olives on the side.

Not wanting to go hungry on my own excursions, I got into the habit of taking along a jar of my preferred mid-day snack,

SAVORY GRANOLA

In a large mixing bowl, mix 2 quarts of old-fashioned oat meal – barley, wheat, or quinoa flakes may also be used – with 1 cup of ground flaxseeds, 2 cups of any combination of sliced almonds, pumpkin seeds, sesame seeds, sunflower seeds or chopped pecans or walnuts, plus 1 ½ cups of warm water and ¼ cup of oil of your choice – anything but canola, which turns rancid in no time, or toasted sesame oil, which is too dominant. Season to taste with salt or soy sauce, a touch of honey or brown sugar, fennel seeds or anise seeds, even fresh rosemary, and white or black pepper. Mix well, kneading it together to form small lumps. Loosely spread the mix out on two parchment-paper lined sheet pans and toast it in a 325° F oven for about 45 minutes, folding it over now and then with a spatula for even toasting, until lightly browned, completely dry and crunchy through and through. Once the granola has cooled down, mix in 2 cups of plump raisins or other chopped-up dried fruit of your choice like apricots or dates. You may also augment it with crushed vegetable chips or even potato chips. Mix well and store in an airtight glass container.

This is a very wholesome and original snack and a welcome alternative to sweet nutrition bars on one hand and the usual salted nuts or commercial trail mixes on the other. Eat it dry with a spoon – not mixed with milk or yogurt the way you would with regular granola – but drink ample water or tea along with it lest it will leave you dehydrated and thirsty.

Only *after* making it for the first time did it occur to me that I had in fact created an elevated form of what the German's call *Studentenfutter* (student fodder), an economical mix of nuts, oats and dried fruit, perfect for sustenance on those long nights of study.

American butter is very different from European butter, especially for baking. Even organic cultured American butter does not come close to the legendary *beurre demi-sel* from Brittany or Normandy. It is worth going out of one's way to find imported butter at least for some dishes, including this regional specialty I often indulge in during our sojourn on the island, especially on afternoons, after a nap or coming home from the beach for a cup of tea or coffee and something sweet.

This is a very nice specialty from Brittany, though a similar pastry is made in Scotland, where it is called shortbread.

GATEAU BRETON

In a bowl, mix ⅓ cup of sugar, 5 egg yolks and a few drops of Bergamot essence (or orange flower water) until well combined. In a separate bowl, mix 3 ½ cups of flour, 1 cup of sugar, and 1 teaspoon of baking powder. Into this dry mixture, cut 250g (the equivalent of 2 sticks of butter plus 2 tablespoons) of cold imported salted butter (best is *beurre de baratte au sel marin** but a regular beurre *demi-sel* will do, in which case one must add an extra dash of *fleur de sel* or other flaky sea salt), cut into pieces. Working with your finger tips, rub the butter loosely into the flour-sugar mixture until everything resembles coarse meal. Add the egg mixture, toss everything lightly to combine and press it, not too firmly, into a buttered rectangular baking dish. The dough should be at least 1 inch high – if the dish is too large, create a partition out of a triple layer of aluminum foil to keep the dough in place on one side. Brush the dough with an egg yolk beaten with 1 tablespoon

---

* Best quality, cultured French butter seasoned with coarse sea salt.

of water. Draw a fork across the surface to draw a diagonal crisscross pattern. Bake at 375° F for about 35-40 minutes, until a cake tester comes out dry and the surface of the cake is bronze colored. Now lower the oven temperature to 325° F and bake the cake for another 10 minutes to get it as dry as it ought to be. This cake is even better once it has rested for a day or two, wrapped in aluminum foil. Serve it cut it into little squares or diamond shapes. I sometimes line the baking dish with fresh fig leaves before adding the dough. They lend the cake an indelible aroma.

Nothing better can be achieved with such few ingredients, perhaps with the exception of this:

QUATRE QUART
(French Pound Cake)

In a mixing bowl, whisk 4 eggs and 1 cup of sugar until homogenized. Add 1 ½ cups of flour and 1 teaspoon of baking powder. Stir slowly until fully incorporated. Fold in 7 ounces of melted, imported salted butter (or the best butter you can find plus a good pinch of flaky sea salt). Butter and flour a rectangular cake pan and pour the dough into it. Bake at 350° F for 30-40 minutes, until a cake tester comes out clean.

Optional: Drop 8-12 moist pitted prunes or thin slices of 1 tart apple into the dough before baking it, pushing them down to fully submerge them in the dough.

These are very nice ways to highlight the flavor of good quality butter but it will just as well enhance any savory dish. As for the preparation of seafood, fish or shellfish, the best approach is to consider two options, raw or cooked. To some, cooking seafood is a crime. If cooked it must be, this classic is always appreciated:

SOLE MEUNIÈRE
(Dover Sole in the ttyle of The Milliner's Wife)

Take a Dover sole, scrape the scales off the white belly skin and, working from the tail towards the head, strip off the upper, dark skin. Cut off the dorsal fin bones with scissors and cut an incision on each side of the belly to fully eviscerate the fish. Season it with salt and ground white pepper. In a large frying pan, heat ¼ cup of neutral oil – grape-seed, corn, peanut or sunflower – never canola. When the oil is hot but not yet smoking, press both sides of the sole into a bed of flour, shake off the excess flour and carefully lower it into the pan, skin side down. Fry it on one side for about 2 minutes before carefully flipping it with two spatulas. Now add 2 tablespoons of salted French butter to the pan. Once it has melted and merged with the oil, spoon the hot fat over the fish as you are cooking the second side. The sole is done when a wooden pick inserted into its thickest part (below the head) meets no resistance. Lift the sole onto a pre-heated platter. Pour most of the fat out of the frying pan and add a couple of tablespoons of more butter and some chopped parsley to the pan. Shaking the pan, melt the butter over medium high heat until the parsley is tender and the butter lightly browned. Pour it over the sole. Serve with lemon wedges.

POISSON EN PAPILLOTE AVEC SON BEURRE NOISETTE
(Whole Fish Baked In Parchment Paper with Browned Butter)

Any medium-size fish like *branzino*, loup de mer, pompano, red snapper or dorade are all well suited for this preparation. The fish must be scaled and eviscerated and have its gills removed. Rinse under cold water and pat dry. Season the cavity with salt and pepper and stuff it with aromatics – any choice or combination of fresh herbs like thyme, parsley, dill, fennel fronds, cilantro, as well as some sliced garlic and a bay leaf. Rub the outside of the fish with very little olive oil and season it with salt and pepper. Lay the fish on a thin bed of very thinly sliced blanched shallots, celery stalks or fennel bulb piled onto a large piece of parchment paper placed over a sheet pan. Fold the paper loosely over the fish as you would to wrap a box, crimp the paper's edges or tuck them under to seal in the air. Bake in a 350° F oven until just done, about 20 minutes, depending on size. The fish is fully cooked when piercing its thickest part right below the head with a wooden pick meets no resistance (remember on which side of the package the head lies so you can find the spot without unfolding the paper which would let the steam you might need for further cooking escape all at once). Once the fish is done, carefully fold open the paper and slide it, with its juices and the softened vegetables onto a pre-heated oval platter.

To make the *beurre noisette³,** melt some top-quality, salted cultured butter, about 2 tablespoons per person, in a sauce pan set it over medium heat. Cook it until it is no longer foamy and the milk solids have curdled and caramelized on the bottom of the pan. Whisk lightly and serve on the side in a preheated sauce boat or bowl with a sauce ladle. This is a revelation – indeed you will feel like you have never tasted melted butter before.

There was shellfish of every variety available at the seafood store. Not just shrimp of all sizes, lobsters, oysters, all sorts of clams and mussels but also sea snails, octopus and crabs. *Coquilles Saint Jacques*, wild scallops, were only in season in the winter and the ones on sale in the summer were imported. Neither Filip Noterdaeme nor I care all that much for scallops – celebrated as they are – but from time to time they add a pleasantly sweet note to a menu. Sliced raw and dressed with a bit of lemon juice or raw diced rhubarb and olive oil, or pan-seared in butter to medium rare, they have their place as an appetizer. One day a neighbor who had a fishing boat brought us a basket with several live *arraignées de mer*, spider crab. Filip Noterdaeme and I loved the delicate flavor of their succulent meat but were not too fond of the laborious task of first throwing them alive into boiling water to cook them and then painstakingly scraping the small nuggets of meat out of their carcasses and thin legs.

My parents' friends on the island were surprised to learn that the cuisine I cooked as a private chef in New York wasn't, as a rule, French. They found it hard to imagine that anything other than French food could be acceptable for entertaining. So I convinced my parents to host a large cocktail party for all their friends and let me showcase my style of cooking for them. The difference between my food and what they were used to was quite extraordinary, except that I had only used local ingredients, some of which, as I told them, I had been gathering in the wilderness of the island. Everybody asked me questions on how I had prepared this or that dish. From then on, my annual cocktail party at my parent's house became a highlight of the season. After three or four years my mother decided it did not have to be every year.

---

* The name, hazelnut butter, is not to be taken literally. No hazelnuts are ever used to make it (although I have to my amusement once seen it prescribed in a very earnest, well-meaning but badly researched American cookbook). The name merely refers to its brown color and nutty flavor.

There was still another kind of shellfish which was quite common on the island, called *encornets*, which most people know as calamari but are called squid in American seafood stores.

The American-Italian chef Lidia Bastianich, whose television cooking show I used to watch occasionally when Filip Noterdaeme and I still had a TV set, is one of the few cooking show hosts whose demonstrations I found noteworthy. From her I learned the best way of preparing calamari. And it was on the French island that I first got to try it out. A friend had invited me to join him on a boating trip to catch squid *à la turlutte*, a technique that involves a special weighed cylinder with sharp hooks at the end of a fishing line that one had to simply drop onto the bottom of the sea and then continuously move up and down like a yoyo in order to attract an unsuspecting squid. We did not catch any *encornets* that day but having built up an appetite for them by having discussed at great length how to best to cook them as we sat lifting and dripping our yoyos, we ended up buying two dozen of them at the seafood store.

Skinned, eviscerated and cleaned[*], the bodies are best steamed until tender and the tentacles are best fried to a crisp with fresh garlic, chili flakes and parsley. Slice the bodies into thin rings and season them with generous amounts of salt. Squeeze the juice of a lemon into a bowl, place the lemon halves into a medium size pot along with enough water to cover its bottom by 1 inch. Bring the water to a boil, place a steaming insert over it, place the sliced squid into it, cover the pot with a lid and cook for about 1 minute. Stir and salt the squid once more, cover again and cook for another minute. Repeat this step one or two more times, until the rings are opaque. Do not be afraid of over-salting them, the salt merely tenderizes them and most of it will drain away through the steaming basket as it cooks. Serve immediately, drizzled with a few drops of olive oil and the reserved lemon juice and garnished with the tentacles that must be fried to a crisp in olive oil with garlic, parsley and a few chili flakes, added towards the end so they don't burn. There are so few people who know the true flavor of calamari, but this way of preparing them is a revelation.

From the United States we always brought a packet of Korean chili powder with us. It is an important ingredient for making Kimchee. At the time no one in France knew much about Korean food. The French grow Napa cabbage but no one really knows what do do with it – usually, they use it like lettuce for a salad or cook it with bacon and heavy cream. When they heard that I was fermenting it with chili powder and cooking with it, they considered us savages. Telling them that Kimchee was the Korean

---

[*] Cleaning squid is in principle quite similar to cleaning cuttlefish, which is described in Chapter VI, in the recipe for *Seppie in Humido.*

choucroute, sauerkraut, did not entice their appetite for it any more. The French don't really care about spicy food, they occasionally use minimal amounts of *Harissa* – Moroccan hot sauce – for their couscous but most of the heat in their food comes from mustard, pink and black radishes and, at least in Alsace, horseradish, which can be quite strong in its own way.

It had been from cooking with my friend Julie Johnson Staples, who was originally from Iowa but whose job as a lawyer in Manhattan had often forced her to travel to Korea that I had become aware of Korean food. We once made a trip to Koreatown in Queens together and bought alarming quantities of Korean pantry items. Back at her home in Brooklyn, we cooked enough Korean food for a week, quite to the delight of her husband who often had to dine alone as she was at the time frequently traveling abroad. We had not considered making Kimchee from scratch – not because we were lazy but because it is so widely available ready-made across the city, not just in Koreatown.

This delicious dish does not need radishes, but 1 cup of pink radishes (or 1 black radish), cut into thin juliennes could be added along with the other garnishes.

KIMCHEE-FRIED RICE

Made with leftover, plain cooked rice from the previous day, this meatless dish is exquisite. Short grain rice is traditional but I prefer lighter, more fragrant long grain varieties like Basmati or jasmine rice.

Working over a colander set over a bowl to catch the juices, squeeze 2-3 cups of Kimchee until quite dry and chop it roughly. Chop half a sweet onion and stir-fry it in a large frying pan until translucent in 2 tablespoons of neutral-tasting oil. Add the Kimchee to the onions along with a few pieces of star anise. Stir-fry it for a few minutes before pushing it to the sides of the pan and pouring a tiny bit of oil into the center. Heap the rice onto the sizzling oil and cook it for a few minutes without stirring. When the rice is hot and starts to crisp up on the bottom, add the Kimchee juice and stir-fry everything until lightly caramelized. For even better flavor, mix 1 tablespoon *Gochujang*, Korean fermented red chili paste, into the Kimchee juice before adding it to the rice (or use a mix of miso paste and Korean chili flakes). Transfer the rice to individual serving bowls and top it with flaked pieces of smoked whitefish or hake, scrambled eggs, a bit of sesame oil, chopped scallions, scissor-cut strips of *Nori* (dried, pressed seaweed leaves, the kind used for sushi rolls), and toasted sesame seeds. To make it a more substantially balanced meal, add steamed broccoli florets and

BRAISED EGGPLANT

Quarter small Italian eggplants lengthwise, salt them, pat them dry after 10 minutes, fry them in batches along with a couple of whole garlic gloves in a sauce pan, using very little oil. When they are browned, stack them all into the pan, sprinkle them with a bit of brown sugar and cover them with a mixture of oyster sauce, rice wine and soy sauce as well as a touch of sesame oil. Cook them without stirring, covered and set over low heat, until very soft, basting them with the juices now and then.

This is one of the very best of rice dishes. Here is another one I also often make on the island, also an exquisite dish.

BASMATI RICE WITH MELTED TOMATOES AND GOAT CHEESE

This can only be made with really sweet and succulent, vine-ripened tomatoes of late summer. Chose firm, small ones over watery large ones, about half a pound per person. To peel them, score a little cross into their bottom and drop them into a pot of boiling water for about a minute or less. Transfer them immediately to an ice bath. Peel off the skin and carve out the stems and tough part of the core. Chop the tomatoes roughly.

Cook Basmati rice according to directions in Chapter I.

In a non-stick pan, cook thinly sliced yellow onion, one per four servings, and a branch of fresh basil in several tablespoons of water until the onions have softened and all the water has evaporated. Add a pad of butter, the chopped tomatoes and a pinch of salt and bring everything to a simmer. Remove and discard the wilted basil. To serve, heap a mound of warm rice onto individual soup plates, spoon some tomatoes over it, add two slices of mild fresh goat cheese, a drizzle of olive oil, flaky sea salt, and a mix of chopped fresh tender herbs like parsley, basil, cilantro, celery fronds or fennel fronds. A green hot chili pepper, pierced with a fork (to prevent it from exploding) and charred over a gas burner, is a welcome addition if you like it hot.

The food I prepared for us on the island was usually light and cooked simply, but in late August, when temperatures dropped, more on the side of hearty fare. Rich and wholesome dishes seemed appropriate after a day of swimming in cold water and biking for hours against the wind and occasional rain. Nevertheless we rarely had a craving for chicken or meat – although I am known for my disparaging opinion of vegetarianism or veganism – and the local mutton, as pretty as it was to see the sheep run freely across the meadows, seemed to us too tough and its flavor a bit sharp, nothing like the mild lamb we both have gotten used to in America.

Monkfish cheeks provided a great alternative as a main ingredient for a dish I am usually more likely to prepare with chicken.

CURRY DE JOUES DE LOTTE
(Monkfish Curry)

Monkfish is a prized delicacy in France, more succulent than in America, and much larger, hence its medallion-size cheeks. I have never seen them on sale in American seafood stores, but monkfish filet, cut into thick slices, is a fine substitute.

Season about 1 pound of monkfish cheeks (or filet medallions) with salt and white pepper, dredge them in flour and briefly panfry them in batches, using very little butter, turning them once and removing them from the pan before they begin to brown. Wipe out the pan, add a tablespoon of butter and 3 chopped shallots, one chopped garlic clove, 1 finely diced stalk of celery, a peeled and finely diced small knob of ginger and 1 diced jalapeno or serrano pepper, seeds and membranes removed according to your tolerance of hot spice. Sauté until translucent, add 1 teaspoon of powdered turmeric, stir-fry everything until it is fragrant, then add 2 peeled, seeded and diced vine-ripened tomatoes, a few finely chopped cilantro stems, 1 cup of coconut milk and 1 cup of coconut water. Bring the sauce to a simmer, reduce it until it is slightly thickened, season it with salt to taste, add the precooked fish chunks, turn the heat to its lowest setting and cover the pot. When the fish is warm and fork tender – it should not take more than a few minutes – the dish is ready. Garnish with chopped cilantro leaves and serve with lime wedges on the side for drizzling. Tastes best with plain Basmati rice or even soft egg noodles. Crispy fried shallots add texture.

This was another pleasant change from the usual French flavor combinations of the region. The exotic aroma of ginger, hot pepper and turmeric was quite invigorating.

The island is very proud of its traditional specialty, cold-smoked tuna filet, so good that a cook has nothing to do but choose the right ingredients to pair it with.

SMOKED TUNA FILET WITH FINGERLING POTATOES

American smoked tuna filet is not quite as tender as the version found in Brittany, but it makes for an acceptable substitute when sliced as thin as you would slice smoked salmon. On the island, only the center-cut tenderloin of the tuna filet, no wider than 2 ½ inches, is used, tied into a tight netting and cold-smoked to such buttery tenderness that it can be served cut into ½-inch thick slices.

Par-boil fingerling potatoes in well-salted water to which you have added a bay leaf. Do not cook them all the way through lest they get too soft and their starch disastrously turns to sugar. Peel them when cool enough to handle and cut them lengthwise in half. Pan-fry them, cut side down, in salted butter until browned and crisp. Add a handful of chopped parsley and coarsely ground black pepper and toss for a few minutes until fully coated. Serve with slices of smoked tuna, a dollop of crème *fraiche*, finely chopped shallots and a lemon wedge.

Canned tuna can be made appetizing, though it will never be as delicate as smoked or raw tuna. Once upon a time, the island's main industry had been the canning of tuna and sardines but today, only one of its tuna canning factories is still in business. All kinds of things are made there, from tuna *rillettes* to tuna *patés*, though one wonders why. The patés are most frequently used for canapés by hostesses without imagination. Regular canned tuna at least can be used for a variety of things.

Here is a recipe for a tart attributed to the women who worked in the tuna factories, where it was served for lunch. It is still sold on the daily local farmer's market.

TARTE AU THON
(Tuna Tart)
Make a simple yeast dough out of 1 ½ cups of flour, 1 teaspoon of salt, 1 teaspoon of dried yeast and about 1 cup

of water. Kneed it deftly until it is no longer sticky and let it rise, covered, in a warm place for a good hour. When it has doubled in size, punch it down, kneed it once more and roll or stretch it out as thin as possible. Transfer it onto a sheet pan you have previously oiled and dusted with cornmeal. Cover it with a towel and let it rise once more for about 15 minutes. Pierce the dough all over with a fork, brush it with just a little olive oil and evenly spread a few tablespoons of Dijon mustard mixed with a tablespoon of crème fraiche onto it. Cover the entire width of the *tarte* with very thin slices of ripe tomatoes and season them with salt, pepper and a few fresh or home-dried thyme leaves. Scatter some drained canned tuna over the tomatoes (1 large can should suffice) and top it with two handfuls of shredded Gruyère. Bake at 400° F for about 25 minutes, until the borders of the tart crust are browned. Serve at room temperature with a simply dressed green salad.

In a hurry or a pinch, this tart can also be made with frozen puff pastry. If you do, omit the olive oil and crème fraiche – it will be rich enough even without it – and par-bake the puff pastry for 15 minutes.

As for the local conger eel, its reason for being seems mainly the many horror stories that are frequently told about its ferociousness and frequent attacks on overly curious snorkelers. This recipe however brings out this particular eel's surprising tenderness.

CRU DE CONGRE
(Conger Eel Crudo)

Conger eel is a very firm-fleshed, lean fish. Monk fish is a close substitute. Slice raw filets as thinly as you can, as you would cut smoked salmon. It helps to freeze the fish for 30 minutes before putting a knife to them. Squeeze some lime juice onto a chilled serving plate, enough to just cover its surface, and align the fish slices on it in an overlapping pattern. Drizzle them with a bit of excellent olive oil and season them with flaky sea salt. Top with a few chopped cilantro stems and finely sliced, fresh hot chili peppers and serve with corn chips or toast points.

Besides the fish, there are the crabs and the oysters. Besides the oysters there are the small local surf clams, another of the region's local species – so popular that fishing them had to be restricted years ago. There have been years when they were not available for purchase at all until an agreement was made with environmental agencies. They are a lovely sight, smaller than other, more common bivalves, with very smooth, pale yellow shells. When they are available on the market, people stand in line to get them. I never liked mussels or clams all that much and did not expect to like these either, but they were in fact quite different from any I had ever had and a delicious revelation. Fishing them commercially is an act of love – not only must they be dug out of the sand in the deep waters that harbors them, between the island and the continent, but they must be rinsed multiple times to give up the sand they harbor between their shells. They are traditionally cooked simply with white wine, garlic, cream and parsley and served with *pommes frites*. As it seemed a bit of an exaggeration to do any deep-frying in a rented summer house, we opted to make an exception and seek out a restaurant that served them prepared this way whenever we felt an appetite for it. Of the handful of seasonal restaurants on the island there was only one we deemed acceptable. It was mostly known for serving the typical Breton *galettes* and *crêpes* but as a nod to local tradition also served surf clams in cream sauce with French fries. Unquestionably, it was the most popular restaurant on the entire island, and for good reasons. The food was always simple and straightforward. What a strange life it would be to cook nothing but crêpes, galettes, clams and French fries every day.

In France not much attention is given to the Italian pasta tradition, and there are never more than three or perhaps four shapes of pasta available at any *supermarché*. The surf clams are very sweet, flavorful and plump. They are perfectly suited for this Italian classic.

SPAGHETTI ALLE VONGOLE
(Spaghetti With Clams)

Rinse and scrub the smallest surf or littleneck clams you can find (New Zealand cockles are a fine substitute) – a good handful per serving – in plentiful of cold water and leave them to rest in a bowl filled with very cold water so they may give up any sand they are still holding. Bring a large pot of water to a boil and add enough salt to render it as salty as the sea. Add as many spaghetti as needed and stir them just once in the pot once the water has come to a full boil again. Heat a large

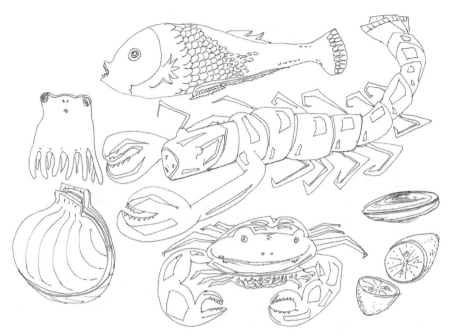

enameled cast iron pot. While it is heating, lift the clams out of their bath – do not simply drain them or you will end up with the sediment from the bottom of the bowl clinging to their shells. Add a bit of olive oil and sliced garlic to the pot. When the garlic begins to brown, add the clams and immediately cover the pot with a lid. Shake the pot a couple of times and leave it covered for about two minutes over a medium high flame. Uncover, add chopped parsley and some chili flakes. By that time, the pasta ought to be al dente. Reserve a cup of the pasta water, drain the pasta and add it to the clams with a splash of olive oil or a piece of butter. Toss over high heat and add a bit of the reserved pasta water if it seems too dry. Serve immediately, garnished with quartered cherry tomatoes. Do not serve any cheese with this pasta dish.

This can also be made with linguini. In France, spaghetti and linguini are most commonly eaten with canned tomato sauce and grated Swiss cheese. This is regarded as mere convenience food, suitable for children. There are those who disgrace the Italian culinary arts even further by cutting their spaghetti into small pieces with a knife and fork, arguing that eating them as they are is vulgar – arrogantly, one cannot help thinking.

Every summer we spend on the island, the mosquitoes that come out at night pose a challenge. French windows are not, cannot be equipped with screens like American windows since they open outward. Neither are air conditioners common or even desirable in northern European climates. The trick to avoid nightly attacks by mosquitos, even though there are rarely numerous – still enough to disturb one's sleep – is to keep the bedroom dark for several hours, windows shut, before opening the windows at bedtime to the agreeably chilly night air. At this point, no light whatsoever can be lit in the room. But even this would be ineffective were it not for a special aroma diffuser, available in every French hardware store. It is a little electric plug equipped with a heating pad on which one places a tablet infused with a mosquito-repellent essence, sometimes scented with lemon balm. I have often wished that these very practical little devices were available in America, but Americans seem to in any case prefer to sleep in air-conditioned rooms, windows closed. Despite all our precautions, there are times when one or two mosquitos would flutter their wings around our sleepy noses and ears. Filip Noterdaeme does not care for them. He can deal with them during the day but when they attack him in bed at night he calls for help, refusing to get up. The only solution then is to close the window, turn on the light, scan the white walls for the beast, and exterminate it. The instruments for the battle are determination, a chair to stand on and a folded *Le Monde* newspaper. This is always effective.

A charming story of wifely and husbandly teasing is one of my parents. She did not wish my father to slow down with age. When they got married she was impressed with his athleticism. In later years, when she felt that he was getting complacent, she would send him up to the top floor of our house in Munich to fetch something and then, once she heard he reached the top of the fourth floor, called up to him that there was someone on the phone for him. He would come flying down the stairs to take the call. Evidently, there was no one at the other end of the line. My mother would smile and say, I knew you still had it, dearest.

Of late, the island has tended to become very crowded in the summer. In my youth, much of my time there had been taken up by socializing but now that I am going there with Filip Noterdaeme I prefer a quiet vacation. When word spread that I was back on the island after all these years, many of the old acquaintances reached out with welcoming gifts and invitations. There was the imminent danger of being pulled back into a social scene that would have required too much attention, never-ending strings of being invited here and there and, naturally, of having to return the favor. In New York, when our apartment used to house The Homeless Museum of Art, we had installed a collection of objects called the *Oh Thank You Collection,* named after the common practice of art collectors bequeathing their collection to an art institution in exchange for a prominent display of their name. Ours had displayed "Useless Gifts from Friends and Acquaintances" – that is, mundane things people brought to endear themselves and that were nevertheless either useless to begin with or simply did not interest us. On the little island this phenomenon of bringing useless gifts is very prominent, for everyone. Once a year, a flea market is being held, and everyone pretends not to notice when acquaintances offer received gifts for sale. In any case, the practice keeps a great many useless things in constant rotation.

Like all shrubs, blackberries flourish on the island. In spite of the municipal landscapers cutting back twice a year the bushes that grow along the many paths that cross the island, nothing can stop them. Sometimes entire parcels of them have to be eroded. To gather the berries is risky because the biggest and juiciest ones always seem just out of reach. It isn't practical to lean too far into the thorny bushes, but by carefully balancing on tiptoes and reaching up with one hand while pushing back with the other, the difficulty can be overcome unless, as it happened to us one day, one stumbles and falls into the shrubs, upending the bucket, half filled with berries! Scratched arms and legs and the loss of an hour-long, painstaking harvest put an end for a while to our blackberry adventures.

The local tomatoes, grown organically by a local farmer who had been a biologist before moving to the island to raise sheep, are the best we have ever had. When in America people praise beefsteak tomatoes from New Jersey, I can only pity them. I once asked the French farmer what it was that made his tomatoes so much more savory and sweeter than others. He simply replied, They have to suffer.

With the farmer's permission, I took a few seeds with me to America where I gave them to a friendly gardener who did everything to make them feel at home, but to no avail, they would not even sprout. That left us no option but to simply omit fresh tomatoes from our New York meal plan and wait all year until we were back on the island to indulge in them once again. Another thing we only eat on the island are croissants. They are better there than anywhere else, perhaps because we get to eat them outdoors, on a beautiful terrace surrounded by a beautiful garden.

Riding our bicycles into the closest village first thing each morning is a daily delight. We always buy two croissants and enough bread for the day – one or two baguettes. Filip Noterdaeme always unfolds and carefully shreds his croissant into small pieces before dabbing it with a few drops of locally made peach or strawberry jam. I call this his deconstructed croissant.

Meanwhile in New York, our annual disappearing act was looked upon with envy – friends and clients became curious. Everybody wanted to find out more about where we were traveling to. We did not volunteer many details. As we were always returning to New York tanned and rejuvenated, more and more people asked us for directions so they could follow us. A famous wedding planner whom Filip Noterdaeme likes to refer to as the wedding planner for future divorcés resolutely asked me one spring to arrange for a hotel reservation in the summer for him and his boyfriend. But, I told him, there are no hotels on this island, this is a family island, not a resort. At that, his eyes lit up. Perhaps, he said, one should explore the business opportunity of building a hotel there. When I avoided giving him the name of the island, he set out to find out about it behind my back. Inevitably he made a wrong conclusion and ended up renting a summer house on another island nearby. In any case, he found the local climate not suitably soothing and ruefully returned to his privileged life in New York City and South Beach.

At the end of our annual stay on the island, we are always so occupied with trying to take advantage of every last moment that we nearly forget to think of useful gifts to take home for friends. Fennel flowers have to be gathered and placed in the sun for 2 days to dry, then crushed and rubbed through a fine-mesh sieve to catch the fragrant pollen which I then mix with locally harvested *fleur de sel*. This is the only souvenir we ever take with us. Every year, looking at the dozen little linen bags, tightly packed with fennel-flavored salt makes me inordinately happy. Not only are they original and useful gifts, we always keep three bags for ourselves. The flavored salt, meant not for cooking but as an elegant table salt, lasts us until next year's spring, when we begin to make plans to return to the island for the summer. It means more to me than the condiments we used to delight in bringing home from Europe and that are no longer allowed in our carry-on luggage: pear butter from Belgium; fresh, white wine-based Dijon mustard from Paris; artisanal honey from Germany. Filip Noterdaeme never gets involved with any of the packing of our luggage. He simply trusts that, on our usual stopover in Brussels, I will procure his favorite Belgian specialties – chocolates from *Pierre Marcollini* and gingerbread from *Dandoy* – both of which are still allowed in carry-on. But he always fears that I could give away too much of it in New York and reminds me that these are mostly and foremost meant for our own enjoyment. Traveling across the Atlantic with four pounds of salt and chocolate is without a question utterly ridiculous, but from the point of view of the sensual memory that scents and flavors can evoke, it is priceless.

One important, life-changing surprise came on one of our last days on the island two summers ago, all the more thrilling considering our feelings of wistfulness about our vacation having come to an end. My parents declared that they had decided to put their house under my name. I was suddenly overcome with memories of the many happy hours we had already spent there. Ah, to know that we now truly had a home in this place to return to, possibly to one day make it our last home. And so we returned to New York, confident that we would always be able to come back.

And now it amuses me to remember how many people have over the years told me that I ought to write a cookbook. It is a comment that was often given at the end of a meal I had prepared. I used to think, How very flattering. Then, perplexed, *But these people don't ever cook.* As if reading a cookbook had anything to do with cooking.

RECIPE LIST

VII. Favorites

VIII. Food in Germany before I came to New York

IX. French Dishes from my Childhood

X. Serving and Being Served in New York

XIII. The Markets on the Island in Brittany

ABOUT THE AUTHOR

Daniel Isengart is a writer, cabaret entertainer and private chef living in New York City. He is the author of *Queering the Kitchen: A Manifesto*, also published by Outpost19 and based on his popular series at *Slate* Magazine. He has written on hidden gay culinary history for *Jarry* Magazine and elsewhere. Daniel is also the subject of *The Autobiography of Daniel J. Isengart*, written by his partner Filip Noterdaeme.

CPSIA information can be obtained
at www.ICGtesting.com
Printed in the USA
BVHW04s2328180518
516359BV00007B/5/P